# THE FARMER

# Country Kitchen Cook Book

— a collection first
published in 1894

*Illustration from the 1917
Country Kitchen Cook Book.*

*Coverplate from the original,*
*1894 Country Kitchen Cook Book.*

# THE FARMER

# Country Kitchen Cook Book

— a collection first
published in 1894

*edited by*
MARGARET LANDIN

*Home economics consultant*
VERNA MIKESH

*Illustrator*
EDWARD LANDIN

**HAWTHORN BOOKS, INC.**
*Publishers/New York*
A HOWARD & WYNDHAM COMPANY

# FOREWORD

"The trouble with most cookbooks is that they are not practical, everyday affairs, but are fit to be consulted only on special occasions." So wrote editors of the first *Country Kitchen Cook Book* in 1894.

"The demand among farmers' wives is for a simple, common-sense recipe book," the statement continues, "specially adapted to their particular use. Such a book is *Country Kitchen*."

Eight-five years and twenty-two printings later, *Country Kitchen Cook Book* continues to stand by that original statement.

Women who love to cook, whether they live in the country or in town, like a recipe book that is really usable — convenient to handle, with easy-to-follow instructions and illustrations which show, for example, how to braid a coffee cake or what a flat whisk looks like.

This new *Country Kitchen Cook Book* is more than an ordinary cook book, however. It is a recipe record of country living in the Upper Midwest. It includes a "from scratch" collection of classic, pioneer, country cookery, as published in *The Farmer's* early cook books and magazine pages.

Combined with these old-fashioned favorites are recipes from World War I, the depression, World War II rationing and a wealth of completely modern recipes, including accurate cooking, roasting, canning and freezing charts.

There is a bonus collection of recipes from Clara Sutter — Iowa's first extension home agent and much-loved "Your Poultry and Mine" columnist for *The Farmer* from 1930 until her death in 1969, at age 94. Clara's wise, homey advice on poultry, life at her farm and throughout the world made her a legend. The *Country Kitchen Cook Book* would not be complete without her egg and chicken dishes.

Three criteria have been applied to each recipe in this collection which dates from the 1880s:

- Are the recipes accurate and dependable? Has each one been tested with today's cooking methods, tasted and approved?

• Are the recipes useful? Are they suited to the modern farm family's needs and resources?

• Do the recipes and kitchen utensils used to illustrate the book accurately represent 100-or-more years of country cookery throughout this Upper Midwest area?

Many people have made this project exciting and valid. Farm homemakers, agricultural associations, food companies and institutes have, over the years, helped build the files of Country Kitchen tested recipes from which this collection was gleaned.

Margaret Landin, Home Editor of *The Farmer* from 1964 to 1973, spent more than two years selecting and testing for the fifth edition. She also gathered a fascinating collection of authentic old and new farm kitchen utensils and serving pieces which her artist-writer-educator husband, Ed, illustrated in careful detail.

A special thank you goes to Verna Mikesh, retired University of Minnesota professor and nutritionist, for her careful reading of the text. Verna's 15 years of experience at the U of M, plus 15 more as an extension home agent and 4-H Club agent in Minnesota, were a particular help in consultation and tracking down authentic, hard-to-find material.

Several sources have supplied special food data or art objects for this book, and so deserve acknowledgement: University of Minnesota Agricultural Extension Service; Minnesota Historical Society; National Livestock & Meat Board; National Turkey Growers Association, and Kerr Glass Manufacturing Corporation.

*Sharon Ross,*
*Home Editor,* The Farmer

# DEDICATED TO
# COUNTRY COOKS
## *— for your health, happiness and fame as good providers*

*Illustration from the 1917
Country Kitchen Cook Book.*

*Illustration from the 1917*
*Country Kitchen Cook Book.*

# TABLE OF CONTENTS

Foreword ........................................... v
Hot and Cold Beverages ........................... 1
Canapes, Snacks and Dips ......................... 9
Salads and Salad Dressings ....................... 17
Vegetables, Legumes, Grains ...................... 33
Meat, Poultry, Fish and Game ..................... 63
Eggs and Cheese for Every Meal .................. 163
Barbecue, Camp and Field Meals.................. 177
Hot and Cold Sandwiches ......................... 193
Yeast and Quick Breads .......................... 205
Bars, Cookies and Candy ......................... 243
Pies, Cakes and Other Desserts .................. 273
Canning and Freezing ............................ 327
Recipes for Large Groups ........................ 371
Measures and Substitutions ...................... 385
List of Illustrations ............................. 390
Index of Recipes ................................ 396

# HOT AND COLD BEVERAGES

## COFFEE

For fragrant, clear coffee, follow these rules; use:

A good grade of coffee, freshly ground or packed in vacuum tight cans.

A freshly-scalded, clean pot or container. Clean after each using with hot, soapy water, then scald with clear, boiling water.

Fresh water below boiling temperature. A bitter flavor is developed and more caffeine drawn out if coffee boils.

Liquid strained from the grounds or immediately removed from near grounds, to keep flavor mild and coffee clear.

*"Boiled" coffee:* Measure 1 rounded tablespoon of regular grind coffee to each 8-ounce cup of water. Mix slightly beaten egg (1 tablespoon for 5 to 6 servings) with the coffee before adding water. Stir thoroughly, then add hot water and bring slowly to a boil, stirring down occasionally. Remove to a warm place immediately and let stand for 3 to 5 minutes. Add a little cold water to settle grounds, then serve immediately or strain from the grounds, using a fine strainer or cheesecloth. Pour the strained coffee in a clean, warm pot or pitcher and serve. If coffee made by this method is not clear, it usually is due to using too fine a grind of coffee, to overcooking, or to lack of settling. For home use, the beaten egg not used can be stored in a cool place in a covered glass to use as needed.

*Steeped coffee* is measured as above, without the egg, and put in a preheated coffee pot. Pour fresh, boiling water over the coffee. Stir vigorously for about 30 seconds. Cover tightly;

let stand in warm place 3 to 5 minutes. Strain at once from grounds or a bitter flavor will develop.

*Perked Coffee:* For percolated coffee, use 1 rounded or heaping tablespoon of regular or perk grind coffee to each cup of water. Start with cold water. Let it percolate gently for 10 to 15 minutes. Coffee is clearer and milder in flavor if slowly percolated than if allowed to percolate rapidly. As soon as coffee is perked, remove the grounds from over the coffee, as they absorb flavor.

*Drip or Filter Coffee:* Drip or filtered coffee is nearly a foolproof method. Use a fine or "drip" grind. Preheat the container with hot water which is poured off. Pour freshly boiling water over the grounds; let it filter through once: remove grounds, as they absorb aroma and flavor.

## CAFFE CAPPUCCINO
*Serve with dessert — pass cookies and candy.*

2 tablespoons instant coffee *or* instant expresso coffee
1½ cups warm half-and-half cream
1½ cups boiling water
¼ cup sugar
Whipped cream
½ teaspoon cinnamon

Place coffee, sugar and cinnamon in coffee pot or carafe. Stir in boiling water and cream. Pour into tall cups and top with a spoonful of whipped cream. A cinnamon stick may be used as a stirrer. Yields 6 demitasse servings.

## SPICED DESSERT COFFEE
*Rich and elegant.*

¼ cup instant coffee *or* instant expresso coffee
4 cups boiling water
24 cracked cardamom seeds (taken out of pods)
Sugar to taste
Whipped cream
4 half slices of orange (optional)

Combine coffee, cardamom seeds and hot water in coffee pot or carafe. Add sugar to taste. Serve in small cups. Garnish each cup with a dollop of whipped cream and a halved orange slice. Yields 6 to 8 demitasse servings.

# TEA
*Stop and sip a cup or glass of tea when you're especially busy.*

*Hot Tea:* The important points in brewing tea are — good tea, fresh boiling water and a clean, hot teapot. An earthenware, pottery, or glass pot is ideal. Put tea in a freshly scalded pot and add freshly boiling water (2 teaspoons tea to 1 pint water). Let steep for 5 minutes, remove tea ball or strain tea from the leaves into another heated pot. Serve with milk or lemon and sugar to taste.

*Afternoon Tea:* A cup of freshly-made tea, daintily served, is an easy and refreshing expression of hospitality. Serve in pretty china cups. Accompany with a plate of thin sections of lemon or orange, each stuck with a clove if desired, and wafers, cookies, or thin sandwiches, trimmed of crusts.

*Iced Tea:* Make a quantity of strong black tea (as English Breakfast or Orange Pekoe) in advance. Make stronger than for hot tea (1 tablespoon to 1 pint water), steep just 5 minutes. Strain tea and chill. Then dilute with ice or cold water. If you have plenty of ice, the best results are secured by pouring hot tea over cracked ice.

## MINTED TEA

1½ quarts boiling water          4-5 mint leaves
2 tablespoons orange
   pekoe tea

Pour the boiling water over the tea and mint leaves and allow it to stand for 5 minutes. Pour off the liquid; chill and dilute or pour over cracked ice. Serve with a fresh mint leaf and a slice of orange in each glass. Yields 6 to 8 cups tea.

## SPICED TEA MIX
*Most people prefer this without the additional sugar.*

Mix: 1 cup unsweetened instant tea, 2 cups orange flavored instant breakfast drink, 1 cup sugar (optional), 1 teaspoon cinnamon and ½ teaspoon cloves. Use 2 heaping teaspoons to a cup of boiling water.

## SLEIGH RIDE CHOCOLATE
*Old-fashioned warmer-upper.*

4 squares (4-ounce each)
   unsweetened chocolate
4 cups strong, hot coffee
½ cup sugar

1 tablespoon vanilla
2 cups whipping cream
Red sugar
Candy canes

Melt chocolate over hot water and add hot coffee and sugar. Stir until sugar dissolves. Remove from heat and add vanilla. Pour 1½ cups cream into a bowl, add hot coffee mixture and beat with rotary beater until very foamy. Pour into mugs. Whip remaining cream and top each mug with a spoonful. Sprinkle with red sugar. Use one candy cane in each mug as a decorative and flavorful stirrer. Yields 6 to 8 servings.

## CHOCOLATE EGGNOG SIX
*Real teen party pleaser!*

⅔ cup chocolate syrup
4 cups cold milk
4 beaten egg yolks

4 stiffly-beaten egg whites
Dash cinnamon

Combine chocolate, milk and egg yolks. Fold in egg whites. Serve plain or over cracked ice. Sprinkle with cinnamon just before serving. Use clean, sound-shelled eggs for eggnogs. Yields 6 glasses of eggnog, 12 ounces each.

## EGGNOG
*Tasty pick-me-up anytime.*

1 egg *or* 2 yolks
⅔ cup milk
1 teaspoon sugar

2 drops vanilla
Nutmeg

Beat egg, add chilled milk, sugar and seasoning; mix together well. Whipped cream may be added for variety. One teaspoon of chocolate syrup or honey may be used for sweetening rather than sugar. Use clean, sound-shelled eggs for this recipe. Yields 1 serving.

## MAPLE SHAKES
*Refreshing with lunch.*

3 pints vanilla ice cream,
softened

½ cup maple-flavored
syrup
3 cups milk

Place softened ice cream in large mixer bowl. Beat ice cream at low speed just until smooth. Do not overbeat. Blend in syrup and milk. Pour into tall glasses and sprinkle with nutmeg. Yields 5 to 6 servings.

## BROWN COW
*Nifty version of the old soda fountain favorite.*

Pour 6 ounces cola-flavored beverage into a tall glass. Add 2 heaping teaspoonfuls sweetened instant chocolate drink and stir until dissolved. Add 2 scoops vanilla ice cream and stir quickly until foamy. Serve at once. Yields 1 Brown Cow.

## LEMONADE SYRUP
*Keep some on hand all summer.*

2 teaspoons finely-grated
lemon peel
2 cups fresh lemon juice
2 cups sugar
1½ cups water

Water *or* charged water
Almond, anise *or* mint
extract (optional)
Lemon wedges

Combine lemon peel, juice and sugar; stir to dissolve sugar. Add 1½ cups water; cover tightly and store in refrigerator.
*To serve,* use ⅓ to ½ cup lemonade syrup for each tall, ice-filled glass. Add water or charged water. Flavor to taste with almond, anise or mint extract. Garnish with lemon wedges. Yields syrup for 12 to 14 servings.

## ORANGE PUNCH
*Refreshing!*

In a large punch bowl, combine 1 quart chilled, fresh, orange juice, 1 quart orange sherbet. Add 2 quarts chilled ginger ale. Garnish with orange slices. Yields 1 **gallon** beverage.

## CITRUS-PEACH JULEP
### *Summer delight.*

¼ cup fresh lemon juice
2 cups fresh orange juice
2-3 ripe, fresh peaches,
　　peeled and sliced
½ cup sugar

¼ cup honey *or*
　　maple syrup
1 cup crushed ice
　　Cinnamon *or* nutmeg

Combine lemon, orange juice and peaches in electric blender. Cover and blend at high speed until smooth, about 30 seconds. Add sugar, honey. Blend at high speed until frothy. Pour into tall glasses over crushed ice. Sprinkle with cinnamon or nutmeg. Yields 4 servings and 1 quart beverage.

*Don't dilute iced beverages.* Freeze ice cubes from the beverage you are serving — coffee, tea, lemonade — and your drinks will be cool and will stay tasty.

## GOLDEN GLOW PUNCH
### *Gay and pretty.*

½ cup orange-flavored,
　　instant, breakfast drink
1 can (6-ounce) frozen,
　　lemonade concentrate
4 cups water

1 pint fresh strawberries,
　　sliced *or* 1 package
　　(10-ounce) frozen straw-
　　berries, partially thawed
2 bottles (7-ounce each)
　　charged water, chilled
　　Ice cubes *or* ice ring

Combine instant breakfast drink, lemonade, water and strawberries. Stir until instant breakfast drink is dissolved. Chill. Just before serving, gently stir in charged water. Pour over ice cubes or ice ring. Yields about 2 quarts beverage.

## RHUBARB PUNCH
*Early summer favorite from the*
*1934 Country Kitchen Cook Book.*

1 quart diced pink rhubarb
1 quart water

Grated rind of 1 lemon
*or* orange
¾-1 cup sugar

Simmer rhubarb in water until very tender. Strain, add the grated lemon and sugar, stirring until the sugar is dissolved. Cool and chill on ice before serving. Yields 2 quarts beverage.

## SPICED GRAPE JUICE
*Slow heating blends flavors.*

1 quart grape juice
¼ cup sugar
6 whole cloves

2 short pieces of stick cinnamon
A few whole allspice

Heat all ingredients together in a double boiler or over a slow fire. Do not boil. Strain out spice. Serve hot with a whole clove on top of each cup of spiced juice. Yummy with fresh sugared doughnuts or salty pretzels and cookies. Yields 1 quart beverage.

## MULLED CIDER
*Use for family or a crowd.*

2 quarts sweet cider *or* apple juice
1 teaspoon whole cloves
1 teaspoon whole allspice

1 3-inch stick cinnamon
½ unpeeled lemon, thinly sliced
¼-½ cup brown sugar

Place all ingredients in a large, covered pan, bring to a boil and boil 10 minutes. Strain and serve hot. You can avoid last-minute straining by tying cloves, allspice and cinnamon in a piece of cloth that can be easily lifted from the hot liquid. Let lemon float in cups. Yields 2 quarts beverage. Better double the recipe if you've more than four guests.

# CANAPES, SNACKS AND DIPS

## SPREADS AND FILLINGS FOR TEA SANDWICHES
*Best when mixed to your taste.*

Use bread at least one day old, unless otherwise specified. Remove crusts. Cream butter before spreading. Use cookie cutters to cut bread into various shapes. Spread butter and filling after bread has been shaped. Keep fresh by wrapping in waxed paper, then in slightly damp cloth; refrigerate.

*Cream cheese,* ground walnuts, ground stuffed olives and mayonnaise;

*Deviled ham,* butter, lemon juice, grated apple;

*Peanut butter* and applesauce;

*Tuna or salmon,* mayonnaise, lemon juice, grated onion or chives;

*Minced cooked turkey* or chicken, cream cheese, olive spread, peanut butter or marmalade;

*Chopped dried apricots,* grated orange peel, orange juice, mayonnaise, cream cheese;

*Ground, cooked frankfurters,* chopped walnuts, prepared mustard, mayonnaise;

*Minced avocado,* chopped, cooked shrimp, mayonnaise, lemon juice.

## BURNING BUSH
*Make ahead and refrigerate.*

| | |
|---|---|
| 1  package (4-ounce) sliced, dried beef, finely chopped | ½ pound cream cheese 1 tablespoon minced chives |

Divide the cream cheese into 32 cubes, then roll each cube into a ball using butter paddles or your hands. Toss each ball into the chopped dried beef and roll around until entirely coated. Spear each ball with a toothpick and serve stuck into a grapefruit or a large apple.

## SESAME PORK SPREAD CANAPES

Spread your favorite small crackers, toast rounds, pastry circles, slices of cucumbers or 3-inch lengths of celery with Sesame Pork Spread, page 201. Garnish attractively with bits of pimiento, stuffed or ripe olives, or a sprinkling of toasted sesame seeds.

## HORS D'OEUVRE DATES
*Keep these warm in a chafing dish.*

Fill each of 24 pitted dates with a walnut or pecan half. Marinate several hours in ½ cup clear French or Italian dressing. Drain dates; reserve dressing for salads. Wrap each date in ⅓ strip of bacon; secure with a toothpick. Set aside until party time. Broil quickly on each side, until bacon is brown and crisp. Serve immediately. Yields 24 stuffed dates.

## CREAMY CRAB SALAD
*Easy and elegant.*

1 cup diced celery
1 can (4-ounce) drained, flaked crab meat
½ cup large-curd cottage cheese

¼ cup chopped, stuffed olives
1 tablespoon lemon juice
1-2 teaspoons finely-chopped onion

Combine all ingredients and chill until ready to fill tiny Cream Puffs, page 307, or spread on buttered bread rounds. Refrigerate puffs until serving time. Yields filling for 4 dozen small puffs.

## CHICKEN-HAM SALAD
*Very nice in tiny cream puffs.*

⅔ cup mayonnaise
⅓ cup whipping cream
1 cup cooked, finely-diced chicken
1 cup finely-diced ham
2 hard-cooked eggs, chopped

¾ cup finely diced celery
½ cup slivered almonds
¼ cup minced green pepper
1 teaspoon lemon juice
¼ teaspoon salt

Whip cream, fold in mayonnaise. Mix remaining ingredients and toss lightly with dressing. Fill puffs or small buttered sandwiches shortly before serving. Refrigerate until serving time. Yields filling for 4 dozen small puffs.

## TINY BEEF BALLS
*Economical canape.*

2 pounds lean ground beef
2 tablespoons finely-
  chopped onion
1 egg, slightly beaten
1 tablespoon Worcester-
  shire sauce

1½ teaspoons salt
¼ teaspoon pepper
¼ teaspoon nutmeg

Combine ingredients; mix. Shape into balls, using 1 tablespoon meat per patty. Arrange on shallow baking pan, cover with plastic film or waxed paper. Refrigerate until serving time. Remove covering and bake balls in preheated, 400° F. oven until done, 10 to 12 minutes. To serve, skewer each meat ball with a toothpick so it can be dipped in hot cheese sauce. Yields 3 dozen beef balls.

*Cheese Sauce:* Stir ¾ cup half-and-half cream and 1 teaspoon mustard into 1 can (10¾-ounce) cheddar cheese soup; heat. Yields about 2 cups sauce.

*To freeze:* Arrange uncooked beef balls on baking sheet; freeze. When frozen solid, remove from pan and store in freezer container. Take meat from freezer 2 to 3 hours before serving time. Arrange on baking pan; cover; store in refrigerator. Bake as directed above when meat is thawed.

*Olive Beef Balls:* Flatten about 1½ teaspoons of meat mixture in your hand. Place a small stuffed olive in the center and roll meat into a ball around olive. Broil or pan fry until brown. Stick on picks and serve hot. *Do not freeze.*

## BACON WRAP-UPS
*Make both kinds for your party.*

Dip pineapple chunks or water chestnuts in soy sauce and wrap in half strips of lean bacon. Fasten with a toothpick. Broil about 3 minutes on each side. Serve crisp and hot.

## SUNFLOWER SEEDS
*Use as snacks.*

*Place shelled meats* in a shallow pan in a preheated, 300° F. oven for about 30 minutes. Stir occasionally. After taking meats from oven, add 1 teaspoon melted butter to each cup of

meats. Stir to coat, then spread meats on absorbent towel and
salt to taste.

*Salt sunflower seeds in the shell* by adding 1 tablespoon
salt to 1 pint water and bringing mixture to a boil. Immerse
seeds in boiling brine; soak overnight or until seeds are
damp. Drain, then heat and salt according to directions
above.

## NUTS AND BOLTS
### *Greatest nibbles — ever!*

½ cup butter
2 teaspoons Worchester-
   shire sauce
1 teaspoon garlic salt,
   season salt *or* savor salt
3 cups square-shape wheat
   breakfast cereal

3 cups square-shape corn
   breakfast cereal
2 cups doughnut-shape
   breakfast cereal
2 cups stick pretzels
1 cup salted peanuts *or*
   cashews

Preheat oven to 250° F. Place butter, Worcestershire sauce
and salt in a large, shallow roasting pan. Place pan in oven
until butter melts; mix ingredients. Add remaining ingredients and mix thoroughly. Return pan to oven for 1½ hours.
Stir mixture every 15 minutes. Cool. Yields 11 cups snacks.

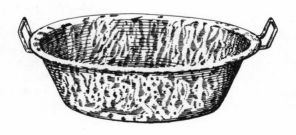

## DIPPABLE GARDEN VEGETABLES
### *Superb with or without a dip.*

Arrange a tray of these vegetables for weight-conscious
friends to nibble on during parties: cherry or pear tomatoes;
cauliflowerettes; tiny green onions; carrot sticks or curls;
celery sticks; red and white radishes; crisp, sweet turnip or
rutabaga sticks; spears of green pepper.

## ZESTY DIP FOR VEGETABLES
*Weight watchers appreciate vegetable snacks.*

1 cup cottage cheese
1 package (3-ounce) cream
cheese
1 teaspoon prepared
horseradish

¼ teaspoon salt
Few drops Tabasco
sauce
⅓ cup chopped fresh dill *or*
dry dill weed

Use blender or mixer and beat together until smooth and fluffy, cottage and cream cheese, horseradish, salt and Tabasco sauce. Blend in dill. Serve in a large, hollowed-out cucumber or zucchini. Use as a dip for celery, carrot or green pepper strips and cauliflowerettes. Yields 1¼ cups dip.

## TUNA PATE
*Tasty tree to highlight a snack party.*

3 cans (about 7-ounce
each) tuna in oil,
well drained
1 package (8-ounce)
cream cheese
1½ teaspoons dry mustard

1-1½ teaspoons salt (to
taste) *or* ¾ teaspoon
Accent with smoke
¾ teaspoon Tabasco
sauce
¼ cup minced onion
2 tablespoons finely
chopped parsley

Combine all ingredients in large bowl of electric mixer. Beat at low speed until smooth and well blended. Turn onto waxed paper and shape into Christmas tree. Garnish with vertical strips of pimiento and chopped parsley. Chill. Delicious with assorted thin crackers. Yields 3½ cups pate. Recipe may be cut in thirds for a small portion.

## PUMPKIN-HOLLOW DIP
*Great on crackers, rye bread sticks, chips.*

Cut top off small pumpkin. Remove seeds and line hollow with double thickness of foil. Crumble foil in bottom to partially fill hollow.

Fill with this dip: Blend ½ pound liver sausage with 3-ounce package cream cheese, 2 tablespoons caraway seed (optional, but very good) and 2 teaspoons onion juice. Use electric mixer. Yields 1 cup.

## CHRISTMAS CHEESE BALL
*Mix and shape the ball a day ahead.*

1 package (8-ounce) cream cheese
¾ cup (4-ounce) crumbled blue cheese
1 cup (4-ounce) shredded, sharp cheddar cheese
¼ cup minced onion

1 tablespoon Worcestershire sauce
Cuts of pimiento, green pepper, pimiento-stuffed olives and cocktail onions

Soften cheeses and mix in a medium-size bowl. Add onion, Worcestershire sauce; blend on low speed of electric mixer. Beat on medium speed until fluffy, scraping bowl frequently. Cover; chill 3 to 4 hours. Mold mixture into large ball; cover and chill 2 hours until firm.

*Before serving.* Decorate ball to resemble Christmas tree ornaments with cuts of pimiento, green pepper and stuffed olive slices. Circle base with tiny cocktail onions and stuffed olives. Surround ball with crackers and serve as a spread.

## DEVILED DIP
*Mix in a jiffy.*

1½ cups creamed cottage cheese
1 can (2¼-ounce) deviled ham
1 teaspoon finely-chopped parsley

1 tablespoon finely-chopped onion
Dash freshly-ground pepper

Combine all ingredients and mix until well blended, either by hand or with an electric mixer. Yields 1½ cups.

## PARTY DIP FOR APPLES
*Nice way to serve apples from your own trees.*

1 cup cottage cheese
1 tablespoon brown sugar
½ teaspoon Worcestershire
   sauce

¼ teaspoon salt
⅛ teaspoon cinnamon
⅛ teaspoon nutmeg
1 cup plain yogurt

Beat cottage cheese until fairly smooth; add sugar and seasonings and continue to beat. Fold in yogurt; cover and chill. Yields about 2 cups of dip.

Core and slice 2 or 3 eating apples. Dip in lemon juice mixed with a little water to keep apples from browning. Place bowl of dip in center of platter and surround with apple slices.

## BRUNCH FRUIT-DIPPING SAUCE
*A brunch treat with crisp bacon and muffins.*

1 cup dairy sour cream
1 tablespoon honey
3 tablespoons finely-
   chopped, preserved
   ginger

1 can (1-pound, 14-ounce)
   pineapple chunks,
   drained

Combine sour cream, honey and ginger. Pour into a small serving dish. Place the dish in center of a large glass or china serving plate. Surround it with pineapple chunks, into which long wooden picks have been plunged (or place a small container of party toothpicks on one edge of the plate for guests to use when picking up pineapple chunks). This dip also is good with strawberries and bananas dipped in lemon juice to prevent discoloring. Yields 8 to 10 servings.

# SALADS AND
# SALAD DRESSINGS

E Landin

## SPUR-OF-THE-MOMENT SALADS
*Serve these tasty combinations on greens and
top with your favorite dressing.*

*Mound cottage cheese* with diced green or red pepper,
cucumber and onions.

*Combine sliced, cooked beets* with very thin raw onion
rings. Sprinkle with a little marjoram, a grating of nutmeg
and a few slivers of garlic. Excellent with French dressing.

*Add thinly sliced radishes,* raw cauliflowerettes, wafer-thin
slices of raw turnip to mixed salad greens.

*Top cooked asparagus* tips with grated cheese. Serve on
thick tomato slices.

*Mix green pepper rings,* onion rings and sliced water
chestnuts *or* raw mushrooms.

*Combine a cup* of broken, raw spinach, ½ cup shredded
cabbage, ½ cup chopped celery and 8 sliced radishes. Very
tasty with French dressing.

*Arrange tomato slices* and red onion rings in a flat serving
dish. Marinate for several hours in a combination of ½ cup
red wine vinegar, ½ cup salad oil, 1 tablespoon sugar, 1
teaspoon salt, ½ teaspoon dry mustard and 1 clove crushed
garlic.

*Slice three heads of chickory* into ½-inch slices; combine
in salad bowl with a large bunch of water cress *or* nasturtium
leaves. Excellent with an oil-vinegar dressing.

*Serve a mixture* of cherry tomatoes, pineapple chunks and
green pepper strips in lettuce cups. Pass French or Thousand
Island dressing.

*Toss together leftover* canned vegetables — carrots, peas,
green beans, corn, lima beans — with your favorite salad
dressing and add shredded cabbage or lettuce and a few
chunks of tomato.

## SPINACH SALAD
*Garden time must!*

2 quarts young spinach,
    washed and dried
2 hard-cooked egg whites

½ cup crumbled, fried
    bacon *or* ham julienne
    (cut in thin strips)

Tear tender leaves of spinach into bite-sized pieces. Press

hard-cooked egg whites through a sieve onto the leaves in a salad bowl. Add bacon or ham. Just before serving, pour dressing over spinach and toss lightly. Yields 6 to 8 servings.

*Zippy Dressing:* Press 2 hard-cooked egg yolks through sieve into a bowl. Add ½ cup olive oil, 2½ teaspoons lemon juice, ⅛ teaspoon dry mustard, ¼ teaspoon paprika, ½ teaspoon dry *or* 1 teaspoon fresh chervil, 1 very small clove garlic, 1 teaspoon salt, dash pepper, 2 teaspoons water. Whisk until blended smooth. Taste to check seasoning. Yields about ¾ cup dressing.

## BACON-WILTED LETTUCE
### *A German speciality.*

| | |
|---|---|
| 1 quart leaf lettuce | 2 tablespoons water *or* |
| ¼ cup sliced green onions | half-and-half cream |
| 6 slices bacon | ½ teaspoon salt |
| 2 tablespoons bacon | ⅛ teaspoon pepper |
| drippings | ½ teaspoon dill weed |
| 2 tablespoons vinegar | |

Tear lettuce into salad bowl. Add green onions. Cook bacon until crisp. Drain and crumble. Add vinegar, water or cream, salt and pepper to drippings and bring to a boil. Pour over lettuce and green onions. Add crumbled bacon and dill weed. Toss lightly. Serve immediately. Yields 4 servings.

*One quart young spinach* may be used in place of lettuce.

## THOUSAND ISLAND DRESSING

*Thousand Island Dressing:* Spoon 1 quart salad dressing into a large bowl. Place 1½ cups chili sauce, ½ cup drained sweet pickle relish, 1 large cut-up onion, 1 cut-up green pepper and 1 bottle (3-ounce) stuffed green olives into blender. Cover and blend until well chopped and mixed, about 10 seconds at "chop" speed. Stir into salad dressing. Store in refrigerator. Use for lettuce salads, breaded shrimp or fish sticks. Yields about 6 cups dressing.

## MIXED BEAN SALAD
*Use fresh vegetables in summer, canned vegetables in winter.*

2½ cups wax beans, cut
2½ cups green beans, cut
2½ cups scraped, diced
    carrots
1 teaspoon salt

2 cups canned, drained
    kidney beans
1 large onion, sliced
1 small green pepper, diced

In a saucepan, cover fresh beans and carrots with water; add 1 teaspoon salt. Boil until tender; drain and cool. Add diced green pepper, onion and kidney beans. Mix all ingredients in a glass bowl. Pour on hot Boiled or cold Italian Dressing; mix. Refrigerate overnight. Yields 12 to 15 servings.

*Boiled Dressing:* In a saucepan, combine ¾ cup sugar, ¾ cup vinegar, ⅓ cup salad oil, ⅓ cup water, 1 teaspoon celery seed or dill seed. Bring mixture to a boil. Yields about 1½ cups dressing.

*Italian Dressing:* Place 3 medium cloves garlic, ¾ cup salad oil and ⅓ cup white vinegar in blender. Cover and blend 2 minutes at "blend" until garlic is completely liquified. Stop blender and add 1 tablespoon pimiento. Cover blender and run at "whip" until pimiento is chopped, about 5 seconds. Yields 1 cup dressing.

## CAULIFLOWER AND BEET SALAD
*Pretty, tasty combination to serve with beef.*

1 medium cauliflower (do
    not overcook)
1 cup sliced, cooked beets

2 green onions, finely
    chopped
Grated Parmesan cheese
    (optional)

Separate cooked cauliflower into flowerettes and place in bowl. Drain beets and add to cauliflower. Add green onions. Toss lightly with Cheese Dressing just before serving and sprinkle with Parmesan cheese.
*Herbed Dressing:* Mix ¼ cup salad oil, ¼ cup white vinegar, ⅛ teaspoon crumbled oregano, salt, pepper. Yields about ½ cup dressing.

## OREGANO GARLIC OLIVES
*Superb mixed into green salads.*

Pour 6 tablespoons salad *or* olive oil into a sterilized, pint-size jar. Add 3 diced cloves of garlic, ½ tablespoon black pepper, 1 tablespoon crushed red pepper, 1 tablespoon crushed oregano. Fill the jar with black, pitted olives; cover, and place in the refrigerator for several days. Shake occasionally so that olives absorb the spiced oil.

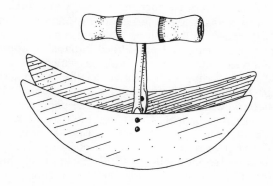

## ORANGE-CHICKORY SALAD
*Very good with roast poultry or game.*

1 quart chickory
2 large oranges, peeled and sliced

½ large Bermuda onion, sliced

Tear chickory into bite-sized pieces in bowl. Arrange orange and onion over chickory. Pour dressing over salad just before serving and toss lightly.

*Oil-Vinegar Dressing:* Combine 1 clove garlic, 6 tablespoons salad oil, 2 tablespoons tarragon vinegar, 1 teaspoon sugar, 1 teaspoon salt, 1 teaspoon paprika, in a bottle, shake well. Remove garlic. Yields about ½ cup dressing.

## SHREDDED CABBAGE OR CARROT SALADS

These two vegetables have many interesting possibilities alone, in combination, or with any of the ingredients below. A fine shredder is best for carrots, although a food chopper will do. Cabbage may be cut on slaw cutter, shredder, or by hand with a sharp knife. Freshen, if necessary, by standing in very cold water until crisp. Then drain thoroughly. Sprinkle with salt. Mix with salad dressing, Honey Dressing or Syrup Dressing — recipes follow.

*With 3 cups shredded cabbage or 2 cups shredded or ground carrots, add one of the following:* ½ cup chopped peanuts; ½ cup shredded cocoanut; 1 cup shredded pineapple; 2 diced oranges and 4 large, cut-up marshmallows; ½ cup finely-chopped, mild onion; 1 cup diced celery and 2 tablespoons green pepper; 1 cup cubed banana or apple and ½ cup chopped nuts; ⅔ cup raisins which have been "plumped" by standing in hot water. Yields 4 to 5 servings.

*Cabbage-Pepper Cole Slaw:* Shred 4 cups cabbage. Dice 2 large ribs celery. Cut fine, ½ medium green pepper and/or ½ medium, sweet, red pepper. Cover vegetables with ice water and stir in 1 teaspoon salt. Refrigerate 1 hour. Drain vegetables and pour on desired amount of Syrup Dressing or Honey Dressing (recipes follow). Chill. Yields 6 servings.

*Vegetable Cole Slaw:* Toss together — 4 cups shredded cabbage, 1 tablespoon minced onion, ½ cup chopped celery, ¼ cup chopped green pepper, 1 grated carrot, ½ cup sliced radishes. Mix with Sour Cream Dressing (recipe follows). Yields 6 servings.

## COLE SLAW DRESSINGS

*Honey Dressing:* Combine ¼ cup lemon juice, ¼ cup water, ¼ cup honey, ½ teaspoon celery seed, 1 teaspoon salt. Toss desired amount of dressing with chilled cole slaw. Yields ¾ cup dressing.

*Syrup Dressing:* Boil to a syrup — 1 cup sugar, ⅓ cup water, ½ cup white vinegar, 1 teaspoon mustard seed. Cool. Stir in 1 teaspoon grated onion, if desired. Toss desired amount of dressing with cole slaw. Yields about 1⅔ cups dressing.

*Sour Cream Dressing:* Combine ½ cup dairy sour cream, 1 tablespoon tarragon vinegar, ¼ teaspoon sugar, ½ teaspoon salt. Toss with chilled cole slaw. Yields ½ cup dressing.

## TOMATO SALADS

*Fresh Tomato Shells:* Remove center part of the top of a large tomato and carefully scoop out pulp, seeds and juice. Set pulp mixture aside for possible use in the recipe.

Invert shells to drain. Season with salt and pepper before stuffing with any of the mixtures below. Bake or chill as directed.

*Fresh Tomato Flowers:* Allow a whole peeled and chilled tomato for each serving. Cut nearly through 3 times to make 6 sections so the tomato can be spread apart, flower-like. Fill center with one of the following.

*Use these fillings* for tomato shells or flowerette salads; Deviled egg half. Cottage cheese, plain, or mixed with cucumber or nuts. Egg salad mixture. Chicken, fish, or meat salad. Mixed vegetable salad. Cabbage salad combinations.

## TOMATO ASPIC
*Excellent with cold roast beef.*

| | |
|---|---|
| 2 tablespoons unflavored gelatin | 2 peppercorns |
| ½ cup cold water | ¼ bay leaf |
| 4 cups tomatoes | 1 teaspoon salt |
| 1 slice onion | 1 tablespoon sugar |
| 3 cloves | 2 tablespoons lemon juice |

Soften gelatin in cold water. Cook tomatoes and seasonings (all but lemon juice) 5 to 10 minutes. Strain. Pour 2 cups of this hot tomato puree over softened gelatin. Add lemon juice, pour into oiled molds to set. Unmold on lettuce or cabbage slaw. Top with mayonnaise or cooked dressing.

*Aspic with Peas and Celery:* Add 1 cup peas and 1 cup celery cut fine to thickened jelly. For party occasions, make in a ring mold and fill center with tuna, salmon or chicken salad.

*Aspic with Cucumber:* Add 2 cups diced cucumbers to thickened jelly.

*Sour Cream Dressing:* Measure ½ cup dairy sour cream, 4 teaspoons vinegar, ½ teaspoon sugar, ¼ teaspoon salt and 1½ teaspoons minced onion into a jar. Cover tightly and shake well. Chill. Shake thoroughly before serving. Yields about ¾ cup dressing for aspic or green salads.

## HOT POTATO SALAD WITH CHEESE
### Variation of a German speciality.

¾ cup French dressing
⅓ cup sliced green onions
¼ cup chopped green
    pepper
6 cups sliced, cooked
    potatoes
1 cup sliced celery

12 slices crisply-cooked
    bacon, crumbled
1½ teaspoons salt
    Dash pepper
1 cup (¼-pound) shredded
    sharp, cheddar cheese

In a large skillet, combine dressing, onions and green pepper; simmer 5 minutes. Add potatoes, celery, bacon, salt and pepper; mix lightly. Cover and simmer 15 minutes. Sprinkle with cheese; cover until cheese melts. Yields 6 to 8 servings.

*Basic French Dressing:* Measure 1 cup corn oil, ⅓-½ cup cider vinegar, 1-3 tablespoons sugar, 1½ teaspoons salt, ½ teaspoon paprika, ½ teaspoon dry mustard and 1 clove garlic into a jar. Cover tightly and shake well. Chill several hours; remove garlic. Use part lemon juice for vinegar, if desired. Store in refrigerator. Yields 1⅓ to 1½ cups dressing.

## DELICIOUS POTATO SALAD
### Buffet supper must from
### The 1945 Country Kitchen Cook Book.

1 quart cold, cubed,
    boiled potatoes
1 teaspoon salt
    Dash of pepper and
    cayenne
¼ teaspoon paprika
1 tablespoon vinegar
2 tablespoons salad oil
1-2 cups chopped celery *or*
    shredded lettuce *or*
    cucumber and sliced
    radishes

2 tablespoons chopped
    onion
4 hard-cooked eggs (cut in
    eighths)
2 tablespoons green
    pepper, pimiento *or*
    parsley
½ cup chopped sweet
    pickle (optional)
2 cups salad dressing

Marinate (coat lightly and let stand) cubed potatoes in vinegar, seasonings and salad oil about an hour. Add the other ingredients. Blend with dressing. Part of the dressing may be mayonnaise if desired. Salad is improved by standing, except for shredded lettuce which should not be added until just before serving. Yields 8 to 10 servings.

*Use Carrots:* Add ½ to ¾ cups shredded carrots to the dressing, omitting some of the other vegetables.

*Marinate with Sour Cream:* Omit oil, and instead heat ½ cup soured cream with vinegar and seasonings. Pour over potatoes and let stand until cold before mixing with the other ingredients.

*Marinate with French Dressing:* Soak warm, cubed potatoes in ¼ cup French Dressing for about 1 hour. Omit vinegar, oil and paprika.

## WHIPPED APPLE-ORANGE FRUIT SALAD
*Take to a pot luck supper.*

1 package (3-ounce) lemon-flavored gelatin
½ cup hot water
¼ cup lemon juice
½ cup undiluted evaporated milk

1 cup diced oranges
1 cup diced, unpeeled apples
1 tablespoon grated orange rind

Dissolve gelatin in hot water. Add 3 tablespoons lemon juice. Chill until consistency of unbeaten egg whites. Chill evaporated milk in refrigerator tray until soft ice crystals form around edges of the tray (10 to 15 minutes). Whip until stiff (about 1 to 2 minutes). Add remaining 1 tablespoon lemon juice and whip *very* stiff (about 2 minutes longer). Fold *whipped* evaporated milk, oranges, apples and grated orange rind into chilled gelatin. Spoon into 1½-quart mold. Chill in refrigerator until firm (about 1 to 2 hours). Unmold. Serve on salad greens. Yields 4 to 6 servings.

## CUCUMBER-PINEAPPLE SALAD MOLD
### *Summer cooler.*

1 tablespoon unflavored
  gelatin
¼ cup cold water
¾ cup boiling water
¼ cup sugar
½ teaspoon salt

¼ cup vinegar
¼ cup juice drained from
  crushed pineapple
1 cup diced cucumber
1 cup drained, canned,
  crushed pineapple

Soften gelatin in cold water. Dissolve in boiling water. Add sugar, salt, vinegar and pineapple juice. Cool until mixture begins to congeal, then add cucumber and pineapple. Pour into 1-quart or individual molds. Chill until firm. Unmold on lettuce. Serve with mayonnaise or French dressing. Yields 5 to 6 servings.

*Blender Mayonnaise:* Break 1 egg into blender jar. Add juice of ½ a lemon *or* 2 teaspoons white vinegar, pinch of dry mustard, ⅓ cup salad oil, salt and pepper to taste. Cover jar and blend for 5 seconds at "liquify." Without turning off motor, remove cover and add ⅓ cup salad oil to center of mixture in a slow, steady stream. Stop blender when last drop of oil has been added. Store mayonnaise in glass jar in refrigerator. Yields about 1 cup dressing.

## MANDARIN ORANGE FRUIT SALAD
### *Midwest company favorite.*

1 cup mandarin oranges
  (11-ounce can), drained
  *or* 1 cup green, seedless
  grapes
1⅔ cups pineapple chunks
  *or* crushed pineapple

1 cup flake cocoanut
1 cup dairy sour cream
1 cup miniature *or* cut-up
  marshmallows
⅓ cup maraschino cherries,
  drained

Combine above ingredients. Chill in refrigerator several hours or overnight. Do not freeze. Yields 8 servings.

*Sweet Cream Fruit Salad:* Omit sour cream. Just before serving, add 1 large, peeled, sliced banana to chilled fruit. Whip 1 cup cream and mix with 3 tablespoons mayonnaise. Fold into fruit mixture. Serve at once.

## FROZEN SALAD
*Make a day or two ahead.*

1 cup drained, crushed
  pineapple
1 cup drained, maraschino
  cherries
3 tablespoons sugar

1 package (3-ounce) cream
  cheese, softened
½ cup salad dressing
½ pint whipping cream

Beat cheese and dressing with electric mixer. Stir in fruit and sugar. Whip cream and fold into cheese mixture. Spread in a single-size ice cube tray, cover with plastic wrap and freeze. Serve on a lettuce leaf and pass more salad dressing. Yields 6 servings.

## RASPBERRY GELATIN MOLD
*Party salad or dessert.*

Place 2 heaping cups marshmallows in top of double boiler. Cover and place over hot water until melted. Stir melted marshmallows into 1 cup dairy sour cream and pour into the bottom of a salad mold. Chill until set. Meanwhile, dissolve 1 package raspberry gelatin in 1 cup boiling liquid made from the juice drained from 1 package of frozen raspberries plus enough water to make 1 cup. Add another scant cup water and the drained berries. Pour cooled mixture over set marshmallow layer in mold. Refrigerate until set. Serve with mayonnaise for a salad or whipped cream for dessert. Yields about 8 servings.

## GRAPEFRUIT-AVOCADO SALAD
*Dressing makes this salad . . .*
*also good with tossed salad greens.*

Combine slices of avocado, 2 cans (303 size) drained grapefruit segments and a few thin onion rings on individual salad plates. Pass Patio Creamy Dressing. Yields 6 servings.

*Patio Creamy Dressing:* Measure ⅔ cup half-and-half cream, 3 tablespoons vinegar, ¼ cup corn oil into a jar. Add 2 teaspoons sugar, ½ teaspoon salt, ¼ teaspoon paprika, few grains pepper and 1 small garlic clove. Chill several hours. Shake well before serving. Yields 1 cup dressing.

## BANANA SALAD WITH CREAMY DRESSING
*Winter favorite!*

| | |
|---|---|
| 1 medium head lettuce | 2 tablespoons chopped |
| 1 large banana, sliced | walnuts |
| | Creamy Dressing |

Break lettuce into bite-size pieces. Lightly toss lettuce, banana slices and walnuts together. Mix in dressing. Sprinkle with paprika. Serve at once. Yields about 6 servings.

*Creamy Dressing:* Blend ¼ cup corn syrup, ¾ cup mayonnaise, 1½ teaspoons prepared mustard and ¼ cup light cream together. Toss salad with some of dressing. Yields about 1¼ cups dressing.

*Note:* Creamy Dressing also is delicious served with orange or grapefruit salad.

## WALDORF SALAD
*Popular in the 1934 Country Kitchen Cook Book.*

| | |
|---|---|
| 2 cups cored, unpeeled, | ½ cup chopped walnuts |
| diced apples | ½ cup mayonnaise |
| 1 tablespoon lemon juice | Milk to thin mayonnaise |
| 1 cup diced celery | ½ teaspoon confectioners' |
| | sugar |

Sprinkle apples with lemon juice to prevent discoloration. Add celery and walnuts. Blend with thinned mayonnaise to which the confectioners' sugar has been added. Yields 5 to 6 servings.

*With Dates:* Substitute ½ cup cut up dates for celery in recipe; *or* dates for nuts.

*With Bananas:* Substitute diced banana for part of celery.

## MELON RINGS
*Serve with hot rolls.*

Arrange rings or "fingers" of chilled melon on a bed of lettuce as the foundation of a cool, fresh fruit salad. Add grapes and cubes or slices of fresh pears dipped in lemon juice. Serve with a peak of sherbet or a fruit dressing.

*Fruit Dressing:* "Puree" the following ingredients in a blender for 15 seconds — 1 package (3-ounce) softened cream cheese, ¼ cup orange juice, ¼ cup crushed pineapple, ¼ cup lemon juice, ¼ cup sugar, ¼ teaspoon salt, ½ thinly-sliced orange peel with white membrane scraped out, ¼ cup whipping cream. Flash blend if cheese becomes lodged in blades. Blend an additional 10 seconds for creamier dressing. Yields about 1½ cups dressing.

*Creamy Maple Dressing:* Gradually add ⅓ cup maple-blended syrup and a dash of salt to ½ cup mayonnaise, mixing until smooth. Whip ½ cup whipping cream until stiff and fold into syrup mixture. Chill. Yields about 1¾ cups dressing. Use for fresh or canned fruit salads.

## BROILED BREAKFAST GRAPEFRUIT SALAD
*So special and so easy!*

3 large grapefruit, halved    ½ cup after-dinner mints,
                              crushed

Cut around grapefruit sections. Place on broiler rack. Sprinkle mints on each half. Broil 4 inches from heat source for 6 to 8 minutes. Yields 6 servings.

## CANNED FRUIT SALADS
*Quickies from the 1934 Country Kitchen Cook Book.*

*Allow 1 or 2 halves* of peach, pear *or* a pineapple slice for each serving. Place on lettuce and top with dressing and/or one of the following—
*Cheese:* Grate cheese over top of the dressing. *Or* spoon a little cottage cheese in the center. Cottage cheese may be mixed with green pepper, preserved ginger, chopped nuts, candied cherries *or* bright preserve.
*Fruit:* Dates *or* prunes *or* white cherries, stuffed with cheese or nuts.
*Peanut Butter:* Mixed with cream or cottage cheese.
*Three-in-One Party Salad:* Arrange a canned pear half and canned peach half (curved side down) and a slice of pineapple on each plate, with crisp lettuce or water cress beneath. Top the pear with a little dab of peanut butter mixed with salad

dressing; the peach with a dab of whipped cream mixed with salad dressing; the pineapple slice with grated cheese.

*Fill a drained peach half* with chopped celery and nuts. Serve on a lettuce leaf; pass mayonnaise to those who want dressing.

*Surround apricot halves* with sliced bananas dipped in lemon juice. Sprinkle with cocoanut.

*Fill pear halves* with red sour pitted cherries and cream cheese.

*Alternate grapefruit* sections with bright unpeeled apple wedges on a leaf-lined salad plate.

## CHERRY CHICKEN SALAD
*A party salad.*

| | |
|---|---|
| 1 cup pitted, halved sweet cherries | ½ cup pineapple tidbits |
| 2 cups cubed, cooked chicken *or* turkey | ¼ cup sliced almonds |
| ½ cup diced celery | Salad greens |
| | Piquant Dressing |

Mix cherries, chicken, celery, pineapple and almonds. Place in salad bowl lined with greens. Toss lightly with dressing. Garnish with more cherries, if desired. Yields 6 servings.

*Piquant Dressing:* Combine ½ cup mayonnaise, ¼ cup sour cream, ⅛ teaspoon horseradish, ¼ teaspoon salt; mix well. Yields ¾ cup dressing.

## TURKEY SALAD
*Serve on lettuce leaves or in cream puff shells.*

| | |
|---|---|
| 3 cups diced, cooked turkey | 1 teaspoon dry mustard |
| 1½ cups chopped celery | 1½ teaspoons salt |
| 3 tablespoons lemon juice | ½ teaspoon pepper |
| 1 cup green, seedless grapes | ¼ cup cream |
| 1 cup sliced almonds | 1 cup salad dressing |
| | 2 hard-cooked eggs |

Mix first 5 ingredients lightly. Combine next 5 ingredients and mix into a smooth dressing. Toss dressing lightly with salad ingredients. Garnish with sliced eggs. Yields about 8 servings.

*Chicken* may be substituted for turkey.

*Tuna,* tart apple and broken walnuts may be substituted for turkey, celery and almonds.

## CHEF'S SALAD BOWL
*Hot weather treat with toast,*
*plus cake and coffee for dessert.*

1 clove garlic
1-2 heads lettuce
1½ cups diced cucumbers
1 green pepper cut in narrow strips
4 tomatoes cut in wedges
4 hard-cooked eggs, sliced

1¼ cups cooked ham, cut in thin, narrow strips (julienne)
1¼ cups cooked chicken, *or* turkey cut julienne
¾ cup Swiss cheese cut julienne
French dressing

Rub salad bowl with cut clove of garlic. Break lettuce in bite-sized pieces in salad bowl. Add cucumbers, green pepper, ham, chicken, eggs and tomatoes. Add French dressing and toss lightly. (Canned chicken and luncheon meat may be used instead of ham and chicken.) Yields about 12 servings.

## BEEF WITH GREENS
*Julienne cut means cut in thin, match-like strips.*

1 cup julienne cooked beef
¼ cup olive oil
¼ cup white vinegar
Salt and pepper
3 bunches leaf lettuce *or* 1 medium head of lettuce

2 large tomatoes
1 large onion *or* 6 green onions
1 large green pepper

Marinate beef (left-over roast or steak works nicely) in the oil, vinegar, salt and pepper for 2 hours. Just before serving, toss beef and marinade with the lettuce, torn into bite-sized pieces, the thinly-sliced onion and green pepper rings. Garnish bowl with tomato wedges. Yields 4 to 6 servings.

## EGG SALAD
*Serve with toast and a cup of soup.*

8 hard-cooked eggs, diced
2 cups diced cucumbers
1 cup diced celery
4 tablespoons chopped
  pimiento *or* relish

2 tablespoons chopped
  onion
½ teaspoon salt
¼ teaspoon paprika
⅔ cup salad dressing

Mix and chill ingredients. Serve in bowl lined with lettuce. Yields 4 to 5 servings.

## TURKEY COLE SLAW
*Serve with toasted cheese sandwiches.*

Combine 4 cups shredded cabbage with 2 peeled and sectioned oranges, 1 teaspoon grated onion, 1½ to 2 cups julienne (thin match-like strips) cooked turkey and 1 tablespoon lemon juice. Season with salt and pepper. Moisten with 1 cup salad dressing. Toss lightly with fork to blend. Arrange in salad bowl, garnish with orange slices and keep chilled until served. Yields 6 to 8 servings.

## EGG AND HAM SALAD
*This hearty salad goes together in minutes.*

6 hard-cooked eggs, diced
1 cup diced, cooked ham
  *or* luncheon meat
6 sweet pickles, diced *or*
  1 cup tart apple, diced

1 cup chopped celery
10 stuffed olives, chopped
¼ cup French dressing *or*
  mayonnaise

Combine all ingredients; chill; serve on salad greens or fill Tomato Flowerettes (page 23). Yields 4 to 6 servings.

# VEGETABLES, LEGUMES, GRAINS

## ASPARAGUS AND EGGS
*This is a good supper dish.*

2 cups asparagus, canned *or* cooked
2 cups medium white sauce, page 57

⅛ teaspoon pepper
4 hard cooked eggs
Buttered crumbs

Put alternate layers of asparagus and sauce in greased baking dish. Cut eggs in halves, lengthwise, and put over the top. Top with buttered crumbs. Bake in preheated, 350° F. oven about 20 minutes.

## QUICKIE GREEN VELVET SOUP
*Hard to believe it's canned soup.*

1 can (10½-ounce) condensed cream of mushroom soup
1 can (10½-ounce) condensed cream of asparagus soup
1 can (10½-ounce) condensed cream of chicken soup

2 soup cans milk
1 soup can water
Chopped toasted almonds (optional)
Grated orange rind (optional)

Stir mushroom soup until smooth in large saucepan. Gradually blend in other soups, milk and water. Heat, but do not boil. Garnish with almonds and orange rind. Yields 6 to 8 servings.

## BROCCOLI CASSEROLE
*Spinach, Swiss chard, artichoke hearts or asparagus also are delicious cooked in this way.*

2 cups chopped, cooked broccoli
½ cup thick white sauce, page 57
½ cup mayonnaise

1 tablespoon onion juice
3 eggs, well beaten
½ teaspoon salt
⅛ teaspoon pepper

Combine all ingredients in order given. Pour into a well-greased, 1-quart casserole. Set in a pan of boiling water and bake in preheated, 350° F. oven for about 45 minutes or until firm. Yields 6 servings.

*Add cheese:* ½ cup grated cheddar cheese may be sprinkled on top.

*Prize-winning* centerpiece features a cluster of fresh asparagus in a deep bowl or cream-colored butter crock. Tie with wide blue ribbon . . . or a colored ribbon which complements tablecloth color. Sprinkle asparagus with water and cover with plastic wrap until used.

### GLORIFIED CABBAGE
*Nice with beef pot roast.*

1 medium head cabbage
2 eggs, beaten
1 tablespoon butter, melted

½ cup half-and-half cream
⅛ teaspoon paprika
½ teaspoon salt
Grated Parmesan cheese

Remove outer leaves from cabbage. Quarter cabbage and shred finely. Place cabbage in boiling, salted water to cover. Cook 5 minutes; drain well. Arrange cooked cabbage in greased 1½-quart baking dish. Season with salt. Pour mixture of beaten eggs, cream and paprika over cabbage. Bake, uncovered, in preheated, 325° F. oven until top is lightly brown and mixture is slightly thickened. Do not overcook. Remove dish from oven and sprinkle Parmesan cheese liberally over top; return to oven and continue baking until cheese is melted. Takes about ½ hour, in all, to bake. Yields about 6 servings.

## CABBAGE TOMATO CASSEROLE
*A favorite vegetable dish with pork chops and cornbread.*

5 cups shredded cabbage
1 cup ripe tomatoes *or*
    drained canned tomatoes
¼ cup medium cracker
    crumbs

½ cup tomato juice
1½ teaspoons salt
⅛ teaspoon pepper
½ cup grated *or* shredded
    processed cheese

Steam cabbage in covered saucepan with a small amount of water until tender-crisp. Drain, if necessary. In a greased, 1-quart casserole, arrange alternate layers of cabbage, tomatoes, onions and crumbs. Add juice and seasonings. Bake, covered, in a preheated, 350° F. oven for 30 minutes. Remove cover; bake 10 minutes more. Sprinkle cheese over top and continue baking another 5 minutes or until cheese is melted and bubbly. Yields 6 servings.

*A copper* pot or silver bowl makes a gleaming nest for a lush, green head of cabbage. Choose one with great, curling leaves that are nearly perfect. Check the garden carefully because you want to avoid trimming if you can. Picking a perfect specimen is the hardest part of this arrangement. After that, simply set cabbage in the bowl, tuck in several sprigs of dill or baby's breath. Sprinkle arrangement with water, cover loosely with a large plastic bag and refrigerate until it's time to call guests. Use cabbage later in cooking.

*Scrape vegetables!* Scrape, rather than peel vegetables like carrots, parsnips and salsify. This is because you peel the best most nutritious part away. — The Farmer, 1933.

## BAKED CARROTS
*Good and quick!*

2 cups scraped, thinly-
  sliced carrots
2 tablespoons grated onion
¼ cup butter

1 teaspoon sugar
½ teaspoon salt
⅛ teaspoon pepper

Brown onion in butter. Add remaining ingredients. Place in 1-quart covered baking dish and bake in preheated, 325° F. oven for 35 minutes, or until tender. Yields about 5 servings.
  *Orange Carrots:* Add 1 small, peeled orange, cut into bite-size pieces, to above ingredients.

## CARROTS AND GREEN BEANS AU GRATIN
*Colorful, tasty, nourishing!*

2 cups diced carrots,
  cooked
1 cup green beans,
  cooked
½ teaspoon salt
3 tablespoons butter,
  melted

1 cup milk
½ cup grated cheese
1 egg, beaten
1 cup bread crumbs
1 tablespoon butter,
  melted

Combine first 7 ingredients and place in 1½-quart baking dish. Mix crumbs and melted butter and sprinkle over vegetables. Bake in preheated, 350° F. oven for 30 to 40 minutes. Yields 6 to 8 servings.

## GLAZED CARROTS AND ONIONS
*Bake along with roast or meat loaf.*

1 dozen small young
  carrots
½ pound small white
  onions

¼ cup butter
½ cup honey
2 tablespoons hot water

Precook carrots and onions in salted water approximately 10 minutes. Drain. Place in casserole. Combine remaining ingredients. Pour over vegetables. Bake in preheated, 350° F. oven for 20 minutes. Yields 4 to 5 servings.

## MASHED CARROTS AND POTATOES
*Light and pretty.*

Boil potatoes and carrots in about equal quantities. Run both through a ricer, mix, season with cream, butter and salt as for mashed potatoes. Pile on a hot dish and serve. This may be piled in baking-serving dish and reheated in a preheated, 350° F. oven.

## SPECIAL OCCASION CARROT RING
*Carrots are generally in good supply and become so "every day" after a while. So, for holidays, company or a special family treat, use this carrot recipe.*

4 cups mashed, cooked
   carrots
2 tablespoons cream
½ teaspoon grated onion
½ teaspoon salt
1 tablespoon melted butter

2 tablespoons brown sugar
½ teaspoon pepper
¼ teaspoon nutmeg
¼ cup melted butter
¼ cup sliced almonds
¼ cup fine bread crumbs

Mix first 8 ingredients together. Grease a 4-cup ring mold. Combine the last 3 ingredients and spread on bottom of mold. Pour carrot mixture over crumbs and bake in preheated, 350° F. oven for 45 minutes. Unmold to serve and fill center with meat balls, little pork sausages or buttered peas. Yields 6 servings.

## CROWN CAULIFLOWER WITH PEAS
*So pretty on a dinner buffet.*

2 packages (10-ounce
   each) frozen cauliflower
1 package (10-ounce)
   frozen peas

1 can (10¾-ounce) con-
   densed cheese soup
½ cup milk

Cook cauliflower and peas according to package directions. Meanwhile, combine milk and soup; heat. Place cooked and drained cauliflower on serving platter; crown with cheese sauce. Drain peas well and sprinkle over sauce for jeweled effect. Yields 6 to 8 servings.

*Pick the* prettiest footed bowl or compote in your cupboard — silver, antique white china, clear or tinted glass. Then pick a fat, perfect head of cauliflower from your garden. Strip away the leaves; set the cauliflower into the bowl and fringe it with lacy, bright green parsley. Sprinkle parsley generously with water; then cover loosely with a large plastic bag. Refrigerate until ready to use so that the parsley stays crisp. Later, cook cauliflower for a family meal.

### BAKED CELERY AND CARROTS
*From the 1942 Country Kitchen Cook Book.*

Cut outside ribs of celery into small pieces; scrape carrots and slice. Combine in a baking dish with soup stock or half-and-half cream to half fill the dish. Season, cover and bake in preheated, 350° F. oven about 45 minutes or until tender.

### BAKED SWEET CORN
*From The Farmer, 1893.*

Take 1 dozen good ears of corn; with a sharp knife cut off the smallest possible portion; then take the back of the knife and scrape off all of the pulp. Season with butter, pepper, salt and cream. Also put in about 1 tablespoon of sugar. Put in a dish; cover closely and put in a preheated, 350° F. oven and bake. Yields about 6 servings.

## ESCALLOPED CORN
*Prepare an entire meal in the oven when you use this recipe.
Small potatoes can be baked in this time;
meat loaf, pork chops or steaks taste good with the corn.*

2 cups whole-kernel corn
  (fresh, canned *or* frozen)
1 cup cold milk
4 tablespoons butter,
  melted

2 eggs, beaten
1½ cups soda cracker
  crumbs
½ teaspoon salt
⅛ teaspoon pepper

Mix all ingredients in a 1½-quart buttered baking dish and bake in preheated, 350° F. oven for 40 minutes. Yields 5 to 6 servings.

## STEWED CORN AND TOMATOES
*From The Farmer, 1886.*

Take the pulp of 8 ears of corn and mix this with 1 quart of ripe, peeled tomatoes, cut in small pieces. Season with salt and pepper, adding a little butter and 3 soda crackers rolled fine. Stew slowly for 1 hour and serve. Yields about 8 servings.

## CUCUMBER A LA DILL
*Cucumber slices add zesty tang to meals.*

3 cucumbers
1 cup dairy sour cream
½ cup thinly-sliced onion
3 tablespoons vinegar

2 tablespoons chopped dill
1 tablespoon sugar
1 teaspoon salt

Peel and slice cucumbers. Blend, then add remaining ingredients. Chill at least 2 hours. Yields about 3 cups cukes.

## FRIED EGGPLANT
*Delicate flavor favorite.*

Pare an eggplant, cut in ½-inch slices. Sprinkle them with salt and pepper; dip in a thin batter, flour, or egg and crumbs. Fry on both sides until brown. Yields 4 to 6 servings.

## GREEN BEANS SUPREME
*"This is by far my family's favorite way to eat green beans,"*
*says a Jackson County, Minnesota, farm wife.*

4 slices bacon
2 tablespoons bacon
  drippings
¼ cup chopped onion
1 can (10½-ounce) con-
  densed cream of celery
  soup

⅓ cup milk
1 pound fresh green
  beans, cooked and
  drained; *or* 2 packages
  (9-ounce each) frozen
  beans

Cook bacon until crisp; cool and crumble. Cook onions in bacon drippings until tender. Blend in soup, milk and beans. Heat slowly, stirring occasionally. Place in serving dish; sprinkle bacon on top. Yields 4 servings.

*Bake it:* Mixture may be placed in a casserole and baked 20 to 30 minutes in preheated, 350° F. oven. Top with crushed potato chips or canned, French fried onion rings during last 10 minutes of baking. This is a fine dish for a buffet meal as the vegetable stays hot in the casserole.

## HERBED GREEN BEANS
*Good with roast pork and sliced tomatoes.*

1 quart (4 cups) frozen
    green beans
¼ cup water

¼ cup butter
½ teaspoon salt
¼ teaspoon sweet basil

In saucepan, place beans, water, butter and salt; cover and bring to boil. Stir to break up beans. Bring to boil again; reduce heat to simmer and cook beans until just tender, about 8 minutes. Toss with sweet basil. Yields 4 to 6 servings.

## BRAISED GREENS

The success of greens depends largely upon: Thorough washing to remove all grit; short cooking to retain fresh color and good texture; thorough draining, and good seasoning. Greens such as spinach, dandelion, mustard, beet and turnip tops are easily cleaned, if rinsed 3 or 4 times in fresh water. Lift greens from water; sand stays in bottom of pan. Most greens can be cooked, covered, without water as enough water for cooking clings to the leaves.

Clean and cut young, tender greens with scissors (dandelion, lettuce, spinach, chard, kale, mixed greens). In a heavy skillet, melt 3 or 4 tablespoons butter or bacon fat, or fry out diced salt pork. Add 1 slice onion, chopped, and cook until soft. Add cut greens, cover skillet tightly and cook until greens are wilted and tender. Uncover; season with salt and pepper; drain off excess liquid, if necessary, and serve. Garnish with hard-cooked egg slices or bacon.

## BAKED MUSHROOMS
*Rich and creamy.*

Wash about 1 pound mushrooms and slice if very large. Sprinkle generously with 2 tablespoons flour. Put in baking dish. Add 1 cup cream, salt and pepper to season. Cover and bake in a preheated, 350° F. oven about 30 minutes, uncovering at the last. Serve on toast. Yields 4 to 5 servings.

*When frying onions,* add unpared, quartered apples to the pan. Arrange with onions on the platter with meat.

## BATTER-FRIED ONIONS
*Better make a lot.*

Onions, preferably mild,
  sliced in ¼-inch to ½-inch
  slices
Flour for dipping

Thin batter for coating
Fine bread *or* cracker
  crumbs

Cover sliced onions with water and let stand about ½ hour. Separate into rings, drain and dry, using paper towels. Dredge rings in flour; shake off loose flour. Dip rings in thin batter coating and drain. Dredge in sifted crumbs. Spread out and let dry about an hour, several hours if convenient. Heat lard, oil or shortening to 365° F. Put a few rings into a frying basket and lower slowly into hot fat. Fry two minutes, stirring gently. Drain on absorbent towel, then put in preheated, 300° F. oven to keep warm until all rings are fried. Serve hot.

*Thin Batter Coating:* Combine 1 beaten egg, 4 tablespoons flour, 1 teaspoon salt and ¼ cup milk. Batter may also be used for batter-fried chicken or fish.

*If parsley is eaten* with onions or a salad containing onions, the odor of the onions will not affect the breath. The sprigs of parsley should be eaten as you would eat celery. — The Farmer, 1896.

# ONIONS AU GRATIN
*Inexpensive flavor treat.*

5 cups coarsely-cut sweet
    onions
Water
1 can (10½-ounce) con-
    densed cream of mush-
    room soup

½ cup grated cheese (any
    cheddar-type leftover will do)
1 teaspoon salt
¼ teaspoon pepper
2 tablespoons butter
½ cup bread crumbs

Boil onions gently in a little water until tender; drain. Mix onions, soup, salt, pepper and cheese and place in 1-quart ovenproof serving dish. Brown crumbs in the butter and sprinkle over top of onions. Bake in preheated, 350° F. oven for 30 to 45 minutes. Yields 4 to 6 servings.

# SCALLOPED PARSNIPS AND CARROTS
*From The Farmer, 1896.*

Wash and scrape and slice thin; put in alternate layers, sprinkling each layer with chopped parsley, pepper, salt and bits of butter. Add sweet milk or cream till it shows between the slices. Cover and bake an hour or more at 350° F.

# SHELLING PEAS

Pour boiling water over the pods and let stand a minute or so until the pods are toughened, so that when you squeeze the pod of peas, the pod will open and the peas come out so easily. You can shell peas in half the time this way, so it helps a great deal when one has a lot to shell, especially for canning. Children will like to shell them this way for the pods pop like a firecracker — The Farmer, 1933.

# PEAS WITH A GOURMET TOUCH

*Add 1 teaspoon finely chopped onion* and ½ teaspoon crushed, dried mint leaves to 2 cups fresh *or* frozen peas *or* peas and carrots. Cook until just tender in lightly salted water.
*Toss a handful of snipped watercress* in cooked green peas just before serving.

*Mix a few chopped, stuffed olives* with drained, cooked, seasoned green peas.

*Add canned, sliced or button mushrooms* which have been sauted in a little butter, to drained, cooked green peas just before serving.

## PEPPERED PEAS
*Doctoring improves canned peas flavor.*

2 cans (13¼-ounce each) peas
2 tablespoons butter

½ cup green pepper strips
2 tablespoons chopped onion

Drain liquid from peas into saucepan; add butter, green pepper and onion. Simmer 3 minutes. Add peas and heat to serving temperature. Spoon peas and liquid into sauce dishes and serve. Yields 6 servings.

## DUTCH STYLE PEAS
*A new zing!*

2 cups fresh green peas *or*
1 package (10-ounce) frozen peas
2 tablespoons butter

2 tablespoons brown sugar
2 teaspoons vinegar
Salt and pepper

Cook peas, drain. Add seasoning. Heat and serve. Yields 3 to 4 servings.

*Dutch-Style Green Beans:* Substitute 2 slices cubed bacon for butter. Saute cubed bacon, add cooked beans and other ingredients listed above; heat and serve.

*Celery seed* takes the place of celery for soup or stews, when the vegetable is scarce — also parsley and parsley seed. — The Farmer, 1897.

# POTATO PANCAKES
*These are traditionally served with sauerbrauten,*
*a German sweet-sour beef roast; but good, too, with*
*bacon, sausage or ham.*

4 eggs
1 quart (4 cups) finely-
   grated raw potato
2 teaspoons salt

4 tablespoons all-purpose
   flour
2 teaspoons grated onion

Beat eggs, add grated potato and salt; mix. Stir in flour and onion. Drop from a tablespoon onto a hot, buttered griddle or skillet. Brown on both sides; turn once. Keep cakes as thin as possible. Serve, spread with butter and sprinkled with salt and pepper. Yields about 8 servings.

# CREAMED NEW POTATOES AND PEAS
*Traditionally served with the first home-raised,*
*fried chicken in the summer.*

2 pounds tiny, new potatoes
2 cups freshly-hulled
   green peas

2 cups thin, well-seasoned
   white sauce, page 57

Scrub and brush the new potatoes, then cook quickly in salted water until tender, about 15 minutes. Cook peas in lightly-salted water until tender, about 5 minutes. Fold potatoes and peas into hot, seasoned white sauce and serve. Yields about 6 servings.

# FRIED SWEET-SOUR POTATOES
*German style — so serve with wieners, sausage or ham.*

4 slices bacon
2½-3 cups peeled, diced,
   raw potatoes
¼ cup finely-chopped
   onion

1 tablespoon sugar
¾ teaspoon salt
½ cup water
¼ cup vinegar

Cook bacon in a fry pan until crisp, remove from pan and chop. Using 2 tablespoons of the bacon fat, cook potatoes over medium heat, without turning, for 15 to 20 minutes, or until they are brown on the bottom. Turn the potatoes with a wide spatula. Add onion and cook for 5 minutes more. Add sugar, salt and water. Cover and simmer for 15 minutes, or until potatoes are tender. Remove from heat and pour vinegar over potatoes. Cover and let stand for 15 minutes. Add chopped bacon, and reheat. Yields 4 to 5 servings.

## POTATOES WITH HERBS
*Delicious with ham or cold cuts.*

2 onions, thinly sliced
2 tablespoons butter
4 medium boiling
   potatoes, peeled and
   thinly sliced
1½ cups water

2 bouillon cubes
1 bay leaf
¼ teaspoon thyme
   Salt and pepper
   Snipped parsley

Cook onion in butter until yellowed, but not brown. Add potatoes, water, bouillon cubes, bay leaf and thyme. Cover and simmer about 15 minutes, until potatoes are tender. Season to taste with salt and pepper. Serve garnished with parsley. Yields 2 to 4 servings.

## POTATO STRIPS WITH CHEESE
*Nice with steak or pork chops.*

3 cups raw, potato strips
   (cut as for French fries)
½ cup milk
1 tablespoon butter
1 teaspoon salt

   Pepper
½ cup thinly-shaved
   processed cheese
1 tablespoon finely-cut
   parsley

Put the strips into a greased baking dish and pour the milk over them. Dot with butter and sprinkle with salt and pepper. Cover and bake in preheated, 425° F. oven for 40 minutes, or until the potatoes are tender. Sprinkle with cheese and parsley and bake, covered, for 5 minutes more. Yields 4 servings.

## STUFFED POTATOES
*Let the kids help fix this good-natured treat using the
first few garden peas — from The Farmer, 1905.*

Take large, smooth, uniform boiling potatoes. Scrub, but
do not peel. Cut a small round hole in one side. Insert a
button hook, boiled until clean (a melon scoop works better).
Gouge out a cavity inside the potato. Fill cavity with green
peas. Make a cork to fit the hole out of a small potato.
Prepare enough potatoes to serve your family. Boil in salted
water; drain, and serve hot.

## SOUR CREAM POTATO SOUP
*Best potato soup we've ever eaten,
staff members said during testing.*

| | |
|---|---|
| 4-6  cups peeled, diced boiling potatoes | 1  bay leaf |
| 4  cups water | 2  cups cut green *or* wax beans, fresh |
| 1  tablespoon salt | 1  cup sour cream (fresh- |
| 1  medium onion, chopped | soured, *or* dairy sour cream) |
| ½  clove garlic | 1  tablespoon flour |
| 1  teaspoon dill weed | 1  tablespoon vinegar |

Boil water, potatoes, salt, onion, garlic, dill and bay leaf
until potatoes are tender. Add beans and boil 15 minutes
more. Add sour cream mixed with flour and vinegar. Simmer
a few minutes until mixture thickens a bit. Yields 8 servings.
*Break whole eggs* into the boiling soup, and cook until they
are hard before adding the sour cream. This makes an old-
fashioned Czech supper dish.

## FROZEN BAKED POTATOES
*A grower's recipe — always on hand for guests and
great with steak.*

Bake baking potatoes until tender. While hot, cut a slab
off the top, horizontally. Carefully scoop out potatoes, saving
shells. Place potato in a bowl and mash with butter and milk
until light and smooth. Return to shells. Cool, wrap and
freeze. If to be kept frozen more than 1 month, use dry milk
crystals and water instead of whole milk.

When ready to use, remove potatoes from freezer and thaw at room temperature about 15 minutes. Top with grated cheese, a little sauerkraut, tiny canned shrimp, tuna, finely-cut ham or crumbled bacon. Lay foil over top of potatoes and bake in preheated, 350° F. oven for 15 minutes. Remove foil and bake 5 minutes more.

## POTATO PUFF
*Man-pleaser from The Farmer, 1895*
*Add an omelet for an easy supper.*

Take 2 teacupfuls of highly seasoned, mashed potatoes. Add 2 tablespoons melted butter and beat to a cream. Beat the yolks of 2 eggs and add to the potatoes, then mix in ½ cup sweet milk. When this is thoroughly mixed, stir in, as lightly as possible, the stiffly-beaten whites of 2 eggs. Pour into a buttered pie plate and bake 30 to 40 minutes in a preheated, 450° F. oven. Yields 3 to 4 servings.

*German way* is to serve with fried salt pork or crisp bacon bits and finely chopped green onion tops. Yields 4 servings.

*Spices and herbs* are merry mates for summer vegetables when added with a subtle touch. Try oregano, sweet basil, coriander, allspice or rosemary, just to name a few.

## CRANBERRY GLAZED YAMS
*Good with roast beef or turkey.*

6 medium yams cooked, *or*
  1 large can (about 1-pound)
  whole-packed yams
1 cup whole cranberry
  sauce

½ cup water
¼ cup brown sugar
½ teaspoon grated orange rind
1 tablespoon butter

Peel fresh yams and cut in halves, or drain canned yams. Arrange in a buttered baking dish. Mix next 4 ingredients in saucepan and bring to boil, cooking gently 5 minutes. Add butter and pour mixture over potatoes. Bake in preheated, 350° F. oven for ½ hour, basting frequently with syrup in dish. Yields 4 to 6 servings.

## BAKED STUFFED SWEETS
*Kids love these.*

6 medium sweet potatoes
6 tablespoons mayonnaise
2 tablespoons milk
2 tablespoons grated onion

1 teaspoon salt
⅛ teaspoon pepper
Marshmallow tidbits

Scrub potatoes and bake in preheated, 375° F. oven for 40 to 45 minutes or until tender. Cut in half and scoop out pulp. Mash with fork and add mayonnaise, milk, onion, salt and pepper. Beat until fluffy. Refill shells. Place marshmallow tidbits on top. Place under broiler, set at 375° F. until marshmallows are brown and bubbly. Yields 6 servings.

## CREAMED PUMPKIN OR SQUASH WITH ALMONDS
*Serve with barbecued spare ribs or beef short ribs.*

6 cups cubed fresh
  pumpkin *or* winter
  squash
2½ cups medium white
  sauce, page 57

½ teaspoon salt
¼ teaspoon pepper
2 tablespoons soft butter
½ cup slivered, blanched
  almonds

Peel pumpkin; discard seeds and fiber; cut into cubes. Simmer pumpkin cubes in lightly salted water until tender; drain. Combine cubes with white sauce, salt and pepper. Pour into baking dish, brush with butter and sprinkle with almonds. Brown quickly under flame of broiling oven until almonds are slightly golden. Serve immediately. Yields 8 servings.

## BAKED PUMPKIN OR SQUASH
*Good with ham or pork.*

2 pounds fresh pumpkin
  *or* winter squash
½ cup butter
¼ cup brown sugar

¼ cup preserved ginger *or*
  a sprinkle of powdered
  ginger
Salt
¼ cup butter, melted

Preheat oven to 350° F. Cut pumpkin into serving pieces; peel wedges; discard seeds and fibers. In a small saucepan melt butter; add sugar and ginger. Score pumpkin with knife. Brush with some of butter mixture and sprinkle lightly with salt. Bake pumpkin in a shallow baking pan in ¼-inch water for 1½ to 2 hours, or until tender. Brush twice more with butter mixture. Yields 6 servings.

*Rutabagas, carrots, cabbage or beets* are nice boiled, then chopped fine and heated up with vinegar, butter, pepper and salt; exact proportions cannot be given. One must suit her taste. — The Farmer, 1896.

*Mashed rutabaga flavor* improves when a little sugar is stirred in with butter and other seasonings.

*Vegetables that are strong* can be made much milder by tying a bit of bread in a clean white rag and boiling it with them — The Farmer, 1897.

## APPLE BAKED ACORN SQUASH
### *Complements pork.*

Cut squash in half lengthwise. Remove seeds. Place in baking dish and fill centers with cubed apple. Cover and bake in preheated, 350° F. oven for 30 minutes. Remove cover, sprinkle with salt, brown sugar, nutmeg and dot with butter. Continue to bake, uncovered, for 45 minutes more. Yields 2 servings per squash.

## SQUASH TREAT
### *Superb with chicken.*

6 cups cubed winter
  squash
1 teaspoon salt
¼ teaspoon pepper

½ cup dark corn syrup
½ cup half-and-half cream
3 tablespoons brown sugar
¼ cup butter

Peel and remove seeds from squash; cut into cubes and place in greased casserole. Season with salt and pepper. Combine syrup, cream and brown sugar; pour over squash. Dot with butter. Bake in preheated, 350° F. oven about 45 minutes, or until tender. Yields 4 servings.

## SUMMER SQUASH
*Tasty with beef roast.*

2 pounds zucchini
  *or* other summer squash
1 small onion

1 clove garlic, peeled and
  minced
4 slices bacon, cut into
  squares

Wash, but do not peel, squash. Cut into ½-inch slices. Cook, covered in small amount of boiling, salted water, until tender — about 8 to 10 minutes. Saute onion, garlic and bacon. Mix with hot, cooked squash. Season with salt and pepper. Yields 4 servings.

## FRIED SUMMER SQUASH
*Serve with pork chop casserole.*

1 summer squash *or*
  4 small zucchini
3 tablespoons flour

¼ teaspoon salt
1 egg, slightly beaten
2½ tablespoons cooking oil

Wash and cut the squash crosswise into ¼-inch slices. Roll in flour. Dip in egg (when beating egg put in salt). Fry slowly in a small amount of oil until light brown on both sides. Yields 4 to 6 servings.

## SALSIFY
*From The Farmer, 1912.*

When preparing salsify drop into cold water with a little vinegar, as it darkens if exposed to the air.

*Escalloped:* Slice and cook thoroughly in salted water; drain and make a medium white sauce, page 57. Flavor salsify nicely. Put a thin layer of this in a shallow dish, then a layer of bread crumbs (alternate layers). Pour on white sauce and cover top with crumbs. Sprinkle with lemon juice, and brown in oven, preheated to 350° F.

*Fritters:* Scrape, boil and mash salsify. Add 1 beaten egg, salt, pepper, 4 teaspoons of cream and flour enough to make batter that will drop from spoon. Fry in deep kettle of hot fat, 375° F.

## SPINACH LOAF
*Make a delicious supper dish from leftovers —*
*The Farmer, 1920.*

2 cups milk
4 tablespoons flour
4 tablespoons butter
½ teaspoon salt
1 cup chopped, cooked
  spinach, green beans,
  asparagus, chard *or*
  beet tops

4 cups boiled rice *or*
  bread crumbs
½ cup pimiento, optional

Make a thick white sauce of the milk, flour, butter and salt. First melt fat and mix in flour; add milk and stir over fire until thickened. Mix with rice, chopped vegetable and pimiento. Form into a loaf and bake in preheated, 350° F. oven for 20 to 30 minutes. Yields about 6 servings.

*Dig chives,* soil and all, from the garden and transplant into a foil or glass-lined basket. Tuck a few bachelor buttons into the moist soil. Sprinkle arrangement with water, cover with plastic wrap and refrigerate until ready to set on the table. Use a natural-color wicker basket or one which has been sprayed with gilt or a brightly-colored lacquer to match the dishes you're using. Replant chives later . . . or give the basket of chives and bachelor buttons to the guest of honor.

# SWISS CHARD
*A most valuable garden green, states the*
*1919 Country Kitchen Cook Book.*

1 quart chard greens, after
  cooking
1 cup medium white
  sauce, page 57

Pepper to taste
1 tablespoon bacon
  drippings *or* butter
1 teaspoon salt

Strip green from the thick midrib, then steam or boil like spinach. Cut the thick midrib into ½-inch pieces. Cover with boiling water and simmer 35 to 40 minutes, or until tender. Drain and cover with cream sauce.

Drain cooked greens, chop and season with salt, pepper and bacon drippings. Place greens in center of serving dish and surround with creamed midrib. Three quarts raw greens yield 1 quart cooked.

# BROILED TOMATOES WITH PARMESAN BUTTER
*Nice to prepare along with broiled steak, fish or lamb chops.*

4 medium tomatoes
3 tablespoons butter
½ cup Parmesan cheese

½ teaspoon oregano
Salt and pepper

Wash tomatoes and cut in half, crosswise. Cream butter and cheese together. Sprinkle tomatoes with salt, pepper and oregano. Place under preheated broiler for 10 minutes. Spread with mixture of cheese and butter and broil 5 to 7 minutes longer. Yields 4 servings.

# SCALLOPED TOMATOES
*Keep ingredients on hand for this standby from*
*The Farmer, 1893.*

Skin and slice about 1 quart tomatoes and arrange in pudding dish with alternate layers of finely crumbled crackers (2 cups in all); season highly and dot each layer with bits of butter; pour a pint of sweet cream over all and bake for an hour in a preheated, 350° F. oven. Shavings of dried beef may be used between each layer. When wanted for breakfast, it may be made the day before and merely heated in the morning.

## TOMATO SUPPER SOUP
### *Fast!*

Combine 1 can (10¾-ounce) condensed tomato soup, 1 can (1-pound, 12-ounce) tomatoes, 1 tablespoon sugar, 1 tablespoon butter. Simmer 15 minutes. Yields 4 servings.

## TURNIPS O'BRIEN
### *So easy!*

| | |
|---|---|
| 2 tablespoons butter | 2 tablespoons chopped |
| 2 cups chopped, cooked | green pepper |
| turnips | ½ teaspoon salt |
| | ⅛ teaspoon pepper |

Heat butter in large skillet. Combine vegetables; add salt and pepper. Spread out vegetables in the skillet in a thin layer. Heat slowly for about 10 minutes, without stirring. Yields 4 servings.

*Use carrots:* Substitute carrots in above recipe.

## EARLY GARDEN SOUP
*Use the first few garden vegetables
for this early summer dish.*

Combine fresh peas, green and/or yellow beans, new potatoes, carrots and onions. Cut these, as desired, for soup. Barely cover vegetables with salted water. Cook until just tender; do not pour off liquid. Add milk — as much as you need for the amount of soup you want. Heat until scalding. Mix a little soft butter and flour together; add to hot milk. Simmer, stirring, until liquid thickens slightly. Season again.

## SPECIAL BUTTERED VEGETABLES
*Try carrots, beans and beets this way.*

1 pint cooked and drained
   vegetable
3 tablespoons butter,
   melted

¼ cup brown sugar
½ teaspoon salt
¼ teaspoon pepper

Melt butter; add brown sugar and stir. Mix in salt and pepper, then add vegetables. Simmer until thoroughly heated. Yields 4 to 6 servings.

## SEASONED BUTTERS FOR VEGETABLES
*Use for corn on the cob, potatoes or cooked green vegetables.*

*Chili Butter:* Blend 1 teaspoon chili powder, ½ teaspoon salt and a dash of pepper into 4 tablespoons soft butter. Yields about 2 servings for corn or potatoes; 4 for other vegetables.

*Curry Butter:* Substitute 1 teaspoon curry powder for chili powder.

*Garlic Butter:* Substitute 1 teaspoon garlic salt for chili powder.

*Onion-Parsley Butter:* Substitute ¾ teaspoon finely-snipped parsley and ¾ teaspoon finely-minced onion for chili powder.

*Herb Butter:* Blend ⅛ teaspoon powdered thyme, ⅛ teaspoon powdered rosemary, ⅛ teaspoon garlic powder, ⅛ teaspoon dry mustard, 1½ teaspoons finely-snipped parsley, ⅛ teaspoon pepper and 1 teaspoon lemon juice into ½ cup soft butter. Let stand ½ hour. Stir well before serving. Yields about 4 servings for corn or potatoes; 8 servings for other vegetables.

## HOLLANDAISE SAUCE
*From the 1934 Country Kitchen Cook Book.*

½ cup soft butter
2 egg yolks
⅓-½ cup boiling water

Salt
Cayenne pepper
1 tablespoon lemon juice

Cream butter, add egg yolks; mix thoroughly in top of double boiler. Add speck of cayenne and few grains of salt.

Set saucepan over hot water. Add ⅓ to ½ cup boiling water; stir until right consistency. Add lemon juice, stirring rapidly. Serve with asparagus, broccoli, fish.

*A less expensive* Hollandaise sauce is made by adding 1 beaten egg yolk, a dash of cayenne and 1 tablespoon lemon juice to 1 cup medium sauce, page 57. Stir rapidly.

## WHITE SAUCE TABLE

*Variations, below, are based on 1 cup medium white sauce.*

|  | FAT | FLOUR | MILK | SALT | USE: |
|---|---|---|---|---|---|
| Thin | 1 tbsp. | 1 tbsp. | 1 cup | ½ tsp. | Cream soup vegetables |
| Medium | 2 tbsp. | 2 tbsp. | 1 cup | ½ tsp. | Vegetables, meat, fish |
| Thick | 3 tbsp. | 3 tbsp. | 1 cup | ½ tsp. | Croquettes, souffles |

Melt fat; add flour; blend, and cook until smooth and bubbly. Remove from heat; add milk, cook and stir until thickened. Yields 1 cup sauce. *Based on 1 cup medium white sauce you can make:*

*Cream Sauce:* Substitute part cream for milk.

*Cheese Sauce:* Add ½ cup cheese cut in small pieces.

*Egg Sauce:* Add 1 or 2 diced, hard-cooked eggs.

*Parsley Sauce:* Add 2 tablespoons finely-snipped parsley either to egg or plain sauce.

*Carrot Golden Sauce:* Add 2 tablespoons minced, cooked carrot or ¼ cup finely-shredded raw carrot.

*East India Sauce:* Add ½ to 1 teaspoon curry powder.

*Pimiento Sauce:* Add 2 tablespoons chopped pimiento or red and green sweet pepper, mixed.

*Lobster, Shrimp or Oyster Sauce:* Add ¼ cup of one of these ingredients, minced finely, to cream sauce. Use over rice or toast.

*Paprika Sauce:* Add 1 or 2 teaspoons paprika. Use for white vegetables such as cabbage and onion.

*Tomato Sauce:* Substitute strained tomatoes for milk and season with onion juice or scraped onion, and cayenne or black pepper. Or use canned tomato soup.

## BOSTON BAKED BEANS
*Cook these old favorites all day!*

2 cups (1-pound) navy
  beans
1 small onion
¼ pound salt pork
½-1 tablespoon salt
¼ cup catsup

2 teaspoons dry mustard
¾ cup molasses
3 cups hot bean water *or*
  meat stock
1¼ cups brown sugar

Wash and soak beans in cold water overnight. In the morning drain, cover with fresh water, and cook slowly until skins break. Drain. Place onion in bottom of earthenware bean pot, pour in beans. Score rind of the salt pork. Mix seasonings and hot water together. Bury pork in the beans, leaving rind exposed. Add molasses and hot water mixture. Cover bean pot and bake in 300° F. oven 6 to 8 hours. Add water from time to time when necessary. Bake uncovered the last hour. Yields 6 to 8 servings.

*Or, cover* dry beans with water; bring to a boil; cook for two minutes. Let soak 1 hour. Boil gently for 45 minutes, and then prepare for baking as described above.

*Make baked beans special* — top with pineapple rings or peach halves during last ½ hour of baking.

*Lay strips of bacon on top* of beans about half way through baking period.

## BEANGO
*Three fast, delicious dishes with canned, baked beans.*

*Fruited beans:* Put 2 cans (1 pound each) pork and beans with tomato sauce in a shallow baking dish. Arrange 10-12 drained, canned apricot halves on top with round sides of apricots up. Mix ¼ cup brown sugar and a dash of cinnamon. Sprinkle over fruit and beans. Bake in preheated, 375° F. oven about 20 minutes. Yields 4 to 6 servings.

*Skillet Beans:* Heat 2 cans (1 pound each) pork and beans in a skillet. Sprinkle top with ¼ cup finely chopped onion and/or green pepper. Cover and simmer a few minutes more. Yields 4 to 6 servings.

*"Doctored" Baked Beans:* Mix together 2 cans (1 pound each) baked beans with tomato sauce, ¼ cup catsup, 2 tablespoons brown sugar, 1 tablespoon minced onion, 1½ teaspoons prepared mustard and 2-3 slices cooked bacon, broken into bits. Place in casserole or bean pot and bake 1 hour in preheated, 350° F. oven. Yields 4 to 6 servings.

## BOILED BULGUR
*Serve as breakfast cereal, vegetable or*
*add to soups and stews at the start of cooking.*

1 cup dry, cracked,
  unseasoned bulgur

2 cups water
½ teaspoon salt

Heat water to boiling; add salt. Stir bulgur into boiling water. Cover tightly and cook over very low heat 20 minutes. Do not remove cover while cooking. Yields 6 to 7 servings, ½ cup each.

*Oven-Cooked Bulgur:* Place 1 cup bulgur and ½ teaspoon salt in a 1-quart casserole. Pour 2 cups boiling water over bulgur; stir and cover. Bake in preheated, 350° F. oven for 25 minutes or until tender. Yields 6 to 7 servings, ½ cup each.

## GRANOLA
*High in protein — not low in calories.*

1 cup honey
1 cup vegetable oil
5 cups old-fashioned
  oatmeal
1 cup shelled almonds
1 cup unrefined seasame
  seeds
1 cup unroasted sunflower
  meats

1 cup shredded cocoanut
1 cup raisins
1 cup soy flour
1 cup dry milk
  (non-instant)
1 cup wheat germ

Combine honey and oil. Mix remaining ingredients, then mix in honey-oil blend. Spread mixture out on 2 large cookie sheets and bake in preheated, 300° F. oven for 1 hour, or until slightly browned. Cool. Store in air-tight containers or plastic bags. Especially good snack food or for breakfast with milk or cream and fruit. Yields about 13 cups granola.

## COOKING PASTAS
*Use for all the macaroni-noodle family.*

Bring 5 quarts of water to a boil in a deep saucepan to cook ¾ pound of pasta. Add 1 tablespoon of salt after the water boils. A few drops of oil added to the water helps prevent sticking. Add pasta gradually.

When pasta is longer than the pan, push it down gradually with a wooden spoon. Stir pasta frequently while cooking to prevent sticking.

Follow cooking time specified on package of pasta. Do not over cook. Pasta should be tender, but firm to the bite. Test by tasting a piece as cooking nears completion. When tender, drain and serve immediately in a heated bowl.

## CARAWAY NOODLES
*A favorite with pork roast or pork chops.*

¾ pound medium noodles (other widths may be used)
4 tablespoons butter, melted

1 tablespoon caraway seeds
⅔ cup almonds, slivered

Place caraway seeds and almonds in a dry frying pan over moderate heat and toast, stirring occasionally with a wooden spoon until seeds and nuts are golden. Cook noodles according to package directions. Drain; toss with butter, caraway seeds and almonds. Serve immediately. Yields 6 to 8 servings.

## NOODLES PARMESAN
*Delectable with beef pot roast cooked with tomatoes.*

1 package (8-ounce) wide noodles
¾ cup grated Parmesan cheese

¼ cup melted butter
Salt and pepper

Cook noodles according to package directions. Drain well, turn into hot serving dish. Sprinkle with the cheese, toss with forks until evenly coated. Add melted butter, seasonings, toss again. Yields 4 servings.

## HOMEMADE NOODLES
*Easy recipe from The Farmer, 1912.*

Beat 2 eggs until very light. Mix with 3 tablespoons milk, ¼ teaspoon salt and enough flour to make a real stiff dough (about 1½ cups). Roll dough thin on floured surface. Let stand to dry until firm but still pliant. Cut just as fine as you can. Cook in soup broth at once, if desired, so noodles do not soak up much broth. Or, air dry cut noodles and store in plastic bag until ready to use. Yields about 3 cups dry noodles.

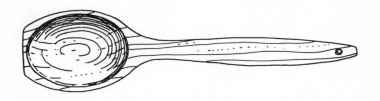

## BOILED WHITE RICE
*To preserve nutrients, do not wash rice before or after cooking and use only the amount of water the rice will absorb during cooking.*

1 teaspoon salt  
2 cups water  

1 cup white, uncooked rice  
1 teaspoon butter *or* oil

Add salt to water and bring to boil. Stir rice into rapidly boiling water. Add fat to reduce foaming. Bring back to a boil and lower heat until water is just bubbling. Cover tightly and boil gently 20 minutes. Don't stir during cooking or rice will get gummy. Remove pan from heat. *Do not uncover.* Let rice stand 10 to 15 minutes, covered tightly, to finish cooking in its own steam. Fluff rice with a fork. Yields 6 servings, ½ cup each.

*Softer Rice:* Increase water to 2¼ cups and boil gently 25 minutes. Let stand 10 minutes, covered. Best for rice rings, patties, croquettes and puddings.

*Oven-Cooked Rice:* Place 1 cup rice and 1 teaspoon salt in 1-quart casserole. Pour 2 cups boiling water on rice; stir and cover. Bake 30 to 35 minutes, or until rice is tender, in preheated, 350° F. oven. Yields 6 servings, ½ cup each.

## OVEN-BAKED  RICE

2½ cups hot water
2 tablespoons butter
1 package (6-ounce) long-
grain white rice, brown
rice *or* long-grain white
and wild rice mix

¾ cup sliced celery
1 medium onion, chopped
(optional)

In a 1½-quart casserole, place water, butter, rice and celery. Cover and bake in preheated, 400° F. oven, stirring occasionally, about 45 to 60 minutes, or until all water is absorbed. Yields 6 servings.

## FRIED  RICE
*Stir gently while food fries.*

6 slices bacon, cut in half
½ cup diced onion
2 cups cooked white *or*
brown rice

¼ cup soy sauce
½ cup water
4 slightly-beaten eggs

Cook bacon in skillet or wok at 350° F. until crisp, about 6 minutes. Remove bacon, drain on paper toweling and crumble. Stir-fry onion in bacon drippings for 2 minutes. Add rice and stir-fry for 7 to 8 minutes. Add soy sauce, water and crumbled bacon. Reduce heat to 250° F. Pour eggs on top of rice mixture. Stir-fry for 3 to 4 minutes, or until egg is cooked.

*Subgum Fried Rice:* When adding soy sauce and bacon, also add ¼ cup bean sprouts, ¼ cup sliced mushrooms, ¼ cup diced green pepper.

## FRIED  WILD  RICE
*Serve as a side dish or as a bed for wild game.*

Wash 1 cup wild rice well in several pans of cold water, pouring off foreign material from the top. Slowly stir rice into a saucepan containing 4 cups boiling water and 1 teaspoon salt. Cook rice slowly, without stirring, for about 30 minutes. Rice will be nearly tender. Melt ¼ cup butter in a skillet. Drain rice and add to melted butter. Brown rice slowly; stirring and turning often. Add salt to taste. Do not allow rice to harden by overcooking. Yields 4 to 6 servings.

# MEAT, POULTRY, FISH AND GAME

## MEAT CONDIMENTS

*Lamb condiments:* Mint jelly, mint sauce, mint apples, ginger pears.

*Condiments for beef:* Brown sauce or variations, East India sauce, chili sauce, tomato sauce, mustard pickle or cranberry sauce (with corned beef), horseradish sauce (tongue).

*Fresh fish condiments:* Egg sauce, parsley sauce, cream cheese sauce, pimiento sauce, tomato sauce (with white fish), maitre d' hotel sauce, horseradish sauce, tartar sauce.

*Condiments for fowl:* Currant jelly, cranberry sauce or jelly; game sauce.

*Condiments for ham:* mustard pickle, spiced gooseberries, plum, cherry, honey or jewelled sauces, apple sauce, horseradish sauce.

*Veal condiments:* Currant jelly, chili sauce, grape catsup, gingered pears, bread-and-butter pickles.

*Pork condiments:* Apple sauce, cinnamon apples; chowchow, cranberry jelly.

## HORSERADISH SAUCE
*Treat from the 1934 Country Kitchen Cook Book.*

Blend together ¼ cup cream, whipped; 1½ teaspoons horseradish; ⅛ teaspoon salt; 1 teaspoon vinegar. Serve with beef and pork. Yields about ½ cup sauce.

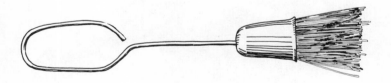

## GLAZED ROLLED ROAST
*Easy, elegant!*

Combine ¼ cup cranberry sauce, 1 teaspoon orange marmalade and 2 tablespoons orange juice; beat together. Prepare and oven-roast your favorite rolled beef roast. Thirty minutes before roast is done, remove it from the oven and spread glaze over top. Return to oven and complete roasting. Garnish meat platter with canned pear halves, filled with cranberry sauce or relish.

## TIME-TABLE FOR ROASTING BEEF

| CUT | APPROX. WEIGHT | OVEN TEMPERATURE | MEAT THERMOMETER READING | APPROX. COOKING TIME |
|---|---|---|---|---|
| | *Pounds* | *Degrees F.* | *Degrees F.* | *Min. Per Lb.* |
| Standing rib* | 6 to 8 | 300°-325° F. | 140° F. (rare) | 23 to 25 |
| | | | 160° F. (medium) | 27 to 30 |
| | | | 170° F. (well) | 32 to 35 |
| | 4 to 6 | 300°-325° F. | 140° F. (rare) | 26 to 32 |
| | | | 160° F. (medium) | 34 to 38 |
| | | | 170° F. (well) | 40 to 42 |
| Rolled rib | 5 to 7 | 300°-325° F. | 140° F. (rare) | 32 |
| | | | 160° F. (medium) | 38 |
| | | | 170° F. (well) | 48 |
| Delmonico (rib eye) | 4 to 6 | 350° F. | 140° F. (rare) | 18 to 20 |
| | | | 160° F. (medium) | 20 to 22 |
| | | | 170° F. (well) | 22 to 24 |
| Tenderloin, whole | 4 to 6 | 425° F. | 140° F. (rare) | 45 to 60 (total) |
| Tenderloin, half | 2 to 3 | 425° F. | 140° F. (rare) | 45 to 50 (total) |
| Rolled rump (high quality) | 4 to 6 | 300°-325° F. | 150°-170° F. | 25 to 30 |
| Sirloin tip (high quality) | 3½ to 4 | 300°-325° F. | 150°-170° F. | 35 to 40 |

*Ribs which measure 6 to 7 inches from chine bone to tip of rib.

*Use a sharp knife* or scissors to cut these attractive lemon or orange garnishes from slices of the fruit. Trim centers with a slice of stuffed olive, a snip of parsley, a clove or two, strips of pimiento. Use these garnishes to trim meat platters, vegetables, salads — your favorite cold beverages.

## BRAISING MEATS

Braise less tender cuts of meat. Some tender cuts are also best if braised, including pork steaks, chops and cutlets; veal chops, steaks and cutlets, and pork liver. Follow these steps for best results:

*Brown meat slowly,* on all sides, in a heavy utensil. Pour off drippings after browning. The browning develops flavor and color. Fat is usually added to prevent meat from sticking as it browns. A slow brown stays on the meat better than a quick brown at a high temperature.

*Season with salt, pepper,* herbs and spices, if desired. Season meat after browning, unless seasoning is added to the coating.

*Add a small amount of liquid,* if necessary. Liquid is added to less tender cuts, but may be omitted when cooking tender cuts such as pork chops and pork tenderloin. The liquid may be water, vegetable juice or soup.

*Cover tightly* to hold in steam needed for softening the connective tissue and making meat tender.

*Cook at low temperature* until tender. This means simmering, not boiling. It may be done on top of the range or in a 300° F. to 325° F. oven.

*Make sauce or gravy* from the liquid in the pan, if desired. Gravy is often what makes a braised dish exceptional.

## TIME-TABLE FOR BRAISING MEATS

| CUT | AVERAGE WGT. OR THICKNESS | APPROXIMATE TOTAL COOKING TIME |
|---|---|---|
| *Beef* | | |
| Pot-Roast | 3 to 5 pounds | 3-4 hours |
| Swiss steak | 1½ to 2½ inches | 2-3 hours |
| Fricassee | 2 inch cubes | 1½-2½ hours |
| Beef birds | ½ inch | 1½-2½ hours |
| | (x 2 in. x 4 in.) | |
| Short ribs | Pieces | 1½-2½ hours |
| | (2 in. x 2 in. x 4 in.) | |
| Round steak | ¾ inch | 1-1½ hours |
| Stuffed steak | ½ to ¾ inch | 1½ hours |
| *Pork* | | |
| Chops | ¾ to 1½ inches | 45-60 minutes |
| Spareribs | 2 to 3 pounds | 1½ hours |
| Tenderloin | | |
| Whole | ¾ to 1 pound | 45-60 minutes |
| Fillets | ½ inch | 30 minutes |
| Shoulder steaks | ¾ inch | 45-60 minutes |
| *Lamb* | | |
| Breast—stuffed | 2 to 3 pounds | 1½-2 hours |
| Breast—rolled | 1½ to 2 pounds | 1½-2 hours |
| Neck slices | ¾ inch | 1 hour |
| Shanks | ¾ to 1 pound each | 1-1½ hours |
| Shoulder chops | ¾ to 1 inch | 45-60 minutes |
| *Veal* | | |
| Breast—stuffed | 3 to 4 pounds | 1½-2½ hours |
| Breast—rolled | 2 to 3 pounds | 1½-2½ hours |
| Veal birds | ½ inch | 45-60 minutes |
| | (x 2 in. x 4 in.) | |
| Chops | ½ to ¾ inch | 45-60 minutes |
| Steaks or cutlets | ½ to ¾ inch | 45-60 minutes |
| Shoulder chops | ½ to ¾ inch | 45-60 minutes |
| Shoulder cubes | 1 to 2 inches | 45-60 minutes |

## BEET RELISH
*Good with cold, sliced beef roast.*

1 cup coarsely-chopped
   pickled beets
½ cup coarsely-chopped
   raw, tangy apple

1 tablespoon horseradish
1 tablespoon pickled beet
   juice

Mix all ingredients and marinate overnight in glass, enameled or plastic covered container. Yields 1½ cups of relish.

## EVERYDAY POT ROAST
*Add a bay leaf with the vegetables and omit the*
*horseradish for a different flavor.*

3-4 pound beef chuck
⅓ cup horseradish
   Salt and pepper
6-8 small boiling onions

6-8 carrots
6-8 ribs of celery
6-8 small new potatoes,
   with skins

Brown meat well on both sides in hot fat. Spread with horseradish. Season with salt and pepper. Add a little water; cover and cook slowly 2 to 2½ hours, adding more water if necessary. Add vegetables and continue cooking 1 hour. Yields 6 servings.

## SUNDAY BEST POT ROAST
*Rich flavor — hot or cold.*

4-5 pound beef blade pot
   roast
2 tablespoons flour
1 teaspoon chili powder
1 tablespoon paprika
2 teaspoons salt
3 tablespoons lard *or*
   drippings

2 medium onions
16 whole cloves
⅓ cup water
1 cinnamon stick
2 tablespoons flour
¼ cup water

Combine flour, chili powder, paprika and salt. Dredge pot roast in seasoned flour. Brown meat in fat. Pour off drippings. Stud each onion with 8 whole cloves. Add water, onions and cinnamon stick to meat. Cover and cook slowly

2½ to 3 hours or until meat is tender. Remove meat to hot platter. Discard onion and cinnamon stick. Measure cooking liquid and add water to make 2 cups. Mix 2 tablespoons flour and ¼ cup water. Add to cooking liquid and cook, stirring constantly until thickened. Serve pot roast with gravy. Yields 6 to 8 servings.

## SPICY POT ROAST
*Like sauerbraten.*

2 cups apple juice
1 tablespoon brown sugar
½ teaspoon cinnamon
¼ teaspoon ginger
2 whole cloves
4 pounds beef rump
¼ cup shortening

1 cup sliced onions
1 teaspoon salt
⅛ teaspoon pepper
5 cups cooked, sliced apples
12 small gingersnaps, crumbled

Combine apple juice, brown sugar, cinnamon, ginger and whole cloves. Place meat in bowl which will leave only very little space around it, pour apple juice mixture over meat, cover tightly and let stand in refrigerator 24 hours. Drain, save liquid, saute meat on all sides in the shortening. Saute onion in the same fat, add apple juice mixture, simmer, covered 3 to 4 hours. One hour before time is up, add salt, pepper, gingersnaps and half of the sliced apples. If desired, thicken gravy in kettle with a little flour mixed to a smooth paste in cold water. Garnish platter of sliced meat and gravy with remaining apple slices. Yields 8 servings.

## FARMERS' STEAK
*Melts in your mouth.*

1 round steak, 1½ to 2 inches thick
Flour
1 tablespoon shortening
1 can (10½-ounce) condensed onion soup

1 can (10½-ounce) condensed chicken gumbo soup
1 teaspoon salt
¼ teaspoon pepper

Cut steak in serving pieces; dip in flour and brown well in melted shortening. Add soups, salt and pepper. Cover and bake in preheated, 350° F. oven for about 1 hour, or until tender. Yields 4 servings.

## BAR-B-QUED SHORT RIBS
*Zesty!*

5-6 pounds beef short ribs;
  trim off excess fat
1 large onion, diced
1 can (10½-ounce) con-
  densed tomato soup
1 soup can water
2 teaspoons salt

½ teaspoon pepper
3 tablespoons Worcester-
  shire sauce
3 tablespoons powdered
  mustard
2 tablespoons A-1 sauce
¼ cup vinegar

Brown short ribs in a heavy skillet. Remove fat and add a mixture of the remaining ingredients to the skillet. Simmer 1 to 1½ hours, or until tender, turning several times. Yields about 6 servings.

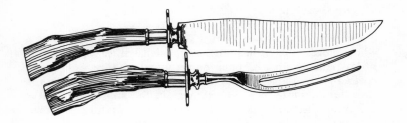

## FLANK STEAK SUPREME
*Serve for a hearty fall supper.*

1 flank steak, 1½-2 pounds
1 teaspoon salt
  Flour
2 tablespoons shortening
1 medium onion, sliced

2 cups cooked tomatoes
1 green pepper, sliced
  *or* 1 cup diced celery
1 teaspoon chili powder

Have meat dealer score steak into diamond shapes. Season with salt and pepper if desired. Sprinkle with flour. Brown on both sides in hot shortening or bacon drippings in skillet or roasting pan. Cover with sliced onions, tomatoes and sliced green pepper, or diced celery. Cover the skillet or pan. Bake in preheated, 350° F. oven for about 2 hours. Mix chili powder with ¼ cup cold water. Stir into the gravy around steak and spoon gravy over meat. Serve on hot rice or spaghetti. Yields 4 to 5 servings.

## PARTY BEEF STEW
*Accompany with fresh fruit salad and fresh hot rolls.*

3 pounds beef chuck, cut in 1½-inch cubes
3 tablespoons flour
1 tablespoon salad oil
2 cups (1-pound can) tomatoes
2 medium onions, sliced
1 teaspoon celery salt
1 teaspoon salt
¼ teaspoon pepper
⅓ cup vinegar
⅓ cup molasses
1 cup water
6 carrots, peeled and cut in pieces
½ cup raisins
½ teaspoon ginger

Sprinkle beef with the flour. Brown in oil in heavy saucepan; add tomatoes, onions, celery salt, salt and pepper. Combine vinegar, molasses and water; add to meat. Cover and simmer until meat is tender, about 2 hours. Add carrots, raisins and ginger. Cook until carrots are tender. Serve over hot, cooked rice. Yields 8 to 10 servings.

## SAVORY BEEF
*Make a double batch for the freezer.*

3 slices bacon
2 pounds ½x4-inch beef strips
1 clove garlic, crushed
2 cans (8-ounce each) mushrooms
1 bay leaf, crushed
1 tablespoon parsley
2 teaspoons salt
½ teaspoon thyme
½ teaspoon pepper
¼ cup butter
¼ cup flour
1¼ cups water
1 beef boullion cube

Fry bacon crisp. Brown beef (round or chuck, cut thin) in some of bacon fat. Add garlic, mushrooms, bay leaf, parsley, salt, pepper, thyme and crumbled bacon. Make a roux of butter and flour and cook until flour browns. Add water and boullion to flour mixture; stir until thick. Add to beef mixture. Simmer, covered, until beef is tender, about 1 hour. Freeze until ready to use. Marvelous with hot rice and salad. Yields 6 servings.

## BROWN  SAUCE
*Savory base for other sauces and dishes — or a meat gravy.*

2 tablespoons minced onion
1 tablespoon minced green
  pepper
3 tablespoons butter
5 tablespoons flour
1 pint soup stock, page 87

1 tablespoon lemon juice
¼ bay leaf
¼ teaspoon thyme
Pepper
Salt

Fry onion and green pepper in butter 5 minutes, stirring. When butter is brown, add flour and stir till brown and smooth. Gradually add soup stock, stirring constantly. Simmer slowly until smooth and thick. Add lemon juice and seasonings. Yields about 2½ cups sauce.

*Mushroom Sauce:* Add 3 or 4 mushrooms, chopped and cooked in butter.

*Sauce Piquant:* Add ¼ cup coarsely chopped green olives.

*Game Sauce:* Add ½ cup melted currant jelly.


## MULTI-PURPOSE HAMBURGER MIX
*Freeze it for future use in any
of nine scrumptous dishes.*

4 medium onions,
  chopped
3 cloves garlic, finely
  chopped
2 cups chopped celery tops
¼ cup fat
4 pounds lean ground beef

4 teaspoons salt
½ teaspoon pepper
3 tablespoons Worcester-
  shire sauce
2 bottles (12-ounce each)
  catsup

Pan-fry the onion, garlic, and celery in fat in a large kettle. Add hamburger and stir and cook until all redness of the meat disappears. Add salt, pepper, Worcestershire sauce, and catsup. Simmer 20 minutes. Skim off excess fat. Yields 10 cups (five 1-pint containers).

*To Freeze:* Cool quickly. Spoon the mixture into five, 1-pint containers. Seal. Label with name and date. Freeze at 0° F. or lower. Do not stack until thoroughly frozen.

*To Thaw:* Place container of the mix in hot water or under running hot water just long enough to allow mixture to slip out of the container.

*Hamburger-Rice Skillet:* Heat 1 pint Hamburger Mix in a skillet. Add 2 cups cooked rice, 1 cup canned whole kernel corn, ¼ teaspoon thyme, and ½ cup chopped green pepper, if desired. Simmer a few minutes to blend flavors and to cook the pepper. Yields 4 to 6 servings.

*Stuffed Green Peppers:* Use the Hamburger-Rice Skillet mixture to stuff 8 hollowed out green peppers. Bake in a shallow pan in a preheated, 375° F. oven about 50 minutes. Yields 4 servings, 2 peppers each.

*Hot Stuffed Rolls:* Allow Hamburger Mix to thaw in refrigerator. Mix in some shredded cheese, if desired. Spoon generously into hollowed out frank buns or French rolls. Wrap the rolls individually in aluminum foil and heat in a preheated, 350° F. oven or on a picnic grill about 30 minutes.

*Hamburger Stroganoff:* Heat 1 pint Hamburger Mix in a table skillet until completely thawed. Add 2 cups sliced fresh mushrooms (one 6-ounce package) and a 10½-ounce can condensed cream of mushroom soup. Stir and simmer 5 minutes. Carefully spoon 1 cup dairy sour cream over surface. Sprinkle with chopped parsley. *Do Not Stir.* Simmer 1 minute more. Serve from skillet over hot cooked rice, noodles, toast or toasted buns. Yields 6 servings.

*Hamburger Buns:* Heat Hamburger Mix slowly in a skillet or chafing dish. Use as filling in hot buttered hamburger buns. (Allow ¼ cup per bun.)

*Chili Con Carne:* Heat Hamburger Mix in a skillet with an equal measure of canned red kidney or pink pinto beans. Season with chili powder.

*Spaghetti with Hamburger Mix:* Heat Hamburger Mix in a saucepan or skillet. Add a dash of cayenne pepper and garlic salt, if desired. Serve on hot cooked spaghetti and top with grated Parmesan cheese.

*Hamburger-Noodle Skillet:* Heat 1 pint of Hamburger Mix in a skillet with 2 cups cooked noodles and 1 cup canned mixed vegetables. Stir to combine. Sprinkle ½ cup shredded quick-melting cheese and ½ teaspoon chopped parsley over top. *Do Not Stir.* Heat just long enough to melt the cheese. Serve from skillet. Yields 4 to 6 servings.

## CHEESE-FILLED MEAT LOAF
*Cheese is a delicious surprise.*

1½  pounds ground beef
 1  can (8-ounce) tomato
     sauce
 ¾  cup quick-cooking
     rolled oats
 ¼  cup chopped onion
 1  egg
 1  tablespoon Worcester-
     shire sauce

1½  teaspoons salt
 ¾-1  teaspoon oregano
 ¼  teaspoon pepper
 1  package (6-8 ounce)
     sliced Mozzarella
     cheese

Combine all ingredients, except cheese; mix well. Divide meat mixture in thirds. Pat ⅓ in bottom of 9½x5x3-inch loaf pan; cover with ½ the cheese. Repeat layers, ending with meat. Bake in preheated, 350° F. oven for 1 hour. Yields 5 to 6 servings.

*Apple-Raisin-Tomato Filling:* Spread half of meat loaf mixture in baking pan. Omit cheese, above, and cover meat with a cupful of mixed chopped apples, cooked tomatoes and seedless raisins. Spread remaining half of meat on top, press together and bake as above.

## DELUXE MEAT BALLS
*A North Dakota Beef Cook-Off winner.*

 2  pounds lean, ground beef
 ½  pound ground pork
 2  eggs, slightly beaten
 2  slices bread
 2  teaspoons salt
 ¾  teaspoon pepper
 ¼  can (10½-ounce)
     condensed chicken soup

 2  medium onions,
     chopped fine
 ⅛  can (2-3 tablespoons)
     condensed onion soup
 ½  cup milk
 1  tablespoon cornstarch
     Dash allspice, nutmeg,
     sage

Cut bread into very small cubes. Combine ground meats, eggs, bread cubes, seasoning (except salt), onion, milk and soups. Blend salt and cornstarch together; add to meat mixture. Blend thoroughly but lightly. Use a teaspoonful of meat mixture for each meat ball. Saute in hot fat until brown, turning frequently to brown evenly. Pour off excess fat. Combine soups and water for gravy; pour over browned meat balls. Cover, simmer about 20 to 30 minutes.

*Gravy:* ¼ can condensed chicken soup, ¼ can condensed onion soup, ¼ soup can water. For more gravy, use all of the remaining chicken and onion soups. Thin with additional water if necessary.

*Easy Casserole Toppings:* Use instant mashed potatoes for a quick potato topping on meat pies. Instead of bread crumb toppings, try crushed cereals, crackers, potato chips or corn chips.

## PASTIE
### A tradition on Minnesota's Iron Range.

| | |
|---|---|
| 3 cups all-purpose flour | 6 small, raw carrots, diced |
| 1½ teaspoons salt | 6 stalks celery, diced |
| 1½ teaspoons baking powder | 12 teaspoons onion, chopped |
| 1 cup shortening | 1¼ pounds ground beef, *or* other ground *or* diced meat |
| 1 egg, slightly beaten | Salt |
| 1 tablespoon vinegar | Pepper |
| 6 tablespoons water | Basil |
| 6 small, raw potatoes, diced | Cream |

Combine first 3 ingredients. Work in shortening as for regular pastry. Combine vinegar and egg and add to flour mixture. Add water gradually, mix lightly. Divide into 6 balls. Roll out pastry and fill with a mixture of remaining ingredients. Place filling on half of each pastie. Fold over top. Seal edges well. Make several slits on top of pastry to allow steam to escape. Pour cream into pastie half way through cooking. Bake on cookie sheet in preheated, 375° F. oven for 40 to 60 minutes. Yields 6 Pasties.

## CORN-CHIP-STUFFED  TOMATOES
*Different, tasty.*

8-10 prepared, fresh
tomato shells, page 23
1 medium onion, sliced
fine
½ cup diced celery
2 tablespoons fat
1 pound ground beef

1 teaspoon salt
1 can (8-ounce)
tomato sauce
1 cup crushed corn
chips
8-10 sprigs parsley

Brown onion and celery in hot fat; add ground beef and salt; stir well. Cover and cook mixutre 10 minutes. Add tomato sauce and cook until meat is done. Add corn chips and mix thoroughly. Fill tomato shells and bake in preheated, 350° F. oven for 25 minutes. Garnish with parsley. A tasty supper dish with a cup of potato soup. Yields 8 servings.

*Stuff Onions:* Peel and par-boil 8 to 10 medium-large onions for about 30 minutes, or until almost tender. Slice off end of each onion and remove all but ¾ inch of outside shell. Chop pulp of onion and add 1 cup to filling above. Place stuffed onions in casserole. Spoon extra filling, if any, on top. Add a little water to pan to prevent scorching and bake for 35 minutes, or until onions are tender.

## STUFFED  CABBAGE  ROLLS
*A favorite when chilly weather comes.*

12-14 large cabbage leaves
1 teaspoon salt
Boiling water
1 pound ground beef
1 cup cooked, salted
rice
2 medium onions, cut
fine

1 egg
2 teaspoons salt
¼ teaspoon pepper
1 cup water
2 cups condensed
tomato soup

Carefully remove the cabbage leaves from the head. Sprinkle with 1 teaspoon salt and pour on boiling water to cover. Soak cabbage 10 minutes to wilt leaves.

Mix next 6 ingredients and place a large spoonful on each cabbage leaf. Wrap carefully and place, folded side down in casserole. Pour water and soup over the "pigs." Bake 1 hour in preheated, 350° F. oven. Yields about 4 to 5 servings.

*Sauce variation:* In a saucepan, combine 2 cups stewed tomatoes; 1 medium onion, chopped; 2 tablespoons vinegar; 2 tablespoons sugar and 5 to 6 mashed gingersnaps. Simmer until sauce begins to thicken; pour over cabbage rolls and bake as directed above.

## HAMBURGER PIE
### *Fast!*

Season 1½ to 2 pounds of hamburger, as desired. Press down into the bottom and sides of a pie pan. Bake in preheated, 350° F. oven, until browned lightly. Remove and pour over the crust one can undiluted vegetable soup (or another kind of your choice). Put mounds of mashed potatoes on top and bake until lightly browned. Cut into pie wedges to serve. Use instant mashed potatoes to save time. Yields 4 to 6 servings.

## OLD-FASHIONED HOT DISH
### *A Midwest macaroni classic.*

3 pounds ground beef
2 large onions, chopped
3 cans (10¾-ounce each) condensed tomato soup
1 soup can water
1 can (6-ounce) tomato paste
2 cans (28-ounce each) tomatoes
2 teaspoons salt
¼ teaspoon pepper
1 package (10-ounce) frozen mixed vegetables, thawed
1 large green pepper, chopped
3 tablespoons salt
6-9 quarts boiling water
6 cups (1½ pounds) elbow macaroni

In Dutch oven, brown meat, stirring frequently; add next 7 ingredients. Simmer, covered, for 30 minutes. Stir in mixed vegetables and green pepper; cook 15 minutes longer or until vegetables are tender.

Meanwhile, add 3 tablespoons salt to rapidly boiling water. Gradually add macaroni so that water continues to boil. Cook, uncovered, until tender; drain. Combine macaroni and meat sauce in large shallow roasting pan (about 17x11½x 2¼-inch). Bake, covered, in preheated, 375° F. oven for 30 minutes or until hot. Serve, sprinkled with Parmesan cheese, if desired. Yields 12 servings.

## MEAT SAUCE FOR SPAGHETTI
*An Italian family's favorite.*

1½ pounds ground round
  steak
1 slice pork steak
4 cloves garlic, chopped
3 medium onions,
  chopped
2 cans (Number 2½)
  solid-pack tomatoes
2 cans (Number 2½)
  water
3 cans (6-ounce each)
  tomato paste

1 teaspoon salt
¼-½ teaspoon crushed
  red pepper
1 heaping teaspoon
  sweet basil
1 heaping teaspoon
  oregano
1 pound long thin
  spaghetti

Have butcher grind the slice of pork with the beef round. Brown meat in skillet. Place meat and juice in large, heavy kettle. Add remaining ingredients (except spaghetti). Simmer mixture over low heat until reduced by nearly one-half to a thick sauce . . . about 5 to 6 hours. Stir occasionally to prevent sticking.

Cook long spaghetti in 5 quarts of boiling, salted water until tender. Drain. Place on hot platter; pour sauce over spaghetti and serve.

Pass grated Parmesan cheese and crushed red pepper with this spaghetti dish. Yields about 2 quarts of sauce for eight servings. This sauce freezes well.

*Add variety:* During the last three hours of cooking, add 1 pound pepperoni sausage sliced into rounds and 6 to 8 rib-cut pork chops. Pork will cook apart somewhat.


## CHILI
*Warming! Filling!*

1½ pounds ground beef
1½ teaspoons salt
2 tablespoons shortening
1 cup chopped onions
¾ cup boiling water
1 tablespoon chili powder

3 tablespoons cold water
2 cans (Number 303)
  tomatoes
1 tablespoon sugar
1 can (Number 303) red
  kidney *or* pinto beans

Season beef, brown in shortening. Mix chili powder and water to a paste. Add this, onions, tomatoes and sugar to ground beef. Cover and simmer 1 to 1½ hours. Uncover and cook ½ hour over low heat. Add beans and simmer until hot. If chili gets thicker than desired, add a little more water. Yields 6 servings.

## BROILING BEEF

Broiling is suitable for tender beef steaks and ground beef, ham slices and bacon. Steaks should be at least ¾ inch thick.

For best results, the following steps should be followed for broiling:

*Set the oven regulator for broiling.* The broiler may be pre-heated or not as desired.

*Place meat on rack of broiler pan, 2 to 5 inches from the heat.* The preferred distance is 2 to 3 inches for steaks, chops or patties ¾ to 1 inch thick; 3 to 5 inches for cuts which are 1 to 2 inches thick. The heat output of broilers may vary causing a modification of the recommended distances of the surface of the meat from the heat.

*Broil until top side is brown.* The meat should be approximately, or slightly more than, half done by the time it is browned on top. (Refer to the time and temperature chart.)

*Season the top side with salt and pepper, if desired.* Omit this step for ham or bacon. Broiled meats are seasoned after browning since salt tends to bring moisture to the cut surface and thus delays browning.

*Turn and brown the other side.* The time-table offers a good guide for broiling time. For the most accurate determination of the degree of doneness of a thick steak or chop, a meat thermometer may be used. Thermometers designed especially for broiling may be inserted and left in the meat throughout the broiling period. Roast meat thermometers may be used to test doneness by inserting them in the steak or chop shortly before the end of the estimated total broiling time.

*Season, if desired,* and serve at once.

## BROILED OR GRILLED STEAK TOPPINGS

*Sunflower Sirloin:* During final 5 minutes of broiling, sprinkle steak generously with roasted, salted sunflower meats.

*Steak Roquefort:* Blend ⅛ pound Roquefort or blue cheese, 2 tablespoons vegetable oil, 1 small clove of crushed garlic. Broil steak to taste; spread on cheese mixture and broil again quickly, close to heat, for 1 to 2 minutes. Sprinkle with salt and pepper; serve at once. Yields spread for 2-pound, 1½-inch-thick steak.

*Mustard-Buttered Steak:* Spread steak rather thickly on both sides with a mixture of equal quantities of butter and dry mustard. About 2 tablespoons of each is sufficient for one sirloin, 1-inch thick. Broil over hot coals a total of 15 minutes, turning once. Sprinkle on salt and pepper; serve.

*Sesame Seed Steak Spread:* Combine ¼ cup butter, 1 teaspoon garlic powder, 2 teaspoons sesame seeds. Stir thoroughly and let stand about ½ hour. Spread on hot, broiled steak just before serving. Yields ¼ cup spread, enough for about 2 large sirloins.

| TIME-TABLE FOR BROILING BEEF* | | APPROXIMATE TOTAL COOKING TIME | |
|---|---|---|---|
| CUT | WT. *Pounds* | RARE *Minutes* | MED. *Minutes* |
| Chuck steak (high quality)— 1 in. | 1½ to 2½ | 24 | 30 |
| 1½ in. | 2 to 4 | 40 | 45 |
| Rib steak—1 in. | 1 to 1½ | 15 | 20 |
| 1½ in. | 1½ to 2 | 25 | 30 |
| 2 in. | 2 to 2½ | 35 | 45 |
| Rib eye steak—1 in. | 8 ozs. | 15 | 20 |
| 1½ in. | 12 oz. | 25 | 30 |
| 2 in. | 16 ozs. | 35 | 45 |
| Club steak—1 in. | 1 to 1½ | 15 | 20 |
| 1½ in. | 1½ to 2 | 25 | 30 |
| 2 in. | 2 to 2½ | 35 | 45 |
| Sirloin steak—1 in. | 1½ to 3 | 20 | 25 |
| 1½ in. | 2¼ to 4 | 30 | 35 |
| 2 in. | 3 to 5 | 40 | 45 |
| Porterhouse steak—1 in. | 1¼ to 2 | 20 | 25 |
| 1½ in. | 2 to 3 | 30 | 35 |
| 2 in. | 2½ to 3½ | 40 | 45 |
| Ground beef patties 1 in. thick by 3 in. | 4 ozs. | 15 | 25 |

*This time-table is based on broiling at a moderate temperature (350° F.). Rare steaks are broiled to an internal temperature of 140° F.; medium to 160° F.; well done to 170° F.

## COWBOY'S STEAK
*What flavor!*

Chuck roast (1½-2 inches thick)
2 cloves garlic, minced
2 tablespoons salad oil
1 tablespoon soy sauce
½ teaspoon rosemary
¼ teaspoon dry mustard
⅓ cup wine vinegar

Non-seasoned meat tenderizer
½ teaspoon coarse-ground pepper
2 tablespoons catsup
1 tablespoon Worcester-shire sauce
1 tablespoon steak sauce

Place roast in baking dish. Combine next 6 ingredients and pour over roast; let stand 24 hours, turn often. Sprinkle roast with meat tenderizer; let stand 30 minutes. Place in broiler 5 inches from heat. Add last 4 ingredients to remaining sauce; pour half of sauce over meat and broil 20 minutes; turn, cover with remaining sauce and broil 15 minutes, or until desired doneness. Steak looks charred. Allow about ½ pound meat, including fat and bone, per serving.

## FONDUE SERVING SUGGESTIONS

*Place fondue pot in the center* of the group using it. Arrange a plate or platter of dippables on each side of the pot on lettuce-lined plates.

*Circle the pot with bowls* of sauces or pass a lazy susan with sauce bowls on it, so that guests can spoon their choices onto their own plates.

*Fondue pot for cooking with oil* should be deep and should narrow at the top to hold heat.

*Serve a sauce variety.* Try to include a tomato, a butter and a creamy sauce.

*Take great care* with the hot oil in which the meat is browned — and with the alcohol or canned heat burner. Keep watch that guests are treating both oil and burner with respect.

*Serve a vegetable salad* with beef and cheese fondue. Make a fruit salad for seafood or turkey fondues. Fondue sauces may be used as dressing, if you like.

*Warmed French bread* or hard rolls are excellent with beef, turkey and seafood fondues. And, because many men often feel a meal isn't complete without potatoes, you might want to serve each guest a baked potato . . . with butter and/or dairy sour cream.

*Have a tray or mat* beneath the fondue pot to prevent spattering and drips from spotting the tablecloth.

*Use an alcohol burner* for meat fondue. Synasol — a type of alcohol available in most paint and hardware stores — will give a hot flame.

*Bring fondue* meat and seafood to room temperature. This helps keep oil from cooling.

*"Dry"* meat before arranging it on serving platter. Blot it in a paper towel to absorb juices which cause spattering.

*Watch* that too many pieces of meat or seafood aren't put into the pot at once . . . or oil will cool. Four to six people cooking in one pot is enough.

*Do make sure* that there is some meat cooking in the pot at all times, so there is a constant supply ready to eat.

*Skewer* meat, seafood or vegetable so about ¼ inch of fork is pushed through it. This keeps food from sticking to bottom of pot.

*Experiment* with a variety of meats. Try ½ inch cubes of duck, pheasant, sausages, chicken, venison.

*For interest,* have both a pot of oil and a pot of broth (see recipe for Mixed Fondue Supper, page 83) simmering for guests to use.

*When* the group is small, supply each person with two forks.

## BEEF FONDUE

Trim the fat from 2 pounds of beef tenderloin or beef sirloin and cut it into 1-inch cubes; cover and refrigerate. Bring to room temperature before serving time. Prepare 2 or more sauces — numbers 1, 2, 3, 5, 6, 7, 8, 10 and 12 are especially good with beef. See page 84.

About 15 minutes before dinner, mound pieces of meat on a bed of greens. Measure salad oil or peanut oil into a deep, narrow-topped metal fondue pot to a depth of 1½ inches to 2 inches. Heat oil on stove until hot enough to brown a cube of bread in 1 minute (about 425° F.). *Carefully* place pot on stand on table and ignite denatured alcohol burner or canned cooking fuel.

To eat beef fondue, spear a cube of meat with a long-handled fork; dip meat into hot oil and cook until meat is crusty on outside and juicy inside. Remove meat from long-handled fork. Dip meat into sauce of your choice and eat with table fork. At stand-up parties, toothpicks may be used for eating. Yields 4 servings.

*Meatball variation:* Season 2 pounds of lean, ground round steak to taste with salt, pepper, onion powder or garlic powder. Shape into ¾-inch-diameter meatballs. Serve, cook and eat as described above.

## MIXED FONDUE SUPPER
*Meats and vegetables cooked in tasty broth*
*[and oil if you like]*
*provide a great evening with friends.*

3 cans (10½-ounce each)
  condensed chicken broth
2 soup cans water

4-5 cups peanut oil
  (optional)

Combine soup and water. Heat to boiling in fondue pot on stove; then place over alcohol flame. Have a tray of assorted foods ready for simmering in the pot — and bowls of assorted dips. Choose from the following:

*Dippables:* Small, paper-thin slices of round or flank steak (slightly frozen meat slices more easily); thin squares of chicken or turkey breast; sliced or diced canned bamboo shoots; shelled, deveined green (raw) shrimp with tails left on; bite-size pieces of fresh spinach; 2-inch pieces of Chinese cabbage; sliced, fresh mushrooms; Pepperoni or Chinese sausage, sliced.

Use long-handled fondue forks or bamboo skewers. Each person skewers a piece of uncooked food and dips it into the boiling broth, holding it there a minute or two until cooked. Cooked food may be dipped into one of the following sauces:

*Sauces:* Peanut butter plus sesame oil; tabasco sauce or vinegar. Sauces 1, 3, 5, 6, 7, 8, 9, 10, 11 and 12 also may be used. See page 84.

After everyone has finished eating the meat and vegetables, heat cooked, thin, egg noodles (or transparent, bean thread noodles) in the broth for 3 to 5 minutes. Ladle broth into soup bowls and pass one to each person.

## MEAT AND SEAFOOD FONDUE SAUCES

*1. Garlic Butter:* Whip ½ cup softened butter until fluffy. Stir in 1 tablespoon snipped parsley and 1 clove garlic, crushed. Refrigerate. Let come to room temperature before serving. Yields ½ cup sauce.

*2. Blue Cheese Sauce:* Combine ½ cup dairy sour cream, ¼ cup crumbled blue cheese, 1 teaspoon Worcestershire sauce and ¼ teaspoon salt. Refrigerate. Bring to room temperature before serving. Yields ¾ cup sauce.

*3. Horseradish Sauce:* Combine 1 cup dairy sour cream, 2 tablespoons horseradish, ½ teaspoon lemon juice, ¼ teaspoon Worcestershire sauce, ⅛ teaspoon salt, ⅛ teaspoon pepper. Refrigerate. Bring to room temperature before serving. Yields 1 cup sauce.

*4. Curried Fruit Sauce:* Combine 2 cups dairy sour cream; 1 can (8¾-ounce) crushed pineapple, drained; 1 unpared medium apple, chopped (about 1 cup); 1 teaspoon curry powder; ½ teaspoon garlic salt. Refrigerate. Bring to room temperature before serving. Yields 3 cups sauce.

*5. Curry Sauce:* Stir together 1 cup dairy sour cream, ¾ teaspoon curry powder and ¼ teaspoon salt. Refrigerate. Bring to room temperature before serving. Yields 1 cup sauce.

*6. Mustard Sauce:* Use bottled, hot Dijon-style mustard.

*7. Red Sauce:* Combine ¾ cup catsup, 2 tablespoons vinegar, ½ teaspoon prepared horseradish. Chill; bring to room temperature before serving. Yields ¾ cup sauce.

*8. Thin, Hot, Barbecue Sauce:* Combine ½ cup butter, ½ cup vinegar, ½ cup water, ½ teaspoon dry mustard, 1 tablespoon finely-chopped onion, ¾ teaspoon sugar, ¼ cup Worcestershire sauce, ¼ cup tomato sauce, ¼ cup chili sauce, ½ clove garlic, juice of ½ lemon. Simmer mixture, covered, for 30 minutes to blend flavors. Remove garlic. Sauce may be made ahead and stored in refrigerator. Serve warm or at room temperature. Yields about 1 cup sauce.

9. *Cranberry-Olive Sauce:* Combine 1 cup jellied cranberry sauce, ½ cup finely-diced stuffed olives, ¼ cup finely-diced celery, 1 teaspoon lemon juice, ½ teaspoon minced onion. Heat thoroughly. Refrigerate. Serve warm or at room temperature. Yields 1½ cups sauce.

10. *Hickory-Smoked Barbeque Sauce:* Buy bottled and serve warm or at room temperature.

11. *Melted Butter:* Warm ¼ pound butter over low heat until just melted. Yields ½ cup sauce.

12. *Soy-Oil Sauce:* Mix ¼ cup soy sauce with 1 tablespoon olive or seasame oil. Yields about ¼ cup sauce.


## COOKING MEATS IN LIQUID

*Brown meat on all sides, if desired.* The browning develops flavor and increased color. Exceptions to browning are corned beef and cured and smoked pork.

*Cover the meat with water or stock.* The liquid may be hot or cold. By entirely covering the meat with liquid, uniform cooking is assured without turning the meat.

*Season with salt, pepper, herbs, spices and vegetables, if desired.* (Cured and smoked meat and corned beef, of course, do not require salt.) Wisely used, seasonings add much to the variety and flavor of meats which are cooked in liquid. Some suggestions are: bay leaves, thyme, marjoram, parsley, green pepper, celery and onion tops, garlic, cloves, peppercorns and allspice.

*Cover kettle and simmer [do not boil] until tender.* Boiling and overcooking shrink the meat and make it dry, detract from flavor and texture and make it difficult to slice.

*If the meat is to be served cold, let it cool and then chill in the stock in which it was cooked.* The meat is more flavorful and juicy and it will shrink less if cooled in its stock.

*When vegetables are to be cooked with the meat, as in "boiled" dinners, add them whole or in pieces, just long enough before the meat is tender to cook them.*

For stews, remove meat and vegetables when done to pan or platter and keep hot. Thicken cooking liquid with flour for gravy. Use 2 tablespoons flour for each cup liquid and just enough water to make a paste of the flour. Stir flour-water mixture into cooking liquid. Bring to a boil and boil 3 minutes or until thickened. Serve over meat and vegetables or pass in a sauce boat.

## TIME-TABLE FOR COOKING IN LIQUID

| CUT | AVERAGE WEIGHT | APPROX. TIME PER POUND | APPROX. TOTAL COOKING TIME |
|---|---|---|---|
| | *Pounds* | *Minutes* | *Hours* |
| Smoked ham (old style and country cured) | | | |
| Large | 12 to 16 | 20 | |
| Small | 10 to 12 | 25 | |
| Half | 5 to 8 | 30 | |
| | | | |
| Smoked ham (tendered) | | | |
| Shank or butt half | 5 to 8 | 20-25 | |
| Smoked picnic shoulder | 5 to 8 | 45 | |
| Fresh or corned beef | 4 to 6 | 40-50 | |
| Beef for stew | | | 2½-3½ |
| Veal for stew | | | 2-3 |
| Lamb for stew | | | 1½-2 |

## LET 'EM BE LATE BEEF STEW
*Great during busy field days.*

1 pound lean beef, cut in
  ½-inch cubes *or* 1 pound
  lean ground beef shaped
  into small balls
  Water
1 teaspoon sweet basil
  Salt
2 carrots

2 potatoes
2 ribs celery
8 onions, boiling size
1 cup eggplant, cubed
1 cup peas, frozen *or* fresh
2 tomatoes
1 package (8-ounce)
  refrigerated biscuits

Dredge beef cubes in flour and brown in small amount of fat. Add water to cover and season with salt and sweet basil. Simmer just below the boiling point until meat is tender, about 2 hours. Add carrots, potatoes, celery, onions and eggplant. Simmer about 15 minutes. Place mixture in 2-quart casserole and keep hot in preheated, 350° F. oven until men head into the yard. Then, stir in peas and tomato wedges. Increase oven temperature to 425° F. While oven is heating, break open biscuits and arrange around edge of casserole.

Bake stew and biscuits for 15 minutes or until biscuits are browned. Yields 4 servings.

*Try Rutabagas:* Use 2 cups diced rutabagas in place of peas and eggplant.

*Lamb Stew:* Use 1 pound boneless, cubed lamb in place of beef. Omit tomatoes; increase carrots and potatoes to 3 each, and add ½ teaspoon rosemary.

## SOUP STOCK

*The 1934 Country Kitchen Cook Book states that this recipe will make a brown stock if part of the meat is browned in the fat marrow from the bone before it is put on to simmer. If meat is not browned, a clear stock results.*

3 pounds lean beef, cut in 1-inch cubes
3 pounds veal knuckle, sawed in pieces
3 quarts cold water
⅓ cup diced carrot
⅓ cup diced turnip
⅓ cup diced celery

2 tablespoons butter
2 tablespoons salt
1 teaspoon peppercorns
4 whole cloves
1 sprig parsley
1 bay leaf

Cover meat and bones with cold water. Bring to simmering and simmer for about 4 hours. Remove scum which has formed. Add vegetables and seasonings; simmer until tender.

The bones may be removed and the mixture served as a vegetable soup; or the liquid may be strained off at once, clarified and used as a clear broth or soup stock. The meat can then be utilized in other dishes. Stock freezes well. Yields about 2½ quarts stock, plus meat.

*To clarify:* For each quart of broth, beat 1 egg white and 1 tablespoon cold water together. Add to soup along with egg shell. Bring to a boil, stirring. Boil 2 minutes. Let stand 20 minutes. Strain through double cheesecloth.

## BOILED BEEF SOUP
*Summer specialty.*

3 quarts water
5 tablespoons salt
½ teaspoon pepper
3 pounds beef short ribs,
   trimmed

3 zucchini, cut into 1-inch
   slices (about 1¼ pounds)
4 large carrots, cut into
   ¼-inch slices
4 ears corn, cut into thirds

Place the first 3 ingredients into large pot. Bring to boil; add short ribs and simmer, covered, 1 hour and 40 minutes. Add zucchini and carrots; cook, covered, 10 minutes. Add corn; cook 10 minutes, or until meat and vegetables are tender. Remove meat from bone; cut into bite-size pieces. Place with vegetables in large serving dish. Pour in broth. Yields 8 servings, about 2 cups each.

*Or use* 1 can (1-pound, 1-ounce) whole kernel corn, drained. Add to soup in place of fresh corn and heat through.

*For winter soup:* Use celery potatoes, turnips, rutabagas, onions or canned tomatoes in place of the zucchini and corn.

## BREAD CROUTONS
*Soup-er toppers!*

*Buttered Croutons:* Melt 2 tablespoons butter in a skillet. Add 2 cups of toasted, ½-inch bread cubes and stir until all sides are coated with butter. Serve with all varieties of soups. Yields 2 cups croutons.

*Cheese Croutons:* Melt 2 tablespoons butter in a skillet. Add 2 cups toasted, ½-inch bread cubes and stir until all sides are coated with butter. Sprinkle 2 tablespoons finely grated Parmesan cheese over top of croutons. Serve with French onion soup or cream of tomato soup. Yields 2 cups croutons.

*Garlic Croutons:* Combine 1½ teaspoons garlic salt with 2 tablespoons corn oil and heat in a skillet. Add 2 cups toasted, ½-inch bread cubes and stir until all sides are coated. Serve with creamed vegetable soups. Yields 2 cups croutons.

*Lemon-Buttered Croutons:* Combine 1 tablespoon soft butter, 1 teaspoon lemon juice and 1 teaspoon grated lemon rind. Toast 2 slices bread on one side. Spread lemon-butter on untoasted side of bread slice. Toast under a preheated, 400° F. broiler for 5 minutes, or until golden brown. Cut toast in ½-inch cubes. Serve with fish chowder and bisques. Yields 2 cups croutons.

*Herb Croutons:* Melt 3 tablespoons butter in a skillet. Add 3 cups soft, ½-inch bread cubes and saute until brown. Sprinkle with ⅛ teaspoon onion salt and ⅛ teaspoon celery salt. Stir until all sides of croutons are seasoned. Serve with creamed vegetable soups. Yields 2½ cups croutons.

## PRESSED BEEF LOAF
*Picnic delight from the 1911 Country Kitchen Cook Book.*

| | |
|---|---|
| 6 pounds lean beef | ½ teaspoon dry mustard |
| 1 tablespoon salt | ½ teaspoon cloves |
| ½ teaspoon cinnamon | ½ teaspoon celery seed |

Cover beef with cold water; add salt. Bring to boil, simmer slowly until meat is tender and ¼ liquor is left. Remove meat from liquor and, when cold, remove any fat. Chop meat very fine. Mix in cinnamon, cloves, mustard and celery seed. Pack meat firmly into enamel or glass pan. Pour over just enough liquor to bind the meat. Pack firmly again and let refrigerate for 24 hours. Serve cold. Garnish unmolded loaf with green olives and pimiento. Yields 1 large loaf.

## SHEPHERD'S PIE
*A savory supper, offered to readers in January, 1912.*

Next time you have a bit of cold roast or even steak left, try a Shepherd's Pie. Put meat through the grinder (measure about 1½ cups); add a cup of boiling water or cold gravy, if you have it, and a few slices of onion. Season to suit. Set on the stove to simmer in an iron skillet. Then put your cold potatoes through ricer (measure about 2 cups), add ¼ cup of cream or milk and a bit of butter, pepper and salt. Beat to a light mass.

If you have no ricer, warm the potatoes slightly in the milk and mash. If your meat has been simmering in water, thicken to make gravy and add ¼ teaspoon of Kitchen Bouquet or soy sauce to color. Spread potatoes over meat for a crust and bake until a rich brown. Yields 4 servings.

## QUICKIE CREAMED MEAT
*Stretch a little meat into a good, hot supper.*

2 cups ground or finely
diced, cooked meat
1 can (10½-ounce) con-
densed cream of mush-
room, tomato, chicken
*or* celery soup

1 teaspoon salt
2 teaspoons catsup *or*
Worcestershire sauce
1 teaspoon celery salt, chili
powder *or* garlic salt

Heat all ingredients together. Taste. Add salt and pepper if
needed. Serve on hot buttered toast, rice, macaroni, noodles,
toasted cornbread or hot baking-powder biscuits. Yields 4 to
5 servings.

## CREAMED DRIED BEEF AND PEAS
*Pass grated cheese to sprinkle over cream sauce.*

⅓ cup butter *or* bacon fat
⅓ cup flour
3 cups milk

¾ cup shredded, dried beef
2 cups cooked peas

Soak dried beef if it is very salty, and drain. Shred and
frizzle in fat until edges curl. Remove, add flour and milk to
make a gravy. Add peas and beef and heat through. Serve hot
on toast. Yields 6 to 8 servings.
*Dried Beef Gravy:* Omit peas and serve with baked
potatoes or pour over hot biscuits or toast.

## MEAT ROLL
*From the 1934 Cook Book.*

1 cup chopped, cooked
meat
Seasonings

1 recipe baking powder
biscuit dough, page 233

Roll dough until about ¼ inch thick. Spread meat over top,
sprinkle with salt and pepper and onion juice, and roll like a
jelly roll. Cut slices about ¾ inch thick. Place cut end down
on a greased pan. Bake in a moderately hot oven for about ½
hour or until well browned. Serve with tomato sauce or gravy.
Yields about 4 servings.

*To make toast cups,* cut crusts from slices of bread. Butter both sides of each slice and press each into a muffin cup, allowing corners to turn up. Toast in preheated, 375° F. oven until golden brown. Cups may be made ahead and heated just before serving. Fill with creamed meats, seafood or eggs.

## BAKED HASH
*Serve with poached eggs and*
*serve more people.*

1 can (10¾-ounce) beef gravy *or* 1⅓ cups leftover beef gravy
2 cups ground, cooked beef
1 cup finely diced cooked potato

1 small onion
½ green pepper, ground
½ teaspoon prepared mustard
Dash pepper

Combine all ingredients in a 10x6x2-inch baking pan. Bake in preheated, 350° F. oven for 1 hour. Serve with chili sauce if desired. Yields 4 servings.

## GOULASH SOUP
*Homemade taste!*

¼ cup chopped green pepper
1 teaspoon paprika
2 tablespoons butter

1 can (10¾-ounce) condensed tomato soup
1 soup can water
1 cup cubed, cooked beef
½ teaspoon caraway seed

Cook green pepper and paprika in butter until green pepper is tender. Add remaining ingredients and heat together. Stir often. Keep over low heat 4 minutes to mellow flavors. Yields 2 to 3 servings.

## CANNED STEW PLUS
*Dumplings make a fast, hearty meal.*

Pour 2 cans (1-pound, 8-ounce each) beef stew into a skillet. Spoon 1 can (1-pound) drained green beans or peas around edge of pan; cover and heat thoroughly. Top with dumplings, recipe below. Yields 4 to 6 servings.

*Cheese Dumplings:* Mix ⅓ cup milk with 1 cup biscuit mix; dough will be lumpy. Spoon 4 to 6 dumplings onto hot stew; cover at once and cook until dumplings are done, 15 to 20 minutes. Sprinkle ½ cup shredded cheddar cheese over dumplings and allow to soften.

### TIME-TABLE FOR ROASTING VEAL

| CUT | APPROX. WT. IN LBS. | OVEN TEMP. | INTERNAL TEMP. | MIN. TO COOK PER LB. |
|---|---|---|---|---|
| Leg | 5 to 8 | 300°-325° F. | 170° F. | 25 to 35 |
| Loin | 4 to 6 | 300°-325° F. | 170° F. | 30 to 35 |
| Rib (rack) | 3 to 5 | 300°-325° F. | 170° F. | 35 to 40 |
| Rolled shoulder | 4 to 6 | 300°-325° F. | 170° F. | 40 to 45 |

### VEAL WITH CASHEWS
*A crunchy, company dish.*

1 cup long grain, raw rice
2 cups boiling water
1½ pounds veal cubes
2 tablespoons shortening
2 tablespoons chopped pimiento
2 cans (10½-ounce each) condensed chicken rice soup
1 can (10½-ounce) condensed cream of mushroom soup
1 large onion, diced
1 green pepper, diced
1 cup cashew nuts

Pour boiling water over the rice and let rice soak overnight. Drain rice. Cube and brown steak in shortening; combine all ingredients. Place mixture in 2-quart casserole and bake in preheated, 375° F. oven for 1½ hours. Yields 8 servings.

## CITY CHICKEN
*Mock chicken legs.*

1½ pounds fresh veal
1½ pounds fresh pork
2 eggs, beaten

Flour, salt, pepper
Bread crumbs
10 wooden skewers

Cut pork and veal about ½ inch in thickness and in 1½-inch squares. Place alternately on skewers until they are ⅔ filled. Roll in seasoned flour, then beaten eggs, then bread crumbs. Brown on all sides in a small amount of fat. Put in roaster, add 1 cup water. Cover and bake until tender, about 1 hour. Yields 5 servings.

*Remember that braising* is good for veal cuts because the combination of browning and steaming tenderizes the meat and develops its flavor.

## KALVSYLTA
*Royal jellied veal.*

2 pounds veal neck
1 veal knuckle, sawed
   through 2 or 3 times
   Water
1½ teaspoons salt
½ teaspoon pepper

6 whole cloves
8 whole allspice
1 tablespoon gelatin
¼ cup cold water
1 tablespoon vinegar
1 bay leaf

Cover meat and knuckle with cold water, add seasonings and spices. Bring to boil, skim, cover and simmer 1½ hours, or until meat is tender. Remove meat and cut in small cubes. Strain stock; cook down to 4 cups. Add chopped meat and vinegar, then gelatin softened in cold water. Cool and skim off fat. Pour into oiled mold. Mixture should be nearly solid meat. If there is a layer of liquid on top of meat, pour or spoon it off. Chill until firm. Unmold.

If sliced, stuffed olives are arranged in the bottom of the mold, the veal loaf will have an attractive pattern on top when unmolded. Or, when loaf is unmolded, spread top with mayonnaise and garnish with pimiento strips, green peppers, radish slices or pickled beets. Yields 8 to 10 servings.

## VEAL LOAF
### — From The Farmer, 1890.

Take 2½ pounds of veal; plus ¼ pound fat salt pork, all chopped fine; 4 soda crackers rolled fine; 2 well-beaten eggs. Season with salt, pepper and sage. Form into a loaf and bake in preheated, 350° F. oven. Baste at intervals with salted water. Yields about 10 servings.

## BRAIN-AND-EGG SAUTE
### From a country butcher's wife.

| | |
|---|---|
| 1 veal brain | 2 eggs, beaten with fork |
| Salted water to cover | ¼ teaspoon salt |
| brain | ¼ teaspoon pepper |
| 2 tablespoons butter | ½ cup bread crumbs |
| 2 tablespoons chopped | |
| onion | |

Soak brain in salt water about 1 hour; pull off membrane; cut brain into bite-sized pieces. Melt butter in skillet and saute onion about 2 minutes. Add brain to skillet and saute lightly.

Stir together eggs, salt, pepper and bread crumbs. Add to skillet mixture and stir in. Fry about 10 minutes over medium heat until mixture is lightly brown — turn now and then. Yields 2 to 3 servings.

## BAKED HEART
### Hearty meal with green peas and gelatin salad.

| | |
|---|---|
| 1 fresh beef heart *or* | 1½ cups rice dressing |
| 2 veal hearts | (below) |
| 4 slices bacon | Paprika |
| 2 cups diluted tomato soup | |

First wash 2 beef or 1 veal heart carefully; remove veins, arteries and blood. Tie heart with string and place on a rack in an ovenproof dish. Add tomato soup and lay bacon on top of heart. Cover dish and bake in preheated, 325° F. oven until tender — 3 to 5 hours for beef heart, about 2 hours for veal heart.

Remove heart to plate and cool slightly. Fill cavity with hot dressing, sprinkle heart with paprika and return it to a hot oven, 400° F., for about 10 to 15 minutes. Tomato sauce may be thickened to serve with meat. Yields 4 to 6 servings.

*Rice Dressing:* While heart is cooking, prepare stuffing. Beat 1 egg. Add ½ cup milk, 2 tablespoons finely chopped parsley, 1 clove finely chopped garlic, 1 tablespoon minced onion, 1 cup cooked rice, ¼ cup grated, sharp cheese, ½ teaspoon salt. Mix well. Place in greased baking dish and bake in oven along with heart for 25 minutes. Remove both heart and dressing — stuff heart and return it to oven as directed above.

## HEART CREOLE
*Slow cooking makes meat fork-tender.*

1 small beef heart *or*
  2 veal hearts
¼ cup all-purpose flour
½ teaspoon salt
¼ teaspoon pepper
¼ cup butter, lard *or*
  drippings
¼ cup finely-chopped
  onion

1 clove garlic
1 can (4-ounce) sliced
  mushrooms
1 can (16-ounce) tomatoes
¼ cup thin green pepper
  strips
1 tablespoon chopped
  parsley
1 teaspoon sugar
  Cooked rice

Wash the heart thoroughly and remove fat, veins and any hard parts. Cut into ¾-inch cubes. Combine flour with salt and pepper, dredge meat in the seasoned flour and brown in butter or fat. Drain off excess fat. Drain mushrooms, save broth and add to the meat along with the onion, garlic and tomatoes. Cover tightly and simmer about 1¼ hours; add mushrooms, green pepper, parsley and sugar; cover and continue simmering until heart is tender and vegetables are done. Serve with hot, cooked rice. Yields 6 to 8 servings.

## KIDNEY RAGOUT
*Serve over hot rice or fluffy mashed potatoes.*

2 teaspoons salt
2 pounds veal *or*
  lamb kidneys
3 tablespoons bacon fat *or*
  butter
2 cups canned tomatoes
⅓ cup diced celery
¼ cup diced green pepper
3 tablespoons onion flakes

1 teaspoon sugar
½ teaspoon salt
½ teaspoon basil
½ teaspoon oregano
¼ teaspoon ground black
  pepper
1 can (4-ounce) whole
  mushrooms, drained

Rub 2 teaspoons salt over kidneys and let stand 2 hours to remove some of the strong flavor. Rinse in cold water; pat dry. Remove membrane and white tubes and cut into slices ¼ inch thick. Saute 5 minutes in fat. Add next six ingredients, cover and simmer 30 minutes. Add remaining ingredients. Cover and cook 10 minutes. Yields about 6 servings.

## LIVER DUMPLINGS
*Grandma's speciality!*

⅛ teaspoon poultry
  seasoning
⅛ teaspoon nutmeg
¾ teaspoon salt
¼ teaspoon pepper
¾ teaspoon lemon rind,
  grated
1½ pounds raw calf *or* beef
  liver, finely ground

2 small cloves garlic,
  finely minced
1 teaspoon onion, grated
6 tablespoons butter
4 eggs
1½ cups stale bread
  crumbs
  Soup or clear broth

Combine poultry seasoning, nutmeg, salt, pepper, lemon rind, garlic, onion, and ground liver. Cream butter and add one egg at a time, beating well. Gradually add dry bread crumbs alternately with liver mixture to the creamed butter and eggs. When all is blended, cover and allow to stand in the refrigerator for ½ hour. Sprinkle flour on hands and form small dumplings 1 to 1½ inches in diameter. Cook vigorously in boiling, clear soup. When dumplings rise to the top, lower heat, and cover. Cook for 4 to 5 minutes more. Yields 4 to 6 servings.

## LIVER CASSEROLE
*Serve with fluffy, mashed potatoes.*

8 slices liver, each ⅜ to ½
   inch thick
Flour for dipping
Butter *or* bacon
   drippings for browning
1 large onion, sliced

½ cup catsup
½ cup water
1 teaspoon salt
¼ teaspoon pepper
⅛ -¼ teaspoon sage

Dip liver slices in flour and saute in melted butter or bacon drippings. Do not cook over high heat or liver will harden. Slice onion over meat, cover and cook a few minutes. Transfer meat, onions and juices to casserole. Mix catsup, water, salt, pepper and sage; pour over meat. Bake in preheated, 325° F. oven for about ½ hour. Yields 4 to 6 servings.

*Add more vegetables:* Casserole is extra-nice when you add 3 thinly sliced carrots and ½ cup chopped celery.

## TURKEY LIVERS EN CASSEROLE
*Delicious budget-stretcher!*

1 pound turkey livers (part
   or all chicken livers
   may be used)
¼ cup butter
¼ teaspoon ground black
   pepper
1 large bay leaf, crumbled
1 tablespoon minced onion

1 can (4-ounce) mush-
   room caps, drained
1 can (1-pound) stewed
   tomatoes, slightly
   drained
1 package (10-ounce)
   frozen, mixed vegetables
1½ cups soda cracker
   crumbs

Saute livers in butter. Add remaining ingredients, reserving 2 tablespoons cracker crumbs for topping. Mix well. Cook over medium heat 5 minutes, stirring occasionally. Pour into 1-quart casserole. Bake in preheated, 350° F. oven for ½ to ¾ hour. Yields 4 servings.

## LIVER WITH SOUR CREAM GRAVY
*Try this gravy with steak.*

6 slices calf's liver
6 slices bacon

Flour, salt and pepper
1 cup soured cream *or*
dairy sour cream

Cook bacon until crisp and remove to a hot platter. Trim liver and dredge with flour, salt and pepper. Cook liver in bacon fat slowly 15 minutes, turning as necessary. Cover and steam 5 minutes. Put on platter with bacon. Add cream to the drippings and heat until blended. Season and pour around the meat.

## FRESH TONGUE
*Delicious in sandwiches.*

1 fresh beef tongue, about
    4 pounds
1 medium-sized onion
3 whole cloves, stuck into
    onion
1 carrot, sliced
2 ribs celery, with leaves,
    sliced

2 tablespoons chopped
    parsley
1 bay leaf
6 peppercorns
Boiling water
2 teaspoons salt

Wash the tongue, place in deep kettle, add next seven ingredients and cover with boiling water. Bring water slowly back to a boil. Boil about 5 minutes, then remove any scum and add salt. Reduce heat and simmer about 50 minutes to the pound, or until meat is tender.

Cool tongue in stock until it can be handled. Remove it and skin it with a sharp knife. Trim tongue, removing fat and tough portions near throat end.

Serve hot or cold with a tart sauce, or bake in a preheated, 375° F. oven for about 25 minutes, basting frequently with 1 cup tomato sauce. Yields 6 to 8 servings.

*Tongue in Vegetable Sauce:* Cook tongue and prepare it as described above. Then lightly brown 1 cup diced celery, 1 cup diced carrots and 1 cup diced onion in 2 tablespoons butter. Add 3 tablespoons flour and 2 cups of meat stock. Season to taste with salt and pepper. Place tongue in a baking dish; pour sauce over meat and bake in preheated, 325° F. oven for

45 minutes. Or, heat sauce until it thickens, add sliced tongue and heat. Serve on a platter with sauce poured around meat.

## OXTAIL STEW
*Nice enough for company.*

2 pounds disjointed oxtails
3 tablespoons shortening
1 large onion, chopped
  Flour
1 bay leaf (optional)
2 teaspoons salt
¼ teaspoon pepper
1 tablespoon vinegar

2 cups water
3 carrots, sliced
1 cup diced celery
1 green pepper, chopped
  (optional)
4 medium potatoes, cut in
  half
  Flour and seasonings

Wash the oxtails in cold water. Pat dry. Melt shortening in a heavy skillet. Add onion. Roll oxtails in flour and brown in the hot shortening with the onion. Add bay leaf, salt, pepper, vinegar and water. Cover tightly. Simmer gently 3 hours. Add more water if necessary to prevent burning. (Meat may be removed from the bones at this point — and meat returned to broth.) Add carrots, celery, green pepper and potatoes. Cover. Increase heat to start vegetables cooking. Then simmer 45 minutes. Place vegetables and meat in heated bowl. Thicken broth for gravy, taste and correct seasonings if necessary. Pour gravy over meat and vegetables, serve. Yields 4 servings.

## SWEETBREADS-CANADIAN BACON GRILL
*Gourmet treat!*

1 pound sweetbreads
1 quart water
1 teaspoon salt
1 tablespoon vinegar *or*
  lemon juice

6 pineapple slices
2 tablespoons butter
6 slices Canadian bacon,
  cut ¼-inch thick

Wash sweetbreads; add water, salt and vinegar or lemon juice; simmer 20 minutes. Chill in ice water and drain. Remove membrane and divide into 6 servings. Place bacon slices and pineapple on broiler rack. Broil about 3 inches from the heat for 4 minutes, turn bacon and pineapple, top each slice of bacon with a serving of sweetbreads. Brush with melted butter and broil for 3 or 4 minutes longer or until lightly browned. Yields 6 servings.

## TIME-TABLE FOR ROASTING PORK

| CUT | APPROX. WEIGHT Pounds | OVEN TEMPERATURE Degrees F. | MEAT THERMOMETER READING Degrees F. | APPROX. COOKING TIME Min. Per Lb. |
|---|---|---|---|---|
| *Pork, Fresh* | | | | |
| Loin | | | | |
| Center | 3 to 5 | 325°-350° F. | 170° F. | 30 to 35 |
| Half | 5 to 7 | 325°-350° F. | 170° F. | 35 to 40 |
| Blade loin or sirloin | 3 to 4 | 325°-350° F. | 170° F. | 40 to 45 |
| Picnic shoulder | 5 to 8 | 325°-350° F. | 170° F. | 30 to 35 |
| Rolled | 3 to 5 | 325°-350° F. | 170° F. | 40 to 45 |
| Cushion style | 3 to 5 | 325°-350° F. | 170° F. | 35 to 40 |
| Boston shoulder | 4 to 6 | 325°-350° F. | 170° F. | 45 to 50 |
| Leg (fresh ham) | | | | |
| Whole (bone in) | 10 to 14 | 325°-350° F. | 170° F. | 25 to 30 |
| Whole (boneless) | 7 to 10 | 325°-350° F. | 170° F. | 35 to 40 |
| Half (bone in) | 5 to 7 | 325°-350° F. | 170° F. | 40 to 45 |
| *Pork, Smoked* | | | | |
| Ham (cook before eating) | | | | |
| Whole | 10 to 14 | 300°-325° F. | 160° F. | 18 to 20 |
| Half | 5 to 7 | 300°-325° F. | 160° F. | 22 to 25 |
| Shank or butt portion | 3 to 4 | 300°-325° F. | 160° F. | 35 to 40 |
| Ham (fully cooked)* | | | | |
| Half | 5 to 7 | 325° F. | 130° F. | 18 to 24 |
| Picnic shoulder | 5 to 8 | 300°-325° F. | 170° F. | 35 |
| Shoulder roll | 2 to 3 | 300°-325° F. | 170° F. | 35 to 40 |
| Canadian style bacon | 2 to 4 | 300°-325° F | 160° F. | 35 to 40 |

*Allow approximately 15 minutes per pound for heating whole ham to serve hot.

*For interest,* dunk a sugar lump or two in lemon extract, place these on top of the roast, and light the cubes to "flame" the roast.

## CROWN ROAST OF PORK
*Trim with spiced apples or frills, page 131, for a roast almost too handsome to be true.*

1 cup chopped onion
¼ cup butter
1 package (9¾-ounce) triscuit wafers, finely rolled, about 3 cups crumbs
3 cups finely-chopped apple, about 4 medium, peeled and cored
1½ cups chicken broth (use 2 bouillon cubes dissolved in 1½ cups water)

1 cup coarsely-chopped pecans
½ cup chopped dates
½ teaspoon ground cinnamon
1 teaspoon salt
1 teaspoon marjoram
1 teaspoon celery seed
¼ teaspoon pepper
1 crown roast of pork, 10 to 12 pounds

Saute onion in butter. Stir in next 10 ingredients. Pile as much stuffing as possible into center of crown roast. Cover stuffing with aluminum foil. Bake remaining stuffing in covered casserole. Roast meat in preheated, 325° F. oven for 4 to 4½ hours, or until meat thermometer registers 170° F. internal temperature. Yields 14 to 16 servings.

## SAUCE AND GLAZES FOR PORK

*Spicy Barbecue Sauce:* Mix ⅓ cup finely-chopped onion, ¼ cup finely-chopped celery, ½ clove minced garlic, 2 tablespoons brown sugar, 2 teaspoons prepared mustard, 1 can (10½-ounce) condensed tomato soup, 2 tablespoons Worcestershire sauce, 2 tablespoons lemon juice or vinegar, 4 drops Tabasco sauce. Mix well and pour over meat during last 1½ hours of roasting. Yields sauce for a 5-pound roast.

*Apricot Glaze:* Combine ½ cup apricot preserves, 2 teaspoons dry mustard, 2 tablespoons lemon juice. Mix thoroughly. During last 20 to 30 minutes, spread glaze over meat and return to oven to finish roasting. Yields ½ cup glaze.

*Rosy Peach Sauce:* Drain 1 can (16-ounce) sliced peaches, reserving juice. Combine juice, ¼ cup catsup and 2 teaspoons lemon juice. Mix 1 tablespoon cornstarch, ¼ teaspoon cinnamon, ⅛ teaspoon cloves and ¼ teaspoon salt; add to juice mixture and blend. Cook, stirring constantly, over medium heat until sauce thickens. Add peaches. During last 20 to 30 minutes spread glaze over meat and return to oven to finish roasting. Yields 2 cups sauce. Prepare enough sauce so you can glaze the roast, then heat remaining sauce to serve at the table.

## STUFFED PORK TENDERLOIN
*Bake potatoes or scallop corn with the meat.*

Split a pork tenderloin in half lengthwise, but leave the halves joined together. Pound each half slightly, then fill with about 1 cup poultry dressing, page 136. *Or* use 1 cup pork chop stuffing, page 104, to which has been added a few chopped pickles. Stuffing should be arranged so that it will be higher in the center. Fasten edges of meat together and sprinkle with flour, salt and pepper. Roast uncovered about 1 hour in a preheated, 375° F. oven, basting occasionally. Yields 4 to 6 servings.

## CRISPY SPARERIBS
*These disappear fast — make great snacks!*

6 pounds spareribs                 Salt and pepper

Cut each rib apart, sprinkle generously with salt and

pepper. Place on rack in pan in preheated, 300° F. oven and cook 2 to 4 hours. Allow to brown; never raise temperature. Serve, accompanied by a hot chili sauce for dipping. Yields 6 to 8 servings.

## SPARERIBS BAKED ON LENTILS
*Economical flavor treat.*

| | |
|---|---|
| 1 pound lentils | 1 teaspoon salt |
| 5 cups water | ⅛ teaspoon pepper |
| 1 small onion, thinly-sliced | 2 pounds spareribs, |
| 1 bay leaf | cracked |
| | Salt and pepper |

Wash lentils. Bring to a boil and simmer, covered, for about 30 minutes in water with onion, bay leaf, salt and pepper. Pour into baking pan. Cut ribs into serving portions. Brown on all sides; season. Place on top of lentils. Bake, uncovered, in preheated, 350° F. oven for about 1½ hours. Serve with apple sauce, hot rolls and a tossed green salad. Yields 5 to 6 servings.

## BAKED SPARERIBS, CORNBREAD STUFFING
*Excellent use for leftover cornbread.*

| | |
|---|---|
| 2 pounds spareribs | 1 onion, chopped |
| 2 cups crumbled | ¼ cup melted butter |
| cornbread | ½ teaspoon thyme |
| ¾ cup milk | ½ teaspoon salt |

Combine all ingredients, except meat, and mix well. Pat out into a shallow casserole or baking dish. Place spareribs on top. Sprinkle with additional salt and pepper. Bake in preheated, 350° F. oven for about 2 hours.

## STUFFED PORK CHOPS
*Classic from The 1934 Country Kitchen Cook Book.*

8-10 pork chops, 1 inch
    thick
2 cups toasted bread
    crumbs *or* cooked rice
2 tablespoons butter
1 medium onion,
    minced

1 tablespoon minced green
    pepper
Salt and pepper
Water *or* milk to lightly
    moisten dressing

Make a pocket in each chop. Make dressing from other ingredients and fill in pockets. Fasten with toothpicks. Brown in frying pan. Add ¾ cup water, cover, and bake in preheated, 350° F. oven for 50 minutes.

*Bake with sour milk:* Instead of water, use 1¼ cups sour milk or buttermilk to pour over chops during baking.

## ESCALLOPED APPLES, CARROTS AND PORK
*Liven up supper.*

Trim excess fat from pork chops or steaks; dip in flour, seasoned with salt, pepper and sage. Saute in hot shortening until golden brown on both sides. Arrange carrot slices, and apples cut in eighths on top of chops. Add ¼ cup water. Cover and cook over low heat about 45 minutes, or until apples and carrots are tender.

## PORK CHOP AND POTATO SCALLOP
*Moist, tender, delicious.*

8 pork chops (about 2
    pounds) *or* pork tender-
    loin patties
2 cans (10½-ounce each) con-
    densed cream of mush-
    room soup
1 cup dairy sour cream

½ cup water
¼ cup chopped parsley
5 cups thinly sliced
    potatoes
Salt
Pepper

Brown chops. Season with salt and pepper. Blend soup, sour cream, water and parsley. In a 2-quart casserole, alternate layers of potatoes sprinkled with salt and pepper, and sauce. Top with chops. Cover; bake in preheated, 375° F. oven for 1¼ hours. Yields 4 to 6 servings.

## CRANBERRY PORK CHOPS
*Party fare.*

4 pork chops ¾ to 1-inch thick
2 cups cleaned cranberries
¼ cup water

½ cup sugar
¼ teaspoon cloves
¼ teaspoon nutmeg

Brown and season pork chops. Mix rest of ingredients and cover pork chops. Cover and bake in preheated, 350° F. oven for about 1 hour. Yields 4 servings.

## MAKE-AHEAD PORK SAVORY
*Take from the freezer and heat quickly in a double boiler, or more slowly in the oven — delicious!*

3 pounds lean pork, cut in ½-inch pieces
1½ teaspoons salt
½ teaspoon pepper
1 tablespoon fat *or* oil
3 cups water
2½ cups sliced carrots

1 cup all-purpose flour
3 cups dairy sour cream
3½ cups diced potatoes
1 tablespoon finely-chopped onions
1½ cups green lima beans
1 tablespoon salt

Sprinkle pork with salt and pepper. Brown meat in fat; add water, cover and simmer until meat is tender. Cook carrots in a little water until almost tender. Combine flour and sour cream; beat until smooth. Combine with meat and broth. Add vegetables and salt; blend well.

*To serve immediately,* bake covered in preheated, 375° F. oven for 1 hour; remove the cover and continue baking for about 30 minutes to brown the top.

*To freeze,* bake covered in preheated, 375° F. oven for 1 hour. Cool quickly. Pack in pint-size freezer containers for faster thawing; leave head room. Seal and freeze immediately.

*To prepare for serving,* bake uncovered in preheated, 400° F. oven until food is heated through, about 45 minutes for pints, 1 hour for quarts. Or, reheat in the top of a double boiler, stirring as needed to prevent sticking. Yields 25 servings, ¾ cup each.

## SWEET-SOUR PORK
*Fun to fix for company.*

½ teaspoon salt
¼ teaspoon pepper
¼ cup confectioners' sugar
2 tablespoons cornstarch
1 pound lean, boneless
  pork, cut into ½-inch
  cubes
2 tablespoons vegetable oil
2 tablespoons water

1 tablespoon butter
1 cup finely-chopped
  onion
1 can (8½-ounce) diced
  bamboo shoots, drained
1 can (1-pound) peas,
  drained
3 tablespoons lemon juice
¼ cup soy sauce

Combine salt, pepper, confectioners' sugar and cornstarch.
Coat pork cubes with mixture. Pour oil into wok or skillet
and heat, uncovered, to 325° F. Add pork and stir-fry for 10
minutes or until evenly browned. Reduce heat to "simmer."
Add water, cover and simmer for 30 minutes or until pork is
fork tender. Remove cover and turn heat control to 325° F.
Push pork up side of pan. Add butter and melt; add onion
and bamboo shoots and stir-fry for 2 minutes. Push up side.
Add peas, lemon juice and soy sauce. Cook for 2 minutes.
Gently mix all ingredients. Reduce heat to "warm." Serve
with rice or chow mein noodles. Yields 4 servings.

## LASAGNE WITH MEAT SAUCE

¾ pound wide lasagne
  noodles
1 pound pork shoulder,
  cut in 1-inch cubes
1 tablespoon cooking oil
1 small onion, chopped
1 clove garlic, chopped
1 tablespoon minced
  parsley
1 teaspoon salt

¼ teaspoon pepper
1½ cans (6-ounce each)
  tomato paste
2 cups hot water
1 pound Mozzarella
  cheese, sliced
1 pound Ricotta cheese
  *or* 2 cups cream style
  cottage cheese
1 tablespoon warm water
  Parmesan cheese

In a skillet, saute 1-inch cubes of pork in oil until meat is
brown on all sides. Add onion and garlic; cook until onion is
golden. Add parsley, salt, pepper, tomato paste and water.
Cover skillet and simmer for 2 hours. Add a little water from

time to time if needed. Remove pork from sauce and serve as a separate dish.

Cook lasagne noodles about 15 minutes, or until just tender; drain.

Mix Ricotta cheese with 1 tablespoon warm water to make a soft paste. Arrange layers of noodles, Mozarella, Ricotta paste and sauce in large, flat baking dish. Cover each layer with a sprinkle of grated Parmesan. Bake in a preheated, 350° F. oven for 20 minutes. Yields 4 to 6 servings.

## PORK CASSEROLE WITH BISCUIT TOPPING
*Dinner's in a single dish.*

1½ pounds pork shoulder, cut in 1-inch cubes
2 tablespoons flour
2 tablespoons shortening
½ cup water
1 small onion, finely chopped
1 cup chopped celery
½ teaspoon thyme
2 teaspoons salt
¼ teaspoon pepper
1 package frozen, mixed vegetables
1 can (10½-ounce) condensed mushroom soup
Biscuits

Roll meat in flour, brown in hot shortening. Pour off excess fat. Add water, onion, celery, thyme, salt and pepper. Cover; cook 1 hour over low heat. Break up frozen vegetables, add with the soup. Heat to boiling. Pour in a 2-quart casserole, top with biscuits, page 233. Yields about 6 servings.

## BROILING PORK

Fresh pork steaks or chops are usually braised, but pork chops are also popular for broiling, particularly on equipment designed for grilling. Fresh pork chops should be at least ¾-inch thick and cooked well done. When pork chops are broiled or grilled, the temperature used must produce chops which are well done in the center by the time they are browned on the outside. Ham should be at least ½ inch thick for broiling.

See broiling instructions under Broiling Beef, page 79.

## CABBAGE-SAUSAGE CASSEROLE
*The sausage and bacon give the cabbage a fine flavor.*

6 slices bacon
1 medium cabbage, cut in
   6 wedges
1 large onion, chopped
½ teaspoon salt

¼ teaspoon pepper
1 cup broth *or* bouillon
1 pound pork sausages,
   link or patties

Fry out bacon so that it is partially browned, but not crisp. Line a 1½-quart casserole with the bacon slices. Place cabbage wedges over bacon. Add onion, salt, pepper and broth. Top with a layer of pork sausages. Cover and bake in preheated, 350° F. oven for 50 minutes. Uncover and let bake 10 minutes more, or until sausages have browned. Yields 4 to 6 servings.

*Add Caraway:* Lightly crush 1 teaspoon caraway seeds and add with broth.


## PORK CHODDER

*Today we'd spell it chowder; this spelling and recipe are from The Farmer in 1893.*

Put 3 or 4 thick slices of pork steak into a kettle and fry it well. Remove meat from pan, cut into bite size pieces and set aside for later use. Put enough water in the cooking pan (about 3 cups) to cover 5 or 6 potatoes which have been peeled and diced. Add 1 medium, diced onion and season well with salt and pepper. Simmer until potatoes are tender. Just before serving add a cup of sweet milk and the bits of pork, if you wish. Heat and serve. Yields 5 to 6 servings.


## PLAIN SOUSE

*Make it any time with pork hocks plus pork shoulder or steak from the butcher shop — a truly tasty recipe from The Farmer, 1905.*

Have the eyes, brains and snout removed from the pig head, then clean head thoroughly. Lay head in cold water over night. Next day, put cut-up pieces of head and the feet into a large pot and cover with fresh, cold water; bring to a boil. Boil until the meat drops from the bones, then drain off and save broth. Cool meat, then carefully pick out all the bones and cut meat up into small pieces. For 4 cups of meat add 2 teaspoons salt, ¼ teaspoon pepper, ¾ teaspoon sage, ½ teaspoon nutmeg and a little grated onion (optional). Skim fat from cooled broth and pour enough broth over meat to make a soft, jelly-like mixture. Stir well and pour into a stone, glass or enameled pan, then put away to cool and set (in the refrigerator). Cut in dainty slices and serve.

*Sliced, stuffed* olives laid in rows in the bottom of the pan produce an attractive garnish for the unmolded souse.


## PORK HOCKS 'N KRAUT WITH CARAWAY
### *A budget meal with zing.*

Place 4 or 5 pork hocks (cut in pieces) in a kettle and cover with water. Add 1 tablespoon salt, ½ teaspoon pepper, 1 teaspoon caraway seed and 1 medium sliced onion. Cover kettle; bring water to a rolling boil; turn down heat and cook for approximately 3 hours, or until tender.

After first 2 hours, add 1 quart sauerkraut. Ten minutes before serving, fine-grate 1 medium, peeled potato into boiling water and continue to cook. Serve with vegetable and potatoes. Yields about 4 servings.


## PORK HOCK DINNER
### *Dinner's in just one pot.*

| | |
|---|---|
| 4 pork hocks, fresh *or* smoked | 4 medium carrots |
| | 4 medium onions |
| 2 teaspoons salt (for fresh hocks) | 4 medium potatoes |
| | 1 small cabbage |

Wash hocks and place in Dutch oven or other large deep pan. Cover with hot water; add salt if fresh hocks are used. Simmer, covered, until meat is nearly tender, about 1½ hours. Add carrots, onions and potatoes. Cover and cook 15 minutes. Add cabbage cut in wedges and cook, covered, 30 minutes longer or until vegetables are tender. Serve hocks and vegetables on large platter. Sprinkle with salt, pepper and paprika. Yields 4 servings.   Add extra vegetables and you have 6 servings.

## PORK SAUSAGE MEAT
*Keep some frozen — from The Farmer, 1893.*

6 pounds fresh, lean pork
3 pounds fresh, fat pork
4 teaspoons powdered sage
2 tablespoons pepper

2 tablespoons salt
½ teaspoon ground cloves
½ teaspoon ground nutmeg

Run meat twice through the meat grinder; add seasonings and mix thoroughly with a spoon or the hands. Press firmly into pans or into rolls. Cut in slices and fry. Very nice. Yields 9 pounds sausage.

## SAUSAGE WITH CREAM GRAVY ON BISCUITS
*Old-fashioned supper.*

1½ pounds sausage meat
⅓ cup flour

2 cups milk
Salt and pepper

Shape sausage meat in patties and fry slowly until brown. Remove patties from frying pan. Blend ¼ cup of the remaining fat in pan with flour. Add milk gradually and continue cooking until thickened. Return sausage patties to sauce and reheat. Serve on hot, split biscuits, page 233. Yields 6 servings, 12 patties.

## COUNTRY SAUSAGE PIZZA
*Teens like to make these.*

1 recipe baking powder
   biscuits, page 233, *or*
   packaged roll mix
½ pound partially cooked,
   crumbled pork sausage

1½ cups shredded cheddar
   cheese
1 can (8-ounce) tomato
   sauce
¼-½ teaspoon oregano
   Dash of garlic salt

Prepare biscuit dough or packaged roll mix. Roll into a circle about 12 inches in diameter. Place on a baking sheet and cover to within ½ inch of edge with crumbled pork sausage that has been well-drained. Cover sausage with 1 cup of cheese. Spoon tomato sauce over cheese. Sprinkle oregano, garlic salt and the remaining cheese over the tomato sauce.

Bake in a preheated, 450° F. oven for 20 to 25 minutes. Cool, wrap in aluminum foil, label and freeze.

To serve, remove from freezer and place the wrapped pizza in a 350° F. oven for 20 to 25 minutes. Serve hot. Yields about 4 snack servings.

## SAUSAGE-STUFFED APPLES
*Superb for Sunday breakfast or brunch.*

Wash, pare and core large apples. Fill each cavity with pork sausage, either bulk or link. Bake in preheated, 350° F. oven about 1 hour, or until apples are tender and sausage thoroughly cooked.

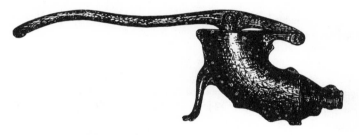

## SQUASH WITH SAUSAGE
*If you want more onions, wrap extras in foil and*
*bake beside the squash halves.*

3 medium acorn squash
3 tablespoons butter, melted
Salt
Pepper

Paprika
6 small, mild onions, peeled
12 pork link sausages

Cut squash in half and remove seeds. Brush edges and center with butter; sprinkle with salt and pepper. Brush onions with butter. Place on baking sheet; cover with inverted squash halves. Bake in preheated, 375° F. oven for 35 minutes, or until tender.

Meanwhile, cook pork sausages as directed on package. When squash is tender, mash it a bit in the shell. Place 2 sausages in each half; put an onion in the center. Brush again with melted butter, sprinkle with paprika. Bake 10 minutes more. Yields 6 servings.

## GLAZES FOR BAKED HAM
### Spark ham flavor.

*Orange-Honey Glaze:* Combine 1 can (6-ounce) of thawed frozen concentrated orange juice, ¾ cup honey and 1½ teaspoons Worcestershire sauce. Score ham fat deeply into 1-inch squares and brush on orange mixture.

*Currant Jelly:* Beat 1 cup of currant jelly with a fork to soften; stir in 2½ tablespoons prepared mustard and ¼ teaspoon ground cloves. Spread over scored ham top.

*Brown Sugar Glaze:* Score ham fat and stud with whole cloves. Combine 1 cup firmly packed brown sugar, 1½ teaspoons dry mustard, ¼ teaspoon cloves and 2½ tablespoons vinegar. Spread over scored ham.

*Applesauce Glaze:* Mix together 1½ cups pureed applesauce, ¼ cup brown sugar, ¼ teaspoon cloves and 3 tablespoons lemon juice; score ham and spread mixture on top.

## HAM SAUCES

*Jewelled Ham Sauce:* Drain 1 can (1-pound, 4½-ounce) pineapple chunks and reserve juice. Combine 2 tablespoons sugar, 1 tablespoon cornstarch and ½ teaspoon salt in a saucepan. Add pineapple juice, stirring constantly. Cook and stir over medium heat until mixture begins to thicken. Add ¼ cup coarsely chopped green pepper and 3 tablespoons prepared mustard. Continue cooking until mixture is thick. Stir in pineapple and 12 sliced maraschino cherries. Serve hot over sliced ham or ham steak. Sauce stores well. Yields about 3 cups sauce.

*Cherry Ham Sauce:* Just before slicing baked ham to serve it, heat a can of cherry pie filling and serve with the sliced ham. Also delicious with smoked pork chops. Yields 2 cups sauce.

*Plum 'n Spice Ham Sauce:* Drain, halve and pit 1 can (1-pound, 15-ounce) purple plums; reserve ½ cup syrup. Combine syrup with 1 tablespoon cornstarch, ¼ cup cider vinegar, 1 teaspoon dry mustard, 2 tablespoons brown sugar, ¼ teaspoon crushed rosemary. Cook over low heat until thick and clear, stirring constantly. Serve with hot ham slices. Yields about 2 cups sauce.

*Honey Ham Sauce:* Combine equal parts of honey, prepared mustard and salad dressing. Serve with baked ham slices or ham loaf.

## SPICED CHERRY RELISH
*Use to garnish ham or roast pork platter.*

1 can (1-pound) dark sweet
  cherries
¼ cup sugar

8 whole cloves
¼ teaspoon nutmeg
2 sticks cinnamon

Drain cherries, reserving syrup in saucepan. Add sugar and spices to syrup; simmer 5 minutes. Pour over pitted cherries and allow to stand several hours. Drain and serve cherries as relish with meats. Yields about 2 cups sauce.

## SAVORY SLICE OF HAM
*Easy to cut and serve.*

Trim fat from slice of ham, cut about 2 inches thick. Stick whole cloves into sides of slice. Chop or cut the fat very fine and mix with 4 tablespoons of maple-blended syrup. Spread over top of slice. Place in a baking pan or casserole and bake slowly, uncovered, until fat begins to brown on top. Cover bottom of dish with water. Cover casserole and continue to bake 45 minutes. Yields about 6 servings.

## HONEY-HAM LOAF
*A party loaf — serve with scalloped potatoes.*

2 pounds ham, ground
½ pound lean, fresh pork,
  ground
1 small onion, finely
  chopped
1 green pepper, finely
  chopped
1 cup bread crumbs

1 tablespoon flour
1 egg
1 teaspoon salt
  Enough milk to
  moisten, (about 1 cup)
1 can pineapple sticks
1 cup honey
  Juice of 1 lemon

Combine ham, pork, onion, pepper, bread crumbs, egg and salt. Add enough milk to moisten. Arrange pineapple sticks in spoke fashion in bottom of deep skillet or pan. Cover with honey, mixed with lemon juice. Pat ham loaf on top. Dust with flour. Bake in preheated, 325° F. oven for 1½ hours. Invert to serve. Yields about 8 servings.

## SWEDISH HAM BALLS
### *For Smorgasbord.*

| | |
|---|---|
| 1 pound ground ham | 1 cup brown sugar |
| 1½ pounds ground pork | 1 teaspoon dry mustard |
| 3 cups fine bread crumbs | ½ cup vinegar |
| 2 eggs, well beaten | ½ cup water |
| 1 cup milk | |

Combine meats, crumbs, eggs and milk. Mix well. Form in small balls. Place meat balls in baking pan. Combine remaining ingredients. Stir until sugar dissolves. Pour over meatballs. Bake in preheated, 325° F. oven for 1 hour, basting frequently. Yields 8 servings.

## HAM TURNOVERS
### *Keep a big batch of these in the freezer and you're ready for unexpected guests.*

| | |
|---|---|
| 6 cups ground, cooked ham, lightly packed | ¾ teaspoon dry mustard |
| ⅓ cup finely-chopped onion, well packed | ¾ teaspoon prepared horseradish |
| 1 cup tomato sauce | 6½ cups sifted, all-purpose flour |
| 2 tablespoons chopped parsley | 2 teaspoons salt |
| ¼ teaspoon pepper | 1¾ cups shortening |
| | 1 cup cold water |

Make filling by combining the first 7 ingredients, above.

Make pastry as follows: Sift flour and salt together. Cut in shortening until mixture is granular. Add water, a little at a time, and mix lightly with a fork. Roll out dough on a lightly-floured board to ⅛ -inch thickness. Cut into rounds or squares, about 5 inches across.

Place 3½ tablespoons of ham filling on each piece of pastry. Fold pastry over from center, forming a half-moon or triangle. Crimp edges with a fork.

*To serve immediately,* bake in preheated, 400° F. oven for 25 minutes. Serve peas or celery heated in cream sauce, cream of celery or cream of mushroom soup poured over.

*To freeze,* wrap unbaked turnovers individually in freezer packaging material and pack in cardboard cartons. Or pack in layers in moisture-proof freezer containers, separating the layers with two sheets of plastic wrap. Seal.

*To serve,* remove wrapping, place turnovers on a baking sheet, and bake in preheated, 400° F. oven for 30 to 40 minutes. Yields 25 turnovers.

## HAM-CHEESE PIE
*Delicious — and a runner-up in a
Minnesota Pork Producers' recipe contest.*

1½ pounds sliced ham
2-3 tart apples, peeled and
    thickly sliced
½ cup brown sugar
2 tablespoons butter

⅓ cup flour
6 slices processed cheddar
    cheese
1 cup dairy sour cream

Butter a low, round casserole or pie plate. Cover bottom with ham slices. Add apple slices in a thick layer. Mix together the brown sugar, butter and flour. Crumble over apples. Top with cheese. Spread sour cream over the top. Bake in preheated, 350° F. oven for 1 hour. Cut in wedge-shaped pieces for serving. This dish may be prepared several hours ahead of time. It's delicious with a green vegetable, crisp relishes, rolls and a simple dessert. Yields 8 servings.

## HURRY-UP HAM AND SCALLOPED POTATOES
*A Minnesota potato grower's speciality.*

2 pounds peeled and sliced
    boiling potatoes
2 cups diced, cooked ham
    Salt and pepper

Flour
Onion salt
Milk
Butter

Boil potatoes for 5 minutes in salted water. Drain. Place a layer in the bottom of a 2-quart casserole. Add a layer of ham; sprinkle with a little flour, salt, pepper and onion salt. Repeat layers twice more. Pour heated milk over potatoes and ham until it just shows around the edges of the potatoes. Dot with butter. Bake in preheated, 350° F. oven for about 1½ hours or until potatoes are tender. Yields 6 to 8 servings.

*With peas:* Cook 1 cup fresh or fresh-frozen peas and sprinkle some over each ham layer.

## HAM 'N RICE DELUXE
*Tote to a church pot luck supper.*

2 cups cubed, cooked ham
2 cups cooked rice, salted
according to package
directions

¼ cup butter
1 cup cubed cheddar
cheese
¼ cup milk *or* soup stock

Grind meat, then cheese, in food chopper, using coarse disk. Keep separate. Spread half of rice in a greased 1½-quart baking dish. Dot with butter. Moisten with the milk or stock. Sprinkle with ⅓ of cheese. Add a layer of ground meat and several dots of butter and ⅓ more cheese. Spread remaining rice, dots of butter and remaining cheese. Bake in preheated, 350° F. oven for 20 to 25 minutes. Serve hot. Yields 4 servings.

## VEGETABLES AND HAM ON TOAST
*Quickie lunch or supper.*

Simmer 1 cup chopped celery in 2 tablespoons water for 5 minutes; drain. Make 1 cup medium white sauce, page 57. Combine celery, 1 cup chopped ham, 1 cup drained and cooked peas and the white sauce. Serve on toast. Yields 4 servings.

## HAM AND CABBAGE SOUP
*Fall speciality.*

2 tablespoons butter
¼ cup chopped onion
¼ cup chopped celery
¼ cup chopped green
pepper
3 tablespoons all-purpose
flour
3 cups boiling water
2 cups shredded cabbage

2 cups cubed, leftover,
cooked ham
1 bay leaf
¼ teaspoon salt
⅛ teaspoon pepper
¾ cup soured cream
2 tablespoons chopped
parsley

Lightly fry onion, celery, and green pepper in melted butter until clear. Remove from heat, stir in flour, and slowly add water, stirring to blend. Return to heat and add cabbage, ham, and seasonings. Cook 8 to 10 minutes, or until cabbage is tender. Remove bay leaf. Add sour cream and sprinkle parsley on top before serving. Yields 4 servings.

## CRISP BAKED BACON
### *Handy for a crowd.*

Lay bacon strips on a rack over a drip pan and bake in a preheated, 400° F. hot oven until crisp, about 20 minutes. Drain fat from drip pan to avoid burned grease odors.

*Sausage cakes* can be baked in the oven on a rack in the same manner. Allow more cooking time, depending on size of cakes.

## SPANISH RICE WITH BACON
### *Fix supper or lunch in a hurry.*

6 slices bacon, diced
2 small onions, chopped
1 green pepper, chopped
1 teaspoon salt

¼ teaspoon pepper
2 cups tomatoes
2 cups cooked white *or* brown rice

Cook bacon until crisp; remove; add onions and green pepper and cook until soft. Add rest of ingredients and simmer gently until heated through. Turn into a serving dish and sprinkle crisp bacon on top. Yields 4 to 5 servings.

## TIME-TABLE FOR BROILING CURED PORK*

| CUT | WEIGHT | APPROXIMATE TOTAL COOKING TIME | |
| --- | --- | --- | --- |
| | | RARE | WELL DONE |
| *Pork, Smoked* <br> Ham slice — tendered <br> ½ in. <br> 1 in. | ¾ to 1 <br> 1½ to 2 | Ham always cooked well done | 10-12 <br> 16-20 |
| Canadian style bacon <br> ¼ in. slices <br> ½ in. slices <br> Bacon | | | 6-8 <br> 8-10 <br> 4-5 |

*This time-table is based on broiling at a moderate temperature (350° F.). Ham is cooked to 160° F. internal temperature. The time for broiling bacon is influenced by personal preference as to crispness.

## TIME-TABLE FOR ROASTING LAMB

| CUT | APPROX. WEIGHT | OVEN TEMP. | MEAT THERM. READING | APPROX. COOKING TIME |
|---|---|---|---|---|
| | *Pounds* | *Degrees F.* | *Degrees F.* | *Min. Per Lb.* |
| Leg | 5 to 8 | 300°-325° F. | 175°-180° F. | 30 to 35 |
| Shoulder | 4 to 6 | 300°-325° F. | 175°-180° F. | 30 to 35 |
| Rolled | 3 to 5 | 300°-325° F. | 175°-180° F. | 40 to 45 |
| Cushion | 3 to 5 | 300°-325° F. | 175°-180° F. | 30 to 35 |

## MINT SAUCE
### *Serve with lamb.*

½ cup vinegar *or* juice of
  1 lemon and
  ¼ cup water

1 tablespoon sugar
⅓ cup chopped mint leaves

Mix sugar and vinegar, pour over leaves, let stand in warm place several minutes. Yields about ½ cup sauce.

## CUSHION SHOULDER OF LAMB
## WITH PRUNE STUFFING
### *Put in the oven before church on Sunday.*

4 pounds cushion-style
  lamb shoulder, boned
1 teaspoon salt
1 small lemon
3 tablespoons butter
1 medium onion, chopped
1 cup diced celery

1 cup bread stuffing
3 cups dried prunes,
  cooked and pitted
½ cup chopped walnuts
½ teaspoon salt
2 tablespoons chopped
  mint (optional)

Sprinkle lamb pocket with 1 teaspoon salt. Slice half of lemon. Chop remaining lemon. Melt butter; add onion and celery, and cook 5 minutes. Add chopped lemon, stuffing mix, prunes, walnuts and ½ teaspoon salt. Mix well. Arrange stuffing mixture in pocket of lamb. Fasten with string or skewers. Top with lemon slices and mint. Bake in preheated, 300° F. oven for 2½ hours. Yields 8 servings.

## LEG OF LAMB WITH CUCUMBER-DILL SAUCE
*Accompany with tiny, new potatoes sprinkled with snipped parsley.*

5 pound leg of lamb
  Dried dill weed
  Slivers of garlic
  Melted mint jelly
½ cup chopped cucumber
¼ cup chopped onion
¼ teaspoon dried dill weed

2 tablespoons butter
1 can (10½-ounce) mush-
  room gravy *or* 1¼ cups
  lamb gravy made from
  roast drippings
2 tablespoons lamb
  drippings

Cut slits in lamb; insert dill and garlic. Place meat in pan and roast in preheated, 325° F. oven for 2½ hours (30-35 minutes per pound). During last 10 minutes of roasting, spread with mint jelly.

*Cucumber-Dill Sauce:* In a saucepan, cook cucumber, onion and ¼ teaspoon dill in butter until vegetables are tender. Add gravy and drippings. Heat; stir now and then. Serve with lamb. Yields 6 to 7 servings.

## LAMB BREAST WITH SAUSAGE
*Special flavor combination that's low priced.*

3 pounds boned breast
  of lamb
½ pound pork sausage
  meat
  Salt and pepper

2 tablespoons fat
1 cup water
¼ cup catsup
1 onion, diced

Spread the breast of lamb with the sausage meat. Roll it up and tie with string or secure with metal skewers. Sprinkle with salt and pepper. Heat fat in a heavy skillet and brown the lamb roll in the hot fat. When well browned, add the water, catsup, and onion. Cover and simmer slowly about 1½ hours or until fork tender. Add small amounts of water during cooking if necessary to prevent burning. Yields 6 to 8 servings.

## SWEDISH LAMB SHANKS
*Good with buttered green beans and fresh homemade bread.*

2 tablespoons salad oil
4 pounds lamb shanks,
   sawed in pieces
1 teaspoon paprika
1 large onion, sliced
1 cup sliced mushrooms
1 cup water

1 tablespoon prepared
   horseradish
¾ teaspoon rosemary
1 teaspoon salt
¼ teaspoon pepper
1 cup dairy sour cream

Add lamb shanks, sprinkled with paprika, to hot oil. Add onion and mushrooms; cook until lamb is lightly browned on all sides. Add water, horseradish, rosemary, salt and pepper; cover and simmer about 1 hour or until meat is tender. Remove the meat, skim off excess fat and add cream to the gravy. Heat, stirring constantly. Do not boil. Serve with, or over, lamb shanks and hot rice or buttered egg noodles. Yields 4 servings.

## ZUCCHINI-LAMB CASSEROLE
*Zucchini ripens early, use it often.*

1½ pounds zucchini (2 or
   3, depending on size)
1½ pounds ground lamb,
   mutton *or* beef
1 medium onion,
   chopped
1 teaspoon salt
¼ teaspoon pepper

1 cup shredded cheese
1 can (10½-ounce) con-
   densed cream of mush-
   room soup
¼ cup milk
   Bread crumbs *or*
   crushed potato chips

Slice unpeeled zucchini and cook in a small amount of lightly-salted water until just tender; drain. Brown ground meat; pour off excess fat. Add onion, salt and pepper to skillet and cook until soft. In a 1½-quart casserole, arrange layers of zucchini, meat and cheese. Combine soup and milk; pour over all. Top with crumbs. Bake in preheated, 350° F. oven for 30 minutes, or until hot and bubbly. Yields 6 to 8 servings.

## HOT POT OF MUTTON AND BARLEY
### *From The Farmer, 1920.*

| | |
|---|---|
| 1 pound mutton (lamb will work) | 2 quarts water |
| ½ cup pearl barley | 4 potatoes |
| 1 tablespoon salt | 3 onions |
| | Celery tops *or* other seasoning herbs |

Cut the mutton in small pieces, and brown with the onion in fat cut from the meat. This will help make the meat tender and improve the flavor. Pour this into a covered saucepan. Add water and the barley. Simmer for 1½ hours. Then, add the potatoes cut in quarters, seasoning herbs and seasoning. Cook, covered, for ½ hour longer. Rice may be used in place of barley. Yields 5 servings.

*Add more vegetables:* 2 diced carrots, 1 small diced rutabaga and 2 ribs of diced celery.

## SOUR-CREAM-LAMB STEW
*Serve a lettuce and cucumber salad plus green beans topped with slivered almonds.*

| | |
|---|---|
| 2 tablespoons butter | 1½ teaspoons salt |
| 1½ pounds cubed lamb shoulder | 2 teaspoons paprika |
| 3 medium onions, sliced | 1 cup water |
| 1 medium green pepper, sliced | 1 cup dairy sour cream |

Melt butter. Add lamb and cook until browned on all sides. Add onions, green pepper, salt and paprika. Cover; cook over low heat 15 minutes. Add water. Cover and cook 1 to 1½ hours, or until lamb is tender. Add sour cream; mix well. Heat to serving temperature over low heat. Serve with noodles or rice, as desired. Yields 4 to 6 servings.

## LAMB SURPRISE
*Fast and satisfying.*

2 cups cooked, diced lamb  
1 package (10-ounce) thawed frozen peas  
1 cup onion rings  
½ cup water, stock *or* bouillon  

1 can (10½-ounce) condensed cream of celery soup  
1 cup crushed potato chips  

Arrange lamb, peas, onions with celery soup diluted with water in casserole. Top with crushed potato chips. Bake in preheated, 350° F. oven for 35 minutes. Yields 4 to 6 servings.

## BROILING LAMB

Lamb chops and steaks should be at least ¾ inch thick. Ground lamb patties are also excellent broiled.

See broiling instructions under Broiling Beef, page 79.

### TIME-TABLE FOR BROILING LAMB*

| CUT | WEIGHT | APPROXIMATE TOTAL COOKING TIME | |
|---|---|---|---|
| | | RARE | MEDIUM |
| Shoulder chops— | | | |
| 1 in. | 5 to 8 ozs. | Lamb chops | 12 |
| 1½ in. | 8 to 10 ozs. | are not | 18 |
| 2 in. | 10 to 16 ozs. | usually | 22 |
| Rib chops—1 in. | 3 to 5 ozs. | served rare | 12 |
| 1½ in. | 4 to 7 ozs. | | 18 |
| 2 in. | 6 to 10 ozs. | | 22 |
| Loin chops—1 in. | 4 to 7 ozs. | | 12 |
| 1½ in. | 6 to 10 ozs. | | 18 |
| 2 in. | 8 to 14 ozs. | | 22 |
| Ground lamb patties | | | |
| 1 in. by 3 in. | 4 ozs. | | 18 |

*This time-table is based on broiling at a moderate temperature (350° F.). Lamb chops are broiled to an internal temperature of 170° F. to 175° F.

## ITALIAN LAMB CHOPS
*These may also be broiled or grilled.*

¼ cup red wine vinegar
2 tablespoons chopped
  fresh mint *or* 1 tablespoon crushed, dry mint
  leaves

1 clove garlic, minced
6 shoulder lamb chops,
  ¾-inch thick
3 tablespoons butter
  Salt

In a shallow dish, combine vinegar, mint and garlic; marinate lamb chops in refrigerator 1 to 2 hours, turning once. In
a large skillet, melt butter, brown chops over medium heat
about 15 minutes. Turn and brown 8 to 10 minutes; salt
lightly and serve. Yields 6 servings.

## WHEN SHOULD YOU THAW A
## FRESH-FROZEN TURKEY?

*If you want to cook it immediately:* Remove wrap. Place frozen turkey on a rack in a shallow roasting pan. Cook for 1 hour in preheated, 325° F. oven. Take turkey from oven and remove neck and giblets from body cavity and wishbone area. Stuff. *Immediately* return turkey to oven and cook until done.

*If you want to cook it later today:* Leave the turkey in its original wrap. Thaw it in running water or water that is changed frequently. Allow 3 to 4 hours for a 5 to 9-pound bird; 4 to 7 hours for a bird over 9 pounds. Cook or refrigerate thawed turkey immediately.

*If you want to cook it tomorrow:* Leave turkey in its original wrap. Place frozen turkey in a brown paper bag or wrap it in 2 to 3 layers of newspaper. Thaw at room temperature. Allow 10 to 18 hours for a bird under 12 pounds; allow 18 to 30 hours for a bird over 12 pounds. Check turkey often during last hours of thawing and refrigerate when thawed.

*If you want to cook it day after tomorrow:* Leave turkey in its original wrap and place on tray or drip pan. Thaw in the refrigerator. Bird over 12 pounds may take up to 3 days.

*Do not:* Allow thawed bird to stand at room temperature. (Refrigerate thawed turkey or cook it immediately.)

*Do not:* Stuff bird until ready to cook.

*Do not:* Thaw commercially stuffed birds.

## ROASTING THE TURKEY

Turkeys of any size may be roasted. Correct roasting is dry heat cooking at low temperature. It requires no water, no searing, no basting, and no cover.

A shallow pan with a rack at least ½ inch high raises the bird off the bottom of the pan, keeping it out of the juices and allowing the heat to circulate, roasting the bird evenly.

Always roast turkey done in one continuous cooking period. Low temperatures assure better flavor and appearance, less shrinkage and less loss of juices. Here are the simple steps:

*Preheat* oven to 325° F.

*Rinse, drain and dry* the bird. Rub cavity lightly with salt, if desired.

*If to be stuffed,* fill wishbone area (neck) loosely and fasten neck skin to back with skewer. Sometimes, the snapped back wing tips hold the neck skin down. Fill body cavity lightly, because dressing tends to expand. Tie drumsticks to the tail.

*Place turkey breast* side-up on rack in shallow roasting pan. Brush skin with butter or fat. If a roast meat thermometer is to be used, insert it so that the bulb is in the center of the inside thigh muscle or the thickest part of the breast meat. Bulb must not touch bone.

*Place in preheated oven.* If desired, baste or brush occasionally with pan drippings or butter — especially any dry areas. When turkey is two-thirds done, cut cord or band of skin at tail to release the legs and permit the heat to reach the heavy-meated part. Cover with a loose tent of aluminum foil or lay a fat-moistened cloth over the legs and breast to prevent excessive browning.

*To test doneness,* a roast meat thermometer placed in the center of the inside thigh muscle or the thickest part of the breast muscle should register approximately 180-185° F. If stuffing is used, it should register 165° F., at the same time. Turkey is done when the thickest part of drumstick feels very soft when pressed between protected fingers.

*For best results in slicing,* allow turkey to stand 20 to 30 minutes to absorb the juices. Remove string and slice with a sharp knife.

## APPROXIMATE TIME-TABLE
## FOR A WHOLE TURKEY

| READY-TO-COOK WEIGHT POUNDS | APPROX. TIME AT 325° F. HOURS | INTERNAL TEMPERATURE WHEN DONE DEGREES F. |
|---|---|---|
| 6 to 8 | 3 to 3½ | 180-185 |
| 8 to 12 | 3½ to 4½ | 180-185 |
| 12 to 16 | 4½ to 5½ | 180-185 |
| 16 to 20 | 5½ to 6½ | 180-185 |
| 20 to 24 | 6½ to 7 | 180-185 |

## LEMON ROASTED STUFFED TURKEY
*Crispy skin — and beautifully brown.*

¼ cup butter
2 tablespoons lemon juice

9 pound turkey
½ teaspoon salt

Melt butter and combine with lemon juice. Set aside. Rub inside cavity of clean, dry turkey with salt; stuff and truss. Heat lemon-butter mixture until butter melts; brush over turkey, repeating every half-hour· during roasting period. Place turkey on a rack in a shallow roasting pan. Bake, uncovered in a preheated, 325° F. oven for 4 hours or until drum stick moves easily when twisted gently. Yields 16 servings.

## BONELESS TURKEY — SPIT-ROASTED

If roast is not pre-seasoned, rub lightly with salt and pepper.

Insert spit rod lengthwise through center of turkey roast. Insert skewers firmly in place in roast and screw tightly. Test the balance. Roast must balance on spit so it will rotate smoothly throughout the cooking period. Place spit rod in rotisserie. Brush roast with melted butter. No further basting is necessary.

Follow manufacturer's directions for rotisserie temperature setting. Roast until done. To test doneness, insert a meat thermometer in center of roast, being careful not to touch spit rod. Thermometer should register 170-175° F.

## APPROXIMATE TIME-TABLE FOR BONELESS TURKEY ROASTS

| READY-TO-COOK WEIGHT POUNDS | APPROXIMATE TIME AT 325° F. HOURS | |
|---|---|---|
| | OVEN | ROTISSERIE |
| 3 to 5 | 2½ to 3 | 2 to 2½ |
| 5 to 7 | 3 to 3½ | 2½ to 3 |
| 7 to 9 | 3½ to 4 | 3 to 3½ |

## APPROXIMATE TIME-TABLE FOR ROTISSERIED WHOLE TURKEY

| READY-TO-COOK WEIGHT POUNDS | APPROXIMATE TIME HOURS | INTERNAL TEMPERATURE WHEN DONE DEGREES F. |
|---|---|---|
| 4 to 6 | 2 to 3 | 180-185 |
| 6 to 8 | 3 to 3½ | 180-185 |
| 8 to 10 | 3½ to 4 | 180-185 |
| 10 to 12 | 4 to 5 | 180-185 |

## ROTISSERIED WHOLE TURKEY

Whole turkeys may be cooked on a rotisserie, provided the weight does not exceed the manufacturer's specifications. Stuffing the bird is not encouraged for rotisserie cooking.

For operation of rotisserie, follow manufacturer's directions.

Follow general instructions on thawing.

Remove neck and giblets, cook promptly and refrigerate until ready to use. Rinse turkey.

Tie drumsticks securely to tail. Fasten neck skin to back with skewer. Flatten wings against breast, then tie string around breast to hold wings securely.

Insert spit rod through center of bird lengthwise from tail end toward front. Insert skewers firmly in place in bird and screw tightly.

Test the balance and readjust if necessary so bird will rotate smoothly throughout the cooking period.

Insert meat thermometer in the center of the inside thigh muscle.

Place spit rod in rotisserie. Brush turkey with melted butter. Barbecue sauce may be used, if desired, the last 30 to 45 minutes of cooking.

## TURKEY PAN GRAVY WITH BACON

Cook ½ pound bacon and cut into ½-inch pieces. Pour drippings from pan in which turkey was roasted into measuring cup. Put ½ cup of the drippings into a skillet. Add ½ cup flour, mix well and brown slightly. Add 2 cups milk to roasting pan and cook up browned bits. Gradually add milk with pan scrapings and an additional 2 cups of milk to mixture in skillet, stirring constantly to make a smooth gravy. Add cooked bacon pieces, 1½ teaspoons salt, ¼ teaspoon pepper and other seasonings if desired. Bring to a boil. Cook 5 to 10 minutes. Serve hot. Yields about 4 cups gravy.

## CRANBERRY-ORANGE RELISH
*Superb with poultry.*

1 large orange                              2 cups granulated sugar
4 cups fresh cranberries

Put rind and pulp of orange and cranberries through food chopper. Mix in 2 cups sugar. Let mixture stand several hours. Yields about 1 quart relish.

## DOUBLE-DRESS THE BIRD

Double the good eating at your holiday table when you double-dress a turkey with two delicious stuffings. Fill the body cavity with an old favorite — fill the expanded breast opening with a new, entirely different treat.

*Here's how to enlarge the breast opening* so it holds a generous bowlful of dressing: Insert fingers beneath skin at the neck opening. *Carefully* work fingers downward over the breast meat. Continue working skin loose until you have loosened it down to the keel bone.

Hold the turkey upright and spoon or pour dressing into the spacious pocket. Stuff loosely — dressing expands during cooking. Fasten opening at the neck with a skewer or sew it shut.

When turkey is done, make a cross slit over the breast and dressing will spoon out easily. You'll also discover that the dressing keeps breast meat more moist and succulent.

Breast pockets of turkeys stuffed during Country Kitchen

testing held half a recipe of stuffing recommended for the size bird stuffed.

Body cavities of turkeys stuffed in Country Kitchen held about three-quarters of the recommended amount for the size bird stuffed.

## OTHER TURKEY STUFFING TIPS

*Use ¾ cup stuffing* per pound of turkey. Filling the body cavity is no longer a slippery, sliding problem if you place the bird, neck-down in a bowl.

*Get the texture dressing you like* by taking a handful of mixed stuffing and pressing it gently to form a ball. If stuffing falls apart lightly when you open your hand, you've the right amount of moisture for dry, fluffy stuffing. If it doesn't fall apart, you'll have a compact ball of moist stuffing.

## FAVORITE BREAD STUFFING

| | |
|---|---|
| 1 cup fat | 1 tablespoon salt |
| 1 cup minced onion | ½ teaspoon pepper |
| 4 cups diced celery | 2 teaspoons poultry |
| 16 cups small bread cubes, | seasoning |
| lightly-packed (use | 1½ cups broth, milk or |
| day-old bread) | water |

Cook onion and celery in fat over low heat until onion is soft but not browned, stirring occasionally. Meanwhile, blend seasonings with bread cubes. Add the onion, celery and fat. Blend. Pour the broth gradually over surface, stirring lightly. Add more seasoning as desired. Yields stuffing for a 14 to 18-pound turkey.

*Apple-Prune Variation:* Remove pits from 1 pound dried prunes which have been cooked or soaked. Cut each prune into 3 or 4 pieces. Add prunes and 2 cups cored, finely chopped apple to bread with seasonings. Include prune juice as part or all of the liquid.

*Cornbread Variation:* Reduce bread to 8 cups. Add 8 cups of crumbled cornbread or cornmeal muffins.

## RICE-ALMOND STUFFING

3 cups cooked, long grain
    rice
1 small onion, finely-diced
⅓ cup butter, melted
1 cup coarsely-chopped
    celery

1 teaspoon salt
¼ teaspoon pepper
½ teaspoon marjoram, sage
    *or* poultry seasoning
1 cup toasted, blanched,
    slivered almonds

Cook onion in butter until soft. Add remaining ingredients. Toss lightly until well mixed. Yields stuffing for 10-pound turkey.

*Giblet Variation:* Chopped cooked giblets and/or a can of drained mushrooms may be added if desired.

## SAUSAGE STUFFING

1 pound pork sausage
    meat
Pork sausage drippings
12 cups bread cubes (about
    16 slices bread)

1 cup chopped celery
½ cup chopped onion
1 teaspoon sage
1 teaspoon salt

Cook sausage thoroughly. Remove from skillet and add to bread cubes. Cook celery and onion in drippings until tender. Add seasonings. Combine with bread cubes and sausage. Mix thoroughly. Stuff bird just before roasting. Yields stuffing for 12-pound turkey.

*Try raisin bread cubes* plus ⅓ cup seedless raisins and 1 tablespoon thyme in above recipe.

## CRANBERRY STUFFING

3 cups fresh cranberries
    (¾ pound)
¾ cup sugar
¾ cup butter, melted
12 cups small bread cubes
1½ cups raisins

1 tablespoon salt
¾ teaspoon cinnamon
Grated rind of 2 lemons
¾ cup broth *or* water

Chop cranberries and blend in sugar. Blend butter and bread cubes. Combine the two mixtures with remaining ingredients. Mix well. Yields stuffing for 12 to 14-pound turkey.

*Sauce Variation:* 1½ cans of whole cranberry sauce and ⅓ cup sugar may be substituted for the fresh cranberry and ¾ cup sugar. Break up cranberry sauce with fork, add sugar and proceed as above.

## WILD RICE DRESSING

2 tablespoons butter
2 tablespoons onion, chopped fine
2 tablespoons celery, chopped

1 tablespoon chopped parsley
1½ teaspoons Worcestershire sauce
Salt and pepper to taste
2 cups cooked wild rice

Brown onion in butter, add celery and saute a few minutes. Combine with parsley, Worcestershire sauce, salt, pepper and wild rice. Yields 3 cups stuffing and can be used with wild duck, pheasant, turkey or chicken. Double recipe for a 10-pound turkey.

## FRILLS FOR TURKEY, LAMB, CROWN ROAST

Make large frills by cutting 7-inch squares of 2 different-colored tissue paper. Place one over the other. Fold in half, mark pencil guideline 1½ inches from folded edge. Cut strips ⅛ inch wide.

Unfold papers carefully and flip so inside is outside. Roll loosely around 2 fingers to 1-inch diameter. Fasten with cellophane tape. Push up center to form 2 tiers.

*Make small frills* by starting with 2 strips of paper 3¼x7 inches. Make cuts from guide to fold line only 1/16-inch wide. Roll frills around 1 finger.

## SKILLET TURKEY AND STUFFING
*Tasty way to serve holiday leftovers.*

⅓ cup diced onion
⅓ cup diced green pepper
3 tablespoons cooking oil
3 cups diced cooked
  turkey
¾ cup chopped celery
3 cups baked bread
  stuffing

3 tablespoons chopped
  pimiento
½ teaspoon salt
⅛ teaspoon pepper
1 cup turkey *or*
  chicken broth
Leftover gravy *or*
  mushroom sauce

Saute onion and green pepper in oil in large skillet until tender. Add turkey, stuffing, celery, pimiento, salt, pepper and turkey broth. Mix lightly. Cook over medium heat until brown on both sides, turning often. Serve with gravy or mushroom sauce, if desired. Yields 6 servings.

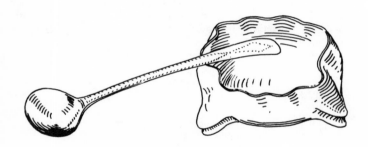

## TURKEY-GREEN BEAN BAKE
*Serve at a New Year's Eve buffet.*

1¾ cups frozen green
  beans
1¼ cups boiling water
2½ cups cooked, diced
  turkey
1 can (10½-ounce) con-
  densed cream of mush-
  room soup

¼ teaspoon salt
⅛ teaspoon black pepper
  *or* a dash of cayenne
1 cup dry, precooked rice
1 can (3½-ounce) French-
  fried onion rings

Cook green beans in boiling water for 5 minutes; drain. Add turkey, mushroom soup and seasonings. Simmer 2 minutes. Stir in rice and half of onion rings. Pour into 2-quart casserole. Top with remaining onion rings. Bake in preheated, 400° F. oven for 20 to 25 minutes. Yields 6 servings.

## WILD-RICE-TURKEY CASSEROLE
*Minnesota speciality.*

3 cups cubed, cooked turkey *or* chicken
1 cup chopped celery
2 medium onions, chopped
1½ cups cooked wild rice
1 can (10½-ounce) condensed cream of chicken soup

3 tablespoons soy sauce
1 can (5-ounce) water chestnuts, sliced
¼ teaspoon pepper
1 small can mushrooms
1 soup can water
½ cup buttered bread crumbs

Mix all ingredients, except crumbs. Pour into greased, 2-quart casserole. Top with crumbs. Bake 1¼ hours in preheated, 350° F. oven. Yields 6 to 7 servings.

## MAKE-AHEAD TURKEY SUPPER DISH
*Serve from a chafing dish or casserole with a candle warmer.*

4-6 cups cooked, cut-up turkey
1 can (10½-ounce) condensed cream of mushroom soup
1 can (10½-ounce) condensed cream of chicken *or* cream of celery soup

1 cup celery, finely diced
¼ cup minced onion
½ cup water
¼ cup sliced, stuffed olives
½ pound salted cashew nuts
1-2 cups chow mein noodles

Combine turkey, soups, salt, pepper, celery and onions in a large saucepan over low heat or in an electric skillet at 225° F. Pour water over mixture. Cover and cook 20 to 25 minutes. Add olives. Put in freezer containers, label, date, and freeze.

To serve, partially thaw and then heat in a double boiler. When thawed, add cashew nuts and continue to cook in double boiler until thoroughly heated. Just before serving, gently mix in chow mein noodles. Yields 10 to 12 servings.

### QUICKIE TURKEY CORN CHOWDER
*Kids like this soup.*

1 can (10½-ounce) con-
densed cream of celery
soup
1 can (10¾-ounce) con-
densed chicken vegetable
soup

1 soup can water
1 soup can milk
1 cup whole-kernel corn
1 cup diced, cooked turkey

Blend soups and liquids in saucepan; add corn and turkey. Heat, stirring occasionally. Yields 6 to 8 servings.

### CREAM OF TURKEY SOUP
*Great blend of flavors.*

1 cup finely-diced celery
¼ cup minced onion
3 tablespoons butter
¼ cup flour
2 cups milk, hot
2 cups boiling turkey *or*
chicken broth
1 cup grated carrots

1 cup finely-chopped,
cooked turkey
Salt and pepper to taste
Sherry flavoring to taste
(optional)
2 tablespoons snipped
parsley

In a saucepan, cook celery and onion in butter until vegetables are soft but not browned, about 10 minutes. Blend in flour with a wire whip; cook and stir 1 minute without coloring. Add milk and broth all at once and beat with a wire whip to blend. Increase heat to moderately high; cook and stir until thickened. Add carrots and cooked turkey. Heat thoroughly. Stir in salt, pepper and flavoring, to taste. Garnish with parsley. Yields 5 cups soup.

### TURKEY FONDUE
*Chicken may be used.*

Cut 2 pounds of turkey white meat into 1-inch cubes. Turkey meat cuts best if partially frozen. Pour peanut or corn oil into a fondue cooker to 2-inch depth. Heat oil on range to near-smoke point (350° to 400° F.). Take hot oil to table; place over alcohol burner. Have turkey meat cubes at room temperature in a serving bowl. Pass small bowls of a variety of sauces. Sauces 1, 3, 8, 9, 10, 11 and 12, page 84, are very good with turkey.

At the table, each guest cooks a turkey cube to desired doneness in hot oil with a long-handled fork. The cooked meat then is removed from the long-handled fork, dipped into one of the sauces and eaten with a table fork. At a stand-up party, toothpicks may be used for eating turkey.

## CRISPY TURKEY
### *Fullbodied treat!*

1 turkey (6 to 8 pounds), cut in serving pieces
1 cup flour
1 tablespoon salt
¼ teaspoon pepper
½ pound butter

Pat washed turkey pieces dry (sometimes thighs and breast are cut into 2 or 3 pieces). Salt meat. Roll meat in mixture of flour, salt and pepper. Melt butter in skillet and fry turkey in skillet until crispy brown. Place covered skillet in preheated, 350° F. oven for 1 to 1½ hours, until meat is tender. Remove cover during last 15 minutes of baking. Yields 8 servings.

## TURKEY STEAK
### *A Minnesota grower's recipe.*

4 turkey steaks (½-pound each), about ½-inch thick
Flour
Salt and pepper
2-3 tablespoons shortening
1 can (10½-ounce) condensed cream of mushroom soup

Have your butcher cut a frozen turkey breast into ½-inch slices (across the bird) on his power saw. If slices are too large for your needs, divide each one through the breastbone. Or, slice a boneless turkey roll.

Thaw slices, sprinkle with salt and pepper, then dip in flour. Melt and heat shortening in skillet, then add turkey steaks and brown on both sides. Remove steaks from skillet and place in a casserole. Mix soup and milk into a smooth sauce and pour over steaks. Cover casserole and bake in preheated, 350° F. oven for 1 hour. Yields 4 servings.

## BAKED CHICKEN WITH GIBLET STUFFING
*Stuffing makes a chicken special!*

2 broiler-fryer chickens
(2½ pounds each), split
lengthwise
6 cups dry bread crumbs
¼ cup chopped celery
Chopped, cooked giblets
¼ cup chopped onion

¼ teaspoon pepper
1 teaspoon salt
¼ teaspoon sage
½ cup butter, melted
Giblet broth
Melted butter

Wash chickens and pat dry with paper towel. Combine bread, onion, celery, giblets, seasonings and ½ cup butter. Add enough broth to just moisten. Mix well. Place each half chicken over stuffing which has been placed in 4 mounds on an aluminum foil-lined, shallow baking pan. Brush chicken with melted butter. Bake in preheated, 350° F. oven for 1 hour. Brush once or twice with melted butter during baking. To serve, cut each half in two, cross-wise. Yields 8 servings.

*Caraway Stuffing:* Mix 4 cups coarse bread crumbs or cubes, ⅓ cup water, ¼ teaspoon pepper, 1 teaspoon salt, ¼ cup finely minced onion, 1 teaspoon crushed caraway seed, ¼ teaspoon fresh or dry marjoram. Blend well. Stuff and truss a 4-pound chicken to bake whole, or proceed as above.

*Stuffed Chicken on a Spit:* Stuff two 2½ to 3-pound chickens, sew up back and front openings; truss wings and legs. Center chickens on spit with necks toward center; fasten securely with prongs. Rotiss until done — when drum stick can be moved up and down and thigh meat is soft when pressed between fingers.

## ORANGE CHICKEN
*Serve with hot rice plus buttered peas and carrots.*

1 can (6-ounce) frozen
orange juice
2 juice cans water
¼ cup butter

3 medium onions, sliced
½ teaspoon salt
2 broiler chickens, cut up
(2½ pounds each)

Heat orange juice, water, butter and onions. Place chicken in roasting pan. Roast chicken at 350° F. for 1½ hours, basting frequently with orange sauce. Yields 6 servings.

## HENS IN THE OVEN
*No last-minute preparation with this Clara Sutter favorite.*

Dress 3 big cull hens. Save back, part of wings and giblets for soup. Cut the rest in pieces. Season with salt, red pepper, ginger and allspice to taste. Roll in flour. Place chicken in a roaster, add hot water to cover. Place in 275° F. oven and bake for 4 hours.

## CARAWAY CHICKEN
*Planted for years in farm gardens in Le Sueur County, Minnesota, caraway now grows wild in many places.*

1 chicken (3½ to 4 pounds), cut up
1 teaspoon salt

1 teaspoon ground caraway
¼ cup water

Wash and dry chicken. Lay pieces in bottom of roaster. Sprinkle on salt and caraway. Add water. Cover roaster and place in preheated, 375° F. oven. Bake chicken, covered for about 1½ hours. Uncover and bake another ½ hour to brown, until tender. Yields 4 servings.

## CINCHY CHICKEN
*While the oven is going, add a casserole of scalloped corn.*

1 frying chicken, cut into serving pieces

1 can (10½-ounce) condensed cream of chicken soup
Salt and pepper

Cut chicken into serving pieces. Sprinkle both sides of chicken with salt and pepper or Clara's Poultry seasoning, page 138. Place pieces, skin side up, in roasting pan. Spoon soup (undiluted) over chicken. Bake, uncovered, in preheated, 350° F. oven for about 1½ hours, or until chicken tests done.

*Creamy gravy* may be easily made after chicken is taken from pan by adding a little milk or water to pan juices and heating mixture just before serving. Yields 4 to 5 servings of chicken.

## SUNFLOWER CHICKEN
*Red River Valley delight.*

Salt
1 cup pancake mix
1 cup water
⅔ cup roasted, salted sunflower meats

1 fryer (3 to 3½ pounds),
cut up
Cooking oil

Wash, dry and salt chicken pieces. Combine pancake mix, water and sunflower meats. Dip chicken pieces into batter. Heat oil in skillet and brown chicken pieces. Transfer chicken to roasting pan and bake, covered, in preheated, 350° F. oven for about 1 hour. Yields 4 servings.

## CLARA SUTTER'S POULTRY SEASONING
*Sprinkle generously on chicken before frying or baking.*

10 teaspoons salt
1 teaspoon black pepper
1 teaspoon red pepper
1 teaspoon dry mustard

1 teaspoon summer savory
1 teaspoon sage
½ teaspoon garlic salt

Mix and have ready to use to make your chicken taste better. Yields about 1 cup seasoning.

## CASSEROLE OF FOWL AND VEGETABLES
*From the 1942 Country Kitchen Cook Book.*

Cut up a cleaned fowl (a roasting or stewing chicken) ready for serving, roll each piece in seasoned flour. Brown slightly and quickly in a spoonful each of butter and lard. Remove and pack into a deep casserole in layers with vegetables. This may include parboiled small onions; potato balls or very small potatoes; minced parsley; sliced carrot or whole baby carrots; a little shredded green sweet pepper; diced celery. Season with salt and pepper, and pour over all 2 cups of hot water which has been first poured in skillet to rinse out the fat. Cover and cook 2 or 3 hours in heated, 325° F. oven until meat and vegetables are tender. Before serving, pour off the liquor, add milk and flour to make a rich gravy, return to casserole and serve. Accompany with a dish of hot buttered toast squares, on which you may serve the contents of the casserole.

*If a tablespoonful of vinegar* is added to the water in which tough meats *or* fowls are boiled it will tend to make them tender. — The Farmer, 1896.

## BOILED CHICKEN
### *Like Mother used to make.*

Clean a mature fowl and cut in pieces for serving. Put in kettle with 1 bay leaf, 2 slices of onion, 1 tablespoon salt and boiling water to cover. Cover and cook slowly until meat will loosen very easily from the bones. For an older fowl, add 1 or 2 tablespoons vinegar.

*Top with Dumplings:* Mix well 1½ cups flour, 2 teaspoons baking powder, ¾ teaspoon salt. Add ¾ cup milk and stir until just blended. Drop spoonsful *onto chicken* in boiling stock. Cook 10 minutes uncovered, cover tightly and cook 10 minutes more. Remove dumplings and meat to hot platter and make gravy from broth.

*Chicken Soup:* Add noodles, carrots, celery and onions to broth to make a delicious soup.

## PRESSED CHICKEN
### *Another Clara Sutter special treat.*

Press chopped, cooked chicken (mixed with chopped hard-cooked eggs if you like) into a bread-type glass or enamel loaf pan. Fill pan ¾ full. Add a "smidgeon — if you know how much that is —" of paprika and red pepper; a bit of ground cloves, allspice and a half dozen crushed cardamom seeds, plus a speck of garlic to 2 cups broth in which the chicken was cooked. Taste broth to see if a little more salt is needed. Add about 1 tablespoon scraped or grated onion if you like it. Pour broth over chicken and refrigerate until broth sets to gelatine. "Vary spices to suit your family taste, just don't use too much of any one. Why use a specific recipe and have your pressed chicken like all the rest? Season as you like, then everyone will ask for yours."

## CREAMY CHICKEN STEW
*Dinner's in one dish!*

1 can (10½-ounce) con-
  densed cream of
  chicken soup
1½ cups water
1 cup sliced celery
1 medium onion,
  quartered
1 teaspoon salt
¼ teaspoon poultry
  seasoning

⅛ teaspoon pepper
1 stewing chicken (4 to 5
  pounds), cut up
4 medium potatoes (about
  1 pound), quartered
6 medium carrots, cut in
  pieces
¼ cup flour

In large, heavy pan, combine soup, 1 cup water, celery, onion and seasonings; add chicken. Cover; cook over low heat 1½ hours, stirring now and then. Add potatoes and carrots. Cover; cook about 45 minutes or until chicken and vegetables are tender. To thicken stew, blend flour and remaining water; gradually stir into stew. Cook 10 to 15 minutes, stirring often. Yields 4 to 6 servings.

## CHICKEN PIE
*Cover pies with foil, wrap in newspaper
and carry to the field for a hearty meal.*

3 chicken breasts (about
  2½ pounds)
1 rib of celery, with
  leaves
1 slice onion
1 can (10½-ounce) con-
  densed chicken broth
1 soup can water
1 teaspoon salt

¼ cup butter
½ cup chopped carrot
⅓ cup chopped onion
½ cup chopped celery
¼ cup flour
Salt
Pepper
Pastry for 2 double-crust,
  9-inch pies

Simmer chicken breasts, cut-up piece of celery with leaves, onion and salt in chicken broth and water. When tender (about 45 minutes), remove chicken; cool slightly. Remove meat from bones and dice into ½-inch cubes. Return bones to broth and simmer to make 2 cups liquid. Meanwhile, saute vegetables in butter until almost tender. Cover skillet so they do not brown. Strain chicken broth. Stir flour into vegetables; stir and cook for 2 minutes. Remove from heat and add hot broth; stir and cook until sauce is thick and smooth. Season to taste. Place chicken into 2 pastry-lined pie plates. Pour vegetables and sauce over meat and cover with top crust. Seal and flute pastry edges; make slits in top crusts. Bake in preheated, 425° F. oven for 35 to 40 minutes or until nicely browned. Serve hot or cold. Yields 8 servings.

## SAUCED CHICKEN SQUARES
### *Luncheon guests enjoy this.*

3 cups chopped, cooked chicken
3 cups white bread crumbs
⅓ cup celery
⅓ cup chopped onion
4 eggs, beaten
¼ cup chopped pimiento (optional)

1 teaspoon salt
Dash pepper
⅓ teaspoon poultry seasoning
2 cups chicken broth
Sauce

Preheat oven to 350° F. In a large bowl mix chicken, bread crumbs, celery, onions, pimiento. Beat together: eggs, salt, pepper, poultry seasoning, chicken broth. Stir in chicken mixture. Pour into buttered, 9x9x2-inch pan. Bake about 1 hour. Yields 6 to 9 servings.

*Sauce:* Heat together, 1 can (10½-ounce) condensed cream of mushroom soup, ½ cup milk and 1 can (3-ounce) mushrooms, drained and diced. Cut cooked chicken mixture into squares and top with sauce.

## CHICKEN HAM SUPPER DISH
### *Quick lunch or supper.*

½ green pepper, chopped
1 can (10½-ounce) condensed cream of mushroom soup
2 cups cooked chicken, diced
1 cup ham, diced

2-3 tablespoons pimiento, sliced
1 can (4-ounce) mushrooms
¼ cup chopped almonds
Salt

Saute green pepper in butter. Add soup that can be thinned with chicken broth, milk or water. Add chicken and ham, pimiento, mushrooms and almonds. Cover and heat thoroughly. Serve on hot rice. Yields 5 to 6 servings.

## CANNED SOUP — DRESSED UP
*From a Clara Sutter "Your Poultry and Mine"*
*column in The Farmer magazine.*

Take a can of chicken noodle soup. Add red pepper, as much garlic salt as would lay on the end of a paring knife, a speck of allspice and a wee bit more of salt. Add a can of water. Blend and heat. After soup is in the dish, add a few snips of parsley. Then, with whole wheat toast, it is fit for a queen — or for a hungry farm woman who knows good soup.

## FRUIT-AND-RICE-STUFFED   DUCKLING
*Company treat!*

5 pound duckling
Salt and pepper
1½ cups cooked rice
1 tablespoon grated onion
1 cup chopped celery
6 tablespoons butter, melted
½ cup dried apricots, cut up

½ cup dried prunes, cut up
¾ teaspoon marjoram
½ teaspoon salt
¼ cup chopped onion
1 can (10½-ounce) mushroom gravy *or* 1¼ cups gravy made from duckling drippings and chopped, cooked giblets

Sprinkle duckling with salt and pepper. Mix rice, onion, celery, 4 tablespoons butter, apricots, prunes, ½ teaspoon marjoram and salt; stuff into duckling and fasten with toothpicks or skewers. Place duckling, breast side up, in roasting pan. Roast in preheated, 325° F. oven about 2½ hours (30 to 35 minutes per pound), basting now and then. Meanwhile in saucepan, cook onion with ¼ teaspoon marjoram in remaining butter until tender. Add gravy; heat, stirring now and then. Serve with duckling and stuffing. Yields 4 servings.

*Bread-Raisin Stuffing:* Lightly toast 2 slices of bread. Mix bread, ¾ cup milk, 2 beaten eggs and 1 tablespoon soft butter. Sift together — ½ cup flour, ½ teaspoon salt, 2 tablespoons sugar, 1 teaspoon baking powder. Add to bread mixture and stir. Add 1 cup raisins and mix well. Stuff duckling lightly. Bake extra dressing in a covered pan for 1 hour.

## DUCKLING AND VEGETABLE CASSEROLE
*Hearty meal men like!*

1 large, *or* 2 medium ducklings, cut up
4 tablespoons shortening
1 medium onion, chopped
3 cups sliced turnips
3 cups cubed potatoes
1 teaspoon salt

⅛ teaspoon pepper
⅛ teaspoon paprika
¼ teaspoon sage
½ bay leaf, crushed
Dash of thyme and cloves
2 cups water

Melt shortening in heavy skillet. Brown duck. Remove meat and saute onions in same drippings. Place ½ of turnips and potatoes in casserole. Place meat on top. Sprinkle with onions and seasonings, and cover with remaining vegetables. Add water to drippings in skillet, bring to boil. Pour over meat. Add more water if needed. Cover and bake in preheated, 350° F. oven for 1½ hours. Remove cover last 15 minutes to brown vegetables and thicken mixture. Yields 6 to 8 servings.

## BRAISED GOOSE

1 goose, cut in serving pieces
½ cup dry white wine
2 cups chicken broth

20 small, white onions
Butter
Salt and pepper
¾ pound mushrooms

Remove heavy fat from goose when cutting into pieces. Brown meat in a small amount of fat in heavy roasting pan or Dutch oven. Remove fat from pan and add wine and broth. Surround meat with onions sauteed in a little butter. Season all with salt and pepper. Cover and place in preheated, 325° F. oven for 1¼ hours. Add mushrooms, re-cover, and continue cooking until meat is tender. Allow a total of about 25 minutes per pound for the goose. Remove meat to heated platter and surround with vegetables. Skim fat from the sauce. Serve sauce in sauceboat with meat. Yields about 2 servings per pound of meat.

## APPLE AND SAUSAGE STUFFED ROAST GOOSE
*Christmas and New Year tradition.*

8-9 pound goose
1 package (7 to 8-ounce)
   prepared stuffing *or*
   stuffing croutons
½ pound ground sausage
   meat
¼ cup butter

2 tablespoons sausage
   drippings
1 cup chopped celery
½ cup chopped onion
¼ cup chopped parsley
½-1 cup broth from giblets
1 cup canned apple-
   sauce

Place goose giblets in a saucepan and simmer in about 2 cups water until tender. Wash goose and pat dry inside and out. Turn stuffing cubes or croutons into a large bowl. In a skillet, lightly brown sausage meat, crumbling it as it cooks. Remove sausage and add to bread. Save drippings in another container. Melt butter in the skillet; add 2 tablespoons sausage drippings. Cook celery and onions in fat until tender but not brown. Combine celery, onion and sausage with the stuffing cubes; add parsley. Lightly toss in applesauce. Rinse the skillet with giblet broth and toss just enough broth with stuffing to make it light and fluffy. Place stuffing in wishbone and body cavity of goose, then truss wings flat, against sides of breast and tie legs securely together.

Place trussed goose, breast down, on a rack in a shallow, uncovered pan. Roast at 325° F. in a preheated oven — 4-6 pounds, 2¾-3 hours; 6-8 pounds, 3-3½ hours; 8-10 pounds, 3½-3¾ hours; 10-12 pounds, 3¾-4¼ hours; 12-14 pounds, 4-4¾ hours. Do not add water or fat. There is no need to baste. Allow an extra ½ hour in case more cooking is needed — especially if the meal is planned for a set time. Goose should be served hot.

During roasting, fat should be spooned or siphoned off as it accumulates in the pan. This assures fat which is light in color and excellent for future use as a shortening. When goose is approximately ⅔ done, according to the timetable, turn breast up and finish roasting. To test for doneness, move the drumstick up and down. Joint should yield readily to twisting and drumstick meat should feel soft.

*Note:* If goose is placed in a brown paper sack on the rack of a shallow roasting pan, fat spattering in the oven can be eliminated. Choose a sack 2 to 3-inches longer than the bird. Fold or crumple opening around drumstick ends. Follow roasting directions, leaving goose in sack during entire roasting period. After goose is ⅔ done and ready to turn, puncture 6 to 8 pencil-size holes in top of bag. After turning, this becomes the bottom and excess fat drains into the roasting pan. For testing, open bag and test as above.

*Sauerkraut Stuffing:* A goose may be stuffed with sauerkraut when it is about ⅔ cooked. Remove goose from oven, drain away fat from cavity. Stuff with heated and drained sauerkraut and complete the roasting.

*Hot mashed potatoes* may be used to stuff a ⅔-cooked goose. Remove from oven and drain away fat. Stuff with slightly dry, hot mashed potatoes which have been seasoned with basil, poultry seasonings, rosemary, sage or thyme.

## FREEZING FISH

*Freeze* only high-quality fresh fish, since freezing doesn't improve quality. Chill fish to below 40° F. as soon as it is caught.

*Remove waste portions* such as head, entrails, backbone, fins and tail to save freezer space. Place enough fish for a family meal in each package.

*Cut large,* dressed fish crosswise into steaks before freezing. Cut steaks about ¾ inch thick.

*Fish fillets* are made by cutting the sides of the dressed fish lengthwise, away from the backbone.

*Package fish* in airtight wrap or containers and it will keep six to nine months and still retain quality.

## COOKING FISH (AND SEAFOOD)

Clear lakes, streams and reservoirs provide fresh fish all year round for country tables. And, because of its high protein content, fish serves as an excxellent substitute for meat. Remember, though, use a moderate temperature during cooking for best texture and flavor.

*Baked Fish:* This method is suitable for any size or cut of fish — saves the mess and spatter of pan frying. Heat oven to 350° F. Place fish on aluminum foil in shallow baking pan or in greased shallow pan. Sprinkle with salt, pepper and dots of soft butter. Bake 20 minutes for fillets, 30 minutes for steaks, 15 minutes per pound for whole fish. Serve with tartar sauce or lemon slices and garnish with parsley flakes.

Fresh fish flavor is enhanced when fish is sprinkled with a small amount of basil, dill, oregano, marjoram or rosemary before cooking.

Lean fish, such as bass, perch, walleyed and northern pike, are best when steamed, boiled or panfried — although they can be baked or broiled by laying bacon strips on top or basting with melted fat.

*Most fish,* with the exception of salmon, mackerel and trout, are low in fat, thus low in calories.

*Pan Fried Fish:* Roll fish in cornmeal or flour, brown in a fairly large amount of fat in a hot skillet.

*If you don't like* the odor of frying fish, pour lemon juice over it before placing in the pan. The lemon eliminates the fish odor.

*Boiled (poached) fish* can be kept from breaking by wrapping it in cheesecloth and lowering it gently into boiling water. Be careful not to overcook the fish. It's done when a fork pierces the flesh easily and the fish flakes.

*If you're puzzled* over how much fish to cook per person, plan on ⅓ to ½ pound of edible fish for each serving. This means that when cooking whole fish, you'll use 1 pound per person; for fillets and steaks, ½ pound each.

*Here is the correct way to carve a large fish:* Run a knife down the back, cutting through the skin. Remove the fins. Then cut into even pieces on one side. When these pieces are served, remove the bones and cut the underside in the same way.

## BAKED STUFFED BASS
*Double recipe for 5 to 6-pound fish.*

1 tablespoon butter
2 tablespoons finely-
chopped onion
1½ cups diced bread
½ cup cottage cheese
1 teaspoon crumbled dill
weed

2 tablespoons finely
chopped dill pickle
½ teaspoon salt
Dash pepper
2 teaspoons lemon juice
1 large mouth bass,
about 3 pounds
Melted fat

Cook onion in butter for 2 minutes, then mix with bread. Add cottage cheese, dill, pickle, salt, pepper, lemon juice. Mix well. Wash fish and dry. Salt inside fish and stuff. Sew, or fasten with toothpicks and lace with heavy white thread. Place fish in lightly greased baking pan. Brush lightly with melted fat. Bake in hot oven, 400° F. for about 10 minutes for each pound of fish, or until flesh easily separates from bone. Yields 4 servings.

## BAKED FISH FILLETS AND VEGETABLES
*One dish meal.*

1 can (1-pound) sliced
potatoes, well drained
1 can (1-pound) whole
green beans, well
drained
1 pound frozen fish fillets,
thawed
¼ teaspoon salt
1 can (10½-ounce) con-
densed cream of mush-
room soup

1½ cups shredded cheddar
cheese
2 tablespoons snipped
parsley
2 teaspoons grated lemon
rind
Tomato slices

Arrange potatoes in bottom of 1½-quart buttered shallow baking dish; layer beans over top. Drain fish on absorbent toweling; place fish over beans and sprinkle with salt. In a mixing bowl, combine soup, cheese, parsley and lemon rind. Spoon soup mixture over fish. Bake in a preheated, 350° F. oven 30 minutes; top with tomato slices. Return to oven to bake 10 additional minutes. Allow to stand 10 minutes before serving. Yields 4 to 6 servings.

## FISH BAKE
*Serve with baked potatoes and green salad.*

| | |
|---|---|
| 1 whole fish, about | 1 small onion |
| 2½ pounds | 4 thin, salt pork strips, |
| ½ small green pepper | 1x2-inch *or* 4 slices bacon |
| 1 medium tomato | 1 bay leaf |

Wash, scale and clean fish. Rub inside with salt. Chop pepper, tomato, onion. Stuff inside fish and fasten fish opening with tooth picks. Place salt pork or bacon and bay leaf on top. Wrap fish tightly in aluminum foil. Bake in preheated, 350° F. oven for about 1½ hours. Serve with white sauce, page 57, or tomato sauce. Yields 4 servings.

## FILLETS IN SOUR CREAM
*Unbeatable flavor.*

| | |
|---|---|
| 1 pound pike *or* bass fillet | ½ cup crumbled, sweet |
| ¼ cup flour | white, round, crackers |
| 1 teaspoon salt | 2 tablespoons butter, |
| ¼ teaspoon pepper | melted |
| ½ cup milk | ½ cup dairy sour cream |

Cut fish in serving-size pieces. Coat with mixed flour, salt and pepper. Arrange in single layer in baking dish. Pour milk over fish. Bake in preheated, 350° F. oven for 45 minutes. Toast cracker crumbs lightly in butter. Spoon sour cream over fish. Sprinkle with toasted crumbs. Bake 10 minutes longer. Yields 4 servings.

## TROUT SAUTEED WITH BACON
*Flavor's unequaled.*

| | |
|---|---|
| 8 slices bacon | Salt |
| 4 trout (heads left on) | ¼ cup slivered almonds |
| Flour | 1 lemon, quartered |
| Pepper | 4 sprigs parsley (optional) |

Cook bacon in a large skillet and put it to drain on a paper towel. Add trout, which have been lightly floured, to the hot pan. Brown quickly in bacon fat, turn, add almonds, brown other side. Season. Serve immediately with bacon, almonds and lemon. Garnish with parsley. Yields 2 to 4 servings.

## POACHED PIKE
*Handsome when served whole and garnished with parsley, pimiento, cherry tomatoes, ripe or green stuffed olives.*

3-4 pounds pike, whole *or* in pieces
Cheesecloth

2 quarts boiling water to cover fish
2 tablespoons salt

Wash and clean fish. If frozen, allow to stand at room temperature about 15 minutes. Bring salted water to rolling boil. Wrap fish in cheesecloth, with long ends of cloth to serve as handles on either side. Use these handles to lower fish into and remove it from the pot. Cover pot and poach (boil gently) until fish flakes easily. Serve hot or cold with a sauce. Yields 6 servings.

## SAUCES TO SERVE WITH FISH

*Herbed Mayonnaise:* Combine 2 cups mayonnaise, ¼ cup chopped parsley, ¼ cup finely chopped chives, ½ cup finely chopped raw spinach, 1 teaspoon tarragon and 1 tablespoon capers (optional). Yields about 3 cups sauce. Try this with cold pike.

*Lemon-Garlic Butter:* Cream 1 cup softened butter. Add 1 clove garlic, pureed; 1 teaspoon salt; ¼ teaspoon pepper — blend well. Add, little at a time: 1 teaspoon grated lemon peel mixed with 2 tablespoons fresh lemon juice, beating after each addition. Yields 1 cup. Excellent with hot fish.

*Maitre d'Hotel Sauce — The Farmer, 1920:* Cream together 3 tablespoons soft butter, 1 tablespoon lemon juice, ½ teaspoon salt, 1 tablespoon finely-snipped parsley (optional). Spread on fish while hot so fat melts. Yields about ¼ cup sauce.

*Tartar Sauce:* Combine ½ cup mayonnaise, 2 tablespoons pickle relish, 1 tablespoon lemon juice and ½ teaspoon Worcestershire sauce in a small bowl. Yields ⅔ cup sauce. Good with hot fish.

## FISH CHOWDER
*Hearty soup, delicate flavor.*

| | |
|---|---|
| 1 pound fresh-water fish fillets | 2 cups finely-diced potatoes |
| ¼ cup chopped salt pork *or* bacon | 3 cups milk |
| ¼-½ cup onion, chopped | 1 teaspoon salt |
| 2 cups hot water | Pepper |
| ¾ cup finely-diced celery | Parsley |
| | 2 tablespoons butter |

Cut fillets in 1-inch cubes. Fry salt pork or bacon until browned. Add onions and brown slightly. Add water and potatoes and cook 5 minutes or until potatoes are partially tender. Add fish and celery; cook until the fish flakes easily when tested with a fork. Add milk, seasonings and heat. Serve immediately with snipped parsley sprinkled on top. Yields 6 to 8 servings.

## LUTEFISK
*An old Norwegian recipe.*

Purchase fish from a local grocer who has the reputation for securing good lutefisk. It should be a nice firm fish, soaked and processed well. Skin the fish, cut off fins and tail, cut flesh into pieces about 4 to 6 inches long. Place pieces of fish into a stone crock with lightly salted water to cover. Keep cold. Change water every day if you are not using the fish immediately. When you are ready to cook the fish, put it in a cheesecloth bag and place in boiling water. When water returns to a boil, boil fish 3 to 5 minutes. Do not overcook. (If fish is cooked in a large piece and has not been placed in cheesecloth, you will see the flakes begin to separate slightly when it is done.) Drain off water and place fish on platter. Serve with whole boiled potatoes and lots of melted butter. (Many Swedish families serve lutefisk with buttery cream sauce sprinkled with freshly grated allspice and pepper.)

*Baked Lutefisk:* Soak fish as described above; drain. Line a shallow baking pan with foil; place fish on foil and cover pan tightly with a lid or foil. Bake a 5-pound side for about 1 hour in preheated, 325° F. oven. This method is recommended for inexperienced Lutefisk cooks since chances of overcooking are slim and a light, flaky fish results.

## TASTY VARIETIES FOR FISH STICKS

*Cook fish sticks according to directions on the package and then try one of these easy, but tempting toppings.*

*Cheese-fish sticks:* Sprinkle the sticks with grated cheese, either the dry grated cheese that comes in shaker cans or any freshly grated cheese.

*Herb-baked sticks:* Sprinkle the sticks with either of these herb mixtures — dried thyme, marjoram and oregano, or a combination of dried parsley, celery flakes and poultry seasoning.

*Deviled fish sticks:* Spread fish sticks with a little chili sauce, or with horseradish and catsup.

*Spicy fish sticks:* Sprinkle sticks with dried mint flakes and nutmeg.

*Savory fish sticks:* Spread sticks with grated onion and a small amount of prepared mustard. Sprinkle with poppy seeds.

### SHRIMP FONDUE
*Serve some with beef fondue.*

Shell and clean 2 pounds of green (raw) shrimp. Arrange on bed of parsley. Heat 2 inches of corn or peanut oil in a fondue pot . . . or heat 3 cups of chicken broth. Spear shrimp on long-handled fondue fork and cook in oil or broth until done. Sauces 1, 4, 7, 8, 11 and 12 are good with shrimp page 84. Yields 4 to 5 servings.

### SHRIMP ALMOND HOT DISH
*Party fare, served with orange, grapefruit, avocado and lettuce salad mixed with a touch of Italian dressing.*

| | |
|---|---|
| 1 can (10½-ounce) con- densed cream of celery soup | 1 cup canned shrimp |
| | ¼ cup toasted, slivered almonds |
| ½ cup milk | 2 tablespoons minced parsley |
| 1½ cups cooked rice | |

Combine all ingredients. Bake in a buttered 1½-quart casserole in preheated, 375° F. oven for 25 minutes. Yields 4 to 6 servings.

## SALMON CASSEROLE
*Hearty!*

Cook 4 ounces of medium-size noodles, following package directions. Drain and pour into a casserole. Add the liquid from a 1-pound can of salmon (or ¼ cup milk for milder flavor) and the salmon broken into chunks. Mix 1 can (10½-ounce) condensed cream of celery soup, 1-1½ cups drained canned peas and 2 tablespoons milk. Season to taste with onion salt and pour over the salmon. Mix lightly but well. Top with coarse cracker crumbs and dot with butter. Bake in preheated, 350° F. oven about 40 minutes. Yields 6 servings.

## SUNFLOWER TUNA
*Make enough for second helpings.*

| | |
|---|---|
| ½ pound potato chips | 1 can (4-ounce) mushroom |
| 2 cans (7-ounce each) tuna | pieces |
| 2 cans (10½ ounces each) condensed cream of mushroom soup | ¾ cup roasted, salted sunflower meats |
| ½ soup can milk | Crushed, roasted, salted sunflower meats |

Crush potato chips, add tuna, soup, milk, mushrooms and ¾ cup sunflower meats. Pour into 2-quart casserole. Top with more sunflower meats crushed with a rolling pin. Bake in preheated, 350° F. oven for ½ hour. Yields 8 to 10 servings.

## CINCHY TUNA RICE
*Speedy!*

| | |
|---|---|
| 1 can (10½-ounce) condensed cream of mushroom soup | tuna, drained |
| ½ cup milk | ¼ pound cheddar-type cheese, grated |
| 3 cups cooked rice | 2 teaspoons crushed tarragon *or* 1 teaspoon |
| 2 cans (7-ounce each) | Worcestershire sauce |

Mix soup and milk thoroughly; add rice; fold in tuna, cheese and tarragon or Worcestershire sauce. Pour into

2-quart casserole and sprinkle paprika over top. Bake in preheated, 350° F. oven for about 20 minutes. Yields 4 to 6
servings.

## TUNA-STUFFED BAKED POTATOES
*Sunday night supper treat.*

2 cans (7-ounce each)
tuna
6 medium baking
potatoes
1 tablespoon butter
1½ teaspoons salt

Dash pepper
1½ tablespoons grated
onion
½ cup chopped parsley
¾-1 cup hot milk
¾ cup grated cheese

Drain tuna. Flake. Bake potatoes in preheated, 425° F.
oven for 45 to 60 minutes, or until soft. Cut slice off the side
of each potato; scoop out insides. Mash potatoes. Add butter,
seasonings and hot milk; blend well. Mix in tuna. Stuff shells
with the tuna-potato mixture. Sprinkle cheese over the top of
each potato. Bake in preheated, 400° F. oven for 25 to 30
minutes. Yields 6 servings.

## SCALLOPED OYSTERS
*Just two layers is the secret to success for this recipe
from the 1911 Country Kitchen Cook Book.*

1 pint oysters
2 cups soda cracker
crumbs
½ cup melted butter

1 teaspoon salt
¼ cup oyster liquid
⅛ cup milk
Salt and pepper

Mix crumbs and butter. Butter a deep earthen or glass
baking dish; put a layer of crumbs on the bottom, then a
layer of oysters, seasoned with salt and pepper. Pour over half
of the oyster liquor and part of the milk. Put on another layer
of crumbs, then the rest of the oysters, the remaining liquor
and milk. Cover the top with crumbs and bake half an hour
in a preheated, 350° F. oven. Never make more than two
layers of oysters, as they do not require much heat and they
cook more evenly. This dish may be prepared several hours
before baking time if kept in a cool place. Yields 4 servings.

## BAKED WILD DUCK AND RICE
*Wild rice is tastiest, but more expensive.*

1 large, 2 medium *or*
  4 small ducks, quartered
Salt, pepper, paprika
4 tablespoons all-purpose
  flour
⅓ cup shortening
1 small onion, chopped
1 tablespoon chopped
  green pepper

¾ cup uncooked, white
  and/*or* washed
  wild rice
2½ cups water *or*
  tomato juice
2 tablespoons catsup
1 teaspoon sage
Dash of cayenne
½ bay leaf

Roll duck in flour seasoned with salt, pepper and paprika. Melt shortening in skillet and brown ducks. Remove to heated casserole. Fry onion, green pepper and rice in drippings about 20 minutes, stirring to brown lightly. Add water or tomato juice and seasonings. Bring to boil and cook 10 minutes. Pour over meat in casserole. Cover and bake in preheated, 325° F. oven for 1½ hours. Stir twice and add liquid as needed. Yields 4 servings.

## WILD DUCK WITH RAISIN-APPLE STUFFING
*Fruit complements duck meat.*

3 wild ducks
Salt
½ cup dark *or* light raisins
3 tablespoons finely-
  chopped onion
⅓ cup thinly-chopped
  celery
¼ cup butter
2 medium-sized cooking
  apples, grated (or ⅓ to
  ½ cup apple sauce)

½ teaspoon salt
½ teaspoon poultry
  seasoning
⅛ teaspoon pepper
4 cups soft bread crumbs
1 egg, beaten
Shortening
Celery ribs and
  quartered apples

To take away gamey flavor, place dressed ducks in salt and soda water (3 teaspoons of each for 3 ducks) for 3 to 4 hours. Then wash birds thoroughly and dry.

*Stuffing method:* The birds must be oven-ready before you mix stuffing. Rinse and drain raisins. Cook raisins, onion and celery slowly in butter for about 5 minutes. Add grated apple, salt, poultry seasoning and pepper. Pour mixture over bread crumbs. Add beaten egg and toss lightly to blend.

Stuff ducks and sew or skewer openings shut. Brush outside of ducks with shortening. Place ducks on a rack in a roasting pan. Place celery and apples around birds. Roast in preheated, 350° F. oven for 2 to 3 hours, depending on size and age of ducks. Yields 3 to 6 servings.

*Unstuffed duck:* Fill cavity with cored, quartered apples or a mixture of 2 tablespoons chopped onion to a cup of chopped celery stems and leaves. Roast as directed above. Remove stuffing before serving.

### ROAST WILD GOOSE
*Tart fruit stuffing sets off rich, meat flavor.*

1 young goose, 6 to 8
   pounds dressed weight
   Juice of 1 lemon
   Salt and pepper
¼ cup butter
¼ cup chopped onion
1 cup chopped tart apple

1 cup chopped dried
   apricots
3 cups soft, day-old
   bread crumbs
½ teaspoon salt
⅛ teaspoon pepper
4-6 slices bacon
   Melted bacon fat

Sprinkle goose inside and out with lemon juice, salt and pepper. Melt butter in saucepan. Add onion, cook until tender. Stir in apple, apricots, crumbs, salt and pepper. Spoon cooled stuffing into cavity, lightly. Close opening with skewers and string. Cover breast with bacon slices and cheesecloth soaked in melted bacon fat. Place breast up in roasting pan, roast in preheated, 325° F. oven 20 to 25 minutes per pound, or until tender, basting often with bacon fat and drippings. If age of bird is uncertain, pour 1 cup water into roaster, cover last hour of cooking. Remove cloth, string and skewers. Yields 6 to 8 servings.

# ROAST GROUSE OR PHEASANT WITH ALMONDS
*A feast for company.*

4 grouse *or* 2 pheasants,
   cleaned
Salt and pepper
4 slices bacon
½ cup butter, melted

¼ cup blanched, slivered
   almonds
1 teaspoon lemon juice
4 slices buttered toast *or*
   4 cups fried wild rice,
   page 62

Sprinkle grouse inside and out with salt, pepper. Cover breasts with bacon, fasten with string or wooden picks. Place breast side up in baking pan. Roast in a preheated, 350° F. oven for about 1 hour, or until tender, basting frequently with ¼ cup melted butter. Combine remaining butter with almonds and lemon juice. Just before grouse is cooked, remove picks, bacon and string. Pour almond mixture over birds, serve on toast or platter of wild rice. Yields 6 servings.

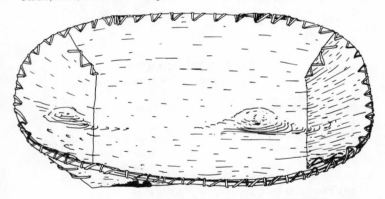

# SMOTHERED PHEASANT OR GROUSE
*Flavor of this brown, succulent bird is enhanced by vegetables. Garnish platter with tiny boiled carrots.*

2 pheasants *or* 4 grouse,
   skinned, washed,
   quartered
1 tablespoon salt
½ cup flour
2 tablespoons butter

¼ cup chopped celery
¼ cup chopped carrot
¼ cup chopped onion
2 tablespoons butter
½ cup boiling water

Mix flour and salt in a brown paper bag. Shake pheasant pieces in the bag, 2 or 3 at a time, until coated. Melt 2 tablespoons butter in skillet. Saute celery, carrot and onion until tender. Place in shallow baking pan. Add 2 more tablespoons butter to skillet and melt. Brown floured pheasant in skillet. Remove meat to baking pan; add water; cover meat with piece of wax paper. Bake in preheated, 350° F. oven for 1 hour, or until meat is tender. Serve at once on a bed of wild rice, page 62. Spoon some of pan juice over meat and rice. Yields 4 to 6 servings.

## PHEASANT OR GROUSE IN CREAM
*Moist and delicately flavored.*

1 pheasant *or* 2 grouse,
  cut up
1 small onion, chopped
¼ cup butter
1 cup half-and-half cream

1 can (10½-ounce) con-
  densed cream of mush-
  room soup
¼ teaspoon ginger
Salt and pepper

Roll pheasant in flour seasoned with salt and pepper. Saute onion in shortening. Remove and brown pheasant in same skillet. After browning, cover and place in preheated, 375° F. oven to bake 35 to 40 minutes. Combine cream, soup and ginger. Add to pheasant last 10 minutes of baking time. Yields 3 to 4 servings.

## SQUIRREL AND/OR RABBIT PIE
*Serve with green salad.*

1 squirrel, quartered
1 small onion, diced
1 teaspoon salt
⅛ teaspoon pepper
  Water

Flour
1 recipe baking powder
  biscuit dough, page 233,
  *or* can of refrigerator
  biscuits

Wash squirrel and soak in salt water 4 to 6 hours. Rinse and pat dry. Place in baking pan, add onion, salt, pepper and enough water to just cover meat. Bake in preheated, 350° F. oven until meat is tender. When tender, thicken broth with flour until gravy consistency. Place a crust of biscuit dough over the top, or cut individual biscuits and set on top of meat mixture. Bake in preheated, 425° F. oven 15 to 20 minutes, or until biscuits are brown. Yields 2 to 3 servings.

## FRIED RABBIT AND/OR SQUIRREL
*There's usually a rabbit and squirrel or two
in every hunter's game bag.*

1 young cottontail (2½ to
  3½ pounds) *or* 2 squirrels
  Shortening
1 egg yolk, beaten

1½ cups milk
⅔ cup flour
½ teaspoon salt

Wash dressed meat under water; soak in salt water 4 to 6 hours. Rinse, dry and cut into serving pieces. Combine egg yolk and milk; add flour and salt gradually and beat until smooth. Dip meat pieces into batter and fry in melted shortening until brown, about 15 minutes. Reduce heat and continue cooking until tender, 30 to 40 minutes. Yields 3 to 4 servings.

## VENISON ROAST
*Moist heat tenderizes meat.*

Place roast on a large enough square of heavy-duty foil to make an air-tight package. Sprinkle roast with ½ package of dry onion soup mix and 1 can of undiluted mushroom soup. Fold foil over the roast. Bake in preheated, 350° F. oven for 1 to 2 hours — about 30 minutes per pound.

## BARBECUED VENISON BURGERS
*Serve these savory burgers with white rice,
thick French bread or round, toasted buns.*

1 pound ground venison,
  ground with pork
½ cup milk

1 teaspoon salt
¼ teaspoon pepper

Mix all ingredients and shape into 6 patties. Place in shallow baking dish and top with barbecue sauce, below. Bake in preheated, 350° F. oven for about 1 hour. Yields 3 to 4 servings.

*Venison Barbecue Sauce:* Heat 3 tablespoons bacon drippings. Lightly brown 3 thinly sliced onions. Add ¾ cup finely chopped celery leaves and cook 3 minutes. Blend in 1 teaspoon dry mustard, 3 tablespoons brown sugar, 1 teaspoon chili powder, 1½ teaspoons salt. Moisten with ¼ cup cider vinegar, ½ cup water and 1¾ cups tomato juice. Cover pan and simmer the barbecue sauce for 20 minutes.

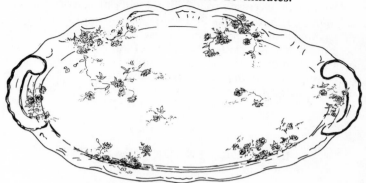

## VENISON, HUNTER STYLE
*Serve this rich, saucy dish with hot wild rice.*

3 pounds venison steak,
   cut in serving pieces
   ¾-inch thick
1 teaspoon salt
4 peppercorns
1 medium onion, sliced
1 carrot, sliced

4 sprigs parsley
½ teaspoon thyme
1 bay leaf
½ cup red wine vinegar
½ cup salad oil
   Sour Cream Sauce

Season meat with salt, place in a bowl or flat glass or enamel pan. Mix peppercorns, onion, carrot, parsley, thyme, bay leaf, vinegar and 5 tablespoons oil; pour over steaks. Cover meat and let stand in refrigerator approximately 24 hours. Turn meat occasionally. Remove meat from marinade; pat dry. Heat 3 tablespoons oil in deep skillet. Cook venison in oil for 3 minutes on each side. Add about ¼ cup of the marinade, cover and cook until well done. Place meat on hot platter; pour Sour Cream Sauce over meat and serve. Yields 6 to 8 servings.

*Sour Cream Sauce:* Pour off and save excess fat from pan in which meat was cooked. Melt 2 tablespoons butter in same pan; add 2 tablespoons flour, ¼ cup finely choppped onion; mix well. Stir in all the browned fat from pan. Gradually add 4 tablespoons vinegar and 2 finely crushed peppercorns; mix well after each addition. Add 1 cup dairy sour cream, juice of half a lemon and a little salt and pepper if needed. Cook and stir until thickened; do not boil. Lemon juice is optional.

## VENISON CASSEROLE
*Savory!*

Cut 2 pounds venison round into serving pieces. Roll pieces in flour and then pound flour into the meat. Brown in hot shortening; remove from skillet. Place half of the pieces in the bottom of a large buttered casserole. Add layers of sliced potatoes, onions, carrots and chopped celery. Top with remaining meat. Pour 3 cups beef boullion over the top; bake in preheated, 350° F. oven for 45 to 60 minutes. Yields 6 to 8 servings.

## MOOSE OR VENISON MEAT LOAF
*Shape into patties and pan broil if you like.*

Combine ⅔ part ground moose or venison and ⅓ part pork sausage. Add 1 chopped onion, 1 egg, 1 cup crushed soda crackers, ⅓ cup catsup, 1 teaspoon celery salt. Salt and pepper. Add enough water or milk to mix well together. Place in greased baking pan. Bake in preheated, 350° F. oven for 1½ hours. Beef can be substituted for moose or venison. Yields 4 to 5 servings.

## MOOSE STEAK TARRAGON
*Meat melts in your mouth.*

| | |
|---|---|
| 2 pounds moose steak, sliced round *or* chuck | 1 teaspoon salt |
| 2 tablespoons bacon drippings | ¼ teaspoon pepper |
| 2 medium-sized onions, peeled and sliced | 1 can (8-ounce) mushroom stems and pieces, not drained |
| ½ cup flour | 1 cup beef boullion |
| ⅛ teaspoon each of marjoram, thyme, sweet basil | ½ cup tarragon *or* red wine vinegar |

In a heavy skillet or casserole, saute onions in bacon drippings until lightly browned; then remove onions to separate dish.

Score meat with sharp knife and cut into serving pieces. Dip meat in herb flour made by mixing the flour, herbs, salt and pepper. Brown meat in same drippings. When browned, sprinkle remaining herb flour over meat; add undrained mushrooms, onions, boullion and vinegar. Cover tightly and bake in preheated, 300° F. oven until tender, 2 or more hours. Yields 4 to 6 servings.

### MOOSE RUMP ROAST
*Marinade tenderizes the meat.*

Trim roast well. Combine ½ pint vinegar and ½ pint water. Add 1 tablespoon salt and 8 bay leaves. Pour over roast. Run sharp knife into meat every square inch to let liquid penetrate. Marinate over night in refrigerator.

1 onion, chopped
1 cup chopped bacon
1 cup beef suet, diced
2 strips of bacon

2 strips beef suet
1 cup water
Salt and pepper

Cut slits in meat with sharp knife, stuff slits (lard) with suet and bacon. Place meat in roaster. Cover with onion. Lay strips of bacon and suet on top. Add water, salt and pepper. Roast in preheated, 350° F. oven, 30 minutes per pound, or until done to your taste.

## BARBECUED ANTELOPE RIBS
### *A nibbler's delight!*

| | |
|---|---|
| 1 side of ribs | 2 tablespoons lemon juice |
| Salt and pepper | ¼ cup Worcestershire |
| 1 large onion, chopped | sauce |
| ¾ cup catsup | 1 tablespoon chili powder |
| ¾ cup water | |

Place ribs with meaty side up in shallow pan. Cover with onion, salt, pepper. Roast in preheated, 375° F. oven for 30 minutes. Mix rest of ingredients together and pour over ribs. Return to 350° F. oven for 45 minutes. Baste occasionally.

# EGGS AND CHEESE FOR EVERY MEAL

E. Landin

## SOFT-COOKED EGGS

*Cold Water Method:* Cover eggs in pan with water to come at least 1 inch above eggs. Bring rapidly to boiling. Turn off heat and, if necessary, set pan off burner to prevent further boiling. Cover, let stand 2 to 4 minutes, depending on individual taste. Cool promptly in cold water for several seconds to prevent further cooking and to make easy to handle.

*Boiling Water Method:* Bring water in pan to rapid boil, using enough to cover eggs as above. To avoid cracked shells, place cold eggs in warm water. Transfer to boiling water with spoon, turn off heat and, if necessary, set pan off burner to prevent further boiling. Cover tightly and let stand 6 to 8 minutes. Cool as above.

## HARD-COOKED EGGS

Hard cook eggs, using boiling water method, above, but let stand 15 minutes. Remove eggs immediately and cool promptly under cold, running water. Overcooking makes white tough, produces hard spots in yellow and turns yolk surface a green-gray color.

## SCRAMBLED EGGS
*Serve with crisp bacon or sausage.*

| | |
|---|---|
| 5 eggs | ⅛ teaspoon pepper |
| ½ cup milk | 2 tablespoons butter *or* |
| ⅔ teaspoon salt | bacon fat |

Beat eggs slightly; add salt, pepper and milk. Melt fat in omelet pan or heavy skillet; turn in egg mixture and cook slowly, scraping from bottom and sides of pan as mixture thickens. Cook until creamy, not dry. Remove from pan the instant eggs begin to set. Serve at once.

*Garnishes:* Parsley; jelly; a bit of butter and paprika; bacon strips; asparagus; tomato sauce; tomato slice; orange slice.

*Egg Buns:* Pile hot scrambled eggs between halves of toasted, buttered hamburger bun. If your family loves cheese, top eggs with 1 tablespoon grated cheese. Place lower half of bun with cooked egg and cheese on cookie sheet under low broiler heat (350° F.) until cheese melts a bit.

*Make herbed eggs* by adding ¼ teaspoon chives, parsley, tarragon, chervil, celery seed or dill to 5 eggs prepared for scrambling.

*Diced cheese,* crumbled cooked bacon, or chipped beef may be added to scrambled eggs for variety.

*Add sliced ripe* olives; instant minced onion; snipped green onion and green pepper; or chives to your favorite scrambled egg mixture.

## HOMESTEAD SKILLET EGGS
*Super with a cup of tomato soup.*

| | |
|---|---|
| 2 boiled potatoes, cubed | ¼ cup milk |
| 6 slices bacon, cut in small pieces | ½ teaspoon salt |
| | ¼ teaspoon pepper |
| 1 medium onion, chopped | Shake of tabasco sauce |
| 6 eggs | (optional) |

Fry bacon over medium heat until crisp. Pour off some of the fat. Add chopped onion to bacon and cook a few minutes. Add potatoes and cook until slightly browned. Beat eggs slightly, add remaining ingredients. Pour over potato mixture. Cook, stirring often, until eggs are set but creamy. Yields 3 to 4 servings.

## SCRAMBLED FRENCH TOAST
*Two easy versions of an old favorite.*

| | |
|---|---|
| 8 slices dry bread | Shortening *or* bacon drippings |
| 3 eggs, well beaten | 8 slices crumbled, cooked bacon (optional) |
| ¾ cup milk | |
| 1½ teaspoons sugar | |
| ½ teaspoon salt | |

Cut bread into small cubes; do not remove crusts. Thoroughly combine eggs, milk, sugar and salt. Pour over bread cubes; toss lightly. Saute in hot shortening in large skillet, turning occasionally until well browned. Sprinkle with bacon. Serve with butter and syrup. Yields 4 servings.

*Molasses French Toast:* Omit sugar and add 2 tablespoons molasses, ½ teaspoon cinnamon, ¼ teaspoon nutmeg and ⅛ teaspoon cloves.

## SURPRISE SAUSAGE 'N EGGS
### Use leftover Easter eggs.

| | |
|---|---|
| 1 pound pork sausage meat | 1 egg, beaten |
| ½ cup quick-cooking *or* old-fashioned oatmeal | ¼ cup milk |
| | 4 hard-cooked eggs, peeled |

Combine sausage meat, oats, egg and milk; mix thoroughly. Divide meat mixture into four parts and shape each part around a hard-cooked egg. Place eggs on rack in a shallow baking pan. Bake in preheated, 375° F. oven for about 35 minutes, or until sausage is cooked. Yields 4 servings.

## CRISP-COATED BAKED EGGS
### Serve on corned beef hash.

| | |
|---|---|
| 3 cups whole wheat cereal flakes | 4 eggs |
| 2 tablespoons butter | Salt and pepper |

Line 4 greased individual custard cups or casseroles with whole wheat flakes; dot with butter. Break egg into each dish on cereal; sprinkle with salt and pepper. Bake in preheated, 375° F. oven for 15 to 20 minutes. Yields 4 servings.

*Use bacon:* Partially fry strips of bacon and line each custard cup with one of the strips. Break egg into cup and bake as directed above.

## SHRIMP FOO YUNG
### Serve with hot white or brown rice.

| | |
|---|---|
| 1 cup shrimp, fresh *or* canned | ½ cup mushrooms, sliced thin |
| 1 cup onions, chopped fine | 5 eggs |
| ¼ cup water chestnuts, sliced thin | 2 tablespoons soy sauce |

Beat eggs until thick; add shrimp, onions, chestnuts and mushrooms. Add soy sauce and continue to beat. Place a small amount of oil in a shallow frying pan; when pan is hot enough, pour the mixture into the pan. Brown on both sides.

Serve hot with sauce. Yields 4 to 6 servings.

*Sauce:* Simmer over a low flame, 1 tablespoon soy sauce, 1 tablespoon cornstarch, ½ cup bouillon and ¼ teaspoon sugar.

## BAKED-EGG-TOMATOES
*Serve at a brunch party.*

| | |
|---|---|
| 6 prepared, fresh tomato shells, page 23 | Salt and pepper |
| | Bread crumbs |
| 6 eggs | 1 tablespoon butter |

Preheat oven to 350° F. Place prepared shells in shallow, greased baking dish with 2 tablespoons water in bottom of dish. Bake shells 10 minutes; remove from oven and break an egg into each shell. Season to taste with salt and pepper. Sprinkle a few bread crumbs over top and dot with butter. Bake another 20 to 30 minutes, until eggs are just firm. Yields 6 servings.

*Make three eggs into four:* Beat eggs, add 1 tablespoon milk for each, salt and pepper to taste. Then break 1½ slices of white bread into small pieces and add to the egg mixture. Pour into a skillet of sizzling butter. Brown on one side; turn and brown on the other.

## CREAMED EGGS
*Grandma's Sunday supper.*

| | |
|---|---|
| ⅓ cup butter | ½ teaspoon curry powder (optional) |
| ½ cup chopped celery | |
| ¼ cup chopped green pepper | 3 cups milk |
| | 6 hard-cooked eggs, sliced |
| ⅓ cup flour | 2 tablespoons chopped pimento (optional) |
| 1½ teaspoons salt | |

Melt butter in saucepan. Add celery and green pepper, and cook slowly until tender. Blend in flour, salt (and curry powder). Add milk and cook, stirring constantly until thickened. Add sliced eggs (and pimento); heat. Serve on hot buttered toast points, toasted English muffin halves or baking powder biscuits. Yields 4 servings.

## DAY OFF TUNA SOUFFLE
*Souffles won't wait for stragglers.*

| | |
|---|---|
| 4 tablespoons butter | 3 egg yolks, well beaten |
| 4 tablespoons flour | 3 egg whites |
| ¼ teaspoon salt | ¼ teaspoon cream of tartar |
| ⅛ teaspoon pepper | 1 can (10½-ounce) con- |
| 1 cup milk | densed cream of mush- |
| 1 can (6½-ounce) drained | room soup |
| tuna, flaked | ½ soup can of milk |

Melt butter, stir in flour and seasonings and cook, stirring, until mixture is smooth and bubbly. Remove from heat and stir in milk. Return to low heat and bring mixture to a boil, stirring constantly. Boil 1 minute, stirring. Remove from heat. Mix in tuna, then egg yolks gradually. Beat egg white with cream of tartar until stiff. Fold gently into tuna mixture. Pour into greased, 1½-quart casserole. One with straight sides works best. Place casserole in pan with 1 inch boiling water in bottom. Bake in preheated, 350° F. oven for 50 to 60 minutes, until puffed and golden brown. (It's better to overcook a bit, rather than undercook.) Serve immediately. Pass mushroom soup mixed with milk and heated as a sauce. Yields 4 servings.

*Plain Souffle:* Omit tuna and serve with sauce made of 1 can condensed tomato soup and ½ can water.

## PUFFY OMELET
*Serve at once!*

| | |
|---|---|
| 5 eggs, separated | Dash pepper *or* paprika |
| 5 tablespoons water | 2 tablespoons butter |
| ½ teaspoon salt | |

Beat egg yolks until thick and lemon-colored; add water and salt. Fold in stiffly beaten whites. Melt butter in a hot omelet pan or skillet with ovenproof handle; turn in egg mixture; spread evenly. Reduce heat; cover pan, and cook slowly so omelet cooks and browns evenly, about 5 minutes. When well puffed up and a delicate brown underneath, put omelet, uncovered, into a preheated, 350° F. oven on the center rack. Cook just until set on the top. When firm to the touch, omelet is done. Groove gently across center, fold in half with wide spatula and turn onto hot platter. Serve at once. Yields 3 to 4 servings.

*Omelet with Cheese and Vegetables:* Before omelet is folded, spoon heated vegetables, grated cheese or chopped, cooked meat such as ham or bacon over half of it. Fold and serve hot.

*Omelet Sauces:* Dilute 1 can condensed tomato, mushroom or celery soup, with ½ soup can of milk; heat and pass with omelet to be ladled over top of individual servings.

### QUICK MUSHROOM CREAM SAUCE
*Serve on omelets and souffles.*

1 can (10½-ounce) mush-    1 egg yolk, beaten
   room soup                    ½ cup milk

Heat soup, add egg yolk and milk. Stir until slightly thickened. Yields 2 cups sauce.

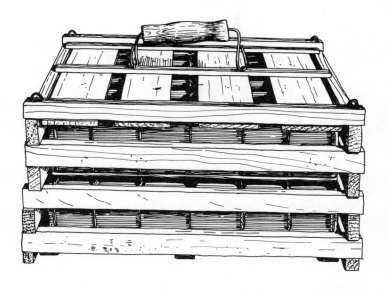

*Save all your egg shells.* They can be used for clearing coffee. They are also good for cleaning bottles. Break up fine and put in a bottle, especially vinegar cruets and the like, with plenty of hot suds and shake the bottle well. They clean charmingly. — The Farmer, 1897.

## PICNIC EGGS

*Clara Sutter's recipe was from her grandmother,
and well over 100 years old. The eggs are pretty and tasty.*

Hard cook eggs about 4 days before you need to use them.
Let eggs cool, then peel. Marinate eggs in juice from pickled
beets for 4 days. Slice eggs in halves or quarters to serve.

## EGGS STUFFED WITH CRABMEAT

*Serve with tomatoes and lettuce, cold cooked asparagus
marinated in French dressing, hot rolls and fruit shortcake.*

| | |
|---|---|
| 6  hard-cooked eggs | ½  teaspoon salt |
| ¾  cup crabmeat | ⅓  cup mayonnaise |
| ½  cup chopped celery | Paprika |
| 1  teaspoon dry mustard | |

Cut eggs in half, lengthwise. Scoop out yolks; mash.
Remove any cartilage from crabmeat and break the meat into
small pieces. Combine crabmeat, egg yolks, celery, mustard,
salt and mayonnaise. Mix well. Fill egg whites with crabmeat
mixture. Sprinkle with paprika. Yields 12 stuffed eggs.

*Eggs Stuffed with Chicken:* Substitute 1 cup finely
chopped, cooked chicken for the crabmeat. Reduce mustard
to ½ teaspoon and mayonnaise to ¼ cup.

*Eggs Stuffed with Ham:* Substitute a 2¼-ounce can of
deviled ham (or 3 tablespoons finely minced cooked ham) for
the crabmeat. Omit salt, mayonnaise and paprika (use ¼ cup
mayonnaise if cooked ham is the ingredient).

## DEVILED EGGS
*Picnic and buffet "musts"!*

4 hard-cooked eggs
¼ teaspoon salt
½ teaspoon prepared
  mustard

⅛ teaspoon pepper
1 teaspoon vinegar
2 teaspoons mayonnaise *or*
  melted butter

When eggs are cold, remove shell and cut each in two, lengthwise. Remove yolks and set whites aside. Mash yolks smooth; mix thoroughly with rest of the ingredients. Roll into balls the size of original yolk. Place a ball in each half white of egg. Add a dash of paprika and serve on bed of crisp lettuce. Yields 8 deviled eggs.

*Leftover egg whites* stored in a tightly covered jar in the refrigerator may be kept a week to 10 days.

*Leftover egg yolks,* covered with water, may be stored in a covered container in the refrigerator two to three days.

## BAKED MACARONI WITH CHEESE
*From the 1934 Country Kitchen Cook Book.*

2 cups cooked macaroni
  *or* spaghetti
1 cup cubed cheese

Salt, pepper
2 cups milk, scalded
1 egg, beaten

Put macaroni (or spaghetti) in alternate layers with cheese in a baking dish. Add egg and seasonings to milk and pour in almost to top layer. Set casserole in pan with 1 inch boiling water in bottom. Bake in preheated, 350° F. oven until milk is absorbed and top is brown. Too high a heat will toughen cheese.

*With Cheese Sauce:* Instead of milk and egg, make 2 cups medium white sauce, page 57. Add cheese and pour over macaroni. Top with buttered crumbs.

*With Celery:* Reduce cheese to ¾ cup and alternate in layers as above, using also 1 cup cooked celery.

*Baked Rice and Cheese:* Substitute cooked rice for macaroni.

*With Peanuts:* Use ¾ cup chopped, salted peanuts and layer these with the cheese.

## CHEESE FONDUE

*A zippy, green salad and good conversation spark this dish.*

1 pound Swiss cheese,
    coarsely grated
3 tablespoons cornstarch
½ teaspoon salt
¼ teaspoon pepper

¼ teaspoon nutmeg
2 cups buttermilk
1 clove garlic
1 loaf French bread (cut in
    bite-size pieces)

Toss cheese with cornstarch, salt, pepper, nutmeg. In a fondue pan, heat buttermilk with garlic clove over low heat. When hot, remove garlic and add Swiss cheese; stir constantly until cheese is melted. Serve from fondue pan over burner. Dip cubes of French bread on long forks into cheese sauce. Yields snack servings for 10 to 12.

## WELSH RAREBIT

*From the 1934 Country Kitchen Cook Book.*

2 cups medium white
    sauce, page 57
½ pound grated cheese
½ teaspoon paprika

¼ teaspoon mustard
2 eggs, *or* 3-4 yolks,
    slightly beaten

Add cheese and seasonings to sauce; stir until smooth. Then add eggs, stirring quickly until blended. Cook and stir 2 or 3 minutes until it thickens a little. Pour over crisp toast or crackers. Yields about 5 servings.

## TOMATO CASSEROLE DINNER WITH CHEESE DUMPLINGS

*This hearty and tasty dish comes from a Martin County, Minnesota farm homemaker.*

1 tablespoon chopped
    green pepper
2 tablespoons chopped
    onion
2 tablespoons shortening
1 tablespoon flour

3½ cups cooked tomatoes
1 tablespoon choppped
    celery tops
1 teaspoon sugar
½ teaspoon salt
⅛ teaspoon pepper

Saute green pepper and onion in melted shortening until tender. Blend in flour and stir until smooth. Add tomatoes, celery tops, sugar, salt and pepper. Continue cooking until mixture comes to a boil, stirring constantly. Simmer over low heat for 5 minutes, stirring occasionally.

*Cheese Dumplings:* Sift together, 1 cup all-purpose flour, 2 teaspoons baking powder, ½ teaspoon salt. Cut in 2 tablespoons shortening. Blend in ½ cup grated cheddar cheese and 1 tablespoon snipped parsley. Add ½ cup milk and mix only until flour is moistened.

Dip tablespoon into cold water. Drop batter, by spoonfuls, onto hot tomato mixture. Cover tightly and steam for 20 minutes. Do not remove cover during steaming process. Serve immediately. Yields 4 to 6 servings.

## QUICHE LORRAINE
*Super-special (but easy to make) for*
*brunch, lunch or late night snacks.*

Pastry for 9-inch,
  1-crust pie
12 slices (½-pound) bacon,
  crisply fried and
  crumbled
 1 cup (about 4-ounce)
  shredded natural Swiss
  cheese

⅓ cup minced onion
 4 eggs
 2 cups whipping cream
¾ teaspoon salt
¼ teaspoon sugar
⅛ teaspoon cayenne pepper

Sprinkle bacon, cheese and onion in pastry-lined pie pan. Beat eggs slightly; beat in remaining ingredients. Pour cream mixture into pan. Bake 15 minutes in preheated, 425° F. oven. Reduce oven temperature to 300° F. and bake 30 minutes longer, or until knife inserted 1 inch from edge comes out clean. Let stand 10 minutes before cutting. Serve in wedges. Yields 6 main dish servings or 8 appetizer servings.

## BAKED SOUR CREAM TACOS
*Party fare, served with hard rolls and green salad.*

12 frozen tortillas
   Oil for frying
2 tablespoons oil
1 small onion, chopped
1 can (1-pound,
   12-ounce) solid
   tomatoes, chopped
1 teaspoon oregano,
   rubbed between palms
   of hands

2 or more tablespoons
   chili sauce, to taste
½ teaspoon salt
1 pound cheese, mild
   cheddar *or* Wisconsin
   brick, shredded
1 pint dairy sour cream,
   salted with ½ teaspoon
   salt

Soften tortillas in a little oil in a skillet. Do not cook very long or they will begin to crisp and will not fold.

For sauce, wilt onion in hot oil. Add tomatoes, oregano, chili sauce and salt. Cool 15 to 20 minutes. Set aside. Put some sauce and a piece of cheese on each tortilla roll. Arrange in a buttered, shallow glass baking dish. Pour remaining sauce over tacos, top with cheese and spoon sour cream over all. Bake at 325° F. for 25 to 30 minutes. Yields 6 to 12 servings.

## GOLDEN CROWN CASSEROLE
*Lenten supper delight.*

1 can refrigerated biscuits
½ pound cooked bacon,
   crumbled
1 can (1-pound) cream-
   style corn
1 tablespoon minced onion

1 can (1-pound) peas and
   carrots
1 cup cubed, soft,
   cheddar-type cheese
10 cubes soft, cheddar-type
   cheese

Combine crumbled bacon, vegetables, cheese and onion. Pour into a buttered 2-quart shallow casserole. Bake in a 375° F. oven for 10 minutes. Remove biscuits from can; place around edge of casserole. Bake at 375° F. for another 15 to 20 minutes until golden brown. Top each biscuit with a cube of cheese, return to oven until cheese begins to melt. Yields 6 to 8 servings.

## CHEESE-CORN CHOWDER
*Favorite harvest-time soup. Great with ham sandwiches!*

| | |
|---|---|
| ¼ cup butter | 2 cups shredded, sharp |
| ¼ cup chopped onion | cheddar-type |
| ¼ cup flour | cheese |
| 1 quart milk | 2 teaspoons salt |
| 2 cans (15-ounce each) | ¼ teaspoon pepper |
| cream-style corn | |

Melt butter over low heat. Saute onion in butter until transparent but not brown, about 5 minutes. Add flour, blend thoroughly. Add milk slowly, stirring constantly; cook until smooth and thickened. Stir in corn, cheese; heat until cheese melts but do not boil. Add seasonings; serve sprinkled with chopped fresh parsley. Yields 6 to 8 servings.

## HUNGARIAN NOODLE HOT DISH
*A favorite Friday night supper.*

| | |
|---|---|
| 3 cups cooked thin noodles | ½ teaspoon salt |
| 1 cup cottage cheese | Dash of pepper |
| 1 cup soured cream | 2 eggs, well-beaten |
| ¼ cup chopped onions | ½ cup cheddar cheese, finely shredded |
| 1 clove garlic, finely chopped | 4 tablespoons butter, melted |
| 2 teaspoons Worcestershire sauce | |

Mix all ingredients together except cheddar cheese and butter. Turn mixture into buttered 1½-quart casserole. Pour melted butter over all. Put casserole in shallow pan. Fill pan with hot water to a depth of 1 inch. Bake in preheated, 350° F. oven for 45 minutes. Sprinkle cheese on top, continue to bake until sharp-pointed knife inserted in center comes out clean. Yields 6 to 8 servings.

## COTTAGE CHEESE
*A modern method.*

1 gallon pasteurized skim milk

½ cup fresh, commercial buttermilk

Cool or heat the skim milk to a temperature of 70° to 72° F. Stir in buttermilk. Let stand at this temperature (room temperature) until it clabbers and the curd settles enough to leave a thin film of whey. This takes 15 to 24 hours.

Cut curd into strips by running a long knife through it in both directions at 2-inch intervals. Then cut the curd horizontally into cubes. Use a U-shaped cheese knife, if you have one, and give it a half turn. Let curd rest 10 minutes. Add 2 quarts water that feels neither hot or cold — 98° to 100° F. Set the kettle of curd on a rack in a dishpan of water and heat slowly until curd reaches 98° to 100° F. Hold at this temperature for 30 minutes to an hour, stirring gently with a wooden spoon every 5 minutes. Do not break curd. Finished curds will settle to the bottom of the kettle as the whey is gradually forced out. Finished curds will break cleanly between the fingers and have a somewhat dry appearance. Too-high temperature or too-long heating will give tough curd.

When heating is finished, pour mixture carefully into a freshly scalded muslin bag, a cone-shaped puree sieve or a fine colander. Rinse curd with clean, cold water while draining to firm it and remove acid taste. Let curd drain as long as whey drips freely, but not long enough for the surface to become dry.

Remove curd from strainer and work in 1½ teaspoons salt. Refrigerate until needed. To make dry curd table-ready, add sweet or sour cream plus any other seasoning desired. Yields about 1½ pounds cottage cheese.

# BARBECUE, CAMP
# AND FIELD MEALS

## BUILDING A COOKING FIRE

Remember, flames are fine for boiling, but coals are best for broiling. The secret to successful barbecuing, is putting food on the grill after a grey ash covers two-thirds of the charcoal pieces. This means you have to allow enough time for the fire to burn, then see no flames (20 to 30 minutes).

With charcoal, there's no hurry to start cooking. A briquette fire usually gives you from 2 to 4 hours cooking time.

A small grill needs only about 16 to 18 briquettes. Too many charcoal pieces make the heat too intense.

Some grills may be raised or lowered for easy control.

You can control heat in several ways: Sprinkle water lightly over coals. A clothes sprinkler works well.

You also may add or remove coals from the fire. If you need to add more, use either started charcoal or warm up some charcoal at the edge of the fire first. This gives more even heat.

## TURKEY ON A SPIT
*A turkey grower's favorite.*

| | |
|---|---|
| 1 cup warm water | ¼ bottle (2-ounce-size) |
| ¼ cup plain salt | Tabasco sauce |
| 1 cup lemon juice, | 1 teaspoon garlic salt |
| strained | 10-14 pound whole turkey |

Dissolve salt in warm water; add lemon juice, Tabasco sauce and garlic salt. Use an internal baster or large hypodermic syringe and needle, to inject the sauce into all the muscle parts of the turkey. Use ¼ cup sauce in each side of breast and each leg-thigh. Also inject sauce into wings and back.

Place injected turkey in a pan, cover with foil and refrigerate overnight. Some of the juices will drain from the turkey. Use this juice to baste the turkey while it is cooking.

When ready to cook, build a bed of coals on the grill and bank some towards the back. Place bird on the spit and get it balanced. Place a foil pan beneath turkey to catch drippings. Cook for about 4 to 5½ hours. Meat is done when leg joint moves easily. Better yet, use a barbecue meat thermometer inserted in turkey breast and cook until internal temperature registers 185° F. Yields 10 to 15 servings.

## BAR-BE-CUED TURKEY
*A grower's own recipe.*

4 turkeys, 4 to 5 pounds
  each
1 cup peanut oil *or*
  olive oil
1 pound butter
2 cups lemon juice
3 cups vinegar
2½ cups water

4 tablespoons salt
1 teaspoon Tabasco sauce
1 tablespoon Wor-
  cestershire sauce
½ cup sugar
1 cup flour

Cut turkeys in half. Remove wings. Soak turkey halves and wings in oil for 2 to 3 hours at room temperature.

Combine remaining ingredients in large sauce pan. Heat. Add flour to thicken to consistency of thin white sauce. Yields about 11 cups sauce. Brush turkey with sauce at least 1 hour before grilling.

Start coals 45 to 60 minutes ahead of cooking time. When coals are ashen grey place turkey on grill 10 inches from coals. Cook 1 hour at this height. Lower grill 8 inches from coals for next ½ hour of cooking. The last ½ hour lower to 6 inches from coals. Baste and turn turkey every 15 to 20 minutes. Test for doneness by pinching leg muscle. Yields about 16 servings.

*Don't baste barbecued meat* until the last 15 minutes of cooking and the sauce won't scorch.

## BEEF KABOBS
*Great on the grill or in your broiler.*

⅔ cup oil
½ cup wine vinegar *or*
  white vinegar
1 clove of garlic, crushed
1 teaspoon salt
¼ teaspoon pepper

½ cup soy sauce
1 tablespoon Worcester-
  shire sauce
1 tablespoon mustard
4 pound chuck roast cut
  in 2-inch cubes

Combine all ingredients but the meat; pour the marinade over meat. Refrigerate 24 hours. Broil on skewers 6 to 8 inches above hot coals, turning as needed. Yields 6 servings.

## KALYPSO KABOBS
*Grilled fruit and lamb tempt every age.*

2 pounds lean, boneless
   lamb shoulder, cut in
   1-inch cubes
1 can (1-pound, 13-ounce)
   pear halves
1 package (8-ounce) pitted
   dates
24 red maraschino cherries
   (about ½ cup)

4 medium bananas, cut in
   1-inch slices
2 tablespoons butter,
   melted
1 tablespoon lemon juice
1 teaspoon cinnamon
¼ teaspoon cloves

Arrange lamb on skewers. Drain pears, reserving syrup. Coat banana slices with syrup. Arrange pear half, 3 dates, 3 banana slices and 3 cherries on each of 8 skewers. Combine melted butter, lemon juice, cinnamon and cloves for basting sauce.

Broil lamb 3 to 4 inches from source of heat or cook on outdoor grill 7 to 10 minutes; turn. Add fruit skewers; brush with basting sauce; cook 7 to 10 minutes longer, turning fruit skewers once. Brush fruit with sauce frequently. Yields 6 to 8 servings.

## TERIYAKI TURKEY KABOBS
*Economical gourmet meal.*

2 pounds boned turkey
   breast, cut in 1-inch
   cubes
1 can (1-pound, 14-ounce)
   pineapple chunks
2 cans (4-ounce each) water
   chestnuts

1 can (4-ounce) button
   mushrooms
1 onion, cut in chunks
   Teriyaki Sauce

Marinate turkey cubes in Teriyaki Sauce 1 hour or longer. Thread turkey, drained pineapple chunks, water chestnuts, mushrooms and onions on skewers. Brush with marinade. Grill over coals, about 4 inches from heat, or broil in oven broiler, 4 inches from heat until tender. Yields 8 servings.

*Teriyaki Sauce:* Beat together ¼ cup syrup from pineapple, ¼ cup honey, ¼ cup cooking oil, ½ cup soy sauce, ½ cup catsup, ⅓ cup white wine vinegar, 1 teaspoon dry mustard and 2 tablespoons minced onion.

## CHARCOAL-BARBECUED SPARERIBS
*Men like to cook and eat these.*

6 pounds pork spareribs
1 cup catsup
½ cup water
½ cup wine vinegar
1 teaspoon garlic salt

3 tablespoons brown sugar
2 tablespoons Worcestershire sauce
1 teaspoon salt
2 teaspoons mustard

Cut ribs into serving portions. Place in a large kettle, cover with boiling water and simmer 45 minutes. Remove and drain. To make sauce, combine remaining ingredients. Dip ribs into sauce. Place on grill. Cook about 6 inches from hot coals for 20 minutes, or until the lean shows no pink when cut and the surface is nicely browned. Baste frequently with sauce during cooking. Serve hot. Yields 6 servings.

*Note:* Simmering the ribs before placing on the grill cuts down on the charcoal cooking time and usually eliminates the need for a drip tray in the grill.

*Barbecued pork chops or steaks:* String 1-inch-thick chops or steaks on rotisserie. Cook at least 6 inches above hot coals for 40 to 45 minutes; or follow instructions with your barbecue equipment. Meat is done when it isn't pink in the center or next to the bone. Thread vegetables between chops, if desired, and brush periodically with your favorite barbecue sauce or salad dressing.

*No motorized skewers?* Support ends of skewers on bricks atop the grill; small bricks for wieners and kabobs, higher bricks for hams and chicken. Turn skewers to brown on all sides.

## GRILLED DINNER IN A PACKAGE
*These make-aheads are fun for picnics.*

Put some fat on a good-sized piece of foil. Make a hamburger patty, seasoned to your taste, and place it on the foil. Add a thin slice of partially-cooked potato, a slice of tomato, some sliced onion and partially-cooked carrots. Sprinkle each layer with salt and pepper. Wrap and fold in ends securely to hold juices. Place package on coals and cook about 20 to 35 minutes. Turn during cooking. Each package yields 1 serving.

*Use muffin pans* to serve a half-dozen paper cupsful of ice tea or pop — or to hold little jars of relish, mustard, catsup and other condiments.

## BARBECUED CHICKEN
*With five super sauces.*

Allow ½ or ¼ chicken for each person. Rinse, pat dry and sprinkle with salt and pepper. Place, skin-side-up, on grate about 5 inches above moderate briquette fire. Broil slowly for 10 to 15 minutes, then turn and broil, skin-side-down, until brown. Turn several times more and begin basting with your favorite barbecue sauce about 10 minutes before chicken is done. Allow about 45 minutes total time for chickens weighing 1½ pounds, 1 to 1½ hours for 2 to 2¼-pound chickens. Chicken is done when the drum stick can be twisted easily. Spoon remaining barbecue sauce over chicken when serving.

*Butter-Rosemary Sauce:* Melt ½ cup butter. Stir in 1 tablespoon salt and 2 tablespoons crushed rosemary. Baste chicken every 10 to 15 minutes. Yields sauce for 2 chickens, 1½ to 2 pounds each.

*Lemon Barbecue Sauce:* Combine 1 small clove garlic, ½ teaspoon salt, ¼ cup salad oil, ½ cup lemon juice, 2 tablespoons finely-chopped onion, ½ teaspoon pepper and ½ teaspoon thyme. Cook until onion is tender; remove garlic. Baste chicken every 10 to 15 minutes. Yields sauce for 2 frying chickens.

*Mustard-Molasses Sauce:* Blend together ¼ cup light molasses, ¼ cup prepared mustard; stir in ¼ cup vinegar, 2 tablespoons Worcestershire sauce and ⅛ teaspoon cayenne pepper. Baste chicken every 10 to 15 minutes. Yields sauce for 3 broilers, 1½ to 2 pounds each.

*Parmesan Sauce:* Melt ½ cup butter; mix in ⅔ cup grated Parmesan cheese and 1 teaspoon salt. Brush chicken with sauce and cook slowly 6 to 12 inches from heat, turning once. Yields sauce for 2 medium fryers.

*Tomato Sauce:* Combine 1 cup tomato puree or catsup, ½ cup water, 1 tablespoon paprika, 1 tablespoon Worcestershire sauce, ⅓ cup lemon juice, ¼ cup soft butter, 1 finely-chopped medium onion, 1 teaspoon salt, 1 teaspoon sugar, ½ teaspoon pepper. Bring to a boil. If sauce thickens while standing, add water to make good spreading consistency. Yields sauce for 2 broilers, 1½ to 2 pounds each.

## GRILL BURGERS
*May be baked in the oven at 350° F.*

Ground luncheon meat mixed with mushroom soup, spread on buns, wrapped in foil and set along the outside of the fire, are ready in a few minutes, and very tasty.

## MARINATED FILLETS
*Real treat from the grill.*

2 tablespoons chopped onion
1 clove garlic, finely chopped
2 tablespoons melted shortening
1 can (8-ounce) tomato sauce

2 tablespoons sherry
½ teaspoon salt
¼ teaspoon oregano
3 drops liquid hot pepper sauce
Dash pepper
2 pounds fresh *or* frozen fish fillets

Cook onion and garlic in shortening until tender. Add next 6 ingredients and simmer 5 minutes, stirring occasionally. Cool. Cut fillets into serving pieces and place in a single layer in a shallow baking dish. Pour sauce over fish and let stand 30 minutes, turning once. Remove fish from sauce; reserve sauce for basting. Place fish in well-greased, hinged wire grills. Cook about 4 inches from moderately hot coals for about 8 minutes. Baste with sauce. Turn and cook 7 to 10 minutes longer, or until fish flakes easily when tested with a fork. Yields 6 servings.

## FRANKS IN A BLANKET
*Kids love these.*

Mix prepared biscuit mix according to package directions and roll out ¼-inch-thick pieces which are large enough to wrap around a frank. Place frank on dough and wrap. Frank should protrude out of dough at each end about ½ inch. Place dough-wrapped franks on single thickness of heavy foil; roll and seal package loosely. Cook 15 minutes on grill near coals, turning frequently. Open 1 pack to see if biscuit is browned. If not, close and continue cooking until biscuit is done — up to a total of 25 minutes.

## ROASTED BRATWURST SANDWICH
*Serve with potato salad or baked beans.*

For each sandwich, spread 2 rye bread slices (or your favorite dark bread) with soft butter, a little mustard and horseradish (if desired). Top a bread slice with well-drained coleslaw *or* heated sauerkraut. Place a grilled bratwurst, split in half lengthwise, on top of the slaw. Cover with second bread slice. Secure with 2 toothpicks and cut in half.

## CHARCOAL GRILLED CORN
*Nothing like it!*

Discard outer husks. Strip inner husks to end of cob; do not tear off. Pull out silk. Soak in ice water about 20 minutes. Drain on towel leaving husks wet. Spread corn generously with butter and rewrap in husks and then in double thickness of heavy duty aluminum foil. Grill 10 to 20 minutes, turning once.

*Special butter:* Mix an equal amount of butter and peanut butter and spread on corn, as directed above.

## BREAD-ON-A-STICK
*If you have a pack of hungry wolves hanging around shouting "when do we eat?" put them to work.*

Have some bread dough or refrigerator biscuits on hand. Shape dough into rolls about 1 foot long, 1 inch wide and 2 inches thick. Let each person cut a stick about 2 feet long. Flour the stick well and twist the dough in a spiral around the stick. Hold stick-with-dough over the coals, turning it until it is cooked through and browned. Then slip roll off the stick, butter and eat it — delicious.

*One of the secrets of cooking fresh vegetables* in foil packets on an outdoor grill is to cut small pieces or slices and so shorten cooking time. Slices of carrots, celery, eggplant, green peppers, onions and summer squash cook quickly when cut on a long angle about ¼-inch thick. Green pepper strips have better color and flavor when blanched in hot water before putting in foil.

*Make individual gelatin salads* by pouring fruited gelatin mixture into paper cups. Place in muffin tins and chill until set. Great for picnics and back yard meals.

### GRILLED POTATOES
*Three choices from a South Dakota farm homemaker.*

*Parboil potatoes to be grilled:* The all-time favorite vegetable with steak is baked potato. One of the ways to hurry the cooking is to leave the skin on and boil the potato until half cooked, then seal it in a foil packet and put on the grill to finish baking.

*Bundled Potatoes:* On a 10-inch square of heavy aluminum foil, place a potato cut into ½ inch slices, a ¼ inch slice of onion and 1 tablespoon butter. Season with salt and pepper. Fold foil to make tight package. Bake on coals or low grill for 45 minutes. Make a bundle for each person to be served.

*Sweet Potato Packs:* Slice canned sweet potato for each pack. Place potato slices on a large square of heavy foil. Add 2 tablespoons brown sugar and a sprinkling of salt and pepper. Fold foil into secure package and cook on grill. Bake until heated through, about 15 to 20 minutes.

### FRUIT-SAUSAGE KABOBS
*Try these for brunch barbecue, a pre-supper snack or a before-bed treat — they're really great!*

Mix ¼ cup pancake syrup and 1 teaspoon orange *or* lemon *or* lime juice. Cut 6 brown-and-serve sausages in half. Cut 2 large, firm bananas into 24 pieces. Measure out ½ cup of well-drained pineapple chunks. String the fruits and sausages on 6 long skewers or long green sticks. Brush with syrup mixture. Cook over medium coals, about 6 inches from source of heat. Baste and turn occasionally until sausages are browned, about 8 to 10 minutes. Yields 6 kabobs.

*Make a roasting shield* for small hands by inserting wiener stick or fork through a disposable aluminum pie tin.

## BEEF JERKY
*Keeps and keeps! Add chewy strips, with water, to dry soup mixes when camping and simmer, covered, about ½ hour.*

Use a piece of top beef round about 3 inches thick. Slice it thinly into strips about ⅛ inch thick. Dip each strip into garlic salt (or plain salt and allspice), then brush off excess. Lay a wire rack in a flat pan (like a jelly roll pan) and place strips of meat on the rack. Or, line your oven with foil and lay the meat right on the oven racks. Set the oven as low as possible, about 140° F. and begin drying meat. Leave oven door open a bit until meat is partially dry. This allows moisture to leave oven. Then close oven door. Dry meat about 8 hours . . . it should still be chewy. For crispy chips, continue drying until desired consistency is obtained. Store in covered jars. Take camping or use as snacks. One-and-one-half pounds trimmed meat yields ½ pound jerky.

## POPPY SEED POTATOES
*Campers love 'em!*

| | |
|---|---|
| 1 can (about 1 pound) small, whole potatoes | 2 teaspoons poppy seeds |
| | ¼ teaspoon salt |
| 2 tablespoons butter | ⅛ teaspoon pepper |

Melt butter in 9-inch skillet; add seasoning. Drain water from potatoes, slice and add to skillet. Saute potatoes until heated through; stir frequently. Yields about 3 servings.
*Parmesan cheese* sprinkled on just before serving is good, too.

## CAMPFIRE CORNBREAD
*No dirty, sticky bowl.*

| | |
|---|---|
| 1 package cornbread mix | ½ cup milk |
| 1 egg | |

Put egg and milk into bag of cornbread mix (or all ingredients into a plastic bag). Squeeze upper part of bag to force out air. Close top, fold over and squeeze shut. With bag

resting on table, knead ingredients vigorously with fingers —
about 40 seconds — until egg is completely blended. Empty
into greased, 9-inch layer cake pan or aluminum foil pan. Set
pan inside 10-inch, heavy skillet and cover. Place over very
low heat and cook 30 to 45 minutes or until golden brown on
bottom and sides. Do not remove lid during cooking period.
Yields 6 servings.

## FRENCH ONION-VEGETABLE SOUP
### *A quickie to take snowmobiling.*

1 can (10¾-ounce) con-
  densed vegetable soup
1 can (10½-ounce) con-
  densed onion soup
2 soup cans water

4-6 slices French bread,
  each about ½ inch
  thick
Butter
Grated Parmesan
  cheese

Combine soups and water. Heat; let simmer a few minutes.
Meanwhile, arrange bread on skewers or long sticks; spread
one side with butter and sprinkle with Parmesan cheese. Broil
plain side until lightly browned, turn and broil buttered side.
Pour soup into bowls; top each with a slice of cheese toast.
When taking soup on a snowmobile outing, carry buttered
bread along in a plastic bag. Yields 4 to 6 servings.

## QUICKIE BLUEBERRY DUMPLINGS
### *Campfire delight!*

2½ cups fresh blueberries
  Dash salt
½ cup sugar
1 cup water
1 tablespoon lemon juice
  (optional)

1 cup biscuit mix
2 tablespoons sugar
2 tablespoons dry milk
⅜ cup water

Heat first 4 ingredients to boiling. Cover and simmer 5
minutes. Add lemon juice. While berries simmer, mix batter
by combining remaining ingredients. Drop batter by tablespoonfuls into bubbling sauce. Cover tightly and cook over
low heat 15 minutes without peeking. Yields 4 servings.
  *Variations:* Fresh cherries, peaches or berries picked in
camp may be used. Or, heat a large (1-pound, 13-ounce) can
of fruit to boiling, then proceed as above.

## BANANA YUM-YUMS
*Cook-out delights.*

Split a banana lengthwise, right through the skin. Sprinkle brown sugar in the opening. Close skin and wrap banana in heavy aluminum foil. Place package on grill and cook about 15 minutes.

*Shorten legs* on an old card table and you have a sit-on-the-ground table that is great for feeding the pre-school crowd or keeping food off sand at the beach.

*Keep salad relishes crisp by* packing them in the top of a double boiler which has ice in the bottom container. Sprinkle a few drops of water on vegetables and cover.

*Tie a clean carpenter's apron,* the kind with several wide pockets, around the nearest tree. Put silverware, bottle opener, napkins, straws and the like in the pockets where everyone can easily reach them. A shoe bag would work too — hang it on a nail.

*Bring out old-fashioned wire corn popper* for popping corn, toasting walnuts in the shell, heating potato chips and canned French fried onions, warming doughnuts. Best of all, line bottom of popper with hot dogs, close lid and roast the hot dogs in quantity without loss into the coals. Shake popper frequently for even browning.

## SUPER SANDWICHES
*Sandwiches with ground, cooked meats and*
*mayonnaise keep best if transported in a cooler.*

Sliced bologna; cole slaw
Chopped chicken or turkey; apple, celery, mayonnaise
Chopped chicken; walnuts, green olives, mayonnaise
Chopped roast beef; celery, grated onion, chili sauce, mayonnaise
Chopped frankfurter; baked beans, catsup, mustard
Chopped frankfurter; pickle relish, mustard, chili sauce
Ground ham; processed cheese, dill pickle, mayonnaise

Chopped ham; pickle and cottage cheese

Table-ready meat; chopped cabbage

Tuna fish; minced nuts, green pepper, mayonnaise

Salmon; chopped cucumber, onion salt, mayonnaise

Chopped chicken; walnuts, green or ripe olives, sage, mayonnaise

Sliced meat loaf; chopped green olives, mayonnaise

Sliced roast pork; apple-butter

Sliced turkey or ham; canned cranberry jelly

Hard-cooked egg with chopped crisp bacon, chives, mayonnaise

Hard-cooked egg with chopped chicken, celery, onion, mayonnaise

Hard-cooked egg with sliced frankfurter, chili sauce, mayonnaise

Hard-cooked egg with tuna or salmon, celery, pickle relish, mayonnaise

Hard-cooked egg with canned corned beef, onion, chopped with mustard, pickle, mayonnaise

Hard-cooked egg, sliced, on deviled ham and pickle

*Field Lunch Tip: Re-sealable baby food jars* and containers are ideal for individual servings because they're spillproof.

## BEANS AND CHOPS
*Hearty lift on a busy day.*

| | |
|---|---|
| 8 pork chops (2 pounds) | ¼ teaspoon allspice |
| ¼ cup finely-chopped onion | ¼ cup toasted, slivered almonds (optional) |
| ⅔ cup applesauce | |
| 2 cans (1-pound each) pork and beans with tomato sauce | |

In skillet, brown chops and cook onion until tender. Cover and cook over low heat 30 minutes. Add beans, applesauce and allspice; cover and cook 15 minutes or until chops are tender. Stir now and then. Garnish with almonds, if desired. Wrap hot, covered skillet in thick newspaper or place in insulated basket to carry to field. Yields 4 servings.

*Use Wieners:* 2 pounds wieners may be substituted for chops. Add to cooked onion, along with beans and other ingredients.

*Field Lunch Tip: Most important items* to include with dinner are a can of hot water, soap, basin and towels. The men appreciate a chance to clean up — and need to if they've been using fertilizers, treated seed or chemicals.

## SAVORY TURKEY HOT DISH
*Send to the field hot, in wide-mouth vacuum bottles.*

2 cups uncooked noodles
¼ cup butter
¼ cup flour
½ teaspoon salt
2½ cups milk *or* broth
¼ cup shredded cheddar cheese

1 can (4-ounce) mushrooms (optional)
2 pimientos, diced
2 cups cooked turkey, bite-size pieces
Crushed cornflakes

Cook noodles according to package directions; drain. Melt butter in large saucepan. Blend in flour and salt; gradually add liquid, stirring constantly. When sauce is thick and smooth, stir in cheese, mushrooms and pimientos. After cheese melts, stir in noodles and turkey. Pour mixture into 2½-quart casserole. Sprinkle top generously with crushed cornflakes and bake 40 minutes in preheated, 325° F. oven. This hot dish stores well in the freezer. Yields 6 servings.

*Field Lunch Tip: Take along an extra vacuum bottle of ice water,* the first aid kit and the transistor radio so the men can hear news and a little music.

## THERMOS HOT DISH
*Carry a hot dinner and cool beverage plus coffee to the field.*

3-4 onions, sliced
  Cooking oil *or* butter
1½ pounds ground beef
1 teaspoon salt
¼ teaspoon pepper

3 cups cooked macaroni (any shape) *or* rice
1 cup grated cheddar cheese
Chili powder (optional)

Saute onions in oil until clear and tender. Remove onions to 2-quart casserole. Season meat with salt and pepper, then brown in the skillet in which onions were cooked. Place ground beef, macaroni, cheese and chili powder, if you are using it, in the casserole. Stir ingredients well. Taste and add more salt if necessary. Bake in preheated, 350° F. oven for 20 to 30 minutes. Reheat hot dish in the morning then place in wide-mouth vacuum bottles which have been preheated with hot water. Yields 6 to 8 servings.

*Field Lunch Tip: Place a wide-mouth* vacuum bottle in the refrigerator, uncovered, overnight. The next morning, pack it full of ice cream and place it in the freezer. Wrap the bottle in a thick layer of newspaper just before leaving for the field.

*Field Lunch Tip: Hot food keeps best* when taken in the pan in which it is cooked. Pack hot pans on one another in a cardboard box, with flat lids for dividers and newspaper for support plus insulation.

*Field Lunch Tip: A gay little note or funny joke cut out of the papers or a magazine and tucked in on top of the lunch box can please a man if he's tired or in bad humor.*

## FIVE-LAYER FIELD DINNER
*Take along crisp, garden vegetables packed in ice.*

1 can (303 size) cream-style corn
3 good-size potatoes, sliced as for frying
½ teaspoon salt
1 large onion, chopped

1 pound ground beef, browned with 1 teaspoon salt
1 can (1-pound, 14-ounce) tomatoes

Layer ingredients in a casserole in the order given. Bake in preheated, 350° F. oven until done, about 1 hour. Slip the entire casserole, hot from the oven, into an insulated bag — the kind you get when buying frozen foods at the grocery store. Yields 6 to 8 servings.

## OINKY HOT SLAW
*Take along rolls, salad, canned or fresh fruit —*
*and plenty to drink for the hay crew,*
*according to a Northern Minnesota farm wife.*

6 thick pork chops *or* pork steaks
1 teaspoon salt
¼ teaspoon pepper
½ teaspoon paprika
Garlic
2 tablespoons chopped onion

1 quart sauerkraut
2 teaspoons sugar
1 cup hot water
1 cup soured cream
1 cup crushed potato chips, corn chips *or* buttered, dry bread crumbs

Brown chops in heavy skillet over medium heat. Season with salt, pepper, paprika and a trace of garlic. Place 3 chops in the bottom of a greased or foil-lined casserole. Cover with chopped onion and half of sauerkraut. Add remaining chops and kraut. Add hot water to the drippings in the pan. Pour broth over kraut and sprinkle with sugar. Pour sour cream over all and bake in preheated, 350° F. oven for 1½ hours. Uncover, sprinkle with crushed chips or crumbs and bake 15 minutes longer. Wrap well with newspaper or place in insulated basket to take to field. Yields 6 servings.

# HOT AND COLD SANDWICHES

## GULP AND GO BREAKFAST SANDWICHES
### *Great for lunch or supper, too.*

*Grilled Peanut Butter-Bacon Sandwiches:* Spread 1 tablespoon peanut butter on each slice of bread. Crumble a crisp-cooked bacon slice over peanut butter and top with a second slice of bread. Grill sandwiches in butter until golden brown on both sides. Garnish with fresh orange slices.

*Orange Cocoanut Toasties:* Allow 2 slices of ½-inch-thick French bread per serving. For 8 servings, combine ½ cup soft butter, ½ cup thick orange marmalade, 1½ teaspoons grated orange rind and ¼ teaspoon ground nutmeg. Spread 1 tablespoon of this mixture atop each slice of bread. Place on cookie sheet and sprinkle with flaked cocoanut. Bake at 400° F. for 5 minutes or until cocoanut is delicately toasted. Serve warm.

*Oven-Toasted Egg Salad Sandwiches:* Do this the night before — spread bread slices with your favorite egg salad mixture and top off with a slice of processed cheese. Cover with another slice of bread. Brush melted butter over outside surfaces of each sandwich. Place sandwiches on cookie sheet, cover with waxed paper or plastic film. Refrigerate. In the morning, place cookie sheet in 400° F. oven for 5 minutes, then turn sandwiches and toast other side. Or, grill sandwiches on both sides in skillet. Serve hot.

*Broiled Cheese Breakfast Sandwiches:* Place a slice of your favorite cheese on a slice of buttered toast. Slip under broiler until cheese melts — watch, this broils quickly. Top each slice of cheese toast with a slice or two of crisp bacon and a slice of tomato. Serve at once.

*Breakfast (Lunch or Supper) Sandwiches:* 12 bacon strips, 8 slices whole wheat or white bread, butter, maple-blended syrup. Cook bacon until crisp, drain. Place 3 strips for each serving between slices of bread. Spread both sides of the sandwich with the softened butter and saute until brown on both sides. Serve with the hot syrup. Yields 4 sandwiches.

## BOSTON SANDWICHES
### *Hearty!*

For each sandwich, spread a slice of white bread (crusts trimmed off) with mayonnaise and cover with hot, baked beans. Place a slice of mild cheese on each sandwich and top with a slice of partially cooked bacon. Place sandwich under the broiler until cheese melts and bacon is crisp. Garnish with green onions.

## SAVARIN CLUB SANDWICH
*Accompany with a cup of your favorite soup.*

For each sandwich, toast 3 slices of white or dark bread, butter inside slices. Arrange slices of cooked white turkey (breast), thinly sliced cooked ham and a crisply cooked bacon strip (cut in 4 pieces) on the bottom slice of toast, top with second slice of toast buttered on both sides. Top with thinly sliced tomatoes and lettuce leaves. Add third toast slice. Serve with potato chips and pickles. Yields 1 sandwich.

## RED DEVIL TURKEY SANDWICH
*Super supper!*

| | |
|---|---|
| 5 slices buttered toast | 1 can (10½-ounce) condensed cream of mushroom soup |
| 5 slices sharp cheddar cheese | |
| 5 large slices tomatoes | ½ soup can of broth, milk or water |
| Sliced cooked turkey *or* chicken to generously cover each slice of bread | Cayenne and mustard (optional) |
| | Paprika |

Arrange on a shallow baking pan for individual servings — toast topped with the cheese, tomato seasoned with salt and pepper, and the turkey. Blend soup with broth and season with cayenne and mustard, if desired. Top each sandwich with 3 or 4 tablespoons of the soup. Sprinkle with paprika. Bake in preheated, 425° F. oven until cheese begins to melt and top is browned, about 15 minutes. Yields 5 sandwiches.

## HAMBURGER CRUMBLE
*Serve tomato soup and a zippy green salad.*

| | |
|---|---|
| 1 tablespoon shortening | 1 tablespoon prepared |
| 1 pound lean ground beef | mustard |
| ¼ cup onion flakes | ½ teaspoon salt |
| 2 tablespoons flour | ¼ teaspoon pepper |
| ⅓ cup catsup | 1 cup dairy sour cream |
| | Toast *or* buns |

Brown meat in hot shortening. Mix next 6 ingredients. Simmer 5 to 10 minutes to thicken a little. Stir in sour cream. Heat through; do not boil. Serve hot on buttered toast or toasted buns. Yields 4 sandwiches.

## TAVERNS
*Chiliburger mix deluxe.*

| | |
|---|---|
| 2½ pounds ground beef | densed chicken |
| 5-6 large stalks celery, | gumbo soup |
|    cut fine | 2 tablespoons prepared |
| 1 large onion, grated | mustard |
| 1 cup catsup | 1 teaspoon chili powder |
| 1 can (10¾-ounce) con- | 2 tablespoons vinegar |
|    densed tomato soup | 2 tablespoons brown sugar |
| 1 can (10½-ounce) con- | 2 teaspoons salt |
| | ¼ teaspoon pepper |

Brown meat in melted shortening. Place meat in roaster with remaining ingredients and mix. Bake, uncovered, at 250° F. for 2 hours, stirring occasionally. Serve on buttered hamburger buns. Yields ½ cup filling for 12 to 14 buns.

## PIZZABURGERS
*Prepare ahead for evening company.*

| | |
|---|---|
| 1 pound ground beef | ¼ teaspoon oregano for |
|    Salt and pepper | each half a bun |
| 6 hamburger buns, split | 6 square slices of cheese |
| 1 can (6-ounce) tomato paste | cut into 4 strips |
|    *or* fresh tomato slices | |

Season hamburger with salt and pepper. Shape into patties. Pan broil until done. Spread tomato paste on each half of bun. Sprinkle with oregano. Top with hamburger patty and cheese strips in form of cross. Place under preheated broiler. Broil until cheese melts. Yields 6 sandwiches.

## MEAT AND POTATO SANDWICH
*Especially tasty with leftover roast or meat loaf.*

Slice cooked beef or pork and fry lightly in butter, so that the slices are warm. Spread each side with a heavy layer of mashed potato; press the potato down on the meat with a knife, or your hands. Roll the potato-covered meat in breadcrumbs and fry in hot butter or oil.

## HAM-ASPARAGUS DELUXE
*Great for evening company.*

24 spears cooked asparagus  
  6 slices boiled ham

  6 slices buttered Vienna bread  
  6 slices processed cheese

Wrap 4 asparagus spears in each ham slice and place each roll on a slice of bread. Cut cheese slices in half, diagonally. Slightly overlap 2 cheese triangles on each ham roll. Broil on a cookie sheet under low broiler for 5 minutes. Yields 6 sandwiches.

## LIVER SAUSAGE BURGERS
*Onion-lovers special from The Farmer, 1941.*

Cut liver sausage into ½-inch slices; 1 slice per sandwich. Brown in a small amount of fat. Split hamburger buns, toast both halves and spread with butter. Place slice of browned liver sausage on half a bun and put a slice of raw Spanish onion over it. Put the other half of the bun on top. Serve.

## SPECIAL HOT DOGS
*Pass relish, mustard and catsup.*

6 wieners
6 strips of cheese, 2 inches
  long and ⅓ inch thick

6 slices of bacon
6 hot dog buns, sliced

Make a slit in the side of each wiener, and place a cheese strip in it. Wrap a slice of bacon around the wiener and cheese and fasten it with a tooth pick. Broil until the bacon is nice and crisp.
Remove the toothpick, and pop the hot dogs into the buns. Yields 6 sandwiches.

## LOAF OF SANDWICHES

½ cup soft butter
2 teaspoons prepared
  mustard
1 teaspoon fine salad
  herbs
16 slices day-old bread

16 square slices
  process cheese
16 large slices bologna,
  salami *or* thuringer
16 tomato slices
16 green onions

Combine butter, mustard and herbs; mix well. Spread inside surfaces of bread with butter mixture. Fill one sandwich with 2 slices cheese, 2 slices meat folded in half, 2 tomato slices and 2 green onions with tops still on. Close sandwich and make remaining 7 sandwiches. Meat, onion and cheese will overlap edges of sandwiches a bit. Thread a long metal skewer through center of each sandwich and press sandwiches together to look like a loaf. Wrap loaf securely in aluminum foil. Place in preheated, 400° F. oven until cheese melts, about 30 to 40 minutes. Or, heat about 6 inches above low-glowing coals on the grill. Turn loaf once during heating. Yields 8 big sandwiches.

## SAUCY BURGERS
*Keep ingredients on hand for tasty lunches or snacks.*

1 can (12-ounce) luncheon
  meat, cut up
1 package (8-ounce)
  cheddar-type cheese

1 medium onion, cut up
1 can (15-ounce) chili
  without beans
8 hamburger buns

Put meat, cheese and onion in blender; blend until thoroughly mixed and chopped. Stir in chili. Spread on hamburger bun halves. Place under broiler until heated through. Yields 16 sandwiches.

## TUNA WRAP-UPS
*Great supper when you're in a hurry to get to a basketball game.*

1 can (7-ounce) tuna
½ cup salad dressing
½ cup grated, mild,
  processed cheese

1 tablespoon grated onion
6 sandwich buns, split
  and buttered

Mix tuna, dressing, cheese and onion. Spread on bottom half of each bun; top with other bun half. Wrap each sandwich in aluminum foil and bake in preheated, 300° F. oven for 20 minutes. Yields 6 sandwiches.

## PARTY SANDWICH LOAF
*These pretty loaves can be a luncheon meal by themselves.*

Cut the crusts from a 1½-pound unsliced loaf of white or whole wheat bread. Cut the loaf into 4 or 5 lengthwise slices. Butter the inner sides of the slices and spread each layer with a different filling.

Be sure to cut the bread thin enough and spread the fillings thick enough so that the bread does not dominate.

Mix and match the fillings on page 200 to suit your taste. The combinations we liked were: 1, 5 and 7; 4, 8 and 9; 6, 3, 2 and 10.

Wrap the loaf firmly in a moist towel, chill well, unwrap and place on a platter. Frost with a cream cheese frosting.

Store, refrigerated, in a tightly-covered container until serving time. Place on a party serving plate and garnish prettily to complement table decorations. Cut 1-inch-wide slices for each guest as they pass through the buffet line. Or, place sandwich loaf and stack of luncheon plates before hostess at the table where she cuts the loaf and serves guests. Place coffee cups, saucers and coffee pot at other end of table; ask someone to serve coffee at the same time, passing plates and cups of coffee up opposite sides of the table to guests.

*Bread slices* may be used to make a large sandwich loaf. Trim crusts from the number of slices you need. Use 3 slices, placed end to end, for each layer. You'll need 12 slices for a loaf with 3 fillings; 15 slices for a loaf with 4 fillings.

*Individual loaves* may be made by stacking 4 or 5 slices of thin-sliced bread (crusts removed) with filling between. Then cut each stack in half and frost with cheese mixture and garnish.

*Round Sandwich Loaf:* Cut a 1½-pound round loaf of bread into 4 or 5 horizontal slices, trimming off crusts. Spread bread with butter and fill. Many bakeries will make a round loaf of bread on request.

## FILLINGS

1. *Olive Egg Spread:* Mash 3 hard-cooked eggs. Blend in ¼ cup mayonnaise, ½ teaspoon salt, ½ teaspoon prepared mustard, 1 tablespoon chopped parsley and ⅓ cup chopped ripe olives.

2. *Egg Salad Spread:* Lightly mix until just blended — 6 chopped, hard-cooked eggs, 6 tablespoons dairy sour cream, ¼ cup finely-chopped green pepper, 2 teaspoons finely-chopped onion, 1½ teaspoons salt, 1 teaspoon prepared mustard.

3. *Cheddar Cheese Spread:* Mix until smooth, 1 cup (4-ounce) shredded cheddar cheese at room temperature, 2 tablespoons light cream, 1 tablespoon dairy sour cream, 1½ teaspoons minced onion, ½ teaspoon dry mustard, ¼ teaspoon Worcestershire sauce, ⅛ teaspoon celery salt, dash of garlic salt. Cover and chill to blend flavors. Spread as a thin layer.

4. *Cheese-Pecan Spread:* Blend thoroughly, 1 package (3-ounce) softened cream cheese, 1 cup finely-chopped pecans, ¾ cup (9-ounce) well-drained crushed pineapple.

5. *Ripe Olive Spread:* Combine ¾ cup chopped, ripe olives with 2½ tablespoons mayonnaise.

6. *Liver Spread:* Beat together until well blended, ½ pound liver sausage, 1 tablespoon lemon juice, 1 tablespoon grated onion, 1 tablespoon dairy sour cream, 2 teaspoons sweet pickle relish, 2 drops Tabasco sauce.

7. *Deviled Ham Spread:* Combine 1 can (4½-ounce) deviled ham, ⅓ cup chopped, ripe olives and 2 tablespoons well-drained pickle relish.

8. *Chicken-Bacon Spread:* Blend well, 8 slices crumbled crisp bacon, 1 cup finely-chopped cooked chicken, ¼ cup mayonnaise, 1 tablespoon finely-chopped pimiento, ¼ teaspoon salt, ⅛ teaspoon pepper.

9. *Shrimp Spread:* 1 chopped hard-cooked egg, 1⅓ cups (7-ounce can) chopped shrimp, ¼ cup minced celery, 2 tablespoons lemon juice, ¼ teaspoon salt, dash pepper, ¼ cup mayonnaise.

10. *Lobster Spread:* Toss together lightly, 1 can (5-ounce) drained chopped lobster, 1 cup chopped celery, ¼ teaspoon grated lemon rind, 2 teaspoons lemon juice, ½ teaspoon onion salt, ⅛ teaspoon pepper. Gently blend in ⅓ cup dairy sour cream.

## FROSTINGS

*Sour Cream Cheese Frosting:* In a small mixing bowl, beat together 2 packages (8-ounce each) and 1 package (3-ounce) softened cream cheese, 2 tablespoons dairy sour cream and 2 teaspoon grated onion. Spread on sides and top of chilled sandwich loaf. Garnish loaf with slices of radishes, parsley and sliced, stuffed olives. Chill until served.

*Mint Green Frosting:* Mix the following ingredients well and spread over sides and top of chilled sandwich loaf — 2 packages (8-ounce each) softened cream cheese, ½ cup half-and-half cream, 2 drops green food coloring. Garnish loaf with half slices of unpeeled cucumber and snipped parsley. Chill loaf until serving time.

*Light Frosting:* For those who do not want a very thick layer of frosting, blend 1 package (8-ounce) softened cream cheese with 1 tablespoon milk. Garnish with ripe olive quarters, parsley and carrot curls.

## HONEY-SWEET PEANUT BUTTER SANDWICH
*Youngsters love this nourishing combination.*

½ cup peanut butter
¼ cup honey
2 teaspoons grated orange
    rind

½ cup ripe banana, chopped
12 slices whole wheat *or*
    white bread
Butter

Blend peanut butter, honey and orange rind until smooth. Add banana and mix lightly until blended. Spread bread with butter. Spread peanut butter mixture on 6 slices bread. Cover with remaining bread slices. Yields 6 sandwiches.

*Toast it:* Butter outside of sandwich and brown to golden toast on both sides in a skillet.

## TUNA SANDWICH SPREAD
*This make-ahead is really special and great to have on hand.*

1 tablespoon cornstarch
½ cup butter
¼ teaspoon salt
½ cup milk

½ cup processed cheese,
    diced
1 cup mayonnaise
1 can (7-ounce) tuna,
    drained and flaked

Mix first 5 ingredients in double boiler and cook over hot water until smooth. Cool mixture a little; then add mayonnaise and tuna. Mix well to blend. Store in refrigerator until ready to use. Yields filling for about 8 sandwiches.

## JUMBO JIGGS
*Fall special when cabbage is plentiful.*

1 quart cabbage, finely
    shredded
¼ cup green onion,
    chopped
⅓ cup salad dressing

1 teaspoon prepared
    mustard
12 slices corned beef
12 slices rye bread,
    buttered

Combine first 4 ingredients and mix well. Spread on 6 slices of bread. Top with 2 slices of meat and remaining bread. Can be made with hard rolls. Yields 6 sandwiches.

## GOURMET CHICKEN SANDWICHES
*Party-nice if you trim crusts from bread.*

1 can (5-ounce) boned
  chicken
½ cup finely-chopped
  celery
½ cup finely-chopped
  cucumber

¼ cup chopped nuts
  (optional)
⅛ teaspoon salt
⅓ cup mayonnaise
16 slices white *or* whole
  wheat bread

Chop chicken and combine with celery, cucumber, nuts and salt. Add only enough mayonnaise to moisten, about ⅓ cup. Spread bread with softened butter. Use about 3 tablespoons of filling for each sandwich. Yields 8 sandwiches.

*To ground left-over ham,* add chopped raw apple, celery, a dash of salt and a little mayonnaise plus ½ teaspoon of either oregano or marjoram. Mix well and spread on buttered toasted buns.

## SESAME PORK SPREAD
*Use for canapes, too.*

½ cup dairy sour cream
2 tablespoons toasted
  sesame seeds
1½ teaspoons prepared
  mustard

½ teaspoon salt
1½ cups finely-chopped,
  cold, roast pork

Combine first 4 ingredients in mixing bowl; mix. Fold in pork and chill. Yields about 2 cups sandwich spread.

*Sesame Pork Sandwiches:* Spread 8 buttered whole wheat, oat, rye or white bread toast slices with Sesame Pork Spread. Cover with slices of tomato, pickle and crisp lettuce leaves. Top each with a second slice of buttered toast. Cut diagonally to serve. Yields 8 sandwiches.

## BAVARIAN SANDWICHES
*Add a mug of hot, creamy soup to make a meal.*

For each sandwich, spread a slice of rye bread with mayonnaise. Cover with drained sauerkraut, a slice of cooked ham and a slice of Swiss cheese. Top with a stuffed olive on a toothpick.

## MAKING BUTTER
*Country treat.*

1-1½ quarts cream, at least       1 scant tablespoon salt
    30% butterfat                Water

If cream is unpasteurized, heat it until it begins to rise in the pan. Then remove it from heat, let cream settle and repeat the procedure twice more. Cool cream by putting the pan into cold water. Pour cream into a glass container, cover and refrigerate for several days. Cream has to be at least 24 hours old to churn well.

Ripen cream before churning by letting it stand at room temperature 4 to 6 hours. Cream will thicken and become slightly sour, giving the butter its good taste. Cool cream again in the refrigerator.

Next, pour cream into large, electric mixer bowl. Don't use more than 1½ quarts of cream to keep spattering at a minimum. Add a few drops of butter color, if desired. Beat cream at high speed until butter flecks begin to form. Beat at low speed until butter separates from milk. Watch carefully to keep spattering down and use a spatula to push cream down sides of bowl as it whips.

Pour off buttermilk and add about as much cold water as there was buttermilk. Let beater run at lowest speed. Pour off water and repeat. Add salt into butter with mixer. Remove beaters, scrape and work water out of butter by pressing it against side of bowl with spatula. *Work out all water.*

Store butter in container with tight-fitting lid. Refrigerate or freeze. One quart cream yields about 1 pound butter.

*Shaking Method:* Though it's much slower, butter may also be made by shaking prepared cream back and forth in a tightly-covered jar which is larger than the amount of cream used. When butter forms, wash, press out water and form as described above.

# QUICK AND
# YEAST BREADS

## YEAST BREADS

Yeast breads are made light by the growth of the yeast plant, a live thing which needs moisture, food, air and warmth. Under favorable conditions the yeast plant divides and multiplies very rapidly, giving off a gas which is held in by the dough until it is baked. Since it is a live plant, it needs many of the same things that all plants require: warmth, moisture, air, food. Important things to remember in baking bread are:

*Good flour:* Use a kind you can depend upon to be uniform from one season or sack to another.

*Temperature of sponge and dough:* Between 80° and 85° is best. In cold weather when room and flour are cool, use warmer water and set the dough in a closed cupboard with a bowl of hot water beside it. In summer, cool liquids more than usual so that the sponge is not too warm. A dairy thermometer in the sponge or dough is helpful.

*Method used:* The sponge method means that the yeast plant is allowed to develop before the dough is mixed entirely stiff. If a sponge is set overnight, be sure that it doesn't get too cool or too hot, or the bread will be of poor quality. The straight dough method means that all of the flour is added at the start. Many prefer this method since it eliminates one mixing and longer rising.

*Kneading:* This helps develop gluten. Knead with a light, springy motion, using the "heel" part of the palm, near the wrist, for at least 10 minutes. Curve fingers to keep dough round and full.

*Making into loaves:* Shape, using little or no flour. Allow dough to stand a few minutes between cutting for loaves and shaping so it will regain its elasticity and keep alive and tender.

*Baking temperatures:* Oven should be hot enough, pre-heated to 400° F. to 425° F., to set the loaf in the first 15 minutes. Bake loaf until it sounds hollow when tapped sharply with tips of finger — 40 to 50 minutes. A well-baked loaf is brown all over with bottom and sides lighter than top; has a crisp, even crust, and an even texture throughout.

*Using Instant-Blend Yeasts:* Combine yeast, any seasonings and enough flour to equal the total measure of liquid, shortening and eggs in the recipe. Heat milk, fat, sugar and salt until just warm. Stir occasionally to melt fat. Add milk mixture to dry ingredients; add egg, and beat with mixer at low speed for ½ minute, scraping sides of bowl constantly.

Beat 3 minutes at high speed. Continue adding flour to make a kneadable dough, as recipe specifies.

## FLAVORED BUTTERS FOR SUPPER BREADS
*Pre-butter and heat loaf —
or let guests select their favorite spread.*

*Cheese-Garlic Butter:* Blend ½ cup softened butter, ¼ teaspoon garlic powder, ¼ cup grated Parmesan cheese. Yields about ½ cup spread.

*Chili-Olive Butter:* Blend ½ cup softened butter, ¼ teaspoon chili powder, 2 tablespoons finely chopped ripe olives. Yields about ½ cup spread.

*Chivy Butter:* Blend ½ cup softened butter, 1 tablespoon minced chives, 2 teaspoons Worcestershire sauce. Yields about ½ cup spread.

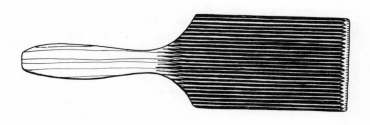

*Serve fancy butter* pats, two or three on a butter plate at each place.

Use firm butter as it comes from the refrigerator. Cut ½-inch-thick slices from each butter stick and form shapes with miniature cooky and garnish cutters available at the variety and hardware store. (Save trimmings for cooking.) Or, cut balls out of butter with your melon ball cutter. Garnish with bits of minced parsley and chill butter designs well before serving.

*Use a heated knife* to cut hot bread and the latter will not be soggy. — From The Farmer, 1887.

## WHITE BREAD
### *Light, moist classic.*

2 cups milk *or* 1 cup milk
and 1 cup water
1 package dry yeast *or*
small square compressed
yeast
¼ cup warm (105°-115° F.)
water for dry yeast or
lukewarm (80°-90° F.)

water for compressed
yeast
2 tablespoons sugar
1 tablespoon salt
2 tablespoons soft
shortening
5-6 cups all-purpose flour

Scald milk, add cold water, or cool milk until it is luke-warm. Soften yeast in ¼ cup warm water. Add sugar to milk mixture; stir to dissolve. Add and blend in yeast. Add 3 cups flour. Beat mixture vigorously until smooth, about 100 strokes, or 2 to 3 minutes with mixer at low speed.

Blend in soft shortening and salt. Gradually add remaining flour to form a ball that clings to the spoon and cleans the bowl. Turn dough onto lightly floured surface. Cover with greased bowl and let rest 10 minutes.

Knead dough 5 to 10 minutes. Add a little flour if necessary to form a smooth, velvety ball. There should be tiny blisters under the surface.

Place dough in greased bowl and turn it over to coat entire surface with a thin film of fat. Cover and let dough rise at 80° to 85° F. until doubled in bulk, 1½ to 2 hours. Punch dough down, let rise until doubled again, about ½ hour.

Turn dough onto lightly floured surface. Divide in half and round into balls. Cover and let rest 10 minutes.

Shape balls into loaves. Place in greased pans. Grease top of loaves lightly with oil or melted shortening. Cover lightly and let rise at 80° to 85° F. until doubled in bulk or until the imprint of your finger remains when you touch the dough lightly on the side.

Bake loaves in preheated, 400° F. oven for 35 to 45 minutes. Turn loaves onto racks. Grease tops lightly with melted butter or shortening; cool. Yields two 1-pound loaves.

*Use ¼ cup nonfat dry milk* mixed with the flour. Use 2 cups warm water for liquid.

*Use half whole wheat or rye flour.* Use brown sugar, honey or molasses for sweetening.

*Add ½ to 1 cup nuts or dried fruit* or both to white or dark doughs.

## BREAD FROM POTATO STARTER-SPONGE

| | |
|---|---|
| 1 potato | 5 tablespoons sugar |
| 4 cups potato water | 3½-4 cups all-purpose flour |
| 1 package dry yeast | |

*Starter-Sponge:* In the evening, peel and cut up potato; cook in water. Remove potato, saving water, and mash. Add mashed potato to potato water and cool until warm. Dissolve yeast in warm potato water; mix well. Beat in sugar and enough flour, about 3½ to 4 cups, to make a batter the consistency of muffin dough. Cover the bowl and leave it on the table, or some place free of drafts, overnight.

In the morning, place one cup of the sponge in a covered jar and put in the refrigerator until ready to make more bread. Use this starter in place of the yeast when setting the sponge (above) in the evening.

*White Bread:* To remaining sponge, beat in 1 tablespoon salt, ⅓ cup shortening, 1 tablespoon sugar and as much flour as possible — about 5 cups. Turn dough onto floured board and knead until blistered in appearance. Set in a warm place to rise, as dough is cool and needs warming. When double in bulk, punch down. Shape into desired rolls or bread loaves; grease tops; cover, and let rise until double in bulk. Bake in 350° F. oven until crust sounds hollow when tapped sharply with your finger. Yields 2 large or 3 medium loaves.

*Cinnamon or Apple Cake:* From The Farmer, 1896. The Germans make a kind of bread that they call by a word meaning "coffee cake." Take enough of your bread sponge to make a loaf of bread; add ½ cup butter and 1 cup sugar, a few raisins, and a little nutmeg if you like; mix and knead with flour to a very soft dough; let rise, roll or spread on tins till not more than an inch thick; let rise again; when nearly ready for oven spread with sweet cream or melted butter, and sprinkle with sugar and cinnamon. Very nice with coffee. Sometimes sliced apples or pie-plant are put on the cakes, when ready for the oven; then cream and sugar. Some consider this superior to pie. Italian plums, pitted and sliced are also very good. Bake in preheated, 350° F. oven.

*Pocket Books:* Instead of putting the dough on tins, roll out thin, cut with biscuit cutter, spread with butter, sugar and cinnamon, fold together, let rise and bake.

## ORANGE RAISIN BREAD
*Freeze some!*

2 packages dry *or*
  compressed yeast
2 cups water
  (105°-115° F.)
1 can (6-ounce) frozen
  orange juice,
  undiluted
⅔ cup sugar

⅔ cup butter
4 tablespoons salt
1 cup raisins, ground
4 quarters fresh orange,
  seeded and ground
About 20 cups
  all-purpose flour

Scald milk; stir in sugar, butter, orange juice and salt; cool to lukewarm. Measure warm water into a large warm bowl. Sprinkle or crumble in yeast, stir until dissolved. Add lukewarm milk mixture. Stir in 8 or 10 cups of flour, beat until smooth. Add ground raisins and orange. Add rest of flour as needed to make a soft dough. Turn out on lightly floured board, knead until smooth and elastic at least 10 minutes. Form into loaves to fit 9x5-inch greased pans. Let rise in warm place until doubled. Bake in preheated, 375° F. oven for 40 minutes, or until loaf sounds hollow when tapped. Yields 6 loaves.

## OATMEAL YEAST BREAD
*Try this for toast, too.*

2 packages dry yeast
½ cup warm water
  (110°-115° F.)
3 cups milk, scalded
⅔ cup shortening
½ cup sugar

2 tablespoons salt
6½-7 cups sifted,
  all-purpose flour
3 cups rolled oats
  (quick or old-
  fashioned, uncooked)
Sesame seeds

Soften yeast in lukewarm water. Pour scalded milk over shortening, sugar and salt. Cool to lukewarm. Stir in 1 cup flour; add softened yeast and oats. Stir in enough additional flour to make a soft dough.

Turn out on lightly-floured board or canvas; knead until smooth and satiny, about 10 minutes. Round dough into ball; place in greased bowl; brush lightly with melted shortening. Cover and let rise in warm place until double in size, about 1 hour. Punch dough down; cover; let rest 10 minutes. Divide dough into 3 equal parts. Shape to form loaves. Place in greased 8½x4½x2½-inch loaf pan. Cut diagonal slashes, about 1 inch apart and ¼ inch deep. Brush lightly with melted shortening. Sprinkle with sesame seed.

Cover; let rise until nearly double in size, about 45 minutes. Bake in preheated, 375° F. oven about 50 minutes, or until golden brown. Remove from pans; brush with melted butter. Yields 3 loaves.

## PUMPERNICKEL RYE BREAD
*Dark and delicious!*

| | |
|---|---|
| 3 packages dry yeast | 1 tablespoon salt |
| 1½ cups warm water (110°-115° F.) | 2 tablespoons soft shortening |
| ½ cup molasses | 2¾ cups sifted rye flour |
| 1-3 tablespoons caraway seeds | 3¼-3¾ cups sifted, all-purpose flour |

Add yeast to warm water in a large bowl; let stand 3 to 5 minutes; stir to dissolve. Stir in molasses, caraway, salt, shortening, rye flour and a little white flour. Beat until smooth — about 100 strokes. Add more flour, a little at a time, until dough is quite stiff; mix in with hands.

Since Pumpernickel dough is rather sticky, rub flour into cloth or board well before kneading, so bread does not pick up too much flour and become too stiff. Grease fingers before kneading for easier handling.

Turn dough onto lightly-floured board or cloth and knead until smooth. Round up and place in greased bowl, turning once. Cover and let rise 1½ to 2 hours. A dent remains when finger is pressed deep into side of dough. Punch down dough. Turn onto board; divide into two parts; cover and let rest 10 minutes.

Round up each part into a smooth ball. Place on opposite corners of a cornmeal-sprinkled baking sheet. Cover and let rise 30 to 45 minutes. Dent remains when finger is pressed gently on side of dough. Just before baking, stab tops of loaves 3 or 4 times with floured skewer or similar utensil. This prevents edges of round rye loaves from cracking.

Bake in preheated, 375° F. oven for 40 to 50 minutes, or until well browned. For a chewy crust, brush tops of loaves with warm water several times during baking, after the first 20 minutes. Remove from pan and cool on rack. Yields 2 loaves.

## BISCUIT AND PANCAKE STARTER
*Keep the starter going as long as you want.*

4 cups warm water  
¼ cup sugar  
1 cake compressed yeast  
   *or* 1 package dry yeast

6 cups sifted, all-purpose flour

*Starter-Sponge:* Dissolve yeast in warm water. Dissolve sugar in mixture. Add flour and beat until smooth. Let mixture stand overnight on kitchen table, in large, covered container, 4 to 5-quart size.

*New Starter:* Use half the batter each time you make biscuits or pancakes. To the other half of starter add 2 cups warm water, 2 tablespoons sugar and 3 cups sifted flour. Beat well, place in a covered container and keep in refrigerator.

*Starter Biscuits:* To ½ of starter add ¼ cup cooled, melted shortening, 2 teaspoons salt. Beat this in well. Add enough flour to make a soft dough, about 1½ to 2 cups. Turn on floured board and knead about 15 times. Make into 16 little round biscuits, and place side by side in greased 9-inch-square pan. Let rise in warm place until double in bulk. Bake at 400° F. about 20 minutes.

*Dark Biscuits:* Follow white biscuit recipe, but substitute 1 cup whole wheat flour for 1 of white. Add 1 tablespoon molasses with shortening and salt.

*Starter Pancakes:* To ½ of starter, add 2 beaten eggs, ⅓ cup melted shortening, 1 teaspoon salt, 1 teaspoon sugar and enough water to make a pouring batter. Pour onto hot griddle. Bake until bubbles break all over tops of cake, turn and brown other side. Turn only once.

## DOUBLE BUNS
*Superb dough to handle! This old-fashioned, Low German roll is distinguished by the tiny, tippy top bun.*

3 cups milk  
1 cup lukewarm water  
2 packages dry yeast  
1¼ cups lard

4 teaspoons salt  
7 tablespoons sugar  
11-12 cups sifted, all-purpose flour

Scald milk and cool to lukewarm. Dissolve yeast in water. Mix lard, milk, salt and sugar. Add yeast mixture, then flour.

Mix well and knead. Dough should be slightly softer than bread dough. Cover and let rise until double in bulk. Form ⅔ of dough into balls about 2 inches in diameter; rest of dough into balls about 1 inch in diameter. Place a small ball on top of each large ball. Cover and let rise about 1 hour. Bake on greased pan in preheated, 400° F. oven for 20 to 25 minutes. Yields about 4 dozen buns.

### FANCY ROLLS — A CINCH TO SHAPE
*Fancy dinner rolls are no more work*
*than any other kind when you follow these*
*simple directions.*

Bake the rolls at 400° F., for 12 to 15 minutes. Brush them with butter when you take them from the oven.

*Fan-tans:* Roll or pat the dough into a rectangle about ¼ inch thick. Brush the top with melted butter. Cut the dough into strips 1 inch wide. Place 5 to 8 strips one on top of another. Cut into pieces about 1½ inches long. Place each short pile on end in a greased muffin cup.

*Crescents:* Roll or pat the dough into circles about 10 inches in diameter and ¼ inch thick. Cut the dough into 12 pie-shaped pieces and brush with soft butter. Begin at the outer edge and roll the dough to the point and press together. Curve the rolled dough slightly to form a crescent and place it, pointed side underneath, on a greased baking sheet.

*Cloverleaf:* Make balls of dough of a size that 3 balls half fill a cup of a muffin pan. Dip each ball in melted butter and place, butter side up, in greased cups of muffin pans.

*Parkerhouse:* Roll or pat the dough about ½ inch thick. Brush the top with soft butter and cut the dough with a biscuit cutter. Fold each circle over, butter side in, to form a half circle. Press the outer edges together firmly and place on a greased baking sheet.

*Sandwich buns:* Divide raised dough in pieces size of a large egg. Shape into balls and let rest on board about 30 minutes, covering to prevent crusting. Shape each into a round or oblong and place on greased tin. Let rise to double bulk before baking.

## BASIC ROLL DOUGH
*Freeze some!*

| | |
|---|---|
| 5 cups hot scalded milk | 4 packages instant dis- |
| 1 cup sugar | solving yeast |
| 1 cup shortening (½ lard, | 16 cups all-purpose flour |
| ¼ butter, ¼ homo- | (about) |
| genized shortening) | 1 cup beaten eggs |
| 2½ tablespoons salt | (4 or 5 eggs) |
| 2 cups boiling water | |

Add sugar, shortening and salt to hot milk; stir to dissolve. Stir in boiling water and set mixture aside to cool. Mix yeast with 7 cups flour and pour into cooled liquid mixture. Stir in eggs. Add more flour until you can't stir dough any more.

Cover and let rest 10 minutes. Knead in enough more flour to make a smooth, elastic dough. Oil dough and bowl; turn dough; cover and let rise in warm, draft-free place until doubled in bulk, about 1½ hours. Punch down, round up, cover top and let rest 5 to 10 minutes. Shape into rolls or buns. Place in oiled pans; cover and let rise until doubled, about 1 hour. Preheat oven to 400° F. Place rolls in hot oven and *immediately* turn oven to 375° F. Bake buns 20 minutes (medium-size parker house rolls 25 minutes) until nicely browned. Remove rolls from pans; spread tops with butter while hot. Place rolls on racks to cool. Yields 9 dozen medium-size rolls.

## KOLACKY
*A really old-time Bohemian recipe from*
*LeSueur County, Minnesota.*

| | |
|---|---|
| 1 cup milk | 1 egg, beaten with |
| 1 cup potato water | beater until frothy |
| ½ cup butter | 1 teaspoon salt |
| 1 large cake | 6-7½ cups all-purpose flour |
| yeast | Sprinkle of nutmeg |
| ½ cup sugar | Pinch of ginger |

Scald milk and potato water together. Add butter to hot liquid and cool mixture to lukewarm. Add broken yeast and stir until yeast dissolves. Mix in sugar, beaten egg, salt and spices. Mix in 4 cups flour; continue adding flour until dough is soft, not sticky, and easily handled. Knead dough about 10 minutes. Place dough in greased bowl, cover and set in warm, draft-free spot. Let rise until double in bulk. Punch down and let rise again. Punch down and shape. Yields about 5 dozen 2-inch squares.

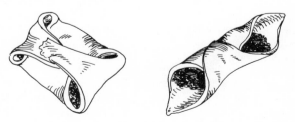

There are several ways to shape kolacky dough. A fast way is to roll a portion of dough out to about ½-inch thickness, then cut into 2-inch squares. Put a spoonful of filling in center then fold points together — see sketch — and pinch to hold in place. Place on greased pan. Cover and let rise again, about ½ hour. Bake in preheated, 375° F. oven about 25 minutes. Just before baking, brush tops with beaten egg mixed with a little milk for a darker, crusty, shiny top.

*Other Shapes:* Cut a circle of dough with a round cutter, make a depression in the center and place a spoonful of filling in the depression. Or, cut the 2-inch squares, but only fold over the two opposite corners.

*Mixed Fruit Filling:* May be made ahead of time. Simmer 1 package (12-ounce) mixed dry fruit in ¾ cup water for 30 minutes. Pour off water and cool fruit. Pit fruits that need pitting. Grind fruit and stir in ½ cup sugar and ½ teaspoon cinnamon. Yields 1 tablespoon filling for 5 dozen kolacky made from 2-inch squares of dough.

*Cottage Cheese Filling:* Mix 2 cups cottage cheese, ¼ cup sugar, ½ teaspoon cinnamon, ⅓ cup seedless raisins, ½ cup shredded coconut, 1 egg yolk. Yields 1 tablespoon filling for 5 dozen kolacky made from 2-inch squares of dough.

*Date Filling:* Boil 4 cups snipped dates, ¾ cup sugar, ½ cup butter for 5 minutes, 'til thick. Remove from heat, stir in 1 teaspoon vanilla. Cool. Yields 1 tablespoon filling for 4 dozen kolacky made from 2-inch squares of dough.

*Poppy Seed Filling:* Mix 2 cups poppy seeds, ground fine, with ½ cup milk, ½ cup dark corn syrup, 1 teaspoon butter and ⅛ teaspoon cinnamon. Cook over medium heat until thickened. Cool. Yields 1 tablespoon filling for 4 dozen kolacky made from 2-inch squares of dough.

## HOT CROSS BUNS
### *Good Friday tradition.*

| | |
|---|---|
| ½ cup lukewarm water | 2 teaspoons cinnamon |
| 2 packages dry yeast | ½ teaspoon allspice |
| 1¼ cups lukewarm milk | ½ cup melted shortening |
| ¾ cup sugar | 2 eggs (⅓ cup) |
| 1 teaspoon salt | 1 cup raisins *or* currants |
| 6½ cups sifted, all-purpose flour | Confectioners' Sugar Icing, page 250 |

Dissolve yeast in lukewarm water 5 minutes. Mix milk, sugar and salt until dissolved. Stir in 2 cups of flour sifted with spices; beat in shortening, eggs and softened yeast. Add currants or raisins, and enough flour to make a soft dough. Turn out on floured board. Knead until dough becomes smooth and elastic and is no longer sticky, about 10 minutes. Place in greased bowl. Grease top of dough and cover with waxed paper. Let rise in warm place (80°-85° F.) until doubled, 1½ to 2 hours. Shape into 2-inch buns and place side by side in greased pans. Let rise until light, about 45 minutes. Before baking, snip top of buns with scissors or knife to form a cross. Bake in preheated, 375° F. oven for 20 to 25 minutes. Remove from oven and brush tops with melted butter or confectioners' sugar icing, page 250. Cool slightly, then fill cross with confectioners' sugar icing. Yields 36 buns.

## BASIC SWEET ROLL DOUGH
*Makes delectable plain rolls or fancy rolls and coffee breads.*

| | |
|---|---|
| 2 packages dry yeast | 1 teaspoon salt |
| ½ cup lukewarm water | 2 eggs |
| ½ cup lukewarm milk | ½ cup soft shortening |
| ½ cup sugar | 4½-5 cups all-purpose flour |

Soften yeast in water for about 5 minutes. Meanwhile, mix milk, sugar and salt. Stir in yeast mixture, then eggs. Mix flour in with a spoon, then your hands until you have added enough to make a dough that is easy to handle. Turn dough onto lightly floured surface and knead until smooth, about 10 minutes. Oil top of dough and place in an oiled, covered bowl. Place in a warm, draft-free place to rise until double in bulk, about 1½ to 2 hours. Punch down, cover and let rise again. After second rising, divide dough for rolls or coffee cakes. Round up and let rest 15 minutes so dough is easy to handle. Shape and let rise until light, 15 to 30 minutes. Bake plain rolls in preheated, 425° F. oven for 12 to 20 minutes. Yields 3 dozen plain rolls.

*Rosebud Rolls* — Roll out a piece of dough 4x4 inches square. Spread with a little cherry, raspberry or strawberry jam. Do not fill full. Fold corners in, pinch together. Snip a cross on top of roll. Use half of sweet roll dough to make 1½ dozen rolls. Place rolls in lightly greased pan, snipped side up. Cover and let rise until double in bulk, about 1½ hours. Bake in preheated, 400° F. oven for 12 to 15 minutes.

*Caramel Rolls* — Mix ⅓ cup melted butter, ½ cup brown sugar, 1 tablespoon corn syrup (and ½ cup broken pecans if desired) in bottom of a 9x13-inch pan. Roll out half of sweet roll dough into a 8x12x½-inch length. Spread with 2 tablespoons soft butter and sprinkle with ½ cup brown sugar and 2 teaspoons cinnamon. Roll up dough tightly, jelly-roll-fashion. Begin at wide side. Seal edges by pinching edges as you roll. Cut roll into 12 slices. Place in pan, cut side up. Cover; let rise until double in bulk, about 35 to 40 minutes. Bake in preheated, 375° F. oven for 25 to 35 minutes.

*Tasty Orange Rolls* — Mix ½ cup sugar, ½ cup soft butter, grated rind of one orange. Roll out half of sweet roll dough into 8x12x½-inch length. Spread with orange mixture. Roll up, beginning at wide side. Roll tightly and seal edges well by pinching together as you roll. Cut into 12 sections and place, cut side up, in greased 9x9-inch pan or 12 muffin cups. Bake in preheated, 375° F. oven for 25 to 35 minutes.

*Easter Egg Buns:* Form ⅓ recipe of sweet roll dough into 12 small balls; place on greased cookie sheet; cover and let rise 15 minutes. Dye 12 uncooked eggs according to dye package directions. Cut each piece of dough half through in center at top of each round; place a colored egg in each cut. Sprinkle buns with sugar. Cover, let rise until double in bulk; about 1 hour. Bake in preheated, 325° F. oven about 25 minutes. Yields 12 buns.

## DANISH COFFEE TWIST
### *Pretty! Delicious warm.*

| | |
|---|---|
| 1 recipe Basic Sweet Roll dough, page 217 | 1 tablespoon soft butter |
| 3 tablespoons sugar | ¼ cup slivered blanched almonds |
| ½ teaspoon cinnamon | Honey Glaze |

Make Basic Sweet Dough. When dough has doubled, punch down. Shape into a ball. Cover and let rest 5 minutes. While dough rests, mix sugar and cinnamon. Flatten ball of dough, then roll out to form long narrow sheet about 6 inches wide and ¼ inch thick. Spread with soft butter. Sprinkle with sugar-cinnamon mixture. Roll up to make long, slender roll. Seal edge by pressing firmly. Twist roll by pushing ends in opposite directions. Lift to lightly greased baking sheet and shape into a large pretzel. Tuck ends of roll under edge of "pretzel" to keep dough from untwisting. Cover and let rise until doubled, about 1 hour. Bake in preheated, 350° F. oven for 25 to 30 minutes. While coffee twist bakes, make Honey Glaze. Brush hot glaze over twist as soon as it comes from oven. Sprinkle with slivered almonds. Remove from baking sheet to cooling rack. Yields 1 large coffee cake.

*Honey Glaze:* Measure 2 tablespoons sugar, ¼ cup honey and 1 tablespoon butter into a small saucepan. Bring to a boil, stirring constantly. While still hot, brush on baked Danish Coffee Twist.

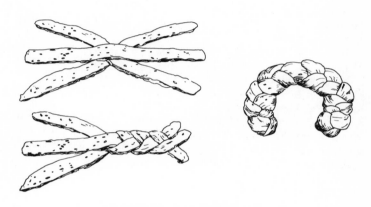

## CARDAMOM COFFEE BRAID
*Swedish delight with butter and honey.*

1 recipe Basic Sweet Roll
  dough, page 217
1 teaspoon ground cardamom
1 cup slivered almonds

Egg yolk mixed with a
  little water
Sugar

Make basic sweet roll dough as directed, adding cardamom and almonds with eggs. After dough rises the second time, punch down and let rest 15 minutes. Roll out into 8x24-inch rectangle. Cut lengthwise into 3 equal strips. Criss cross two strips and place last strip straight up and down on top. Braid coffee cake from the center to each end. Pinch ends together and tuck under cake. Place dough on greased sheet, cover and let rise until light, about 1 hour. Brush with egg mixture and sprinkle generously with sugar. Bake in preheated, 350° F. oven for 25 to 30 minutes. Cool on rack. Yields 1 large coffee cake.

## GERMAN CHRISTMAS COFFEE CAKE
*We divided dough and made 2 coffee cakes.*

2 packages dry yeast
2 cups lukewarm water
3 eggs, beaten
½ cup sugar
1 teaspoon salt
2 cups all-purpose flour
½ cup butter, melted

1 cup flake cocoanut
1 cup finely chopped
Brazil nuts
About 4 cups flour
Confectioners' sugar
icing, page 250
Colored sugar *or* candies

Dissolve yeast in lukewarm water. Stir in eggs. Stir in sugar. Beat in 2 cups of flour; stir in melted butter, cocoanut and Brazil nuts.

Add about 4 cups flour, to make a soft, somewhat sticky dough. Cover dough with damp cloth and let rise until double in bulk in a warm, draft-free place. Punch down dough and place on a large, greased cookie sheet. Work and pat dough into a tree shape. Cover with damp cloth and let rise again until double in bulk. Bake in preheated, 350° F. oven 25 to 30 minutes. Frost with Confectioners' Sugar Icing, while still hot. Sprinkle frosting with tiny candies before it sets. Yields 1 very large coffee cake tree.

## GLAZED PINEAPPLE ALMOND RING
*Frankly fancy, but worth the effort.*

1 package dry *or* cake of
compressed yeast
¼ cup warm water
(105°-115° F.)
¼ cup milk, scalded and
cooled
1 egg
3 tablespoons sugar
1 teaspoon salt
⅛ teaspoon cardamom

¼ teaspoon almond
extract
1 teaspoon grated lemon
peel
2¼ cups sifted flour
Butter
Pineapple Almond
Filling
Pineapple Glaze

Dissolve yeast in warm water in warm bowl. Blend in milk, beaten egg, sugar, salt, cardamom, almond extract and lemon peel. Gradually beat in flour to make moderately stiff dough. Turn out on lightly-floured board and knead until smooth. Place in greased bowl. Cover with damp cloth and let rise in warm place until light and double in size, about 1½ hours.

Turn out on floured board. Roll to a rectangle about 12x15 inches. Spread with 4 tablespoons soft butter. Fold ends to middle, overlapping them to make 3 layers. Roll out dough again. Spread with 2 tablespoons soft butter and fold again. Cover and let stand 15 minutes. Roll out to a 10x18-inch rectangle. Spread surface with cooled Pineapple Almond Filling.

Starting from long side, roll up like jelly roll; pinch lengthwise seam together to seal. Place seam-side down on greased baking sheet. Shape into ring, pinching ends together to seal. With scissors, make cuts ⅓ to ½ of the way through the ring at 1-inch intervals, starting from outer edge. Turn each section on its side. Brush with melted butter and let rise until light and doubled in size, about 35 to 40 minutes. (A small collar of foil placed around outer edge of dough will keep ring from spreading during rising.) Bake in preheated, 400° F. oven 20 to 25 minutes, or until a rich golden brown. Remove ring to rack to cool. Spread top surface with Pineapple Glaze while still warm. Makes an 11-inch ring, about 8 to 10 servings.

*Pineapple Almond Filling:* Open 1 can (8½-ounce) crushed pineapple. Measure out 2 tablespoons pineapple and set aside for glaze. Combine remaining, undrained pineapple, 3 tablespoons brown sugar, few grains of salt, 2 teaspoons cornstarch and 1 tablespoon butter. Cook, stirring over moderate heat until clear and thickened. Remove from heat and add ½ cup almond paste (canned or from bakery) crumbled into small pieces; stir to blend. Cool before using.

*Pineapple Glaze:* Blend together 2 tablespoons crushed pineapple and ¾ cups sifted confectioners' sugar.

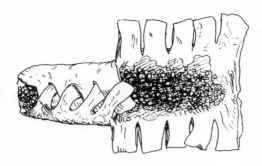

## POPPY SEED COFFEE CAKE
*Special, rich cake with a delectable hint of orange.*

1 package dry yeast
¼ cup warm water
½ cup milk, scalded
¼ cup poppy seeds
½ cup butter
¼ cup sugar
2 eggs
2 tablespoons grated
  orange rind

¼ teaspoon salt
2½-3 cups all-purpose flour
2 cups peeled, chopped
  cooking apples
½ cup sugar
¼ teaspoon cinnamon

Sprinkle yeast over warm water to soften. Add poppy seeds to ¼ cup hot scalded milk; set aside for filling. In a mixing bowl, cream butter; add sugar. Beat in eggs, orange rind and salt. Add 1 cup flour; beat at medium speed of mixer about 2 minutes. Add remaining ¼ cup milk and dissolved yeast. Gradually add enough remaining flour to make a soft dough. On floured surface, knead dough until smooth and satiny. Place in buttered bowl; brush with melted butter. Cover and allow to stand in warm place until double, about 1 hour. Punch down. On lightly-floured surface, roll in rectangle about 16x8 inches; place on greased baking sheet. In a bowl, combine apple, sugar, cinnamon and poppy-seed mixture; spread down center of rectangle. Along each longer side of dough, cut about 1½-inch slits, making strips about 1-inch wide. Fold strips at an angle across filling, alternating from side to side. Cover and allow to stand in warm place until doubled. Bake in a preheated, 350° F. oven for 30 to 40 minutes; remove to wire rack to cool. While warm, drizzle Orange Icing over top. Yields 1 coffee cake.

*Orange Icing:* In a small mixing bowl, beat together ¾ cup confectioners' sugar, ½ teaspoon grated orange rind, 1½ tablespoons orange juice and 1 teaspoon soft butter. Beat until smooth. Drizzle over top of coffee cake.


## RAISED DOUGHNUTS WITH SUGAR GLAZE
*Use a dowel stick for turning doughnuts when frying.*

| | |
|---|---|
| 1 cup water (105°-115° F.) | ⅓ cup sugar |
| 2 packages dry yeast | ½ teaspoon mace |
| 3½ cups sifted, all-purpose flour | ½ teaspoon nutmeg |
| | 1 teaspoon salt |
| ¼ cup dry milk | ⅓ cup shortening |
| | 2 eggs, well-beaten |

Sprinkle yeast over water and set aside while you blend the next 6 dry ingredients thoroughly. Cut in shortening, as for biscuits, until mixture is fine as meal. Make a well in the center. Stir yeast and pour into well in flour. Add eggs. Beat thoroughly, stirring from center out, taking up as much flour as needed to form a thick, elastic batter. Then work in remaining flour to form a soft dough.

Turn dough onto a well-floured board or pastry canvas. Wait 10 minutes (longer if convenient), then knead until smooth and elastic. Cover dough with bowl which has been well-greased, let rise until double. Flatten dough by tapping over entire surface with edge of rolling pin. Then roll to about ⅜ inch thickness and cut into rounds or form into twists for frying. Let rise, *uncovered* until double in bulk.

Deep-fry at 365° F. Turn doughnuts as soon as they come up, then turn repeatedly for even browning. Do not puncture when handling — use dowel for turning. Remove from fat, drain and pass at once through glaze. Yields about 3 dozen doughnuts.

*Glaze:* Combine ½ pound confectioners' sugar, 4 cups boiling water and ½ teaspoon vanilla. Stir until sugar is dissolved.


*Split a doughnut* and spread it with applesauce or apple butter for a special treat. — The Farmer, 1947.

## FLAT BREAD
### *Called Julknockebröd.*

2 packages dry yeast
½ cup warm water
1 cup butter
1½ cups milk
1 teaspoon sugar
1 teaspoon salt

1 teaspoon baking soda
2 cups whole wheat flour *or* quick-cooking oatmeal
4 cups sifted, all-purpose flour

Dissolve yeast in water. Melt butter and add milk. Pour tepid mixture over yeast. Add sugar, salt, baking soda dissolved in 1 teaspoon milk and wheat flour (or oatmeal). Work in the white flour a little at a time. Beat dough smooth and let rise in the bowl under a cover for 15 minutes. Turn dough onto a floured baking board and knead 5 minutes. Divide into 8 parts and roll out each part into a very thin cake. Roll directly onto baking sheet. Use a ridged rolling pin. Cut into 4x2½-inch rectangles, using a pastry wheel, if desired. Let rise, covered, for ½ hour at room temperature. Bake in preheated, 325° F. oven for about 15 minutes. Remove from oven and break into pieces. Cool on rack and store in covered container. Yields about 150 pieces.

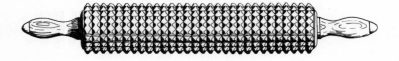

## SPECIAL BUTTERS AND SAUCES
### *Superb with pancakes, waffles, French toast, muffins or biscuits.*

*Whipped Strawberry Butter:* Combine ½ cup soft butter, ¼ teaspoon salt, 6 tablespoons frozen strawberries (drained), 1 tablespoon powdered sugar. Blend in blender or with electric mixer until smooth. Serve additional fresh or frozen strawberries or a mound of strawberry preserves with pancakes or waffles.

*Whipped Honey Butter:* Blend ½ cup soft butter and ½ cup honey in blender or with electric mixer until light and fluffy. Pass a jar of warmed honey, too.

*Brown Sugar Spread:* To 6 tablespoons softened butter add ¼ cup brown sugar and ¼ teaspoon cinnamon. Blend until smooth and creamy. Spread on hot waffles. Yields about ½ cup spread.

*Peach Sauce:* Combine 1 tablespoon corn starch and 1 cup cold water in saucepan and bring to boil, stirring constantly. Cook until thick. Add 2 teaspoons lemon juice and 1 package (10-ounce) thawed, frozen peaches, *or* 1 can (16-ounce) sliced peaches. Simmer 10 minutes, stirring occasionally. Serve warm. Yields 2½ to 3 cups sauce.

*Maple Butter Apple Slices:* Heat together 1 cup maple-flavored syrup and 1 tablespoon butter. Add 2 cups thinly-sliced cooking apples and simmer gently until apples are tender, about 10 minutes. Serve warm. Yields about 2 cups sauce.

*Caramel-Butter Syrup:* Combine 1 cup white sugar and ½ cup butter. Place in heavy saucepan over medium heat, stirring occasionally until a light golden brown. Add 1 cup hot water, keep stirring from bottom of pan, over heat, until mixture is completely dissolved. Add 1 cup brown sugar, stir and heat until smooth. Serve warm over pancakes and waffles. If you wish to have it thinner, add an additional ¼ cup hot water. Yields about 3 cups syrup.

## BUTTERMILK PANCAKES
### Family pleasers!

1 egg
1 cup buttermilk *or* sour milk
¼ cup sugar
½ teaspoon salt
1 teaspoon soda
½ teaspoon baking powder
1¼ cups all-purpose flour
2 tablespoons butter, melted

Sift dry ingredients together. Beat egg; add buttermilk and stir together. Add sifted dry ingredients and beat until smooth. Stir in melted butter. Pour onto hot griddle, 380° F. and bake until bubbles form; turn pancakes and bake until delicately brown. Yields about 16 pancakes, 4-inch diameter.

*Sweet Milk Pancakes:* Use sweet milk instead of buttermilk or sour milk listed in basic recipe. Omit soda and add an extra 1 teaspoon baking powder.

*Ham Cakes:* Fold ½ cup finely-chopped ham or luncheon meat into pancake batter just before cooking.

*Fresh Peach Cakes:* When pancakes are cooked on one side and ready to turn, place a few slices of fresh or thawed peaches over the unbaked side of each cake. Turn, finish cooking. To serve, drizzle with melted butter and sprinkle cinnamon and sugar over top.

*Blueberry Cakes:* Fold 1 cup fresh or unthawed, frozen blueberries into batter before cooking.

*Onion Cakes:* Place a little finely chopped onion on top of each pancake before turning on griddle. Delicious when served with creamed meats for supper.

*Apple Cakes:* Add ¾ cup finely-chopped, peeled, raw apple to batter just before cooking. Pick a tart apple. Serve, sprinkled with a mixture of ½ cup sugar and 2 tablespoons cinnamon.

*Sausage Cakes:* Fold ½ pound cooled, drained, browned pork sausage meat into batter just before cooking.

## GINGERBREAD PANCAKES
*Brunch or dessert special!*

| | |
|---|---|
| 1 egg | 1 package (14-ounce) |
| 1½ cups milk | gingerbread mix |
| | 2 tablespoons butter, melted |

Combine egg and milk thoroughly; blend with gingerbread mix. Stir in butter. Cook on lightly greased griddle, browning lightly on both sides. Serve with butter and orange marmalade or applesauce. Yields about 16 pancakes, 4-inch diameter.

## PAN-SANS
*Really pancake sandwiches — for breakfast, lunch or supper.*

Follow a basic pancake recipe. Then spread one pancake with any filling listed below, cover with a second pancake and serve hot with butter and maple-blended syrup.

*Apple-Nut:* Spread with hot, spiced applesauce and sprinkle with toasted, chopped pecans.

*Scrambled Egg:* Spread with scrambled eggs and sprinkle with minced, cooked bacon, chopped ham or frizzled, fried beef.

*Canadian Bacon with Pineapple:* Use a slice of Canadian bacon and cover with warm, canned crushed pineapple.

*Berry Stack:* Spread each buttered pancake generously with a prepared berry pie filling and stack one atop another. Drizzle some filling on top and finish with a daub of whipped cream.

## WAFFLES
*For the diet-conscious, top waffles with cottage cheese and unsweetened applesauce.*

2 cups flour
½ teaspoon salt
2 teaspoons baking powder
2 tablespoons sugar *or* honey

2 eggs, well beaten
1½ cups milk
6 tablespoons melted butter *or* other shortening

Mix and sift dry ingredients. Combine eggs, milk and fat; beat. Add to dry ingredients and beat. Bake in hot iron. Yields 6 to 8 waffles, 7-inch diameter.

## RICE GRIDDLE CAKES
*Printed in The Farmer, 1893.*

Mix together 1 quart water, 3 well-beaten eggs, 1 tablespoon baking powder, 2 teaspoons salt, 1-2 tablespoons grated onion, 2 teaspoons sugar, 1 cup cold boiled rice and flour to make a good batter (about 4 cups). Whole kernel corn may be used in place of rice in this recipe. Bake in a hot, greased skillet. Two dessert spoonfuls of batter yields 40 griddle cakes, 4-inch diameter.

## REMEMBER MILK TOAST?

The old-fashioned, flip-flop toaster or a carefully watched oven broiler makes the best toast.

Butter 2 to 3 crisp slices of toast per adult serving. Sprinkle on a little cinnamon and as much sugar as you like. Pour on ¾ cup hot (not boiled) milk.

*Try rusks:* Cinnamon rusks taste super-good, too.

## POPOVERS
*Split and fill with creamed dried beef or creamed chicken
for a special breakfast or supper dish.*

1 cup sifted, all-purpose
  flour
½ teaspoon salt

1 cup milk
2 eggs

Beat ingredients together until smooth — use a rotary egg
beater if you have one. Fill well-greased, deep, muffin cups ¾
full of batter. Glass cups make higher popovers. Bake in preheated, 425° F. oven for 35 to 45 minutes — until popovers
are golden brown. Serve at once. Yields 5 to 9 popovers,
depending on cup size.

## YORKSHIRE PUDDING
*Remove beef roast from oven when cooked to desired
doneness, cover loosely and set in warm place
while pudding cooks.*

Sift ⅞ cup flour and ½ teaspoon salt into a bowl. Make a
well in the center and pour in ½ cup milk. Stir milk into
flour. Beat 2 eggs until fluffy, then beat eggs into batter. Add
½ cup water and beat batter well with a fork until large
bubbles rise to the surface. You may permit the batter to
stand 1 hour, then beat it again. When ready to cook, place 3
tablespoons hot beef drippings in the bottom of a 10x10-inch
pan. Heat pan in oven. Pour batter into pan. Bake pudding in
preheated, 400° F. oven for about 20 minutes. Reduce heat to
350° F. and bake 10 to 20 minutes longer. Serve at once.
Yields 6 to 8 servings.

## MUFFINS
*With old and new variations.*

2 cups flour
2 teaspoons baking powder
1 teaspoon salt
2 tablespoons sugar

1 egg, beaten
1 cup milk
2 tablespoons melted
  shortening

Mix and sift dry ingredients. Combine liquids (fat cooled
slightly) and pour all at once into dry ingredients. Stir
vigorously until dry ingredients are just dampened. The
batter should not be entirely smooth. (Overstirring causes

tunnels.) Fill greased tins ⅔ full with as little extra stirring as possible. Bake in a preheated, 425° F. oven for 20 minutes. If iron muffin tins are used, grease and heat thoroughly before pouring batter into pan. Yields 10 to 12 muffins.

*Use Sour Milk:* Decrease amount of baking powder to 1 teaspoon. Mix ½ teaspoon soda with 1 tablespoon water and add to wet ingredients. A little more milk may be needed if it is quite thick.

*Use Sour Cream* in place of milk and omit shortening. Follow directions above for sour milk.

*Blueberry Muffins:* Increase sugar to ¼ cup. Add ⅔ cup fresh berries last. If using canned berries, drain well. If using frozen blueberries, do not thaw.

*Date or Nut Muffins:* Add ½ cup chopped dates or nuts. Mix with dry ingredients before liquids are added.

*Cranberry Muffins:* Use double amount of fat and sugar. Add ½ cup raw cranberries cut in halves and 1 additional teaspoon of baking powder to dry ingredients.

*Whole Wheat, Corn Meal, Graham or Bran Muffins:* Substitute 1 cup dark flour, meal or bran for 1 cup white flour. Increase baking powder to 3 teaspoons; ¼ cup brown sugar may be substituted for white, or sugar left out and ¼ cup molasses added to liquids.

*Cooked Cereal Muffins:* Use ½ cup cooked oatmeal, rice, or hominy and 1¾ cups flour in place of 2 cups flour. Increase baking powder to 3 teaspoons.

*Maple Muffins:* Add ¼ cup maple or maple-blended syrup to other liquids and increase shortening to 3· tablespoons. Proceed as directed in basic recipe.

*Apple Muffins:* Add ⅔ cup finely-chopped Jonathan or Winesap apple to basic recipe just before putting into pans. Do not over-stir. Sprinkle tops with mixture of sugar and cinnamon.

## LIZZIE'S CREAM MUFFINS
*Popover-like flavor men love — The Farmer, 1886.*

Mix well, 1 pint of milk, 1 pint of flour, 3 beaten egg yolks, ¾ teaspoon salt, 1 teaspoon melted butter. Fold in 3 stiffly beaten egg whites. Put in pans and bake in a pretty hot oven (preheated to 425° F.) and bake 20 to 25 minutes. If made and baked right, these cannot be excelled. Yields about 2 dozen muffins.

## BOSTON BROWN BREAD
*Grandma's favorite with ham and baked beans —*
*from the 1934 Country Kitchen Cook Book.*

3 cups coarse flour such
    as 1 cup rye,
    1 cup graham,
    1 cup corn meal
1½ teaspoons soda
1 teaspoon salt

1 egg beaten
2 cups soured milk *or*
    buttermilk
¾ cup molasses
1 cup raisins, optional

Mix and sift dry ingredients, then add raisins if they are used. Combine egg, milk and molasses, then add to dry ingredients. Beat well. Divide dough between two 1-pound coffee cans; cover can tops with heavy greased foil and tie securely. Steam 3 hours. Uncover and bake ½ hour in oven to dry. If using a pressure cooker, steam 1 hour with petcock open, until bread rises. Finish cooking 15 minutes at 15 pounds pressure. Yields 2 loaves.

## INDIAN FRIED BREAD
*Light and flaky — a great taste and texture!*

2 cups sifted, all-purpose
    flour
2 teaspoons baking
    powder

½ teaspoon salt
4 tablespoons shortening
    (½ butter, ½ lard)
¾ cup milk

Sift dry ingredients together. Cut in shortening well; add milk directly to dry mixture and mix with 2 knives or pastry blender until well blended. Roll dough out on lightly floured board and cut into strips about 1½x3 inches. Slash each strip in the center. Fry in deep, hot fat, preheated to 400° F., until bread is puffed and brown on one side, then turn and brown on the other side. Drain on absorbent paper. *Serve at once.* Lard is usually used to fry the bread. Bread may also be fried in a skillet of hot fat about 1 inch to 1½ inches deep. Accompany fried bread with bacon or ham and eggs. Drizzle honey or syrup onto bread, or shake hot, drained Fried Bread strips in a bag of powdered sugar. Yields about 16 pieces.
    *Raisin Variation:* Add ½ cup seedless raisins to dry ingredients.
    *Biscuit Variation:* Roll dough ¼ inch to ½ inch thick and

cut with a biscuit cutter. Bake in preheated, 450° F. oven for 10 to 12 minutes or until biscuits are lightly browned.

## GUIDE TO DEEP FAT FRYING

*Doughnuts, fritters, uncooked mixtures:* Keep fat at 365° F. to 370° F. — a cube of bread will turn golden brown in 60 seconds.
*Croquettes, other cooked mixtures:* Keep fat at 375° F. to 385° F. — a cube of bread will turn golden brown in 40 seconds.
*French fried potatoes:* Keep fat at 385° F. to 390° F. — a cube of bread will turn golden brown in 30 seconds.

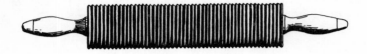

## LEFSE
*Rolled dough should be translucent when held to the light.*

3 cups cold, unseasoned,         ½ cup vegetable oil
  well-mashed potatoes          1 tablespoon salt
2 cups half-and-half cream       5 cups all-purpose flour

Add cream to potatoes and mix until smooth. Mix in shortening. Stir salt into flour and add flour to potatoes to make quite a stiff dough. For each lefse, use 1 tablespoon dough. Roll very thin on a floured surface using a grooved, lefse rolling pin. Bake lightly on both sides on an ungreased electric lefse griddle, in an electric skillet or on top of a wood kitchen cook stove. Bake on medium heat, turn once. Bake until done. Serve warm or cold with butter; butter and sugar; butter, cinnamon and sugar, or butter and hot lutefisk. Lefse may be cooled on racks, then well-wrapped and refrigerated or frozen, and later warmed again before serving.
*Note:* Do not mix large batches of lefse dough at one time unless baking on several griddles at once because the dough tends to absorb flour when standing.

## IRISH BATTER BREAD
*This bread of Clara Sutter's is so good —*
*and men like it on cold winter days.*

2 eggs                          1 tablespoon baking
¾ cup sugar                       powder
1 teaspoon salt                 3 cups flour
2 tablespoons lard              1¾ cups buttermilk
1 cup raisins

Beat all ingredients together until well mixed. Pour into a lightly greased, 10-inch iron skillet and bake 1 hour in a preheated, 350° F. oven. Serve hot. Yields about 8 to 10 servings.

# CORN BREAD
*Great with honey and syrup at any meal!*

| | |
|---|---|
| 1 cup corn meal | 1⅔ cups soured milk *or* buttermilk |
| 1 cup flour | 1 egg, beaten |
| 1 teaspoon sugar | 2 tablespoons melted shortening |
| 1 teaspoon salt | |
| 1 teaspoon soda | |

Mix and sift dry ingredients. Mix egg with milk and shortening. Combine and bake in greased, hot, 8x8-inch pan in preheated, 450° F. oven for about 40 minutes, or until cake tester comes out clean. Yields about 6 servings.

*Bacon Corn Bread:* Add just 1 tablespoon bacon fat to batter. Sprinkle top with partially-cooked bacon squares before baking bread.

# BAKING POWDER BISCUITS

| | |
|---|---|
| 2 cups all-purpose flour | ¼ cup shortening |
| 1 tablespoon baking powder | ⅔ cup milk |
| 1 teaspoon salt | |

Mix and sift dry ingredients; work in shortening quickly with a fork or pastry blender. Add milk all at once and stir lightly to make a soft dough. Turn out on slightly floured board, knead lightly 20 times, roll to ⅓-inch thickness. Cut, dipping 2-inch round cutter in flour after each using, transfer biscuits to baking sheet. Bake in preheated, 450° F. oven for 12 minutes. Yields about 1 dozen biscuits.

*Drop Biscuits:* Use 2 or 3 more tablespoons milk to make dough of drop consistency. Do not roll out.

*Cinnamon Rolls:* Roll dough lightly in an oblong sheet ¼ inch thick, spread with soft butter, sprinkle with a mixture of sugar and cinnamon. Roll up from the long side like a jelly roll. Cut slices ½ inch thick, lay them flat side down on a baking sheet, and bake.

*Orange Biscuits:* Substitute orange juice for part of the milk. On top of each biscuit, put a piece of cube sugar that has been soaked in orange juice long enough to absorb some of it, but not long enough to dissolve. Grate orange rind over top of biscuits.

*Shortcake:* Increase shortening to ⅓ cup in the basic recipe and mix as for biscuits. Pat out dough about ¼ inch thick, cut in large rounds for individual shortcakes. Place in pairs, before baking, with butter between. Or pat dough out in an oblong pan — in a thin sheet (to be used double), or a thick sheet (to be split). To serve, place sweetened fruit between and on top of layers. Top with sweetened, whipped cream.

*Golden Shortcake:* Increase shortening as for shortcake above to ⅓ cup. Add 1 beaten egg to ½ cup milk and use as the liquid in place of plain milk to make a softer dough than usual. Bake in muffin tins. Split to serve.

*Cardamom Shortcake:* Add ½ teaspoon ground or crushed cardamom to your favorite shortcake biscuit dough.

*Bacon Biscuits:* Cut 4 slices of bacon into small pieces and fry until crisp. Drain on absorbent paper. Stir bacon into mixed dry ingredients and proceed as directed in basic recipe.

*Scotch Scones:* Proceed as for regular biscuits, adding 2 teaspoons sugar to dry ingredients. In place of plain milk use ⅓ cup half-and-half cream mixed with 2 beaten eggs, reserving a little egg white. Roll out and cut in triangles, brush with egg white, sprinkle with sugar and bake in preheated, 450° F. oven 12 to 15 minutes. For raisin scones, add ½ cup raisins.

## MAKE-AT-HOME BISCUIT MIX
*So economical and so handy.*

8 cups all-purpose flour
1 cup non-fat dry milk
2 teaspoons salt

4 tablespoons baking powder
1½ cups lard *or* shortening

Combine first 4 ingredients together in large mixing bowl. Do this with an electric mixer on low speed, or by sifting the ingredients together 3 times. Add lard to dry mixture in small pieces for easier blending. Blend in lard until it is evenly distributed and has the appearance of coarse meal. Store mix in tightly-sealed container.

If lard used does not contain a chemical preservative it must be stored in the refrigerator. Keeping time is six weeks.

If lard does contain a preservative, the mix may be stored on the pantry shelf up to four weeks.

If electric mixer is used to combine dry ingredients with lard, do not overmix, because the mixture becomes very fine and will pack during storage and reduce the keeping quality. Yields about 9 cups biscuit mix.

## BISCUITS FROM BISCUIT MIX
*Save time by dropping biscuits onto pan with a spoon.*

Add ⅔ cup milk to 2 cups biscuit mix all at once. Stir with fork to make a soft dough, then beat dough vigorously 20 times. Dough will be stiff and slightly sticky. Roll dough around on well-floured surface, then knead gently 8 to 10 times. Roll out ½ inch thick and cut biscuits with cutter dipped in flour. Bake on lightly greased baking sheet in preheated, 450° F. oven for 10 to 15 minutes. Yields 12 biscuits, 2 inches in diameter.

## MUFFINS FROM BISCUIT MIX

2 cups biscuit mix
2 tablespoons sugar

1 egg, well beaten
⅔ cup milk *or* water

Combine mix and sugar thoroughly in mixing bowl. Combine egg and milk. Add to dry ingredients and mix until flour is barely moistened, about 10 to 20 strokes. Place in greased muffin tins. Bake at 425° F. for approximately 20 minutes. To vary muffins, add about ½ teaspoon of jelly or marmalade on top of batter and bake. Drained fruit or crumbled bacon may be added to dry mixture before combining with liquid. Yields 10 muffins.

## PANCAKES FROM BISCUIT MIX
*Griddle is hot when a few drops of water skitter across surface.*

Beat 2½ cups biscuit mix, 1 egg and 1⅔ cups milk together until smooth with a rotary beater. Cook on a hot, greased griddle until bubbles appear on cake surface, turn and cook until bottom is golden and middle set. Add more milk for thinner cakes. Yields about 18 pancakes.

## SUNDAY BREAD FROM BISCUIT MIX
*Great company fare.*

2 cups biscuit mix
1 cup rolled oats,
    uncooked
¾ cup sugar
¼ teaspoon salt
1 teaspoon baking powder
½ cup snipped dried
    apricots

½ cup golden seedless
    raisins
½ cup broken walnut
    meats
1 egg, well-beaten
1¼ cups milk

Combine first 5 ingredients by stirring (do not sift). Add fruits and nuts. Combine egg and milk and stir in. Beat hard with a spoon for half a minute. Spoon into greased 1½ quart casserole. Bake in preheated, 350° F. oven for 50 to 60 minutes. Cool in casserole 10 minutes, then remove to rack. Cool. If desired, frost with a thin sugar icing. Do not slice until the day after baking. Yields 1 loaf.

## ONION BISCUIT MIX BREAD
*Excellent with barbecued or roast meats.*

Add ⅔ cup milk, all at once, to 2 cups biscuit mix. Stir with fork into a soft dough. Add 1 tablespoon instant minced onion. Beat 20 strokes. Spread on greased baking sheet in 10x8-inch oblong. Bake 10 minutes in preheated, 450° F. oven. Serve hot, broken in pieces. Yields 1 loaf.

## MINCEMEAT-TOPPED COFFEE CAKE

1 cup biscuit mix
⅓ cup granulated sugar
⅓ cup milk
1 egg
¼ cup melted butter
½ cup mincemeat

¼ cup brown sugar
¼ cup flour
¼ teaspoon cinnamon
2 tablespoons melted
butter

Mix first 5 ingredients into smooth batter. Spread into greased and floured 9-inch round layer pan. Spread mincemeat evenly over batter. Sprinkle with mixture of last 4 ingredients. Bake in preheated, 375° F. oven for 20 to 25 minutes or until nicely browned. Serve warm. Yields 6 servings.

## CRANBERRY HONEY BREAD

3 cups biscuit mix
1 cup cranberries, coarsely
   ground
¼ teaspoon salt

½ cup chopped nuts
¾ cup honey
⅔ cup milk
1 egg, slightly beaten

Combine mix, cranberries, salt and nuts. Combine honey, milk and egg. Add to cranberry mixture. Stir until ingredients are moistened. Spoon into greased, paper-lined 8½x4½-inch loaf pan. Bake in preheated, 350° F. oven for 55 to 60 minutes. Yields 1 loaf.

## STREUSEL-FILLED COFFEE CAKE
### *For mid-morning coffee.*

¾ cup sugar
¼ cup soft shortening
1 egg
½ cup milk
1½ cups sifted, all-purpose
   flour

2 teaspoons baking
   powder
½ teaspoon salt
Streusel Mixture

Heat oven. Mix shortening with sugar and egg thoroughly. Stir in milk. Sift together and stir in next 3 ingredients. Spread half of batter in greased and floured 9-inch-square pan. Sprinkle with half the streusel mixture. Add the remaining batter, and sprinkle remaining streusel over top. Bake in preheated, 375° F. oven for 25 to 35 minutes. Yields about 9 servings.

*Streusel Mixture:* Mix together, ½ cup brown sugar, 2 tablespoons flour, 2 teaspoons cinnamon, 2 tablespoons butter, melted and ½ cup chopped nuts.

*Blueberry Coffee Cake:* Gently mix ¾ cup fresh or unthawed frozen blueberries into dough before putting into pan.

## BANANA BREAD
*Makes a great cheese sandwich.*

| | |
|---|---|
| 3½ cups all-purpose flour | 4 teaspoons baking powder |
| ¾ cup butter | 1 teaspoon baking soda |
| 1¼ cups sugar | 2 cups mashed, ripe |
| 4 eggs | bananas |
| 3½ cups all-purpose flour | |

Cream butter and sugar together. Beat in the eggs. Combine flour, baking powder and soda, add with the mashed bananas, and mix well. Place loaves in two 3½x7½x2-inch buttered and floured baking pans and bake in preheated, 350° F. oven for 1 hour, or until well browned. Yields 2 small loaves.

## PUMPKIN BREAD
*Freezes well.*

| | |
|---|---|
| ½ cup cooking oil | 1 teaspoon salt |
| 1½ cups sugar | ½ teaspoon cloves |
| 2 eggs | ½ teaspoon cinnamon |
| 1 cup canned pumpkin | ½ teaspoon nutmeg |
| 1¾ cups all-purpose flour | ½ teaspoon allspice |
| ¼ teaspoon baking | ⅓ cup water |
| powder | ½ cup white raisins |
| 1 teaspoon soda | |

Grease two 3½x7½x2-inch pans; flour pan bottoms. Mix oil and sugar. Add eggs, pumpkin, spices sifted with flour, water and raisins; mix thoroughly. Bake in preheated, 350° F. oven for 1 hour, or until bread tests done. Yields 2 small loaves.

## QUICK NUT BREAD
*Delicious, nutritious — alone or in sandwiches.*

| | |
|---|---|
| 2 cups all-purpose flour | 1 cup chopped nuts |
| 1 teaspoon salt | 2 eggs, beaten |
| 4 teaspoons baking powder | 2 cups milk |
| 2 cups whole wheat flour | 2 tablespoons melted |
| 1 cup brown sugar | shortening |

Mix and sift flour, salt and baking powder; add whole wheat flour, sugar and nuts. Combine egg, milk and shortening. Combine both mixtures; pour in 2 greased 1-pound coffee cans. Let stand 15 or 20 minutes, then bake 45 minutes in preheated, 350° F. oven. Yields 2 loaves.

*Date or Raisin Nut Bread:* Add 1 cup chopped dates or seedless raisins to rest of dry ingredients.

*Prune Bread:* With dry ingredients, sift 1 teaspoon soda and decrease baking powder to 2 teaspoons. In place of sweet milk, use 1 cup each sour milk and prune juice. Add 1 cup prunes which have been stewed, drained, pitted and chopped, omitting nuts if desired.

*Cherry Nut Bread:* Add ½ cup finely cut maraschino cherries and substitute ½ cup cherry juice for ½ cup milk.

## ORANGE SUNFLOWER BREAD
*Red River Valley recipe.*

3 cups sifted all-purpose
    flour
1 cup sugar
1 egg, beaten
3½ teaspoons baking
    powder

¾ cup orange juice
4 teaspoons grated
    orange peel
¾ cup milk
¼ cup butter, melted
¾ cup (4¼-ounce package)
    roasted sunflower meats

Sift the dry ingredients together. Combine egg, orange juice, peel, milk and butter; add to dry ingredients, mixing well. Stir in sunflower nuts. Turn into greased 9½x5x3-inch (2-quart) loaf pan. Bake in preheated, 350° F. oven about 1 hour or until done. Let cool on rack 15 minutes before removing from pan. Yields 1 large loaf.

## MAPLE BRAN LOAF
*Bread slices best the second day.*

1½ cups sifted, all-purpose
  flour
3 teaspoons baking
  powder
1 teaspoon salt
¼ cup sugar
1½ cups bran cereal

½ cup chopped raisins
1 egg, well beaten
½ cup milk
½ cup maple-blended
  syrup
¼ cup shortening, melted

Sift together flour, baking powder, salt and sugar. Stir in
bran and raisins. Combine egg, milk and syrup. Add to dry
ingredients, mix. Add shortening, mix. Pour into 8x4-inch
loaf pan, greased and bottom-lined with waxed paper. Bake
in preheated, 350° F. oven for about 1 hour. Yields 1 loaf.

## HASTY COFFEE CAKES
*Refrigerator biscuit delectables!*

*Biscuit Bubble Ring:* Butter a 6½-cup ring mold. Preheat
oven to 400° F. Blend ¾ cup brown sugar and 1 teaspoon
cinnamon. Melt ½ cup butter and pour 2 tablespoons in
bottom of ring mold; sprinkle in 4 tablespoons sugar mixture.
Open 2 packages (8-ounce each) refrigerator biscuits. Dip
each biscuit in remaining butter; then roll in sugar mixture.
Place 10 biscuits in bottom of mold, overlapping edges
slightly. Repeat with second layer. Bake 12 to 15 minutes;
allow to cool on wire rack about 5 minutes; invert on serving
plate. Yields 8 to 10 servings. May be frozen after baking.
*Pineapple Bubble Ring:* Preheat oven to 375° F. Blend ⅔
cup brown sugar, 1 teaspoon cinnamon and 1 tablespoon
grated orange peel. Melt 6 tablespoons butter and pour 2
tablespoons in bottom of buttered, 6½-cup ring mold.
Sprinkle in ¼ cup sugar mixture. Cut drained slices from
8¼-ounce can of pineapple in half and arrange with

maraschino cherries and 2 tablespoons of raisins in bottom of mold. Open two packages of refrigerator biscuits and proceed as directed in above recipe. Bake 20 to 25 minutes. Yields 8 to 10 servings.

*Caramel Cherry Coffee Cake:* Heat oven to 350° F. Melt ½ cup butter. Mix ⅔ cup brown sugar, 2 tablespoons milk, and 2½ tablespoons melted butter in bottom of a 6½-cup ring mold. Arrange ¼ cup pecan halves and ½ cup maraschino cherries on syrup. Mix 1 cup sugar and 1 tablespoon cinnamon. Open 2 packages of refrigerator biscuits and dip each in remaining butter, then sugar mixture. Place on edge, side by side, in mold. Bake 45 minutes. Cool 20 minutes in pan; invert on serving plate and serve warm. Yields 8 to 10 servings.

## HASTY HOT ROLLS

*Make from brown-and-serve rolls or refrigerator biscuits.*

*Caraway Rolls:* Brush tops of six brown-and-serve rolls with 1 teaspoon melted butter. Sprinkle ¼ teaspoon caraway seeds over each roll. Bake in a greased, shallow pan in a preheated, 400° F. oven for about 12 minutes. Serve at once. Yields 6 rolls.

*Celery Rolls:* Combine 1 tablespoon melted butter and ¼ teaspoon celery salt. Make a lengthwise cut in top of each of 6 brown-and-serve rolls. Spread ½ teaspoon celery butter into cut and over top of each roll. Bake in a greased, shallow pan in preheated, 400° F. oven for about 12 minutes. Serve immediately. Yields 6 rolls.

*Parmesan Butter Roll:* Cream 3 tablespoons soft butter, 2 tablespoons grated Parmesan cheese, ¼ teaspoon oregano, ⅛ teaspoon basil and a dash of garlic powder. Separate 1 package (8-ounce) refrigerated, snowflake dinner rolls and place on jelly roll pan, overlapping to form an 8-inch circle. Spread top with butter mixture and bake in preheated, 375° F. oven for 12 to 15 minutes. Yields 10 rolls.

*Pineapple Sticky Buns:* Mix ¾ cup drained, crushed pineapple, ½ cup butter, ½ cup brown sugar and 1 teaspoon cinnamon. Spoon into 10 greased, large muffin cups. Place a biscuit in each cup and bake 10 to 12 minutes in preheated, 425° F. oven. Cool 5 minutes, invert on serving plate. Serve warm. Yields 10 buns.

*Quick Apricot Biscuits:* Combine ½ cup brown sugar with 2 tablespoons melted butter, a few chopped nuts and 1 tablespoon grated orange rind. Place a well-drained, pitted, canned apricot half in each of 10 muffin cups and sprinkle with some of the brown sugar mixture. Open an 8-ounce package of refrigerator biscuits and place a biscuit in each cup. Bake 8 to 12 minutes in preheated, 425° F. oven. Cool a minute or so before inverting pan on wax paper. Remove pan when biscuits have cooled. Yields 10 biscuits.

*Cranberry-Mincemeat Rolls:* Combine ½ cup mincemeat and ½ cup whole cranberry sauce. Spoon mixture into 10 greased muffin cups. Open an 8-ounce package of refrigerator biscuits and place a biscuit, top-side-down, over mixture in each cup. Bake in preheated, 400° F. oven for about 15 minutes. Let rolls stand in pan a minute, or longer, after removing from oven. Invert pan to remove rolls, so that fruit mixture is up. Serve immediately. Yields 10 rolls.

# BARS, COOKIES
# AND CANDY

E. Landin

## APRICOT SHORTBREAD
*Tangy!*

⅓ cup soft butter
½ cup brown sugar
1 cup sifted, all-purpose
   flour
¾ cup dried apricots
   Water

1 teaspoon grated lemon
   peel
⅔ cup granulated sugar
2 teaspoons cornstarch
⅓ cup chopped walnuts

Beat butter with sugar until light and fluffy with electric mixer. Beat in flour at low speed. Pat mixture evenly into bottom of an 8x8x2-inch baking pan. Bake 12 minutes in preheated, 350° F. oven, or until light-golden in color. Let cool completely in pan on wire rack.

Meanwhile, make filling. Place apricots in small saucepan. Add just enough water to cover; bring to boil. Reduce heat and simmer, covered, 15 minutes. Drain apricots, reserving 3 tablespoons cooking liquid. Chop apricots fine. Combine in small saucepan with reserved liquid, lemon peel, sugar, cornstarch. Bring to boil, stirring constantly; boil 1 minute. Cool 10 minutes. Spread evenly over shortbread crust. Sprinkle with walnuts. Bake 20 minutes more at 350° F. Let cool completely in pan on wire rack. Yields 20 bars 2x1½ inches each.

## ENGLISH TOFFEE SQUARES
*Party fare!*

1 cup butter
1 cup brown
   sugar
1 teaspoon vanilla
1 egg yolk

2 cups all-purpose flour
¼ teaspoon salt
4 bars (7-ounce each)
   milk chocolate
½ cup finely-chopped nuts

Cream butter, sugar, egg yolk and vanilla. Stir in flour and salt until blended. Pat into a rectangle, 13x10-inch, on greased baking sheet, leaving 1 inch around edge of sheet. Bake in preheated, 350° F. oven for 20 to 25 minutes, until nicely browned. Dough will be soft. Remove from oven. Immediately place separated squares of chocolate on top. Let stand until soft; spread evenly over surface. Sprinkle with nuts. Cut into small squares while warm. Yields about 5 dozen 1x2-inch cookies.

## CHERRY COCONUT BARS
*A favorite with Country Kitchen visitors;*
*we always double the recipe.*

½ cup butter
3 tablespoons con-
  fectioners' sugar
1 cup all-purpose flour
2 eggs beaten slightly
1 cup sugar
¼ cup all-purpose flour

½ teaspoon baking powder
¼ teaspoon salt
1 teaspoon vanilla
¾ cup chopped nuts
½ cup flake coconut
½ cup quartered
  maraschino cherries

Mix first 3 ingredients with hands until smooth. Spread thin in 8-inch-square pan. Bake in preheated, 350° F. oven about 25 minutes.

Meanwhile, prepare filling. Stir last 8 ingredients into the beaten eggs, spread on top of baked pastry and bake about 25 minutes more at 350° F. Cool and cut. For holiday use, red and green cherries are festive looking. Yields 16 bars, 2x2 inches each.

## DATE BARS
*Take to the school bake sale.*

1 package (8-ounce) dates,
  snipped into small pieces
⅓ cup boiling water
1 cup sugar
½ cup shortening
2 eggs

1 teaspoon vanilla
1 cup sifted, all-purpose
  flour
½ teaspoon salt
¼ teaspoon soda
½ cup chopped nuts

Pour boiling water over snipped dates and let stand to cool. Cream butter and sugar with electric mixer. Add eggs, one at a time, and beat well after each addition. Beat in vanilla. Mix dry ingredients. Add dry ingredients, dates and nuts to batter and mix in *by hand* until blended. Bake in greased and floured, 9x13-inch pan in preheated, 350° F. oven for 35 minutes or until a tester comes out clean. Do not overbake. Cool and dust with confectioners' sugar. Yields about 24 bars, about 2x2 inches each.

## PECAN SURPRISE BARS
*Country Kitchen visitors ask for this recipe.*

1 package (18½-ounce)
   butter *or* yellow
   cake mix
½ cup butter, melted
1 egg

½ cup brown sugar
1½ cups dark corn syrup
1 teaspoon vanilla
3 eggs
1 cup chopped pecans

Generously grease bottom and sides of a 9x13-inch baking pan. Reserve ⅔ cup dry cake mix for filling. In large mixing bowl, combine remaining dry cake mix, butter and 1 egg; mix until crumbly. Press into prepared pan. Bake in preheated, 350° F. oven for 15 to 20 minutes, until light golden brown.

Meanwhile, prepare filling. Combine ⅔ cup reserved cake mix, brown sugar, syrup, vanilla and 3 eggs. Beat at medium speed for 1 to 2 minutes. Pour filling over partially baked crust; sprinkle with pecans. Return to oven and bake for 30 to 35 minutes, until filling is set. Cool and cut into bars. Yields about 3 dozen 1½x2-inch bars.


## FRENCH BARS
*Unfrosted bars freeze well.*

4 eggs, well beaten
2¼ cups brown sugar
1½ cups heavy,
   soured cream
1½ teaspoons soda
2¼ cups unsifted,
   all-purpose flour

1 teaspoon cinnamon
½ teaspoon salt
1½ cups chopped walnuts
1½ cups dates, cut up
1 cup toasted, flake
   cocoanut

Add sugar to eggs and beat; stir in sour cream. Blend in dry ingredients. Stir in nuts, dates and cocoanut. Do not overmix. Spread into two greased, 15½x10½x2-inch pans or three 13x9x2-inch pans. Bake in preheated, 350° F. oven for 20 minutes. Cool and frost with Orange Butter Frosting. Yields about 6 dozen 2x2-inch bars.

*Orange Butter Frosting:* Combine and beat the following ingredients until creamy — 1 pound sifted confectioners' sugar, 1 cup soft butter, ¼ cup orange juice, ½ teaspoon salt, 1 teaspoon grated orange rind. Spread on cooled bars.

## TOFFEE BARS
*Economical!*

2 cups quick-cooking
    oatmeal
½ cup brown sugar
½ teaspoon salt
¼ cup light corn syrup

⅓ cup butter, melted
½ teaspoon vanilla
1 package (6-ounce)
    chocolate chips
⅓ cup chopped nuts

Combine the first 3 ingredients. Add syrup, butter, vanilla and mix well. Pat into greased 13x9-inch oblong pan. Bake in preheated, 400° F. oven no longer than 10 minutes. Remove from oven and sprinkle with chocolate chips. Return to oven just long enough to melt chips. Spread evenly with spatula. Sprinkle with chopped nuts. Cut immediately. Yields about 2 dozen 2x2-inch bars.

## CHEWY DELIGHTS
*Man-pleasers!*

¼ cup butter
1 cup graham cracker
    crumbs
1 cup flake cocoanut
1 cup semi-sweet chocolate
    pieces

1 cup chopped nuts
1 can (15-ounce) sweetened,
    condensed milk

Combine melted butter, crumbs and cocoanut in ungreased, 9x13-inch pan. Press lightly and evenly in bottom of pan. Cover with layer of chocolate pieces. Sprinkle with layer of chopped nuts. Drizzle sweetened, condensed milk evenly over surface. Bake for 30 minutes in preheated, 350° F. oven. Cool completely before cutting. Yields about 4 dozen 1x2-inch bars.

## MINCEMEAT BROWNIES
*Moist!*

½ cup butter
1 cup sugar
2 eggs
1½ squares unsweetened
  chocolate, melted
½ cup mincement

½ cup chopped nuts
1 teaspoon vanilla
¼ teaspoon salt
¾ cup all-purpose flour
  Confectioners' sugar

Cream butter and sugar. Add eggs, one at a time, and beat after each addition. Add chocolate, mincemeat, nuts and vanilla. Fold in flour and salt. Pour into shallow, 9x13-inch pan, bottom-lined with greased, waxed paper. Bake in preheated, 350° F. oven for 30 minutes. Cut in squares and sprinkle with confectioners' sugar. Yields 24 bars, 2x2 inches each.

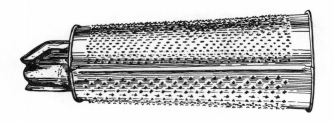

## LEMON BARS
*Elegant for tea time.*

½ cup butter
1 cup all-purpose flour
¼ cup confectioners' sugar
1 cup granulated sugar
2 tablespoons all-purpose
  flour

½ teaspoon baking powder
2 beaten eggs
2 tablespoons lemon juice
  Rind of one lemon

Mix first 3 ingredients well and pack in 8x8-inch pan. Bake 15 minutes at 350° F. Sift the next 3 ingredients together. Add last 3 ingredients. Mix well and pour on baked base. Bake in preheated, 350° F. oven for 25 to 30 minutes, or just until brown around edges. Do not overbake. May be frosted with confectioners' sugar frosting and decorated with red and green candied cherries. Cut into bars. Yields 32 bars 1x2 inches each.

## HONEY FRUIT BARS
### *Published in The Farmer, 1947,*
### *when sugar was scarce.*

Boiling water
1 cup seedless raisins
1 cup dates
1⅓ cups all-purpose flour
1 teaspoon baking powder

¼ teaspoon salt
3 eggs
½ cup sugar
½ cup honey
1 teaspoon vanilla

Pour boiling water over raisins; let stand 5 minutes. Drain and cut into small pieces. Wash dates and cut fine. Sift together flour, baking powder and salt. Beat eggs until foamy. Add sugar and honey gradually, then beat until very light. Add vanilla, raisins and dates; blend. Add sifted dry ingredients and mix well. Pour into a well-greased, 9x13-inch pan. Bake in preheated, 300° F. oven about 40 minutes. Cool and cut into 1x3-inch bars. Yields about 3 dozen bars.

## DOUBLE TAKE BROWNIES
### *The frosting's built in.*

⅓ cup all-purpose flour
⅓ cup dry bread crumbs
⅓ cup brown sugar
¾ cup finely-chopped nuts
⅓ cup butter, melted
2 eggs, well beaten
½ cup butter, melted

¾ cup brown sugar
2 teaspoons vanilla
¾ cup all-purpose flour
⅓ cup cocoa
1 teaspoon baking powder
½ teaspoon salt

Combine first 4 ingredients; mix well. Add ⅓ cup melted butter; blend well. Press mixture firmly into a lightly-greased, 8-inch-square pan. Bake in preheated, 425° F. oven for 5 minutes. Meanwhile, combine eggs, ½ cup melted butter, ¾ cup brown sugar and vanilla. Combine remaining ingredients and add to egg mixture. Mix thoroughly. Remove nut layer from oven; reduce heat to 350° F. Pour chocolate layer over first layer and return to oven. Bake for 40 to 45 minutes, or until firm, but still soft. Yields 16 bars, 2x2 inches each.

## UNBAKED PEANUT BUTTER BARS
*May be frozen.*

½ cup shortening
1 cup creamy peanut
  butter
2 packages (6-ounce each)
  butterscotch chips

1 package (1-pound)
  miniature marshmallows
¾ cup fine, flaked cocoanut
½ cup chopped nuts

Melt shortening, peanut butter and butterscotch chips together. Cool slightly and add marshmallows, cocoanut and nuts. Butter 11x16-inch pan and pat mixture into it. Sprinkle with more cocoanut. Cool until firm in the refrigerator (about ½ hour); cut. Pastel-colored marshmallows give these bars a party look. Yields about 7 dozen 1x2-inch bars.

## LEMON PUDDING COOKIES
*Dainty, yet easy and fun for children to make.*

½ cup shortening
½ cup sugar
1 package (3¾-ounce)
  lemon instant pud-
  ding mix

2 eggs
1½ cups all-purpose flour
½ teaspoon baking soda
¼ teaspoon salt

Cream shortening, sugar and pudding mix well. Beat in eggs. Stir flour, soda and salt together and blend into egg-sugar-pudding mixture. Drop by teaspoonfuls onto ungreased cookie sheets. Bake in preheated, 375° F. oven for 10 to 12 minutes. Do not brown. Cool on racks. Frost with confectioners' sugar icing and sprinkle with colored sugar. Yields 4 to 4½ dozen cookies.

*Confectioners' Sugar Icing:* Combine ½ cup confectioners' sugar, 2 teaspoons water and ¼ teaspoon vanilla. Add a little more water, if necessary, to make icing spread.

## SHREWBURY CAKES
*Delicate and not too sweet — from The Farmer, 1893.*

Cream 2 cups soft butter and 2 cups sugar. Beat in 4 eggs, 1 at a time. Mix in 1 teaspoon ground cinnamon; 2 teaspoons caraway seed, ground. Add 4 cups all-purpose flour and work into a paste. Roll pieces of dough out thin, right on a lightly-greased cookie sheet. Prick with a fork, then cut into diamond shapes by criss-crossing dough with a pastry wheel or knife. Bake in preheated, 350° F. oven for 10 to 12 minutes. Do not brown. Yields about 12 dozen cookies.

## SOUR CREAM DROP COOKIES
*Every farm wife had easy access to fresh-soured cream when the 1934 Country Kitchen Cook Book was published.*

| | |
|---|---|
| ¼ cup butter | 3 cups all-purpose flour |
| ½ cup sugar | 1 teaspoon soda |
| 2 eggs, beaten | 1 teaspoon baking powder |
| 1¼ cups sugar | ½ teaspoon salt |
| 1 cup thick, soured cream | 1 tablespoon grated rind of orange *or* lemon |

Cream butter, add ½ cup of the sugar, cream thoroughly. Add eggs beaten with remaining 1¼ cups sugar and cream. Sift flour with soda, salt and baking powder. Add grated rind, then combine with rest of ingredients to make a drop batter. Drop on greased sheet, top with a plump raisin and a sifting of sugar. Bake in preheated, 400° F. oven about 10 minutes — until edges are lightly browned. Yields about 6 dozen cookies.

## CHOCOLATE CHIP COOKIES
*Better double recipe!*

| | |
|---|---|
| ½ cup soft shortening (part butter) | 1⅛ cups all-purpose flour |
| ¾ cup sugar, (½ brown sugar) | ¼ teaspoon soda |
| 1 egg | ½ teaspoon salt |
| 1 teaspoon vanilla | ½ cup cut-up nuts |
| | 1 package (6-ounce) chocolate chips |

Mix first 4 ingredients thoroughly. Sift next 3 ingredients together; mix into first batter. Stir in nuts and chocolate chips. Drop rounded teaspoonfuls of dough about 2 inches apart on lightly greased cookie sheets. Bake in preheated, 375° F. oven until delicately browned. Cookies should be soft. Cool slightly, then remove from pans. Yields about 3 dozen cookies.

## SUGAR COOKIES
*Best ever used in Country Kitchen.*

½ cup soft shortening
(half butter)
¾ cup sugar
1 egg
1 tablespoon milk *or*
cream
1 teaspoon flavoring

(vanilla, lemon *or*
combination)
1¼ cups all-purpose
flour
¼ teaspoon baking
powder
¼ teaspoon salt

Mix together thoroughly, shortening, sugar and egg. Stir in milk and flavoring. Sift together and stir in flour, baking powder and salt. Chill dough.

Roll dough very thin (1/16-inch). Children will have an easier time working with dough if it is rolled a bit thicker. Cut dough into desired shapes. Place on lightly greased baking sheet and sprinkle with sugar. Bake 5 to 7 minutes in preheated, 425° F. oven until delicately browned. Yields 5 dozen 2½-inch cookies.

*Filled Cookies:* Cut sugar cookies in 3-inch rounds and place a filling on ½ of the cookie. Fold over, press edges together. Filling: Mix together 2 tablespoons flour and ½ cup sugar. Add ½ cup boiling water. Cook until thick. Add 2 cups chopped dates or raisins, ½ cup chopped nuts and 2 tablespoons lemon juice.


## CHAMPION SUNFLOWER COOKIES
*Winners in a Red River Valley*
*sunflower meat baking contest.*

2 cups sugar
3 cups flour
1 teaspoon soda
1 teaspoon baking powder
1 cup butter

1 cup shortening
1 teaspoon vanilla
1 cup toasted, salted
sunflower meats
1 cup flake cocoanut

Measure and mix dry ingredients, cut in shortening and butter. Add vanilla, cocoanut and sunflower meats. Shape into four 2-inch-diameter rolls and refrigerate at least 2 hours. Slice while cold, turning roll as you slice so cookie holds its shape. Bake about 10 minutes in preheated, 350° F. oven. Do not brown. Yields about 9 dozen cookies.

## HERMITS
*After-school favorite from* **The Farmer, 1912.**

1 cup sugar
1 cup butter
3 eggs
1 teaspoon soda
½ cup milk

1 cup molasses
1 teaspoon cinnamon
½ teaspoon cloves
3 cups all-purpose flour
1 cup raisins

Cream butter and sugar. Add eggs, one at a time, and beat after each addition. Next stir in soda, dissolved in milk; then molasses. Mix flour, cloves and cinnamon. Add to sugar-butter-egg mixture and mix well. Stir in raisins. Drop dough from a small teaspoon on a well-greased cookie sheet. Cookies spread. Bake in preheated, 375° F. oven about 5 minutes, until lightly browned. Yields 9 to 10 dozen cookies.


## SPICED OATMEAL COOKIES
*Old stand-by, with variations.*

1 cup shortening
2 cups brown sugar
2 eggs
1 cup soured milk
2½ cups flour
¾ teaspoon salt

1½ teaspoons cinnamon
¾ teaspoon nutmeg
¾ teaspoon cloves
1 teaspoon soda
2 cups oatmeal
2 cups raisins

Cream shortening with sugar. Beat eggs and mix with milk. Mix flour well with soda, salt and spices, and then with the rolled oats and raisins. Add liquid and dry ingredients alternately to the shortening and sugar. Drop on greased pans and bake about 15 minutes in preheated, 375° F. oven. Yields about 4 dozen large cookies.

*Variations:* Use 3 cups whole-wheat flour instead of white flour.

*Or,* use a scant-cup of sweet milk instead of sour milk; decrease soda to ½ teaspoon; add 2 teaspoons baking powder.

*Or,* substitute bran cereal for oatmeal for a bran drop cookie.

*Or,* add 1 cup chopped nuts.

## JUMBO RAISIN COOKIES
*Fill a cookie jar for kids.*

2 cups raisins
1 cup water
4 cups sifted, all-purpose flour
1 teaspoon baking powder
1 teaspoon baking soda
1 teaspoon salt
½ teaspoon cinnamon
½ teaspoon nutmeg
1 cup butter *or* shortening (*or* use ½ butter, ½ shortening)
1¾ cups sugar
2 eggs, slightly beaten
1 teaspoon vanilla
½ cup chopped nuts

Bring raisins and water to a boil. Boil until the raisins are plump — about 3 minutes. Set aside to cool. (Do not drain.) Sift flour with baking powder, soda, salt and spices. Cream butter. Gradually blend in sugar, creaming well after each addition. Add eggs and vanilla; mix well. Stir in the raisins and any remaining water. Gradually add the flour mixture, blending thoroughly after each addition. Stir in the nuts. Drop by tablespoonfuls, about 2 inches apart, onto greased baking sheets. Bake in preheated, 375° F. oven for 12 to 15 minutes. Cool on wire rack. Yields about 3½ dozen cookies.

## ORANGE DROPS
*So simple.*

⅔ cup butter, softened
1½ cups brown sugar
1 egg
1½ tablespoons grated orange rind
⅓ cup orange juice
3 cups sifted, all-purpose flour
½ teaspoon baking powder
1 cup chopped nuts — walnuts, pecans *or* salted, roasted sunflower meats

Cream butter and sugar. Add the egg and mix well. Add orange rind and orange juice. Sift flour and baking powder together and add. Stir in chopped nuts. Drop dough by teaspoonfuls on greased cookie sheet. Bake in preheated, 350° F. oven for 10 to 12 minutes. While still hot, dip in a mixture of 1 cup sugar, ⅓ cup orange juice and 1 teaspoon grated orange rind. Yields about 7 dozen small cookies.

*To freeze,* cool cookies and place in rigid containers with sheet of waxed paper between layers. To serve, allow to thaw in the container.

## GINGER COOKIES
### *Thin and delicate.*

| | |
|---|---|
| 1 cup sugar | ½ teaspoon cloves |
| ¾ cup shortening (½ cup butter and ¼ cup lard) | 1½ teaspoons soda |
| 4 tablespoons molasses | 1 teaspoon baking powder |
| 1 egg | 2 cups all-purpose flour |
| 1 teaspoon ginger | ½ teaspoon salt |

Mix the first 4 ingredients well; add dry ingredients and mix well. Roll teaspoonfuls of dough into a ball and flatten on a well-greased cookie sheet with the bottom of a tumbler dipped in sugar. Cookies are very thin. Bake at 325° F. about 12 minutes. These may be decorated as desired for Christmas cookies. Yields about 5 dozen cookies.

## MOLASSES PEANUT BUTTER COOKIES
### *Tasty — and extra nutritious!*

| | |
|---|---|
| ¾ cup butter | 2 cups all-purpose flour |
| ½ cup sugar | ¼ teaspoon salt |
| ½ cup molasses | ¼ teaspoon baking soda |
| ½ cup peanut butter | 2 teaspoons baking powder |
| 1 egg | |

Cream together butter and sugar. Add molasses, peanut butter and egg, blend well. Combine dry ingredients, stir into molasses mixture. Drop by tablespoonfuls onto ungreased baking sheet. Bake in a 375° F. oven 10 to 12 minutes. Yields about 3½ to 4 dozen cookies.

# PEANUT BLOSSOMS
*Party peanut butter cookies.*

½ cup shortening
½ cup peanut butter
½ cup brown sugar
½ cup sugar
1 egg
1 teaspoon vanilla

1¾ cups all-purpose flour
1 teaspoon soda
½ teaspoon salt
Chocolate candy kisses,
    remove wrappers

Cream shortening and peanut butter. Add white sugar and brown sugar. Beat in egg and vanilla. Add dry ingredients and beat well. Shape teaspoonfuls of dough into ball and roll in sugar. Bake on a greased cookie sheet in preheated, 375° F. oven for 10 minutes. Then remove from oven and place a chocolate candy kiss on each cookie. Press down firmly so cookie cracks around edge. Return to oven and bake 2 to 5 minutes more until golden brown. Yields about 4 dozen cookies.

# ALMOND BUBBLES
*Light as air.*

½ cup soft butter
⅔ cup sugar
⅛ teaspoon salt
⅔ cup all-purpose flour
1 teaspoon grated lemon
    peel

1 cup (4½-ounce can)
    almonds, chopped
½ teaspoon vanilla
Confectioners' Sugar
Icing (below)

Combine all ingredients except icing in large mixer bowl. Mix on lowest speed or by hand until dough forms. If dough doesn't hold together, work with your hands. Chill until firm enough to handle.

Roll dough into 1-inch balls. Place 2 inches apart on ungreased baking sheet. Bake in preheated, 375° F. oven for 8 to 10 minutes, or until flat, light tan and bubbly. Cool slightly; remove carefully from baking sheet. While warm, drizzle with Confectioners' Sugar Icing. Yields about 3½ dozen cookies.

*Confectioners' Sugar Icing:* Combine ½ cup confectioners' sugar, 2 teaspoons water and ¼ teaspoon almond extract. Add small amount of water, if necessary, to make icing spread.

## DOUBLE DECKER COOKIES
*Better double the recipe!*

1 cup all-purpose flour
½ teaspoon baking soda
¼ teaspoon salt
½ cup butter
½ cup sugar
½ cup light brown sugar
1 egg

½ teaspoon vanilla
1 cup corn flake cereal, crushed
1 cup quick-cooking rolled oats
½ cup cocoanut
Chocolate Filling

Combine flour, soda and salt. Beat butter and sugars until creamy. Blend in the egg and vanilla. Stir in the flour mixture. Fold in the cereal, rolled oats and cocoanut. Using a level teaspoonful of dough, shape ⅔ of dough into balls, place on buttered cookie sheet and flatten with the bottom of a glass dipped in flour. Bake in preheated, 350° F. oven for 8 to 10 minutes. Shape ⅓ of the dough by ½ teaspoonfuls into balls, flatten and bake as directed above.

*Chocolate Filling:* Melt over hot water, 1 cup of semi-sweet chocolate pieces, ½ cup sifted confectioners' sugar and 1 tablespoon water. Beat in 1 package (3-ounce) of cream cheese until smooth. Cool and spread over the top of each of the larger cookies and top with the smaller ones. Yields 3 to 3½ dozen double cookies.

## NUT BALLS
*Sometimes called "thumb prints."*

½ cup butter
⅓ cup sugar
1 egg yolk
¼ teaspoon vanilla
¼ teaspoon almond extract

1 cup all-purpose flour
½ teaspoon salt
¾ cup nuts
½ cup apricot *or* raspberry jam *or* red jelly

Cream butter and sugar; add egg yolk, vanilla, almond flavoring. Add flour. Mix well and add chopped nuts. Roll dough into balls about 1 inch in diameter. Put on greased baking sheet. Make an impression in the center of each cookie with your thumb. Bake 25 minutes in preheated, 300° F. oven. Cool and fill with a little jam or jelly. Yields about 3½ dozen 2-inch cookies.

## ORANGE-CRANBERRY COOKIES
*Crisp morsels with the zing of fresh fruit.*

1¼ cups all-purpose flour
½ teaspoon soda
½ teaspoon salt
½ cup butter, softened
½ cup sugar
½ cup brown sugar
1 egg

½ teaspoon vanilla
1 medium orange, unpeeled, finely chopped (½ cup)
¾ cup whole cranberry sauce, drained
1 cup broken walnuts

Mix flour, soda and salt. Cream together butter and sugars until fluffy. Add egg and vanilla; beat until smooth. Add dry ingredients to creamed mixture, alternately with chopped orange and cranberry sauce; blend thoroughly. Stir in nuts. Drop by teaspoonfuls on lightly-greased cookie sheet. Bake in preheated, 375° F. oven for 10 to 12 minutes. Remove from sheet to wire rack; cookies will be crisp when cool. Yields about 4 dozen cookies.

## CHERRY COCOANUT MACAROONS
*Gay and tasty.*

4 egg whites
½ teaspoon cream of tartar
Dash of salt
2 cups sifted, confectioners' sugar
½ cup sifted, all-purpose flour

¼ cup chopped walnuts
2 cups shredded cocoanut
⅓ cup chopped maraschino cherries, well-drained

Add salt and cream of tartar to egg whites and beat until foamy. Gradually add sugar, 1 tablespoon at a time, beating until stiff. Fold in flour, walnuts, cocoanut and cherries. Drop by teaspoonfuls on greased baking sheet. Bake in preheated, 325° F. oven for 12 to 15 minutes. Garnish with additional cherries, if desired.

## CINNAMON ANGELS
*Spicy meringues.*

| | |
|---|---|
| 4 egg whites | 1½ cups sugar |
| ¼ teaspoon cream of tartar | 1 teaspoon vanilla |
| 1 teaspoon ground cinnamon | 1 package (2¼-ounce) slivered almonds |
| ⅛ teaspoon salt | |

Beat egg whites until stiff peaks are formed. Gradually beat in cream of tartar, cinnamon and salt until blended. Beat sugar in gradually until well blended. Add vanilla. Drop mixture by heaping teaspoonfuls onto ungreased, brown-paper-lined cookie sheet. Poke 5 or 6 slivered almonds into top and sides of each cookie, allowing about ½ of each almond sliver to show. Bake in preheated, 300° F. oven for 50 minutes, until almonds are toasted and cookies barely browned and dry. Remove to a wire rack to cool. Yields about 3½ dozen cookies.

## LEMON BONBONS
*Spark a cookie plate.*

| | |
|---|---|
| 1 cup butter | 1 cup sifted, all-purpose flour |
| ⅓ cup confectioners' sugar | ½ cup finely-chopped pecans |
| ¾ cup cornstarch | |

Cream butter and sugar until light. Add cornstarch and flour, beat well. Chill until easy to handle. Shape dough into small balls (about 1-inch in diameter). Scatter chopped nuts on waxed paper, place balls on nuts, flatten out with bottom of small glass dipped in flour. Place cookies on ungreased cookie sheet, nut side up. Bake in preheated, 350° F. oven for 15 minutes. Cool, frost with icing. Yields about 4 dozen cookies.

*BonBon Frosting:* Blend together until smooth: 1 cup powdered sugar, 1 teaspoon butter, juice of ½ lemon. Swirl on top of cookies.

## FRENCH LACE COOKIES
*Rich and delicate.*

1 cup all-purpose flour
1 cup finely-chopped nuts
½ cup corn syrup

½ cup shortening
⅔ cup brown sugar

Measure flour; blend in nuts. Bring syrup, shortening and sugar to a boil in saucepan over medium heat, stirring constantly. Remove from heat; gradually stir in flour and nuts. Drop batter by level teaspoonfuls about 3 inches apart on lightly-greased cookie sheet. Bake only 8 to 9 cookies at a time in preheated, 375° F. oven. Bake 5 to 6 minutes; remove from oven and allow to stand 5 minutes before removing from baking sheet. Yields about 5 dozen cookies.

*Florentines:* Spread with a little chocolate frosting and sprinkle with bits of candied fruit or nuts.

## MINCEMEAT MARVEL COOKIES
*No baking!*

⅓ cup butter, melted
1 cup canned mincemeat
½ teaspoon rum extract

3 cups fine, graham
cracker crumbs

Mix all ingredients well. Shape spoonfuls of mixture into small balls and store them in the refrigerator for several hours or overnight. Before serving, roll each ball in confectioners' sugar. Yields about 3 dozen little cookies. (Cookies will keep best if kept stored in the refrigerator.)

## VIENNA CRESCENTS
*Everyone loves these tender little almond cakes.*

1¾ cup almonds
1¾ cups all-purpose flour

⅓ cup sugar
⅞ cup butter, softened

Put almonds through food chopper. Sift dry ingredients together and mix with ground almonds. Work flour mixture into butter. Work dough into long rolls, about ½-inch in diameter. Chill. When ready to bake, cut off a small piece of dough and shape into a 2-inch crescent. Arrange on cookie sheet and bake in preheated, 325° F. oven about 25 minutes, until tips begin to turn yellow. Do not brown. Cool slightly and sprinkle with confectioners' sugar. Yields 4 to 5 dozen cookies.

*Use Brazil nuts*, instead of almonds, in above recipe.

## NOELS
*Like a candy surprise.*

½ cup soft butter
1 teaspoon vanilla
¾ cup
  brown sugar
1 egg
1¼ cups all-purpose flour
¼ teaspoon baking powder

½ teaspoon salt
½ teaspoon soda
½ cup dairy sour
  cream
36 walnut quarters
36 pitted dates

Cream butter and vanilla; gradually beat in sugar; add egg, and beat well. Sift together flour, baking powder, salt and soda. Add sifted ingredients alternately with cream. Stuff dates with a piece of walnut. Roll in dough and drop from fork on well-greased baking sheet. Bake at 400° F. for 10 minutes. Cool and ice. Yields about 5 dozen cookies.

*Icing:* Cream together 1 cup sifted confectioners' sugar, 2 tablespoons soft butter and 1 teaspoon vanilla. Add about 1 tablespoon milk or cream so that mixture spreads easily.

## PALLILOS ANISE STICKS
*An Italian Christmas cookie, lightly flavored.*

2 cups all-purpose flour
1 teaspoon baking powder
¼ teaspoon salt
¾ cup sugar

¼ cup shortening
2 large eggs, well beaten
2 drops anise extract
Butter

Blend dry ingredients; cut in shortening until particles are the size of large peas. Stir in eggs and anise extract; mix thoroughly with hands. Roll dough, half at a time, on lightly floured board to ¼-inch thickness. Cut into sticks 4x½-inch. Place on ungreased baking sheet, about ½-inch apart, and brush with soft or melted butter. Bake in preheated, 375° F. oven for 10 to 12 minutes. Yields 3 to 4 dozen cookies.

## CHRISTMAS TREE COOKIES
*Sparkling pyramids melt in your mouth —*
*they're worth the work.*

| | |
|---|---|
| 1 cup shortening (part butter) | 1 teaspoon salt |
| 1 cup sugar | ½ teaspoon soda |
| 2 eggs | Green decorators' sugar |
| 1½ teaspoons vanilla | Confectioners' Sugar |
| 3 cups all-purpose flour | Icing |
| | 50 red cinnamon candies |

Mix shortening, sugar, eggs and vanilla. Stir flour, salt and soda together; blend in. Mix thoroughly with hands. Divide dough in half. Press and mold into three 14-inch-long rolls, using ½ of dough for the largest roll, ⅔ of second half for medium roll and the remainder for the smallest roll. Coat outside of each roll evenly with green decorators' sugar. Chill. Cut each roll into ¼-inch slices; place 1 inch apart on ungreased baking sheet. Bake in preheated, 400° oven for 8 to 10 minutes or until delicately browned on edges. Cool. Stack 3 rounds (large, medium, small) together with Confectioners' Sugar Icing (below) to form a tree. Top each with red cinnamon candy dipped in icing. Yields about 50 cookie trees.

*Confectioners' Sugar Icing:* Mix 1 cup confectioners' sugar, ½ teaspoon vanilla and enough cream to make a spreading consistency.

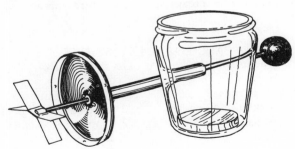

*Decorate with pretty cookies:* Cover a styrofoam cone with red foil paper, top with a glistening red Christmas ornament. Hang crescent, wreath and twisted cookies on toothpicks inserted in the foam. Set tree in center of a large plate filled with cookies that won't hang.

### SWEDISH CREAM WAFERS
*Delectable, tender cookies from Ward County,*
*North Dakota*

1¼ cups all-purpose flour
⅓ cup half-and-half
cream

1 cup butter, softened
Granulated sugar, white
or colored

Mix flour, butter and cream thoroughly. Roll into ⅛-inch thickness. Cut into 1½-inch rounds. Dip each round into granulated sugar. Bake in preheated, 350° F. oven for 6 to 8 minutes — do not brown. Cool and put together with following frosting. Handle with care while frosting. Yields about 5 dozen double cookies.

*Frosting:* Mix ¾ cup confectioners' sugar, ¼ cup softened butter, 1 teaspoon vanilla, 1 egg yolk. Use electric mixer for smoothest, lightest frosting.

### GATEAU BONBONS

⅔ cup soft butter
1 cup sugar
1 egg
1 package (3-ounce) cream
cheese, softened
½ teaspoon lemon juice
1 teaspoon finely-grated
lemon rind

2 cups sifted, all-purpose
flour
2 cups all-purpose flour
½ teaspoon baking powder
½ teaspoon salt
⅛ teaspoon soda
Orange marmalade

Mix first 6 ingredients until light and fluffy. Blend the dry ingredients and then add these to butter mixture; mix well. Chill. Using ¼ of dough at a time (keep rest refrigerated), roll ⅛-inch thick on lightly-floured board. Cut 1-inch rounds. Place half the rounds on lightly-greased baking sheet. Put ¼ teaspoon marmalade in center of each. Cover with remaining half of rounds. Seal edges with floured fingers. Bake in preheated, 350° F. oven for 8 to 10 minutes, or until edges are slightly browned. When cool, frost. Yields 7 dozen cookies.

*Easy Creamy Icing:* Blend 1 cup sifted confectioners' sugar, ¼ teaspoon salt and ½ teaspoon vanilla. Add about 1½ tablespoons cream to make mixture spread easily. If desired, tint with a few drops of food coloring. Spread lightly on cookies.

## DATE PINWHEELS
*Delectable twirls brighten up the cookie plate.*

1 package (8-ounce) dates,
  chopped
½ cup water
¼ cup sugar
2 tablespoons lemon juice
½ cup finely-chopped
  walnuts

½ cup butter
¾ cup brown sugar
1 egg
½ teaspoon vanilla
2 cups all-purpose flour
½ teaspoon baking powder
½ teaspoon salt

Combine first 3 ingredients in saucepan. Bring to simmer; cook 6 to 8 minutes, stirring frequently, until thick. Stir in lemon juice, then nuts. Cool. Cream softened butter and sugar. Add egg and vanilla extract; beat until smooth. Sift together dry ingredients. Add to creamed mixture, stirring until smooth. Chill 1 hour. Divide dough in half. On floured surface, roll one part into 8x11-inch rectangle, about ¼ inch thick. Spread ½ of date mixture evenly over dough. Beginning at long end, roll like jelly roll. Repeat with remaining dough and filling. Wrap each roll in waxed paper; freeze. To bake, slice frozen dough ¼ inch thick. Bake on lightly-greased cookie sheet in preheated, 375° F. oven for 12 to 15 minutes or until lightly browned. Yields about 5 dozen cookies.

## FATTIGMAN
*Scandinavian delicacy.*

4 egg yolks
1 whole egg
5 tablespoons sugar
2 tablespoons cream
1 tablespoon melted butter
1 tablespoon brandy
  flavoring

½ teaspoon ground
  cardamom
1½-1¾ cups all-purpose
  flour
Confectioners'
  sugar

Beat eggs and sugar until very thick and light colored. Add remaining ingredients and blend well. Gradually add flour until dough is stiff enough to roll on floured board. Roll very thin, cut into diamond shapes making a slit in center of each. Fry in 1 to 1½-inch-deep hot fat, 380° F., until delicately browned. Drain on absorbent paper. Yields about 3 dozen cookies. When cool, dip in confectioners' sugar.

## MOLASSES COOKIES
*Cut this dough into many shapes,*
*trim and hang on the tree as delightful edibles.*

| | |
|---|---|
| 4 cups all-purpose flour | 1 teaspoon cinnamon |
| 1 teaspoon salt | 1 teaspoon nutmeg |
| 1 teaspoon baking soda | 1 cup shortening |
| 2 teaspoons baking powder | 1 cup sugar |
| 2 teaspoons ginger | 1 cup molasses |
| 1 teaspoon cloves | 2 eggs, separated |

Sift flour with salt, baking soda, baking powder and spices. Cream shortening; add sugar gradually and beat until fluffy. Add molasses and egg yolks. (Reserve egg whites for frosting.) Mix well. Thoroughly mix in flour mixture. Wrap dough in waxed paper and chill until dough can be easily handled (at least 2 to 3 hours). Roll out small portions of dough about ¼-inch thick on lightly-floured board or pastry cloth. Cut with an 8-inch gingerbread man cutter.* (Use other shapes, too.) Place on ungreased baking sheets. (If you prefer, roll dough out on waxed paper, cut and invert cookies on baking sheet.) Insert a small piece of toothpick in the top of each cookie. (This will form the hole through which string for hanging from Christmas tree branch will run.) Bake in preheated, 350° F. oven about 10 to 12 minutes. Remove from oven. Cool about 2 minutes before removing from the baking sheet. Cool completely. Frost. Yields about sixteen 8-inch cookies, or many more smaller shapes.

*Cut the legs of gingerbread men a bit deeper into the body and move the legs into dancing positions once the cookie is on the baking sheet.

*Frosting:* Blend 2 egg whites with about 3 cups sifted confectioners' sugar until it is proper consistency to go through decorating tube and hold shape. Decorate as desired. Yields about 2 cups frosting.

## CHOCOLATE COOKIE DIP
*Use for sugar and rich butter cookies.*

Melt over hot (not boiling) water 1 cup semi-sweet chocolate bits; add 1 cup sifted confectioners' sugar and ⅓ cup evaporated milk. Beat until smooth. While decorating, keep frosting over hot water so it won't thicken. This amount of chocolate dip will coat 2 batches of sugar cookies.

## ROSETTES
*The bit of extra milk makes thin, delicate cookies.*

2 eggs
1 teaspoon sugar
¼ teaspoon salt

1⅓ cups milk
1 cup all-purpose flour

Beat eggs slightly with sugar and salt; add milk and flour. Stir until smooth but not frothy. Heat oil or fat to 365° F. or 370° F. Heat rosette iron well in fat. Dip hot iron in batter. Be careful not to let batter run over top of form. Return batter-dipped iron to deep hot fat and cook until lightly browned. Pick rosettes from iron using a towel to prevent breaking. Cool; sprinkle with powdered sugar. Yields about 50 cookies.
*Omit sugar* from batter and use shells for creamed meat.

## SANDBAKKELSE
*Serve, tipped upside down, on your prettiest blue plate.*

1 cup butter
1 cup sugar
1 small egg, unbeaten

½ teaspoon almond extract
3 cups all-purpose flour

Cream butter; add sugar, and cream well. Add egg and extract; mix well. Add flour to make a stiff dough. Chill dough 3 hours or overnight. Allow dough to soften slightly before forming. To form, take a small ball of dough and with the thumb, press it evenly to the bottom and up sides of Sandbakkelse tart tins. Cookie must be thin, about 1/16 inch thick. Place tins on cookie sheet and bake in preheated, 375° F. oven about 10 minutes. Do not brown. Take from oven and tip tins upside down at once. Pinch slightly to remove cookie from tin. Yields about 4 dozen cookies.

# TART COOKIES
*Afternoon coffee treat.*

Make pastry for 2-crust pie (or prepare pie crust mix according to package directions). After rolling out pastry, cut into 2½-inch circles or other desired shapes. Cut 2 of the same shape for each cookie. On half of the circles, spread about 1 teaspoon jam (apricot, raspberry, cherry) or mincemeat. For a decorative effect, cut out the center of the remaining circles with a small cutter; place each on a jam-covered circle. Seal edges securely with fork. Place on ungreased baking sheet and sprinkle with sugar. Bake in preheated, 450° F. oven for 10 to 12 minutes. Yields about 1½ dozen filled cookies.

# SPRITZ
*A Christmastime must!*

| | |
|---|---|
| 1 cup butter | ½ teaspoon almond |
| 1 cup sugar | extract |
| 2 egg yolks | 2½ cups flour |
| 1 tablespoon cream | |

Cream butter and sugar. Add egg yolks, cream and flavoring. Blend in flour. Work smooth. Put through cookie press. Bake 8 to 12 minutes in preheated, 350° F. oven. Do not brown. Yields 4 dozen cookies.

# HONEY-SPICED WALNUTS
*Yummy!*

| | |
|---|---|
| 3 cups walnut halves | ½ teaspoon vanilla |
| 1½ cups sugar | 1 teaspoon cinnamon |
| ¼ cup honey | ¼ teaspoon ginger |
| ½ cup water | |

Cook sugar, honey and water over medium heat until it reaches the firm ball stage, 242° F. on candy thermometer. Remove syrup from heat, add vanilla and spices. Beat with wooden spoon. When mixture begins to thicken and looks creamy, stir in walnuts. Stir until very thick and creamy, taking care not to break walnuts. Pour onto waxed paper and spread out to harden. When cool, break nuts apart.

## PEANUT BRITTLE
*Great, inexpensive gift.*

1½ cups sugar
⅔ cup water
½ cup white corn syrup
2 tablespoons butter
1 teaspoon vanilla

1 teaspoon soda
1 tablespoon cold water
½ pound salted peanuts, chopped

Put sugar, water and corn syrup in heavy, 2-quart saucepan and stir, over medium heat, until sugar dissolves. Stir gently so that syrup does not coat sides of pan.

When sugar is dissolved, cover pan and let mixture boil 3 or 4 minutes, then uncover pan and cook mixture to 275° F. on a candy thermometer. (Or until, when a little is cooled and chewed, it clings but does not stick to teeth.)

Add butter and peanuts and stir constantly until peanuts brown a bit — about 1 minute. Remove mixture from heat. Dissolve soda in cold water, add the vanilla and stir vigorously into candy. When candy is through foaming, turn onto a warm and well-buttered cookie sheet, jelly roll pan or marble slab and spread. As soon as candy has cooled a little at the edges, take hold of edges and pull it out as thin as possible. Loosen candy from the receptacle at the center with a spatula and turn the whole sheet upside down; pull again. Break into small pieces when cold. Yields about 1¼ pounds candy.

## BEEF CANDY (LIGHT FUDGE)
*Unique and delicious — from a rancher's wife.*

2 cups white sugar
1 cup brown sugar
½ cup corn syrup
3 tablespoons butter
½ cup milk

½ cup finely ground, lean beef (firmly packed)
½ cup broken nut meats *or* cocoanut
1 teaspoon vanilla

Combine all ingredients except nuts and vanilla. Cook the candy slowly to 241° F. on a candy thermometer. Cool to 120° F., or less, before beating. Beat with an electric mixer until creamy. If fudge stiffens too quickly, add a little cream and beat.

Add vanilla and nuts. Pour into buttered 9-inch-square pan to cool. Cut into squares.

For variation, add 1¾ squares shaved semi-sweet chocolate just before cooling. Do not stir, chocolate melts as candy cools. Yields 36 pieces, 1½-inches square.

## SUPER FUDGE
### *No guessing!*

¼ cup butter
1 cup white sugar
1 cup brown sugar
¼ cup dark corn syrup
½ cup evaporated milk

2 squares unsweetened chocolate, cut fine
1½ teaspoons vanilla
1 cup chopped walnuts (optional)

Melt butter over medium heat. Mix sugars, syrup and milk. Add this to butter and heat to boiling point. Boil rapidly, 2½ minutes, stirring constantly. Add slivered chocolate. Boil 5 minutes, stirring rapidly at first, then more slowly toward the end. Remove from heat and add vanilla and nuts. Stir vigorously until mass thickens. Longer stirring makes smoother fudge. Add a little milk or cream and continue stirring if fudge seems to thicken too rapidly. Fudge should be stirred for several minutes. Pour into 8-inch-square buttered pan and set in cool place to harden. Yields about 32 1x2-inch pieces of candy.

## CHOCOLATE NUT CRUNCH
### *Like an English Toffee.*

½ cup chopped almonds
¾ cup brown sugar
½ cup butter

6 squares semi-sweet chocolate, coarsely chopped

Scatter nuts over bottom of lightly buttered 9-inch-square pan. Combine sugar and butter in a medium saucepan. Bring to a rolling boil, stirring constantly; then boil 7 minutes, to 270° F. on candy thermometer, stirring frequently. Pour mixture over nuts in pan. Sprinkle chocolate over top of hot mixture and cover for 2 minutes. Then spread chocolate evenly. Chill until firm. Remove from pan. Break or cut into pieces. Yields about 1 pound of candy.

## PINOCHE
*Fast, delicious — from The Farmer, 1912.*

Boil together, stirring, 2 cups brown sugar, ¾ cup milk, 1 tablespoon butter until candy thermometer reads 245° F. Remove from heat. Beat until candy is thick and begins to lose its sheen. Add 1 teaspoon vanilla and ½ cup nuts. Pour into buttered, 8x8-inch pan. Cool and cut into 2-inch squares. Yields 16 pieces.

## BURNT-SUGAR CANDY
*Cuts beautifully — from Country Kitchen Cook Book, 1945.*

| | |
|---|---|
| 3 cups sugar | ½ teaspoon orange *or* |
| 1½ cups whipping cream | lemon rind |
| ⅛ teaspoon salt | 1 cup broken pecans, |
| | walnuts *or* black walnuts |

Place 2 cups sugar with the cream into a good-size kettle and bring to a boil. At the same time, put the other cup of sugar in an iron skillet and melt it over hot fire, stirring constantly until dark brown, but not burnt. When melted, and when the sugar-cream mixture is boiling hard, combine both mixtures — these will boil up. Add salt, stir until smooth and cook to soft ball stage, 235° F. on candy thermometer. Cool slightly, add grated rind and beat until mixture thickens and begins to lose its sheen. Stir in nuts and pour into buttered 9x9-inch square pan. Cut into 1½-inch squares. Yields 36 pieces.

## RICH CARAMELS
*Wrap individually in bright foil.*

| | |
|---|---|
| 1 cup half-and-half cream | 1 cup half-and-half cream |
| ½ cup butter | 1 cup broken nuts, optional |
| 2 cups sugar | 1 teaspoon vanilla |
| 1 cup dark *or* white corn syrup | |

Put first 4 ingredients into a saucepan and bring to a boil. Add second cup of cream slowly, so boiling does not stop. Cook, stirring, to hard ball stage, 250° F. on candy thermometer. Stir in vanilla and nuts. Pour into buttered,

8x8-inch pan. Cool and cut into 1-inch squares with knife dipped in water. Wrap in foil or plastic wrap. Yields 64 pieces.

## MAPLE DIVINITY
*Used to be called sea foam.*

| | |
|---|---|
| 2 cups maple-flavored syrup | 2 egg whites |
| ¼ teaspoon salt | ½ cup pecans, broken |

Butter sides of heavy 2-quart saucepan. In saucepan, cook maple-flavored syrup rapidly to hard ball stage, 250° F. on candy thermometer, without stirring. Remove from heat. At once, add salt to egg whites, beat to stiff peaks but not dry. Pour hot syrup slowly over beaten egg whites, beating constantly at high speed with electric beater. Continue beating until mixture forms soft peaks and begins to lose its gloss. Quickly add nuts, drop by teaspoonfuls on waxed paper; swirl each candy to peak. Yields about 3 dozen pieces.

## CANDY APPLES
*Keep caramel melted in top of chafing dish over hot water and let guests make their own treats.*

| | |
|---|---|
| 1 cup granulated sugar | 12 medium-sized apples |
| 1 cup brown sugar | 12 wooden skewers |
| ¼ cup light corn syrup | 2 cups corn soya shreds, |
| ⅔ cup water | wheat shreds |
| 1 teaspoon salt | *or* chopped nuts |

Cook sugars, corn syrup, water and salt together, stirring until sugars dissolve. Continue cooking without stirring to 250° F. (hard ball in cold water). Remove from heat. Insert a skewer in stem end of apple and dip in syrup; let excess syrup drain off. Roll in corn soya, chopped nuts or wheat shreds. Set on waxed paper or greased baking sheet to harden. Yields 12 candy apples.

*Variation:* Two large bags of light caramels may be melted over hot water to make the candy coating for the apples.

## POP CORN BALLS
*Keep a pan of cold water handy to cool off your hands
when handling hot pop corn and syrup.*

2 cups dark corn syrup
  (½ molasses may be used)
2 cups sugar
2 tablespoons butter
1 teaspoon vinegar

1 teaspoon salt
½ teaspoon soda
1 tablespoon hot water
5 quarts freshly-popped
  corn

Cook first 6 ingredients to hard ball stage, 250° F. on a candy thermometer. Remove from fire and add soda dissolved in hot water. Pour the hot syrup over popped corn, stirring until each kernel is well-coated. When mixture can be molded, form into balls with buttered hands. Wrap each ball in plastic wrap. Yields about 15 medium-size balls.

## STUFFED DATES, PRUNES OR FIGS
*Twist individual pieces in plastic wrap
and use for Christmas stocking stuffers.*

Steam prunes or figs until soft. Remove pits from dates or prunes carefully. Fill with: Piece of marshmallow, large pieces of nuts, candied orange or grapefruit peel. Roll in granulated sugar.

## PULL TAFFY CANDY
*Pull vigorously —
from the 1945 Country Kitchen Cook Book.*

2 cups sugar
⅔ cup water
2 tablespoons vinegar

1 tablespoon butter
Flavoring

Mix all ingredients, but flavoring. Stir over heat until sugar dissolves. Then, cook to soft crack stage, 268° F. to 270° F. on a candy thermometer, without further stirring. Pour into a buttered platter. Cool enough to handle. Pull until taffy is white, adding flavoring as you pull. Cut lengths into small pieces with a sharp knife. Candy becomes creamy as it stands. Yields about 4 dozen small pieces.

# PIES, CAKES AND OTHER DESSERTS

E. Landin

## PIE CRUST SUPREME
*Codington County, South Dakota teenager won a state's
4-H fruit pie baking contest using this crust.*

| | |
|---|---|
| 1½ cups sifted, all-purpose flour | ½ cup lard |
| ½ teaspoon salt | 2 tablespoons butter |
| ¼ teaspoon baking powder | 2 tablespoons beaten egg |
| | 3 tablespoons ice water |
| | ½ teaspoon vinegar |

Combine first 5 ingredients and blend with pastry blender.
Add liquid ingredients, a little at a time, until all flour is
moistened. (You probably will not need all of the liquid.)
Divide in half and roll on a floured pastry cloth or between
sheets of floured waxed paper. Line a 9-inch pie pan. Yields
pastry for a 2-crust, 9-inch pie.

*Make tarts easily* by rolling dough to desired thickness on
heavy aluminum foil. Cut foil into 4-inch or 5-inch squares.
Fold up edges of crust and foil; pinch corners so squared-shells
hold their shape. Bake on cookie sheets in preheated, 425° F.
oven for 12 to 15 minutes.


*Seal pie crust edges* by moistening the lower crust edge with
water before putting on the top crust. *Or,* trim the lower crust
even with the pan and the upper crust ½ inch wider. Then fold
this extra crust under the lower crust. Press two crusts together
with a fork or flute between thumb and first two fingers. —
The Farmer, 1941


## MIX AND PRESS CRUST
*If you hate to roll pie crust, hurrah!*

| | |
|---|---|
| 1 cup all-purpose flour | 2 tablespoons butter |
| ½ teaspoon salt | 1 tablespoon cold water |
| ¼ cup shortening | |

Place all ingredients in a small mixer bowl. Beat at low
speed with electric mixer until particles are fine. Use rubber
spatula frequently to push mixture into beaters. Make certain
that there are no large particles of butter or shortening.
Pour crumb mixture into 9-inch pie plate and spread over

bottom. Press crumb mixture evenly and firmly over the sides and bottom of the pie pan with floured fingers. You'll have the nicest fluted edge if you work dough up the sides of the pan first, then press remaining mixture across the bottom.

Flute edges. Do not prick crust. It now is ready to bake or fill, as recipe calls for.

For baked crust, place in preheated, 425° F. oven 12 to 15 minutes, until golden brown (or as directed in recipe).

For more even browning, it is a good idea to place a ring of aluminum foil on the pie crust edge the last 5 minutes of baking. Yields 1-crust, 9-inch pie shell.

*Two crust pie:* Place 2 cups all-purpose flour, 1 teaspoon salt, ½ cup shortening, ¼ cup butter and 2 tablespoons cold water in small mixer bowl. Beat at low speed until all particles are fine, as directed above.

Press 2 cups of the crumb mixture into a 9-inch pie plate, as directed above. Fill as desired. Sprinkle remaining crumb mixture over the filling. Flute edge of crust. For a firmer top crust, press down with fingers. If desired, sprinkle with sugar. Bake as directed in recipe. Cover edge of crust with a strip of foil during last 15 to 20 minutes of baking to prevent excessive browning.

## CORN FLAKE CRUST

3 cups corn flakes
¼ cup butter

2 tablespoons sugar

Crush corn flakes into fine crumbs. Blend butter and sugar. Stir in corn flake crumbs; mix well. Press evenly and firmly around sides and bottom of 9-inch pie pan. Chill.

## CHOCOLATE CRUMB CRUST

1 cup chocolate wafer crumbs

½ cup finely-chopped walnuts
¼ cup softened butter

Mix wafer crumbs, walnuts and butter until crumbly. Press onto bottom and sides of 9-inch pie plate. Bake in preheated, 375° F. oven about 7 minutes. Refrigerate until well chilled.

## GRAHAM CRACKER CRUST

1⅔ cups fine graham　　　　¼ cup sugar
　　cracker crumbs　　　　　¼ cup flaked cocoanut
¼ cup soft butter

Combine graham cracker crumbs, butter, sugar and cocoanut, blend thoroughly. Pour into an 8-inch or 9-inch pie plate, press firmly against sides and bottom of plate. Bake in preheated, 375° F. oven for 7 minutes. Cool; freeze, if desired.

## MERINGUE

3 egg whites, at room　　　　¼ teaspoon cream of tartar
　　temperature　　　　　　　6 tablespoons sugar

Beat egg whites until frothy in a small, deep bowl — several seconds with an electric mixer. Bowl should be completely free of grease or oil, so whites will attain full volume. Add cream of tartar and beat on high speed until whites have just lost their foamy appearance and bend over slightly when beaters are withdrawn, forming soft peaks. (If cream of tartar is old or not available, substitute 1 teaspoon freshly-squeezed lemon juice for ¼ teaspoon cream of tartar.)

Reduce speed to medium while adding sugar gradually, about 1 tablespoon at a time. Return to high speed and beat until whites are fairly stiff, but still glossy and soft, with peaks forming again when beaters are withdrawn.

Place meringue on the hot filling in several mounds around edge of pie. When filling is hot, there is less chance of meringue shrinking and weeping. Use a narrow spatula to gently push meringue against inner edge of pie crust, sealing it well. Cover the rest of the filling by swirling meringue from edge of pie to center, forming decorative peaks with spatula. Bake pie as directed in recipe. Cool on wire rack to room temperature, away from drafts, for 2 hours before cutting and serving. Cut with a sharp knife, dipped into hot water after each cut, and you will have "clean-cut" servings.

*Four-Egg-White Meringue:* Combine 4 egg whites, ¼ teaspoon cream of tartar and 8 tablespoons sugar, as directed above.

## MORE MERINGUE TIPS

*Early addition* of the cream of tartar stabilizes egg whites, permitting them to hold more air without breaking down. *Contrary to popular belief,* salt actually lowers the stability of egg whites.

*The amount of beating* before and after adding sugar is a chief factor in preventing common problems such as beading, weeping, slipping and dryness. The key is soft peak. Stiff, but not dry beating is one stage beyond soft peak but does not give such a tender meringue.

## FRESH LEMON MERINGUE PIE
### *Fantastic!*

1 baked, 9-inch
    pie crust
1½ cups sugar
¼ cup *plus* 2 tablespoons
    cornstarch
¼ teaspoon salt
3 egg yolks, well-beaten
½ cup freshly-squeezed
    lemon juice
½ cup cold water

2 tablespoons butter
1½ cups boiling water
1 teaspoon finely-grated
    yellow part of
    lemon peel
Few drops yellow food
    coloring
1 meringue, using 3 *or* 4
    egg whites

In an even-heating, 2 to 3-quart saucepan, thoroughly mix sugar, cornstarch and salt. A wire whisk works best. Use whisk to gradually blend in cold water, then lemon juice, until mixture is smooth. Add beaten yolks, blending vigorously. Add butter and gradually stir in boiling water, stirring constantly with a rubber spatula. Gradually bring mixture to a full boil, stirring gently and constantly with spatula over medium or high heat. Spatula moves mixture across bottom of pan in greater quantities and prevents uneven thickening and scorching. Reduce heat slightly as mixture begins to thicken. Boil slowly for 1 minute. Remove from heat and stir in grated peel and food coloring. Pour hot filling into baked pie shell. Let stand, allowing a thin film to form while preparing meringue. Top hot filling with meringue and bake in preheated, 350° F. oven for 12 to 15 minutes or until golden brown. Yields 6 servings.

## COCOANUT CREAM PIE
*Custard's like velvet!*

1 baked, 9-inch pie crust with high, fluted edges
⅔ cup sugar
½ teaspoon salt
2½ tablespoons cornstarch
1 tablespoon all-purpose flour
3 cups milk

3 egg yolks, slightly beaten
1 tablespoon butter
1½ teaspoons vanilla
¾ cup moist, flake cocoanut
Sweetened, whipped cream

Mix the sugar, salt, cornstarch and flour in a heavy saucepan. Gradually stir in milk. Cook over moderate heat, stirring constantly, until mixture thickens and boils. Boil 1 minute. Remove from heat. Stir a little of the hot mixture into the beaten yolks. Then blend yolks into hot mixture in saucepan. Boil 1 minute more, stirring constantly. Remove from heat. Blend in butter and vanilla; cool, stirring occasionally. Just before pouring into pie shell, fold in cocoanut. Chill thoroughly, about 2 hours. Serve, topped with whipped cream. Yields 6 servings.

*Banana Cream Pie:* Omit cocoanut. Just before pouring filling into pie shell, slice 3 large bananas and arrange in ½-inch-deep layer in bottom of pie shell. Pour in filling and chill.

## CUSTARD PIE
*Unbeatable — from the 1928 Country Kitchen Cook Book.*

Pastry for 1-crust, 9-inch pie
3 eggs
½ cup sugar

2½ cups milk (scalded)
¼ teaspoon salt
Nutmeg
1 teaspoon vanilla

Line a pie tin with pastry. Make a good rim on the crust to keep filling in. Scald milk and add to eggs slightly beaten with sugar and salt added. Strain mixture into lower crust and sprinkle nutmeg over the top. Bake in preheated, 450° F. oven for 10 minutes to set crust, then bake more slowly at 350° F. until custard is firm and knife dipped in center of filling comes out clean.

*Cocoanut Custard Pie:* Substitute 1 cup cream for 1 cup milk in above recipe. Omit nutmeg. Add ½ cup moist, canned cocoanut before baking.

## CHOCOLATE PIE
*Grandma's specialty — smooth and chocolate-y.*

| | |
|---|---|
| 2 cups milk | Few grains salt |
| 2 squares unsweetened | 2 egg yolks, beaten |
| chocolate, cut | ¼ cup sugar |
| 3 tablespoons flour | 1 teaspoon vanilla |
| ½ cup sugar | Meringue, page 276 |

Scald chocolate and milk in top of double boiler. Place mixture over hot water. Mix well flour, ½ cup sugar and salt. Add to milk, stirring constantly; stir mixture well. Cook over hot water 15 minutes until flour is thoroughly cooked. Add eggs, beaten with the remaining ¼ cup of sugar. Stir quickly until thickened. Remove from heat, add vanilla, cool slightly and pour into baked shell. Cover hot filling with meringue and bake 20 minutes. If pie is to be topped with whipped cream, decrease flour to 2 tablespoons and use 2 whole eggs. Yields 6 servings.

*Note:* Do not scrape sides of pan while stirring filling or a lumpy custard will result. If you forget, simply strain cooked filling into pie shell.

## RHUBARB MERINGUE PIE
*Super!*

| | |
|---|---|
| Pastry for 1-crust, | 2½ tablespoons flour |
| 9-inch pie | 3 egg yolks, beaten |
| 2½ cups rhubarb, cut | Grated rind of ½ lemon |
| 1¼ cups sugar | Meringue, page 276 |

Mix together flour and sugar, add yolks of eggs and mix well. Add rhubarb, mix and pour in unbaked pastry shell. Bake in preheated, 425° F. oven for 20 minutes, reduce heat to 325° F. and bake until tender. Top with meringue, page 276 and bake 20 minutes. Yields 6 servings.

## PUMPKIN PIE
*Freezes well up to 4 months.*

Pastry for 1-crust,
9-inch pie
1¾ cups mashed, cooked *or*
canned pumpkin
¼ cup brown sugar
½ cup white sugar
½ teaspoon salt

1 teaspoon cinnamon
¼ teaspoon ginger
¼ teaspoon nutmeg
¾ cup evaporated milk
1 cup milk
2 tablespoons butter
3 eggs, beaten

Combine pumpkin, brown and white sugar, salt and spices. Heat milk and add the butter. Combine with the pumpkin mixture. Add the beaten eggs and stir until thoroughly mixed. Pour into pie shell and bake at 450° F. for 15 minutes. Reduce heat to 300° F. and continue baking for about 45 minutes or until a silver knife inserted in the center comes out clean. Cool. Yields 6 servings.

*To freeze,* wrap in moisture-vapor-proof material, label and freeze.

Remove from freezer and allow to stand in wrapping at room temperature for about 30 minutes before serving. Then remove wrapping and place in a preheated, 325° F. oven for another 30 minutes. Serve with whipped cream. Do not store in the freezer more than 4 months.

*A carrot variation worth knowing:* From September 20, 1886 issue of The Farmer. "Every farmer's wife in the west, especially in Dakota where we can get so little fruit, is perplexed with the questions how to supply the table with pies. During threshing and harvesting this year we have been feeding our men on pumpkin pie. Rather an expensive luxury when pumpkins are scarce? Not at all. We make them of carrots, which you know we can raise to perfection. Boil the carrots, strain through a colander and prepare it as you do genuine pumpkin, and if there is a reader of The Farmer who can tell the difference, he or she is smarter than the average."

*Response to "carrot variation"* above, from a Valley City, Dakota, reader in October 20, 1886 issue: "We were somewhat amused at the idea of making pumpkin pie out of carrots, but the recipe given by a correspondent last month was tried, and as all our family is fond of pumpkin pies they were delighted at the new and easy way of making them, and declare that if they could forget that it was made from carrots they would be perfectly satisfied."

*Orange Carrot Pie:* Add ½ teaspoon grated orange rind to filling. Add ½ teaspoon grated lemon rind to pastry at the time shortening is cut into flour.

## BUTTERSCOTCH PIE
### *Well worth the effort!*

| | |
|---|---|
| Baked pastry shell for 1-crust, 9-inch pie | 2 eggs, beaten |
| ¼ cup soft butter | ½ teaspoon salt |
| ¾ cup brown sugar | 2 cups milk |
| 2 tablespoons all-purpose flour | ½ cup granulated sugar |
| | ½ cup boiling water |
| | Whipped cream |

Cream butter with brown sugar and flour. Mix in eggs and salt. Scald milk in double boiler.

*Caramelize sugar* in a heavy saucepan by heating and stirring sugar constantly over medium heat until sugar melts and is a rich brown. Add boiling water; stir and boil mixture until syrupy.

Stir caramel mixture into hot milk in top of double boiler. Add creamed mixture and cook over hot water 15 minutes; stirring constantly. Cool slightly. Pour into baked pie shell. Cool, then chill at least 1 hour. Serve with sweetened whipped cream. Yields 6 servings.

## COTTAGE CHEESE PIE
### *German delicacy.*

| | |
|---|---|
| Pastry for 1 crust, 9-inch pie | ½ cup sugar |
| 2 eggs, well beaten | 1 tablespoon flour |
| 1 cup large-curd cottage cheese | ½ cup milk |
| | Milk |
| | Cinnamon |

Line pie plate with pastry, making a high, heavy edge. Mix first 5 filling ingredients and pour into pastry shell. Fill shell with milk nearly to fluted edge. Sprinkle with cinnamon. Bake in preheated, 375° F. oven for about 1 hour, or until silver knife inserted in center comes out clean. Cool and serve. Yields 6 servings.

## PECAN PIE
*Easy classic.*

Pastry for 1-crust,
  9-inch pie shell
3 eggs, slightly beaten
1 cup dark corn syrup
1 cup sugar

2 tablespoons butter,
  melted
1 teaspoon vanilla
⅛ teaspoon salt
1 cup pecans

Combine ingredients, adding nuts last. Pour into unbaked pastry shell. Bake in preheated, 400° F. oven 15 minutes; reduce heat to 350° F. and continue baking 30 to 35 minutes. Filling should be slightly less set in the center than around edges. Yields 6 servings.

*Fudge-Nut Pie:* Follow recipe for Pecan Pie, melting 2 ounces unsweetened chocolate with the butter and reducing eggs to 2.

*Date-Nut Pie:* Follow recipe for Pecan Pie, substituting 1 cup finely-chopped dates and ½ cup walnut halves for pecans.


## WASHINGTON CHERRY CREAM PIE
*So pretty — yet it's made quickly.*

Baked pastry shell for
  1-crust, 9-inch pie
1 package (3¼-ounce)
  vanilla pudding and pie
  filling mix
  Milk (amount directed
  on filling package)
¾ cup sugar

¼ cup cornstarch
½ teaspoon cinnamon
1 can (1-pound) red, sour,
  pitted cherries
  Red food coloring
½ cup whipping cream,
  whipped and sweetened

Prepare filling mix according to package directions. Pour into baked pie shell. Chill. Blend dry ingredients for topping and gradually stir in ¾ cup of juice drained from cherries, adding cold water to juice to make ¾ cup, if necessary. Cook mixture until thick and clear, stirring constantly. Add food coloring and drained cherries. Cool and spread over vanilla cream layer in pie shell. Chill. Top with whipped cream. Yields 6 servings.

## PINK MOON STRAWBERRY-RHUBARB PIE
*A South Dakota state pie contest winner.*

Pastry for 2-crust,
9-inch pie
2¼ cups fresh rhubarb
(frozen rhubarb,
thawed and well
drained, may be used)
½ cup strawberry halves
(thawed, frozen, un-
sweetened strawberries
may be used)
2 eggs
1¼ cups sugar
⅛ teaspoon salt
½ cup cream
2 tablespoons melted
butter
½ teaspoon vanilla

Mix drained strawberries, rhubarb; set aside. For custard, beat eggs, sugar and salt slightly. Stir in cream, butter and vanilla. Cook mixture over low heat until mixture thickens, stirring constantly — 7 to 10 minutes. Roll out a little more than half the pastry and fit into a 9-inch pie pan. Place mixed fruit on pie shell bottom. Pour custard mixture over it. Roll out remaining pastry and cut into strips ½-inch wide and weave lattice crust. Bake pie in preheated, 350° F. oven for 45 minutes . . . or at 325° F. if you use a glass pie plate. Yields 6 servings.

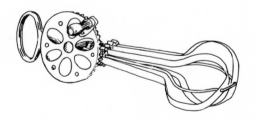

## STRAWBERRY GLACÉ PIE
*Best strawberry pie there is!*

Wash and hull 1 quart strawberries, reserving a few large ones for garnish. Combine half of the berries with 1 cup sugar in a saucepan; crush. Combine 2 tablespoons cornstarch, ½ cup water, 1 tablespoon lemon juice and ¼ teaspoon salt; add to the crushed berries. Cook over low heat until thickened and transparent, stirring constantly. Cool. Halve the remaining berries; gently fold into the thickened mixture. Pour into a baked pastry shell and chill. Serve, topped with whipped cream. Garnish with the whole berries. Yields 6 servings.

## APPLE PRALINE PIE
*Better make two!*

Pastry for 2-crust, 9-inch
  pie
½ cup brown sugar
½ teaspoon cinnamon
½ teaspoon nutmeg
¼ teaspoon salt

4 cups sliced, tart apples
2 tablespoons butter
  Praline Topping, below
¼ cup coarsely chopped
  nuts

Mix sugar, spices and salt. Slice apples into an unbaked, 9-inch pastry-lined pie pan. Sprinkle on sugar-spice mixture. Dot with butter. Cover with top pastry, cutting slits to allow steam to escape. Bake in preheated, 425° F. oven about 45 minutes, or until done. Spread Praline Topping on top crust and sprinkle with nuts; continue baking for 5 minutes. Yields 6 servings.

*Praline Topping:* Cream 2 tablespoons butter until smooth; add ¼ cup brown sugar and 1 tablespoon half-and-half cream; beat until smooth.

*For a shiny crust:* Before baking, brush tops of pies with 1 egg yolk, lightly beaten with 2 tablespoons milk.

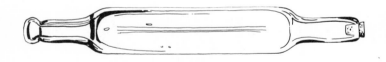

## GERMAN APPLE PIE
*Winter apple treat.*

Pastry for 1-crust, 9-inch
  pie
3 cups sliced, pared apples
½ cup raisins
1 egg
1 cup dairy sour cream

½ cup sugar
1 teaspoon soda
¼ teaspoon nutmeg
¼ teaspoon salt
  Whipped cream,
  optional

Prepare pie shell and bake in preheated, 425° F. oven for 10 minutes. Lower oven temperature to 375° F. Place apples and raisins in pie shell. Combine remaining ingredients. Pour over apples. Bake at 375° F. for 30 to 35 minutes, or until apples are tender. Cool. Top with a daub of whipped cream when served. Yields 6 servings.

## RASPBERRY, GOOSEBERRY, BLACKBERRY OR CURRANT PIE
*You'll use this recipe all summer.*

Pastry for 2-crust,
  9-inch pie
4 cups fresh *or* frozen
  fruit
3 tablespoons cornstarch
⅔-1 cup sugar

⅛ teaspoon salt
1½ tablespoons lemon juice
  *or* ½ teaspoon
  cinnamon
2 tablespoons butter

Line 9-inch pie pan with pastry. Defrost frozen berries just enough to separate. Combine cornstarch, sugar, cinnamon and salt; mix with fruit and let stand about 15 minutes. Place berry mixture in unbaked pastry shell, dot with butter and top with lattice crust. Bake in preheated, 425° F. oven for 35 to 45 minutes. Yields 6 servings.

*Strawberry Pie:* Use 4 cups sliced strawberries and 1 teaspoon grated orange rind in place of raspberries and lemon juice.

## WILD BLUEBERRY PIE
*Northern Minnesotan's specialty.*

Pastry for 2-crust, 9-inch
  pie
4 cups wild blueberries
¾ cup sugar

3 tablespoons flour
½ teaspoon cinnamon
1 tablespoon butter

Roll bottom crust and place in pie pan. Sprinkle dry ingredients over berries and stir gently until blended. Pour into crust. Dot with butter. Let stand 15 minutes. Cover with top crust. Bake in preheated, 450° F. oven for 10 minutes. Reduce heat to 350° F. and bake until crust is golden brown, about 40 minutes. Yields 6 servings.

*Blue Cheese-Blueberry Pie:* Crumble a little blue cheese over blueberry pie filling before fitting it with a top crust.

## BEEF MINCEMEAT
### *From a stockman's wife.*

2 pounds lean beef (from
  any part of carcass)
1 pound beef suet
5 pounds apples, peeled,
  cored and chopped
2 pounds raisins
2 pounds currants
2 quarts apple cider

3 pounds brown sugar
¾ pound citron, ground
2 tablespoons cinnamon
1 tablespoon nutmeg
2 tablespoons mace
1 tablespoon cloves
1 tablespoon salt

Cook meat in a very little water in a covered pan until done, when cool grind with suet and apples. Add the remaining ingredients and bring to a boil. Cook 15 minutes, stirring frequently. Pour into sterile jars; adjust lids. Process 60 minutes at 10 pounds pressure. Yields 7 to 8 quarts mincemeat.

*Especially good if you add* finely chopped rind and juice of 1 orange plus 1 cup molasses to above recipe.


## MINCEMEAT-SQUASH PIE
### *Try this at Thanksgiving.*

Pastry for 1-crust,
  9-inch pie
1½ cups mincemeat
1 cup mashed, cooked
  winter squash
½ cup sugar

½ teaspoon cinnamon
2 eggs
¼ teaspoon salt
¼ teaspoon nutmeg
½ cup milk

Cover bottom of pastry shell with mincemeat. Combine remaining ingredients, using a rotary beater. Pour over mincemeat in a pie pan. Bake in a preheated, 425° F. oven for 30 to 40 minutes. Serve slightly warm. Yields 6 servings.


## MINCEMEAT PASTRY SQUARES
### *Take one to a Farm Bureau Supper.*

Prepare pastry for a 2-crust, 9-inch pie. Roll half of dough into a rectangle, 15x10 inches; transfer to baking sheet. Spread mincemeat evenly over pastry to within ¾-inch of edge. Roll out remaining dough for top crust; place over filling. Pinch edges together; cut slits in top to allow steam to escape. Bake in preheated, 450° F. oven about 20 minutes or until golden brown. Spread glaze over top. Yields 12 servings.

*Lemon Glaze:* Mix thoroughly 1 cup sifted confectioners' sugar, 2 teaspoons grated lemon peel and 2 tablespoons lemon juice.

## CHEESE-MINCE PIE
*Rich, so serve small slices.*

Baked pastry shell for
  1-crust, 9-inch pie
3 cups (24-ounces)
  mincemeat

12 2-inch rounds, thin-
  sliced cheddar cheese

Fill pie shell with mincemeat. Bake 10 to 15 minutes, until filling is hot and bubbly, in a preheated, 350° F. oven. Remove from oven and top with cheese rounds while still warm. Yields 6 to 8 servings.

*Brandied Mince Pie:* Fill pie shell with mincemeat, sprinkle with 1 tablespoon sugar. Bake 10 to 15 minutes. Remove from oven and sprinkle with 2 teaspoons brandy extract. Top with Hard Sauce, page 318.

## CRANBERRY PIE
*Rich winter treat.*

Pastry for 2-crust,
  9-inch pie
4 cups fresh cranberries,
  washed and halved
1½ cups brown sugar

4 tablespoons light
  molasses
½ teaspoon cinnamon
  Whipped cream *or* ice
  cream, optional

Fill 9-inch pastry-lined pan with cranberries which have been lightly mixed with brown sugar. Dust with cinnamon. Sprinkle on molasses. Cover filling with lattice crust made of ½-inch strips of pastry placed about 1-inch apart. Flute edge with remaining pastry. Bake pie in preheated, 425° F. oven for 10 minutes, then reduce heat to 325° F. Bake about 1 hour longer. Serve with whipped cream or vanilla ice cream, if desired. Yields 6 servings.

## CHERRY-ALMOND PIE
*Nuts add a special crunch.*

Pastry for 2-crust,
    9-inch pie
1 cup sugar
3 tablespoons cornstarch
¼ teaspoon salt
1 cup juice from cherries
¼ teaspoon red food
    coloring, optional

¼ cup slivered, toasted
    almonds
2 cans (1-pound each)
    water-pack, tart, red pie
    cherries, about 3 cups
    drained fruit
2 tablespoons butter

Mix sugar, cornstarch and salt in saucepan. Add juice and food coloring; stir until smooth. Cook until thickened and clear, stirring. Remove from heat; add almonds, drained cherries and butter. Pour into unbaked 9-inch pastry-lined pie pan. Cover with top crust. Bake in preheated, 425° F. oven about 40 minutes. Cool. Yields 6 servings.

## PINEAPPLE UPSIDE DOWN PIE
*Try it, you'll love it.*

Pastry for 2-crust, 9-inch
    pie
1 can (1-pound, 4½-ounce)
    pineapple tidbits
    Water
3 tablespoons cornstarch
2 tablespoons lemon juice

¾ cup brown
    sugar
6 tablespoons butter
½ cup pecan halves
    Whipped cream *or*
    ice cream, optional

To syrup drained from pineapple, add enough water to measure 1¼ cups. Combine with cornstarch, lemon juice and ¼ cup brown sugar. Cook, stirring, until clear and thickened. Blend in pineapple and 2 tablespoons butter. Cool slightly. Melt remaining 4 tablespoons butter in 9-inch pie pan. Sprinkle with remaining ½ cup brown sugar and 1 tablespoon water. Arrange pecan halves, rounded side down, around bottom and sides of pan. Carefully line pan with pastry. Spoon in pineapple mixture. Cover with pastry; seal and flute edges. Prick top. Place pie on square of foil in oven to catch drippings. Bake at 425° F. 25 minutes, until richly browned. Turn out, upside down, on serving plate immediately. Cut when cool. Serve with whipped or ice cream, if desired. Yields 6 servings.

## MILE-HIGH APRICOT PIE
### *Tangy!*

1⅔ cups finely-rolled
    graham cracker crumbs
¼ cup sugar
¼ cup butter, softened
¼ cup chopped almonds
⅓ cup apricot preserves
1 can (1-pound, 1-ounce)
    apricot halves

2 tablespoons lemon juice
1 envelope unflavored
    gelatin
⅔ cup sugar
¼ teaspoon salt
4 eggs, separated

Blend crumbs, sugar, butter and almonds. Press firmly against bottom and sides of 9-inch pie plate. Bake at 375° F. for 8 minutes. Cool. Spread apricot preserves over bottom of pie shell. Drain apricot halves. Reserve syrup. Chop apricots fine. In top of double boiler, combine ½ cup apricot syrup and lemon juice. Sprinkle gelatin over liquids and let stand for 5 minutes. Add ⅓ cup sugar, salt and egg yolks. Beat slightly to blend. Cook over hot water, stirring constantly, until mixture is thickened and coats a metal spoon. Remove from heat and add chopped apricots. Chill until thickened. Beat egg whites until foamy. Gradually add remaining ⅓ cup sugar, beating until egg whites are stiff, but not dry. Fold into gelatin-apricot mixture. Pour into pie shell. Chill 3 to 4 hours, or until firm. Yields 6 servings.

## CHOCOLATE-COFFEE PIE
### *Delectable!*

1 baked pastry shell for
    1-crust, 9-inch pie
¾ cup butter, soft
1 cup plus 2 tablespoons
    sugar
1½ squares unsweetened
    chocolate, melted
    and cooled

1½ teaspoons vanilla
1½ tablespoons powdered,
    instant coffee
3 eggs
½ cup nuts, chopped
1 cup whipping cream,
    whipped

Cream together butter and sugar. Blend in chocolate, vanilla and coffee. Add eggs, one at a time, beating 2 minutes after each addition. Pour into pie shell. Chill until set, about 2 to 3 hours. Top with whipped cream and chopped nuts. Yields 6 servings.

## DATE CREAM PIE
### *A delicious quickie.*

Bake an 8-inch pie shell with pie crust mix (or use the extra shell you made last time you mixed up a pie). Prepare a package of vanilla pudding or pie filling mix. When filling has cooled a bit, fold in ¾ cup chopped pitted dates. Turn into pie shell, chill. Yields 4 or 5 servings.

## BLUEBERRY-GRAHAM-CRACKER PIE

½ cup butter, melted
16 graham crackers, rolled
   fine
¼ cup brown sugar
1 package (8-ounce)
   cream cheese, softened
½ cup sugar
2 eggs

1 teaspoon vanilla
Cinnamon
Juice of 1 lemon
1 can (16-ounce) blueberry
   pie filling
Whipped cream *or*
   ice cream

Mix first 3 ingredients and press into bottom and sides of 7½x11½-inch pan. Beat next 4 ingredients with electric mixer and pour over cracker crust. Bake in preheated, 375° F. oven for 15 minutes. While filling is still warm, sprinkle with cinnamon. When cooled, mix lemon juice and pie filling and pour over custard. Refrigerate pie for 24 hours. Serve with whipped cream or ice cream topping. Yields 6 servings.

*Frosting stays nice* when you tote a cake if you cover pan with wax paper that has been rubbed with a small amount of butter. Paper doesn't stick to cake.

# FOUNDATION YELLOW CAKE
*A rich basic recipe for a yellow butter cake.*
*From this you can make white, gold, chocolate, burnt-sugar,*
*spice and other cakes.*
*Printed in the 1934 Country Kitchen Cook Book.*

| *Standard Recipe* | *Smaller Recipe* |
|---|---|
| ¾ cup butter *or* part other shortening | ½ cup butter |
| 1½ cups sugar | 1 cup sugar |
| 3 eggs | 2 eggs |
| 1 cup milk *or* water | ⅔ cup milk *or* water |
| ¾ teaspoon salt | ½ teaspoon salt |
| 3 teaspoons baking powder | 2 teaspoons baking powder |
| 3 cups cake flour | 2 cups cake flour |
| 1 teaspoon vanilla | ⅔ teaspoon vanilla |
| *(Makes 2 large squares or 3 layers.)* | *(Makes 1 sheet cake or 2 layers.)* |

Cream fat thoroughly in deep bowl (have it soft before you start). Add sugar gradually, beating until the mixture is fluffy and light like whipped cream. Add eggs, beaten until light. Sift dry ingredients together and add alternately with liquid, beginning and ending with the dry ingredients. Beat thoroughly and add flavoring. Bake in layers or flat loaf pan in preheated, 375° F. oven for 30 minutes.

## CLASSIC VARIATIONS
*Important: Variations given are based on the standard (larger) recipe.*

*White Cake:* Use 6 egg whites instead of 3 whole eggs in standard recipe (4 whites in smaller recipe). Beat until stiff, but not dry, and fold in at last, lightly but thoroughly.

*Lady Baltimore Cake:* Make white cake in 2 layers. Make 7-minute Frosting, page 303, and divide into 2 bowls. To one part add 1 cup chopped nuts and fruit (as raisins, dates, figs) and put this between layers. Ice top and sides with rest of icing left plain.

*Spanish Cake:* Sift 3 teaspoons cinnamon with dry ingredients. Ice with Creamy Icing, page 301.

*Old-Fashioned Chocolate Cake:* Bake yellow cake in layers and ice with Easy Fudge Icing, page 302.

*Chocolate Cake:* Add 3 squares melted chocolate to the standard recipe before dry ingredients are added. Scant the shortening by 3 tablespoons and increase milk 3 tablespoons. This is not a red cake but chocolate color.

*Fluffy Spice Cake:* Combine 1¾ teaspoons cinnamon, 1 teaspoon nutmeg and ¾ teaspoon cloves with 3 tablespoons boiling water. Let stand. Add to standard yellow cake just before dry ingredients are added. Half-cup strong coffee may be used in place of ½ cup of the liquid if you wish a coffee spice cake.

*Gold Cake or Lord Baltimore Cake:* For a rich egg yolk cake, use 6 yolks instead of 3 whole eggs in the standard recipe. Beat them until very light with a rotary beater and add to the butter and sugar mixture. Increase baking powder 1 teaspoon. Flavor with lemon. Ice with 7-Minute Frosting, page 303.

*Cocoanut Cake:* Ice white or yellow cake with 7-Minute Frosting, page 303.  Pile with fresh grated cocoanut or moist canned cocoanut.

*Burnt-Sugar Cake:* Make a burnt-sugar syrup by caramelizing to a golden brown 2 cups white sugar. Add 2 cups hot water, stir until caramel is dissolved and boil until it makes a thick syrup. Keep in a jar to use as a flavoring for cake, icing, custard and such. Use 3 tablespoons syrup with the standard recipe. Add this syrup to the liquid and combine as usual.

*Orange Layer Cake:* Bake the foundation recipe in 2 layers. Put Orange Filling between layers, page 305. Top with 7-Minute Frosting, page 303, which is flavored with 1 tablespoon grated orange rind.

### HAZEL NUT CAKE
*Fall treat, published in The Farmer, 1891.*

Rub together with tips of fingers (or cream with electric mixer), 2 cups sugar and 1 cup butter. When smooth, mix in ½ cup milk, 4 eggs (1 at a time), 1 teaspoon extract of lemon, 1 cup chopped hazel nut meats, 1 cup raisins and 2½ cups all-purpose flour into which has been sifted 2 teaspoons baking powder and ½ teaspoon salt. Beat well and pour into a greased, flat cake pan (10x13-inch). Bake in preheated, 350° F. oven for about 50 minutes or until a toothpick comes out clean. Cool and frost with a white frosting. Make layers, if desired, and fill with lemon filling, page 305. Yields about 18 pieces cake.

## APPLESAUCE CAKE
*It stays moist for days.*

½ cup shortening
1½ cups sugar
1 egg
1½ cups applesauce
2 teaspoons soda
1 teaspoon cinnamon

¼ teaspoon cloves
2 cups all-purpose flour
¼ teaspoon salt
¾ cup dates, cut up
¼ cup seedless raisins
1 cup walnuts, cut up

Cream shortening and sugar. Add egg and mix well. Mix applesauce and soda. Mix other dry ingredients; add to shortening and sugar alternately with applesauce mixture. Stir in dates, raisins and walnuts. Pour into prepared 9x13-inch loaf pan. Bake at 350° F. oven 40 to 45 minutes. Yields 18 pieces, about 2x3 inches.

*Lemon Icing:* Heat 4 tablespoons butter in 3 tablespoons lemon juice until butter melts. Add 1 tablespoon grated lemon rind and 3 cups powdered sugar. Beat until smooth. Spread on cake.

*Tip from The Farmer, 1897:* Melted butter will not make a good cake.

## DUTCH FAMILY CAKE
*Moist, luscious!*

½ cup shortening
2 squares unsweetened chocolate
1 cup sugar
2 eggs
1 cup applesauce
1 teaspoon vanilla

½ cup pecans, chopped
1 cup all-purpose flour, sifted
½ teaspoon baking powder
¼ teaspoon soda
¼ teaspoon salt

Melt and blend shortening and chocolate together. Cool. Beat eggs and add sugar, applesauce, vanilla, pecans and chocolate mixture. Sift flour, baking powder, soda and salt together. Add to mixture. Pour into greased and floured square 8x8-inch pan and bake 40 to 50 minutes in preheated, 350° F. oven. To decorate top, use paper mat for stencil. Place on top of cake, dust lightly with powdered sugar. Remove mat carefully, lifting straight up. Yields about 9 servings.

## HONEY-ALMOND CUP CAKES
*Sugar rationing recipe printed in The Farmer, 1947.*

| | |
|---|---|
| 1 cup sifted flour | ¼ cup butter |
| 1 teaspoon baking powder | ¼ cup sugar |
| ⅛ teaspoon soda | 1 tablespoon honey |
| ¼ teaspoon salt | ½ teaspoon vanilla |
| ½ cup chopped almonds | 1 egg |
| ¼ cup milk | |

Sift together the flour, baking powder, soda and salt. Grind almonds or chop very fine. Combine almonds, milk and honey and bring just to the boiling point. Remove from heat and cool while creaming together the butter, sugar and vanilla. Cream until very light and fluffy. Add egg yolk and beat. Add nut mixture. Mix well. Add sifted dry ingredients and mix well. Fold in stiffly beaten egg white.

Pour into well-greased medium-size muffin pans, filling about ⅔ full. Bake in preheated, 400° F. oven until cakes shrink slightly from sides of pan and spring back when touched lightly with the finger — about 20 minutes. Remove from pans and cool. Serve while fresh. Yields 8 to 10 cup cakes, depending on size of muffin pans.

## POUND CAKE
*Build the pyramid from The Farmer, 1890.*

| | |
|---|---|
| 2¼ cups sifted, all-purpose flour | 5 egg yolks, well beaten |
| ¼ teaspoon salt | ½ teaspoon vanilla |
| 1 cup butter | ¼ teaspoon lemon extract |
| 1 cup granulated sugar | 5 egg whites, beaten until stiff but not dry |

Sift flour with salt; sift again. Cream butter, gradually add sugar, beating mixture until fluffy. Add beaten egg yolks and beat until batter is very light. Sift in flour-salt mixture, a little at a time and beat well. Stir in vanilla and lemon extracts. Carefully fold in egg whites. Pour batter into greased loaf pan, which has been bottom-lined with greased paper. Bake in preheated, 300° F. oven for 1¼ hours, or until cake shrinks from sides of pan and a cake tester comes out clean. Yields about 20 thin slices.

*Chocolate Pound Cake:* Omit lemon extract in recipe above. Add ¼ teaspoon cinnamon to dry ingredients. Melt 1 package (4-ounce) chocolate chips over hot water; cool. Add to batter with egg yolks.

*Pyramid Pound Cake:* Double either recipe for pound cake, above. Bake batter in a large flat cake pan or pans, spreading batter to about 1-inch depth. When cake has baked (30 to 40 minutes) and cooled, cut into 3½x2-inch pieces. Frost top and sides (use Creamy Icing, page 301). Arrange pieces on a cake stand in a pyramid before icing is quite set. First, lay a circle of 5 pieces with some space between. Over the spaces, lay five more pieces with some space between. Gradually build up the pyramid, drawing in the column toward a peak. Crown top with a small bouquet of garden flowers.

## CORN STARCH CAKE
*Butter-y delight to eat plain, with a thin icing or berries and whipped cream — from The Farmer, 1886.*

Cream 1 cup butter and 2 cups sugar until light. Beat in 3 egg yolks and 1 teaspoon vanilla. Mix 2 cups flour, ½ cup cornstarch and 1 teaspoon soda. Add to batter alternately with 1 cup milk. Beat well after each addition. Beat 3 egg whites until frothy. Add 2 teaspoons cream of tartar and beat until whites are stiff, but not dry. Fold whites into batter. Pour batter into greased and bottom-floured springform or angel food cake pan and bake 1 hour, or until tester comes out clean, in preheated, 350° F. oven. Cool on rack. Yields 16 slices.

## ANGEL FOOD CAKE

*It takes time, and some muscle, to whip a dozen*
*egg whites like Grandma did — but results are worth it.*

1 cup cake flour
1½ cups *plus* 2 tablespoons
   sugar
1½ cups egg whites
   (about 12)
¼ teaspoon salt

1 tablespoon water
1½ teaspoons cream of
   tartar
½ teaspoon almond
   extract
½ teaspoon lemon extract

Sift flour 4 times *after* measuring. Measure sugar. Beat egg whites lightly with a flat wire whisk. Use a copper bowl, if you have one, as whites beat faster. Add salt, water and cream of tartar when whites are half beaten. Beat until whites will hold a peak when whisk is gently lifted. Now, gradually fold in sugar, then flour — a tablespoonful at a time. Fold in extracts. Bake in an *ungreased* tube pan in a preheated, 375° F. oven for 30 to 35 minutes, or until top springs back when lightly touched with finger. Remove cake from oven and invert pan to stand on its legs, or over the top of a funnel or pop bottle. When serving angel food cake, separate into pieces with two forks rather than a knife. Yields about 12 slices.

*Individual Angel Food Cakes* may be made by baking batter in a thick layer in a 9x13-inch pan. Cut cake into squares, diamonds or heart shapes. Frost with Creamy Icing, page 301, and decorate with bits of candied cherry, nuts or orange peel.


## YOLK SPONGE CAKE

*Use the yolks from meringues or an angel food cake.*

½ cup egg yolks (6 to 7
   yolks)
½ cup boiling water
1 tablespoon lemon juice
1 teaspoon grated lemon
   rind
1 cup sugar

1½ cups sifted cake *or*
   1⅓ cups all-purpose
   flour
1½ teaspoons baking
   powder
¼ teaspoon salt

Beat yolks until thick and lemon-colored. Add water and beat again. Add lemon juice and rind. Beat sugar gradually into egg yolks until light and thoroughly blended. Fold sifted dry ingredients gradually into egg and sugar mixture. Bake in an ungreased tube pan in a preheated, 325° F. oven for 45 minutes. Invert pan and cool before removing. Yields 10 to 12 slices.

*Trim a cake* by inverting a small star or heart mold on the frosting, then sprinkle chopped nuts, tinted cocoanut or colored sugar around it. Remove mold.

## BLACK WALNUT CHRISTMAS CAKE
*Superb with rich, fragrant coffee.*

½ cup butter, softened
1 cup sugar
4 eggs, separated
1 teaspoon vanilla
2 cups sifted, all-purpose flour

2 teaspoons baking powder
¾ teaspoon salt
½ cup milk
1 cup finely-chopped black walnuts

Cream butter and sugar until light. Beat in egg yolks, one at a time. Add vanilla. Sift dry ingredients together, reserving ¼ cup. Add to creamed mixture alternately with milk, beginning and ending with dry ingredients. Mix together remaining flour and walnuts; add to batter, mixing just until blended. Beat egg whites until stiff, but not dry; fold into batter. Pour into greased and floured 9x5x3-inch loaf pan or 2-quart mold. Bake in preheated, 350° F. oven for 50 to 60 minutes, or until cake tests done. Cool in pan on wire rack for 5 minutes. Turn onto rack and cool completely. Yields about 16 slices.

*Top cake* with a simple Noel Icing, page 261. Trim with candied cherries.

## WHITE FRUIT CAKE
### *From the 1934 Country Kitchen Cook Book.*

| | |
|---|---|
| 1 cup butter | 1 cup blanched, slivered |
| 2 cups sugar | almonds |
| 1 cup sweet milk | 1 cup shredded cocoanut |
| 2½ cups flour sifted with | ¼ cup maraschino cherries, |
| 2 teaspoons baking | cut up |
| powder | 1 pound white raisins |
| ½ cup lemon and orange | ½ pound dates, snipped |
| juice | ¼ pound candied citron, |
| 2 tablespoons grated | cut up |
| rind, both kinds | |
| 7 egg whites | |

Dredge fruit and nuts with part of the flour. Cream butter, add sugar. Add flour and milk alternately, then add fruit and juice. Add beaten egg whites last. Cut waxed paper to fit bottom of pans. Generously grease waxed paper and sides of pan. Pour in batter and bake in preheated, 250° F. oven for 1½ to 2 hours, until cake tester comes out clean. Yields 5 pounds of fruit cake.

## DARK FRUIT CAKE
### *The country classic!*

| | |
|---|---|
| ½ pound candied cherries | 1 pound margarine |
| ½ pound candied pineapple | 10 eggs, beaten until frothy |
| 1 pound dates | 1 cup sorghum |
| 1 pound seeded *or* seedless | 1 cup honey |
| raisins | ½ cup cider *or* bourbon |
| 1 pound currants | 4 cups all-purpose |
| ¼ pound candied lemon | flour |
| peel | 1 teaspoon baking powder |
| ¼ pound candied orange | 1 teaspoon salt |
| peel | ½ teaspoon cloves |
| ½ pound candied citron | ½ teaspoon cinnamon |
| ½ pound walnut meats | ½ teaspoon mace |
| 1 pound dark brown sugar | |

Cut up fruit and nuts. Cream shortening and sugar until light colored. Add fruits, nuts, beaten eggs, sorghum, honey and cider to creamed mixture. Sift dry ingredients together 3 times and mix into batter. Line bottom and sides of bread pans with heavy, brown wrapping paper; grease paper well. Pour batter into pans, filling pans about ¾ full. Lay a sheet of aluminum foil on oven rack beneath rack on which cakes are set. Bake fruit cake in preheated, 300° F. oven about 2 hours or until cake tester comes out clean. Baking time will depend on size of pans. If cakes seem to be browning too rapidly on top, lay a piece of brown paper loosely across top of cakes. Cool cakes on racks. When cold, cut a rectangle of linen cloth to fit top of each cake; soak cloth in rum; lay on cake. Wrap each cake in waxed paper and store in a tightly covered metal container. If fruit cakes are to be kept several months, open storage container and resoak linen pieces about every month. Yields 5 fruit cakes, 2 pounds each.

## CRANBERRY-ORANGE CAKE
*The glaze makes this buttery cake rich and special.*

1 cup cut-up dates
1 cup finely-chopped walnuts
1 cup cranberries, halved
½ cup sifted, all-purpose flour
½ cup butter
1 cup sugar
2 eggs
3 tablespoons grated orange peel

2 cups sifted, all-purpose flour
1 teaspoon baking powder
1 teaspoon baking soda
¼ teaspoon salt
1 cup buttermilk
⅔ cup sugar
⅔ cup orange juice

In a bowl, combine dates, walnuts, cranberries and ½ cup flour; set aside. In a mixing bowl, cream butter; gradually add 1 cup sugar and beat until light and fluffy. Beat in eggs, one at a time. Add orange peel. Sift together 2 cups flour, baking powder, soda and salt; add to cream mixture alternately with buttermilk. Fold in fruit-nut mixture. Turn into greased 9-inch tube springform or bundt pan. Bake in preheated, 350° F. oven 1 hour, or until cake tests done. Cool on wire rack 15 minutes.

Meanwhile, in a small saucepan, heat ⅔ cup sugar and orange juice until sugar is dissolved. Remove cake from pan; place top side up on a wire rack over a shallow pan. Pour glaze slowly over cake, catching drippings and pouring back over cake. Cover and refrigerate at least 12 hours before serving. Yields 10 to 12 servings.

## LINGONBERRY CREAM CAKE
*Elegant easy treat in an old tradition.*

Bake a yellow cake mix with 2 layers. Cool. Split to make 4 layers. Whip 1½ cups whipping cream until stiff, then fold in ⅓ cup confectioners' sugar. Spread each of 3 layers with ¼ jar (14-ounce) lingonberries *or* cranberry-orange relish, then ¼ of the whipped cream. Top with fourth cake layer. Spread remaining cream on top of cake. Spoon remaining lingonberries in a circle on cream. Refrigerate before serving and to store. Yields about 10 servings.

## TUNNEL-OF-LOVE CAKE

| | |
|---|---|
| ½ pound (50) large marshmallows | 1 cup heavy cream, whipped |
| ¼ teaspoon salt | ⅛ teaspoon almond extract |
| ⅓ cup water | 1 round, 10-inch angel food cake |
| 1 cup (6-ounce package) chocolate chips | |

Combine marshmallows, salt and water in saucepan; place over medium heat until melted, stirring constantly. Remove from heat. Stir in semi-sweet chocolate morsels until melted. Chill about 10 minutes. Fold in whipped cream and almond extract. Cut a slice about 1-inch-thick from top of cake. Set aside. Gently hollow out a 2-inch-wide and 2-inch-deep trench in remaining cake. A grapefruit knife does this job well. Tear pieces removed from cake slightly. Fill trench in cake with half of cream filling. Place torn cake pieces on top; press down slightly. Replace top of cake. Top with remaining filling. Chill several hours. Yields 10 to 12 slices.

*Chocolate Cream Frosting:* If desired, sides of cake may be frosted with ½ cup heavy cream, whipped with ¼ cup instant, sweetened cocoa powder.

*Fruit Cream Filling:* Whip 3 cups heavy cream, adding ⅓ cup confectioners' sugar as cream begins to stiffen. Continue beating until cream mixture is stiff. Fold ¾ cup crushed pineapple (well drained), 1 cup fresh strawberries (cut in half) and 6 large marshmallows (cut in squares) into a little less than half of the cream. Place in cavity of cake. Spread remaining cream on top and sides of cake.

## ORANGE CAKE MIX CAKE
*If serving in the field, take cake in pan.*

1 package white *or* yellow    1 cup sugar
  cake mix                  3 tablespoons orange juice

    Bake cake in 9x13-inch loaf pan as directed on package. Combine sugar and orange juice. Spread over baked cake. Place cake in preheated, 450° F. oven or under broiler until slightly browned. Yields about 12 to 14 servings.

## DRUM CAKE WITH CREAMY ICING
*Bake your favorite cake in three, 8-inch layers, then decorate like this.*

¾ cup butter              1 teaspoon vanilla
1 egg                    1 teaspoon lemon juice
6 cups sifted confectioners'    12 peppermint sticks
  sugar                   Red cinnamon candies
3 tablespoons cream

    Blend butter and egg thoroughly. Add sugar, cream and flavorings; beat until smooth. Spread between layers and frost top, sides of cake. For drum effect, press red and white peppermint sticks at angles on the sides. Press cinnamon candies along top edge and along bottom of cake. Cross two candy sticks on cake top for drumsticks.

*Coffee Creamy Icing:* Use strong, hot coffee in place of cream.

*Orange Creamy Icing:* Use orange juice in place of cream to moisten and 2 teaspoons grated orange rind for flavoring.

*Strawberry Creamy Icing:* Use 1 cup slightly crushed strawberries and juice in place of cream. Add juice gradually to obtain desired consistency.

## CLOWN CUPCAKES

Make cupcakes of dark or light cake batter or a packaged mix. Bake, cool. Cut cone-shaped pieces out of the tops of cakes; turn these pieces upside down, frost with chocolate icing to form peaked hats. Fill cupcake cavities with scoops of vanilla ice cream; make eyes and nose with raisins, set frosted hats on top of clown heads. Freeze.

## EASY CHOCOLATE ICING
### *Either way is good.*

2 tablespoons softened
   butter
1 whole egg *or* 2 yolks
   Few grains of salt
1 square melted, unsweetened
   chocolate

½ teaspoon vanilla
2 cups confectioners' sugar
2 teaspoons milk, about

Put first 4 ingredients in bowl and beat with electric mixer until creamy. Add vanilla and confectioners' sugar and enough milk to spread easily. Put on with even strokes, leaving a slightly ridged appearance. Yields frosting for 2-layer cake.

*In place of chocolate,* add 3 tablespoons cocoa with the confectioners' sugar and increase butter 1 tablespoon.

## 7-MINUTE FROSTING
*Don't stop beating.*

| | |
|---|---|
| 1 cup sugar | 3 tablespoons water |
| ¼ teaspoon cream of tartar | Few grains salt |
| 1 egg white | ½ teaspoon vanilla |

Put all ingredients except vanilla in the top of a double boiler. Cook over boiling water 7 to 10 minutes, beating all the while with a rotary beater. When ready to remove from stove, the icing will be thick and almost ready to spread. Add vanilla, beat until cool and ready to spread. Double the recipe for all but a small cake.

*Chocolate:* Melt 1 square unsweetened chocolate in double boiler; add other ingredients and proceed as above.

*Marshmallow:* Add 8 marshmallows, cut in pieces, when icing is partly cooled to make a fluffier icing.

## UNCOOKED HONEY FROSTING
*Makes gingerbread special.*

| | |
|---|---|
| ¼ teaspoon salt | 1 teaspoon almond |
| 2 egg whites | extract |
| 1 cup honey | |

Add salt to egg whites. Warm honey over hot water. Pour in thin stream over egg whites while beating vigorously. Add flavoring. Continue to beat until thick and fluffy. Yields about 2 cups frosting.

## SWEET CREAM TOPPINGS AND FILLINGS

*Sherry Whipped Cream:* Beat 1 cup whipping cream and 2 teaspoons confectioners' sugar until stiff. Fold in 2 to 3 teaspoons sherry. Yields topping and filling for 9-inch layer cake.

*Orange Whipped Cream:* Beat 1 cup whipping cream and 2 teaspoons confectioners' sugar until stiff. Fold in 2 teaspoons shredded orange peel. Yields filling and topping for 9-inch layer cake.

*Chocolate Whipped Cream:* Beat 3 cups whipping cream until stiff. Fold in ½ cup confectioners' sugar and ⅓ cup sweetened cocoa. Fill and frost entire 9-inch layer cake.

## REFRESHING SWEET OR SOUR CREAM TOPPINGS
*Cream Toppings are also delicious served over gingerbread or spice cake.*

*Orange:* Combine 1 cup sweet cream *or* dairy sour cream, 2 teaspoons grated orange rind, 4 tablespoons orange juice and 2½ teaspoons sugar. Chill in covered container. Serve over halved, lightly-sugared strawberries or other fresh fruits.

*Blueberry:* Combine sweet cream *or* 1 cup dairy sour cream, 1 cup fresh, frozen or canned blueberries, drained, and 2½ teaspoons sugar. Chill. Store in closed container. Serve over lightly-sugared raspberries or other fresh fruits.

*Spicy:* Combine 1 cup sweet cream *or* dairy sour cream, 3 teaspoons brown sugar and 1 teaspoon nutmeg *or* ginger. Chill. Store in closed container. Serve over cantaloupe balls or cubes.

## CREAM CHEESE FILLING
*Spread between layers of warm gingerbread or spice cake or use as a frosting.*

1 package (8-ounce) cream
  cheese *or* 1 cup fine
  cottage cheese
Cream to moisten

½ cup drained chopped
  fruit (cherries, pine-
  apple, apricots)

Run cottage cheese through fine sieve or mash until smooth and season lightly with salt. Or mix softened cream cheese. Add cream and fruit to make a smooth filling.

## PINEAPPLE CREAM FILLING
*Wow!*

1 package (3¼-ounce) vanilla
  pudding and pie filling
  mix

1¾ cups milk
½ cup canned, crushed
  pineapple, drained

Combine pudding mix and milk in saucepan. Cook and stir until mixture comes to full boil. Remove from heat. Cover and chill. Then beat until smooth and creamy. Fold in ½ cup pineapple. Yields filling and topping for 9-inch layer cake. Frost sides of cake with sweetened, whipped cream, if desired.

## PRUNE FILLING
*Split slices of spice cake and fill.*

½ cup sugar
1 tablespoon flour
⅛ teaspoon salt
¼ teaspoon cinnamon

½ cup soured cream
1 cup prune pulp
1 egg, beaten
1 tablespoon lemon juice

Mix dry ingredients, add cream, prune pulp and egg. Cook until thickened, add lemon juice and cool.

## ORANGE FILLING
*Tangy and fresh-tasting.*

1 tablespoon flour
¼ cup sugar
2 egg yolks
2 tablespoons soft butter

1 tablespoon grated
orange rind
½ cup orange juice
1 tablespoon lemon juice

Mix sugar and flour, then beat with yolks in a small bowl. Combine all ingredients and mix well. Cook until thickened in top of double boiler or over medium heat in a heavy saucepan, stirring constantly. Cool thoroughly, spread between cake layers. Yields filling for 2 or 3-layer cake.

*Lemon Filling:* Use 2 tablespoons flour, ½ cup sugar, 2 egg yolks, 2 tablespoons soft butter, 2 teaspoons grated lemon rind, 3 tablespoons lemon juice and ¼ cup cold water. Combine according to directions above.

*Feather white frosting* on a cake by pressing chocolate mixture through narrow opening of decorating tube at 1-inch intervals across cake. With toothpick, lightly cross chocolate lines at 1-inch intervals. Make chocolate mixture by melting ¼ cup chocolate bits and 1½ teaspoons vegetable shortening over hot water.

*Make a tray of checkers.* Frost half a square or oblong cake with light frosting, half with dark. Cut cake in squares; decorate with nuts and other candies. Arrange like checkerboard.

## ELEGANT CHEESE CAKE
*Serve small slices. This is very rich.*

Make crust by combining 1½ cups graham cracker crumbs, ¼ cup confectioners' sugar, 1 teaspoon allspice and ⅓ cup melted butter. Spread in the bottom of a 9-inch spring-form pan, pressing some up the sides to form a ½-inch to ¾-inch rim.

| | |
|---|---|
| 2 packages (8-ounce each) cream cheese, at room temperature | 2 eggs, beaten slightly<br>⅔ cup sugar<br>2 teaspoons vanilla extract |

Stir cheese until soft and creamy. Add eggs, sugar and vanilla. Beat until thoroughly creamed and smooth; pour into crust. Bake in a 350° F. oven 25 minutes. Then top with a mixture of:

| | |
|---|---|
| 1½ cups dairy sour cream | 4 tablespoons sugar<br>2 teaspoons vanilla |

Return to oven, increase temperature to 450° F. and bake 7 minutes. Cool, then chill. Yields 10 to 12 servings.

## DANISH PUFF
*Pastry has a puff topping and rich frosting.*

| | |
|---|---|
| 1 cup all-purpose flour<br>½ cup butter<br>3 tablespoons water<br>½ cup butter<br>1 cup boiling water | 1 teaspoon almond extract<br>1 cup all-purpose flour<br>3 eggs |

Cut 1 cup flour and ½ cup butter together, as for a pie crust. Stir in 3 tablespoons water with a fork to form a soft dough. Divide dough in half and form into 2 oblongs, about 4 inches wide and as long as a cookie sheet. Use your fingers to pat dough into shape.

Melt ½ cup butter in 1 cup boiling water. Remove from heat and immediately add almond extract and 1 cup flour, all at once. Stir until dough leaves sides of kettle. Put in small mixing bowl and beat in eggs, one at a time. Spread on the 2 oblongs and bake about 50 minutes in preheated, 350° F. oven.

While still warm, frost puff with toasted cocoanut icing. Yields 16 slices.

*Cocoanut Icing:* Melt ¼ cup butter in a skillet. Stir in 1 teaspoon vanilla and 1 heaping cup flaked cocoanut. Heat in skillet, stirring, until cocoanut is golden brown. Add ¼ cup milk and thicken with about 2 cups confectioners' sugar. Spread on puffs.


## CREAM PUFFS

| | |
|---|---|
| 1 cup water | 1 cup all-purpose flour |
| ½ cup butter | 4 eggs |

Heat water and butter to rolling boil. Add flour and stir vigorously over low heat for about 1 minute. Mixture will leave sides of pan and form a ball. Remove from heat and beat in 1 egg at a time until batter is smooth. Drop on ungreased baking sheet in 8 mounds, 3 inches apart. Bake in preheated oven at 400° F. for 45 to 50 minutes, or until puffed, golden brown and dry. Cool slowly, away from drafts. Cut off tops with sharp knife and scoop out soft dough. Fill with sweetened whipped cream or one of the fillings below. Yields 8 large cream puffs. Dough may be divided into as many mounds as you wish, up to 40 for tiny, canape-size puffs. Cooking time will vary some — the smallest puffs taking about 30 minutes to bake.

*Freezing Cream Puffs:* Freeze unfilled cream puffs without filling. Filled puffs will tend to become soggy. Cool puffs, cut and remove soft centers. Put puffs in layers in box with waxed paper between; overwrap the box with freezer paper. Label, date. Cream puffs may be stored 9 to 12 months.

When ready to use, fill with sweetened whipped cream or any desired filling while puffs are frozen or slightly thawed.

*Cherry Puffs:* Fill half a cream puff with prepared cherry pie filling, top with a daub of whipped cream and place 1 cherry on top. Yields filling for 8 large puffs.

*Blueberry Puffs:* Use blueberry pie filling, prepare puffs as above. Or, fold fresh or frozen blueberries into sweetened whipped cream.

*Chocolate-Orange Filling:* Melt 1 cup semi-sweet chocolate pieces over hot (not boiling) water. Add 3 tablespoons orange juice. Let mixture cool. Beat 1 cup whipping cream until stiff. Fold in chocolate mixture. Yields filling for 6 large puffs.

## MERINGUE SHELLS
*Serve filled with slightly crushed, sugared fruit
and topped with whipped cream.*

2 egg whites
½ teaspoon vinegar *or*
  lemon juice

½ teaspoon vanilla
⅔ cup sugar

Add vinegar and vanilla to egg whites. Beat until egg
whites hold a very stiff peak. Add sugar gradually, about a
tablespoon at a time, beating well after each addition. Divide
meringue into 6 portions on a lightly greased baking sheet.
Shape into hearts or round shells with about ¼-inch-
thickness on the bottom, and edges built up about ½ inch.
Bake in preheated, 275° F. oven about 25 minutes until
meringue is dry. Cool thoroughly before adding filling. Yields
6 meringues.

## SHORTCAKE TOPPINGS
*Shortcake recipes on page 234.*

*Mixed Fruit Topping:* Combine 1 can (8½-ounce) crushed
pineapple, 1 cup finely chopped, red-skinned apple, 1 cup
cranberry sauce. Let stand at room temperature.

*Banana-Strawberry Topping:* Combine 2½ cups sliced,
sugared strawberries with 1 cup sliced banana. Let stand
while shortcake is baking.

*Berry Topping:* Lightly crush 1 quart strawberries *or*
raspberries with the back of a spoon. Add ¾ cup sugar and
let stand at room temperature 30 minutes.

*Fresh Peach Topping:* Lightly crush 1 quart sliced, fresh
peaches with back of a spoon and marinate for 30 minutes in
1 cup sugar.

## FRUIT SOUP
*Søt Suppe.*

Simmer 1 cup prunes which have been pitted and cut up,
½ cup raisins, ½ cup rice or tapioca in 2 cups of water until
nearly tender. Add ½ cup sugar, 2 cinnamon sticks, ½
orange, very thinly sliced, 4 large apples, diced, ½ lemon,
thinly sliced. Simmer gently for about 30 minutes. Serve
warm or cold. Yields about 6 small servings.

## GINGERBREAD UPSIDE DOWN CAKE
*Flavor innovation!*

¼ cup shortening
¼ cup sugar
½ cup molasses
1 egg
1¼ cups all-purpose flour
½ teaspoon salt
1 teaspoon baking
powder
¼ teaspoon baking soda
½ teaspoon ginger

1 teaspoon cinnamon
¼ teaspoon ground cloves
½ cup hot water
4 pineapple slices, halved
1 whole pineapple slice
9 maraschino cherries
⅓ cup molasses
¼ cup sugar
1 tablespoon butter

Cream shortening and sugar until fluffy. Blend in molasses. Beat in egg. Sift together the 7 dry ingredients. Add to creamed mixture, alternately, with hot water.

Arrange 6 halved pineapple slices around edge of 9-inch round cake pan, 2 inches deep. Place whole pineapple slice in middle; place cherries in center of pieces. Pour in molasses; sprinkle with sugar and dot with butter.

Turn gingerbread batter into prepared pan. Bake in preheated, 350° F. oven for 40 minutes. Invert immediately on serving plate. Spoon juice over cake. Yields 6 large servings. May be served warm or cold with whipped cream.

## JELLY ROLL
*Really easy!*

4 eggs
1 cup sugar
3 tablespoons cold water
¼ teaspoon flavoring

1 tablespoon cornstarch
1 cup flour
1 teaspoon baking powder
1 cup jelly *or* jam

Separate eggs and beat yolks until light. Add sugar, blend, then stir in cold water and flavoring. Mix dry ingredients and add to egg mixture. Fold in stiffly-beaten egg whites. Pour into a pan, bottom-lined with waxed paper cut to fit. Spread the batter about ½ inch thick. Bake in a moderately hot oven, 375° F., 15 to 20 minutes. Remove warm cake onto towel sprinkled with confectioners' sugar. Remove paper, roll cake into towel, cool on rack. Unroll carefully, spread with jam or jelly. Roll, cut cake into two equal pieces. Freeze for future use.

## PINEAPPLE ALMOND TORTE
*Elegant, easy make-ahead.*

1 cup sugar
½ teaspoon cream of tartar
¼ teaspoon salt
4 egg whites
1 teaspoon vanilla
4 drops almond extract

½ cup blanched, slivered
   almonds
1 can (1-pound, 14-ounce)
   pineapple chunks
1 cup whipping cream

Heat oven to very hot (450° F.). Combine sugar, cream of tartar and salt. Beat egg whites with electric mixer until stiff peaks form. Add sugar gradually to egg whites, beating slowly. Fold in flavorings. Pour into lightly-greased, 8-inch ring mold. Stick top thickly with almond slivers, porcupine fashion. Place in oven and turn off heat. Leave torte in oven overnight or until oven is cold. Drain and chill pineapple. Remove cold torte carefully from ring mold with aid of small spatula. Keep almond side up. Frost sides of ring with whipped cream. Fill center with well-drained, chilled pineapple. Decorate plate with grape clusters, and grape, mint or lemon leaves, if desired. Yields 6 to 8 servings.

*Frosted grape clusters* are easy to make: Brush grapes with slightly-beaten egg white, then dip in granulated sugar. Put on a wire rack or paper towel and allow to dry thoroughly. Arrange with other fruit in a bowl for a lovely edible centerpiece.

## CHOCOLATE DREAM DESSERT
*Rich and yummy!*

12 graham cracker squares,
    rolled fine
3 egg whites, beaten stiff
½ pound marshmallows,
    cut in small pieces

¾ cup cut-up walnuts
3 egg yolks
½ cup butter, melted
1 cup confectioners' sugar
½ cup chocolate syrup

Place half of cracker crumbs in bottom of an 8-inch-square pan. Fold marshmallow and nut pieces into beaten egg whites. Place in a layer over cracker crumbs. Beat egg yolks until thick and light yellow, add melted butter and mix well. Add chocolate and stir well. Pour gently over egg white mixture. Sprinkle remaining cracker crumbs on top. Cover pan and refrigerate for 24 hours. Spoon into serving dishes and top with whipped cream. Yields 6 to 8 servings.

## BAKED APPLES WITH DATES
*Supper dessert from the 1917 Country Kitchen Cook Book.*

Core and peel tart apples, then rub over the surface with the cut side of a lemon to keep apples from discoloring. Fill apple centers with 2 or 3 stoned dates. Dredge apples in sugar and cinnamon. Bake in preheated, 350° F. oven until tender, about 1 hour. Each apple yields 1 serving.

*A glass of apple jelly* melted in a double boiler, then mixed with chopped, toasted almonds and poured over baked apples is delicious. Cool and serve with whipped cream.

*Glazed Baked Apples:* Wash, core and peel cooking apples about ⅓ of the way down from the stem end. Turn upside down in baking pan, pour over them a hot syrup of equal parts sugar and water. Bake 15 minutes in hot oven, then turn apples right side up and continue baking, basting every few minutes until tender and top surface is glazed.

## APPLE DUMPLINGS

Pat 1 recipe of biscuit dough, page 233, to ¼-inch thickness and cut into individual servings—squares or triangles. Fill with apple or other fruit and pinch together using milk or water to seal dough. Bake with smooth side up in the syrup made of ½ cup brown sugar and ½ cup water. Yields about 6 servings.

## PIE-PLANT PAN-DOWDY
*A rhubarb delight from a midsummer, 1894 issue of*
*The Farmer.*

This is a quick dessert and may be prepared in a hurry. Cut the pie-plant as for pies; put a good layer in a pudding dish that has a cover; add sugar plentifully and a cup of water; bring to a boil on range. Make baking powder biscuit crust and roll it ½-inch thick; cut a gash across the center and lay over the pie-plant which should be boiling hot. Cover tightly and cook slowly on top of range, but keep it boiling for 20 or 30 minutes. Serve hot with the sweet sauce. (Modern families like a scoop of vanilla ice cream on top).

## PURPLE PLUM COBBLER

| | |
|---|---|
| 4 cups quartered, fresh, purple plums | 2 tablespoons sugar |
| 1 cup sugar | ¼ cup cocoanut |
| 2 tablespoons cornstarch | 2 teaspoons grated orange rind |
| ⅓ cup orange juice | 3 tablespoons salad oil |
| 1½ cups biscuit mix | 6 tablespoons milk |

Place quartered plums in 8x12-inch baking dish. Combine sugar, cornstarch and orange juice, and scatter over plums. Combine biscuit mix, sugar, cocoanut and grated orange rind. Add salad oil to milk. Combine with the dry ingredients. Turn out on lightly-floured board. Knead a few times until smooth. Pat or roll out lightly to pan size. Cut dough into 6 pieces to fit the baking dish. Sprinkle crust lightly with granulated sugar. Bake in preheated, 425° F. oven for 20 to 25 minutes. Serve hot or warm with pour-on or slightly-sweetened whipped cream. Yields 6 servings.

*Apple Cobbler:* Bring to a boil, 2 tablespoons cornstarch, 1 cup sugar, ½ teaspoon cinnamon, 1 cup water, 2 tablespoons butter and 5 cups peeled, cored and thinly-sliced apples. Pour into 8x12-inch baking dish and proceed as directed for topping in recipe above.

## QUICKIE, PEACH COBBLER
*Slip a quickie peach cobbler into the oven*
*for a last-minute dessert.*

Drain 1 can (1-pound, 13-ounce) cling peach slices. Blend peach syrup with 1 tablespoon cornstarch; heat until thickened. Add dash cinnamon, lump of butter, then peaches. Place in buttered baking dish; ring with refrigerated cinnamon buns. Bake in 350° F. oven for about 30 minutes. When done, frost buns with packaged icing. Yields 6 to 8 servings.

## APPLE SNAPS PUDDING
*Speedy treat!*

In a buttered baking dish place alternate layers of cornflakes and thinly-sliced tart cooking apples, sprinkling each layer with brown sugar and cinnamon. Dot with butter. Bake in preheated, 350° F. oven for 35 minutes. Serve warm with half-and-half cream.

## RHUBARB CASSEROLE
*No watching needed.*

1 pound fresh rhubarb                    1½ cups sugar

Wash rhubarb, cut into 1-inch pieces. Place in 1½-quart buttered casserole, sprinkle with sugar and cover tightly with cover or foil. Bake in preheated, 300° F. oven for 30 minutes or until done. Cool and serve.

*Add flavor interest:* As soon as rhubarb is cooked, stir in 1 tablespoon grated lemon rind and a dash of ginger *or* ¼ teaspoon mace *or* 2-3 teaspoons grated orange rind *or* 1 teaspoon cinnamon. Before cooking, add 2 whole cloves *or* 1 stick of cinnamon *or* dash of nutmeg.

## FRUIT ROLLS
*Smells delectable, too.*

Roll biscuit dough, page 233, ¼-inch thick. Spread with softened butter. Cover with sliced apples, rhubarb or berries and sprinkle with sugar. Roll up like a jelly roll and cut in 1-inch slices. Have ready a baking pan (6x10-inch or 8x8-inch) containing hot syrup made of 1 cup brown sugar and 1 cup water. Lay slices in syrup, cut side down, and bake in a preheated, 375° F. oven until dough is thoroughly baked and fruit is done, about 45 minutes.

Serve with thin cream, slightly sweetened and seasoned with nutmeg, if desired. Yields 6 to 8 servings.

## SPICED CHERRIES
*A light delight to serve at the end of a holiday meal . . .*
*or as a fruit soup.*

1 can (1-pound) pitted,
   tart, red cherries
Water
⅔ cup sugar
3 lemon slices, seeded
⅛ teaspoon ground cloves
2 tablespoons cornstarch

2 tablespoons water
Few drops red food
   coloring
½ cup dairy sour cream
Ground cinnamon
   (optional)

Drain cherries and reserve liquid. If necessary, add enough water to liquid to make 1 cup. Pour into saucepan; add sugar, lemon slices, cloves. Bring to a boil, stirring occasionally. Combine cornstarch and water. Stir into spiced cherry liquid. Return to a boil, stirring constantly. Remove lemon slices and blend in red food coloring. Add cherries. Heat thoroughly. Spoon into dessert dishes and garnish with a dollop of sour cream and a sprinkling of cinnamon, if desired. Yields up to 6 servings.

## DANISH CUSTARD
*A company dessert for us because of its secret ingredients—*
*brown sugar and rum flavoring in the bottom*
*of the baking dish,*
*reports a Chisago County, Minnesota homemaker.*

3 eggs
¼ cup sugar
⅛ teaspoon salt

2 cups milk, scalded
1 tablespoon rum flavoring
½ cup light brown sugar

Beat eggs until light, add sugar and salt. Stir in milk slowly and then beat custard until well blended. Sift brown sugar and place in bottom of mold or custard cups; drizzle rum flavoring over sugar. Pour custard on top of brown sugar. Place baking dish in a pan of hot water and bake in preheated, 350° F. oven until custard is firm, about 1 hour (silver knife inserted in center will come out clean). Chill custard. Invert custard on serving plate; brown sugar forms a caramel sauce. Or dish up individual portions with caramel sauce poured over each serving. Yields 5 servings.

*Custards baked too long* or at too high temperatures form watery bubbles throughout the mixture and custard will be watery when spooned.

## IN-A-BOWL BLUEBERRY PUDDING
*Published in The Farmer, 1941.*

½ cup butter
1¼ cups sugar
1 teaspoon cinnamon

5 cups slightly-dry bread cubes
1 quart blueberries
½ cup water

Cream butter and sugar. Add bread cubes, water, and berries, and mix thoroughly. The mixture should look rather dry. Put into a well-buttered baking dish and bake in preheated, 375° F. oven for about 45 minutes. Serve warm or cool, with pour cream. Yields 6 servings.

## SWEDISH RICE PUDDING
*The high point of Swedish holiday festivities arrives on Christmas Eve with a lavish smorgasbord dinner. The dessert is a traditional creamy rice pudding with a whole almond hidden in it. It is said that whoever is served the almond will be the next married.*

2½ cups milk
1 cup long-grain white rice
½ teaspoon salt
3 tablespoons sugar

1 teaspoon vanilla
1 cup whipping cream, whipped
1 whole, blanched almond

Heat milk until bubbles appear around the edges of heavy saucepan. Add rice and salt. Cover tightly and cook over low heat until milk is absorbed, about 25 minutes. Stir rice occasionally with fork. Remove from heat. Add sugar and vanilla. Cool to room temperature. Gently fold in cream and whole almond. Chill at least ½ hour. Serve with lingonberry or cranberry sauce. Yields 8 servings.

## TUTTI-FRUTTI PUDDING
### *Quickie!*

Prepare 1 package (3¾-ounce) vanilla *or* cocoanut cream instant pudding mix, according to package directions, using 1¾ cups milk. Let stand to set — about 5 minutes. Fold in 1 can (8¾-ounce) crushed pineapple, drained, ¼ cup miniature marshmallows, 2 tablespoons chopped nuts and 2 tablespoons chopped, drained maraschino cherries. Spoon pudding into individual dessert dishes. Yields 4 servings.

## GRANDMA'S CUSTARD
### *Sometimes called Cornstarch Custard.*

¼ cup sugar
2 tablespoons cornstarch
¼ teaspoon salt
1 egg *or* 2 egg yolks,
  mixed with a fork

2 cups milk
1 tablespoon butter
1½ teaspoons vanilla

Mix first 4 ingredients in a heavy saucepan. Gradually stir in milk. Cook over low heat, stirring constantly until mixture boils. Boil 1 minute. Blend in butter and vanilla. Chill and serve. A sheet of waxed paper layed directly on surface of custard will prevent "skin" from forming. Yields 6 servings.

## STEAMED CRANBERRY PUDDING
### *So Christmas-y!*

1½ cups sifted, all-purpose
  flour
1 teaspoon baking
  powder
¼ teaspoon salt
½ cup molasses

⅓ cup warm water
2 tablespoons shortening,
  melted
2 teaspoons soda
⅔ cup whole cranberry
  sauce (drained)

Sift flour, baking powder and salt together. Mix molasses, water, shortening and soda; add to flour mixture. Fold cranberry sauce into batter. Pour into greased, 1-quart mold and tie waxed paper loosely over top. Place mold on trivet or wire rack in bottom of deep kettle. Pour in boiling water to half the depth of the mold. Cover and steam 2 hours, replenishing the water if necessary with more boiling water to keep original level. Unmold onto serving platter. Serve hot with hot Vanilla Sauce, page 319. Yields 8 servings.

## ENGLISH PLUM PUDDING
*Make ⅓ of recipe for family use.*

2 pounds seedless raisins
3 pounds currants
2 pounds white beef suet
¾ pound candied citron
¾ pound candied orange peel
¾ pound candied lemon peel
¾ pound blanched, slivered almonds
2 pounds brown sugar

1½ pounds soft, fine bread crumbs (use "cheap" bakers bread)
½ pound (2 cups) all-purpose flour
12 eggs
1 teaspoon nutmeg
1 teaspoon cinnamon
½ teaspoon mace
½ teaspoon cloves
1 teaspoon ginger
4 teaspoons salt
1½ cups milk (about)

Break suet apart; remove membrane, and grind. Cut up fruit and nuts; dredge in some of the flour. Mix rest of flour, suet, sugar and spices; then blend into fruit. Separate eggs. Beat yolks until thick. Mix yolks, bread crumbs and milk into fruit. Beat egg whites until stiff and gently fold into mixture with your hands.

Grease enameled pudding pans or butter crocks well; then flour generously. Fill jars about ¾ full of pudding mixture. Flour top of pudding. Cover jars with foil and tie down tightly. Place on rack in boiling water which comes partway up sides of jar. Cover pan and steam puddings slowly about 6 hours. Slow steaming is important for light pudding. Serve with hard sauce or flavored vanilla sauce, page 319. Yields about 14 pounds of pudding.

*Cooled puddings may be stored* in their jars, on the shelf, for several months. Remove foil and cover top with several thicknesses of waxed paper, tied securely in place. To reheat, remove waxed paper, recover with foil tied in place and steam as above for about 1 hour.

## STEAMED HOLIDAY PUDDING
*Tastes like Great-Grandma's,*
*but a mix makes this superb pudding easy.*

1 package (about 1-pound, 3-ounce) spice cake mix
1 can (10¾-ounce) condensed tomato soup
3 eggs

½ cup finely-chopped pecans
½ cup chopped, seedless raisins
¼ cup chopped, pitted dates

Combine cake mix, soup and eggs; mix as directed on package. Fold in nuts, raisins and dates. Pour into greased, 2-quart mold, ovenproof bowl or casserole. Cover mold by placing two layers of heavy aluminum foil over top and part way down sides. Tie foil tightly around mold with string. Place on a trivet in a large kettle. Add boiling water to ½ the height of mold. Cover kettle; steam pudding 2 hours. Remove mold from water; uncover and loosen edges of pudding with knife. Unmold while hot; serve at once with Foamy Sauce.

*Foamy Sauce:* Beat 1 egg white with a rotary beater until it stands in soft peaks; gradually beat in ¾ cup confectioners' sugar. Stir in fork-beaten egg yolk. Whip ¾ cup of heavy cream; fold into egg mixture along with ½ teaspoon vanilla. Yields 2 cups sauce.

## HARD SAUCE
*Use with steamed puddings.*

⅓ cup butter
1 cup confectioners' sugar

½ teaspoon vanilla
Nutmeg

Cream butter, add sugar gradually. Add flavoring. Yields about 1¼ cups sauce.

*Brown Sugar Sauce:* Use brown sugar, first sifted to remove lumps, and add to butter instead of confectioners' sugar. Then add ¼ cup thick cream and blend.

*Brandy Variation:* Omit vanilla in butter Hard Sauce recipe and add 1 tablespoon brandy extract with cream.

*Orange Variation:* Omit cream and vanilla in butter Hard

Sauce recipe and substitue 2 tablespoons orange juice and 2 tablespoons grated orange rind.

*Cocoa Sauce:* Blend in 2 tablespoons cocoa with confectioners' sugar and add a few grains salt.

## VANILLA PUDDING SAUCE
*Versatile classic for cake, puddings, ice cream —*
*from the 1934 Country Kitchen Cook Book.*

| | |
|---|---|
| 1 cup sugar | 2 cups boiling water |
| 3 tablespoons flour *or* | 1 teaspoon vanilla |
|   2 tablespoons cornstarch | 2 tablespoons butter |

Mix flour and sugar, add water gradually. Boil about 7 minutes; stir constantly. Remove from fire, add butter and vanilla. Serve hot or warm. Yields about 2½ cups sauce.

*Lemon Sauce:* Add 2 tablespoons lemon juice and 1 tablespoon grated rind in place of vanilla.

*Yellow Lemon Sauce:* Beat 1 egg and pour hot lemon sauce over it. Mix thoroughly. Cook 1 minute longer.

*Fruit Sauce:* Substitute fruit juice, as cherry, pineapple, berry, for 1 cup of the water in vanilla sauce recipe. If juice is sweetened, decrease sugar in recipe to ¾ cup.

*Chocolate Sauce:* Blend ¼ cup cocoa with dry ingredients and use just half as much flour or cornstarch as called for in vanilla sauce recipe. If desired, use half water and half rich milk instead of all water.

## BRANDY OR WINE SAUCE
## FOR STEAMED PUDDING
*From The Farmer, 1891.*

Mix ½ cup sugar and 1 tablespoon flour. Slowly add 1 cup water. Stir well and cook as you stir about 6 or 7 minutes. Mix in 4 tablespoons brandy (or wine). Serve hot with steamed pudding.

## BLUEBERRY ANGEL DESSERT
*Make in large pans for shower luncheons.*

1 angel food cake
1 can (1-pound, 5-ounce)
  blueberry pie filling

1 cup whipping cream,
  whipped

Break cake into bite-size chunks. Place half of chunks in 8-inch-square pan. Pour pie filling over cake. Spread 1 cup whipped cream over filling and add remaining cake chunks. Chill before spooning into serving dishes. Yields 8 servings.

*Cherry Angel:* Substitute 1 can cherry pie filling for blueberry in recipe above.

## BERRY SWIRL
*Take it to a pot luck supper.*

1 cup graham cracker
  crumbs
1 tablespoon sugar
¼ cup butter, melted
2 cups slightly-crushed,
  fresh raspberries *or*
  strawberries
2 tablespoons sugar

1 package (3-ounce)
  raspberry-flavored *or*
  strawberry-flavored
  gelatin
1 cup boiling water
½ pound marshmallows
½ cup milk
1 cup whipping cream,
  whipped

Mix crumbs, sugar and butter. Press firmly over bottom of 9x13-inch pan. Chill until set. Sprinkle sugar over fresh berries; let stand ½ hour. Dissolve gelatin in boiling water.

Drain berries, reserving juice. Add water to juice to make 1 cup; add to gelatin. Chill until partially set. Meanwhile, combine marshmallows and milk; heat and stir until marshmallows melt. Cool thoroughly, then fold in whipped cream. Add berries to gelatin, then swirl in marshmallow mixture to marble. Pour into crust; chill until set. Garnish with whipped cream, if desired. Yields 9 generous servings.

## CHERRY MELANGE
*Smashing summer party dessert.*

3 cups pitted fresh *or*
  frozen sweet cherries
1 cup ripe raspberries
1 cup cantaloupe cubes
1 cup fresh *or* frozen
  pineapple chunks

1 cup orange marmalade
⅓ cup hot water
1 tablespoon candied
  ginger, cut fine
Mint leaves
Whipped cream

Early on the day of the party, prepare and chill drained fruits. Combine marmalade with hot water and ginger. Bring to a boil and cool. Two hours before serving, layer fruits in a compote or glass bowl. Dribble syrup over fruit. Chill until ready to serve. Garnish bowl with sprigs of mint, if desired. Spoon fruit over slices of angel food or pound cake and top each serving with a daub of whipped cream. Yields 10 to 12 servings.

## SPEEDY APPLESAUCE DESSERT
*The kids will make this for you.*

1 cup fine graham cracker
  crumbs (about 15
  squares)
½ teaspoon cinnamon

¼ cup sugar
¼ cup butter, melted
1¼ cups thick applesauce
Whipped cream

Mix cracker crumbs, cinnamon, sugar and butter. Place 3 tablespoons crumb mixture in the bottom of a sauce dish or sherbet (fix 5 dishes). Place ¼ cup applesauce on top of crumbs in each dish. Divide remaining crumbs and sprinkle over applesauce. Chill. Top with a daub of whipped cream just before serving. Yields 5 servings.

## STRAWBERRY COOLER
*Only 71 calories per serving.*

| | |
|---|---|
| 6 cups fresh strawberries | 4 teaspoons orange juice |
| 1 cup dairy sour cream | 2½ teaspoons sugar |
| 2 teaspoons grated orange rind | |

Wash and hull strawberries; chill. Combine sour cream, orange rind, juice and sugar. Chill in covered container. When ready to serve, spoon 1 tablespoon cream mixture over ⅔ cup berries. Refrigerate remaining topping for future use. Yields 8 servings.

## STRAWBERRY-RHUBARB SAUCE
*Serve over ice cream with toasted almonds.*

| | |
|---|---|
| 2 cups diced rhubarb (¾-pound) | 1 cup sugar *or* part sugar and part honey |
| 1 tablespoon water | |
| 1 pint strawberries, sliced | |

Cook rhubarb with the water in a covered pan until tender, 3 to 5 minutes. Add sugar, sliced berries and simmer 3 minutes longer. Remove from heat and chill. Yields 3 cups sauce.

## FRENCH VANILLA ICE CREAM
*Beautiful texture!*
*From the 1934 Country Kitchen Cook Book.*

| | |
|---|---|
| 2 cups milk | ⅛ teaspoon salt |
| 4 egg yolks *or* 2 eggs *or* 1 egg and 1 tablespoon flour | 2 cups whipping cream |
| | 1 tablespoon vanilla |
| | ⅔ cup sugar |

Scald milk in double boiler and pour over egg yolks, mixed with sugar, salt and flour, if used. Return to double boiler and cook until it coats the spoon. Chill, add the cream and flavoring and freeze, using ¼ cup plain salt to 2 cups finely crushed ice. Pack ice cream in covered plastic containers and ripen in freezer several hours. Yields 3 pints ice cream. Increase recipe to fit freezer size you are using.

*Chocolate Ice Cream:* Scald 1½ squares chocolate, cut in pieces, with milk and beat with rotary beater. Proceed as above, increasing sugar by 3 or 4 tablespoons.

*Peanut Brittle Cream:* Grind peanut brittle to make 1 cup and add to foundation during freezing or before packing to ripen.

*Peppermint Cream:* Grind peppermint candy to equal 1 cup. Omit vanilla and decrease sugar to ½ cup in foundation recipe. Tint a very faint green if desired, add candy when cream is partly frozen. This gives the ice cream a crunchiness. For a smoother cream, let candy dissolve in the cream before freezing.

## CARAMEL ICE CREAM
### *Double for a gallon.*

1½ cups sugar
½ cup all-purpose flour
1½ cups sugar
1 pint milk
3 eggs

2 pints whipping cream
1 teaspoon vanilla
½ teaspoon salt

Mix 1½ cups sugar and flour. Heat milk over hot water (in top of double boiler). In a heavy, cast iron skillet, melt 1½ cups sugar and carmelize (stir and heat) until a light brown. Keep heat low so that sugar does not burn. Add caramelized sugar to hot milk; stir.

Beat egg until light; add sugar-flour mixture and beat well. Add egg mixture to hot milk and continue cooking over hot water. Stir gently until mixture thickens to a custard; cool. Stir in salt, vanilla and whipping cream. Freeze in crank-type ice cream freezer, as you usually do, *or* see directions with French Vanilla Ice Cream, page 322. Yields ½ gallon ice cream.

## FRESH FRUIT ICE CREAM
*A must in summer,*
*from the 1934 Country Kitchen Cook Book.*

1 quart berries, washed
  and hulled *or* other
  prepared fruit
⅓ cup sugar
⅓ cup flour
¼ teaspoon salt

2 cups sugar
2 cups milk, scalded
6 eggs
1 tablespoon vanilla
4 cups whipping cream

Mash berries with ⅓ cup sugar. Combine flour, salt and 2 cups sugar in top of double boiler; add milk. Cook over boiling water, stirring constantly, until mixture thickens. Cover and cook 5 minutes longer. Beat eggs slightly. Stir a little of the hot mixture into the eggs, then add eggs to custard in a thin stream, stirring constantly. Cook over hot water, stirring, for 1 minute longer. Cool; add vanilla. Blend in cream and berries. Freeze according to directions with your freezer or see directions with French Vanilla Ice Cream, page 322. Yields 1 gallon ice cream.

## PINEAPPLE CREAM SHERBET
*Recipe from the 1942 Country Kitchen Cook Book —*
*may be doubled.*

¾ cup canned pineapple
  juice
¼ cup lemon juice
1½ cups sugar
1 tablespoon unflavored
  gelatin

¼ cup cold water
2 cups cold milk
2 cups whipping cream,
  whipped

Add sugar to fruit juice and let stand several hours, if possible, until a thick syrup forms. Add gelatin to cold water; set over hot water to dissolve. Add to syrup and stir well. Do not have syrup too cold or gelatin may become stringy while it is being added. Add milk slowly, stirring constantly. Partly freeze, according to freezer manufacturer's directions and using 1 part salt to 8 parts finely-crushed ice. When partly frozen, add cream which has been whipped until soft peaks form. Finish freezing. Pack in plastic containers and store in freezer. Yields about 3 pints.

*Orange Cream Sherbet:* Use orange juice instead of pineapple.

*Lemon Cream Sherbet:* Use ½ cup lemon juice and ½ cup water for pineapple juice and lemon juice listed above. Increase sugar to 1¾ cups.

*Banana Cream Sherbet:* Add 1 cup ripe banana pulp to any of the above recipes. Banana adds smoothness and flavor.

## STRAWBERRY SHERBET
*From a Washington County, Minnesota farm family.*

| | |
|---|---|
| 4 quarts fresh strawberries, washed, hulled and sliced | 2⅔ cups milk |
| 4 cups sugar | ⅓ cup orange juice |
| | ⅛ teaspoon cinnamon |

Mix strawberries and sugar; let stand until juicy (about 1½ hours). Mash or puree in blender. Strain seeds. Add milk, orange juice and cinnamon. Mix well. Freeze in a crank-type freezer. (Or pour mixture into freezer trays or loaf pans; freeze about 3 hours; stir 2 or 3 times during freezing.) Pack in plastic containers for freezer. Yields about 1 gallon.

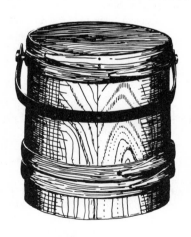

## SNOW CREAM
*Printed in The Farmer, 1893.*

In a large bowl, put 1 egg, beaten until light; 1 cup sugar; 1 cup thick cream; 1½ teaspoonfuls vanilla extract and stir well; add 4 or 5 cupfuls feathery, new-fallen snow. Splendid!

## PECAN BOMBE
*A make-ahead that's easier than it sounds and
well worth the effort.*

1 tablespoon butter
38 pecan halves
¼ teaspoon salt
2 pints coffee ice cream,
   softened

2 pints chocolate ice
   cream, softened
1 cup butterscotch sauce

In a shallow baking pan, melt butter; add pecans and salt.
Toss lightly and toast in preheated, 375° F. oven for 5 to 8
minutes. Set aside to cool.

Chill a 7-cup mold in freezer. Quickly spread coffee ice
cream as evenly as possible with back of spoon or spatula on
inside of mold to make a shell lining about 1-inch thick.
Return to freezer to harden ice cream. Spoon chocolate ice
cream into center of mold to fill; freeze. To unmold, dip mold
into warm water and turn onto plate to catch ice cream drips.
Melted ice cream glazes bombe. Move at once to fancy chilled
plate or cake stand and return to freezer to harden.

Garnish with toasted pecans to conform to design of mold.
Dribble ¼ cup butterscotch sauce over top of bombe; serve
remaining ¾ cup sauce in separate dish. Serve portions of
bombe easily with a large berry or serving spoon. Yields 10 to
12 servings.

## EASY FIXIN' ICE CREAM LOG
*Keep one in the freezer.*

⅔ cup chocolate cookie
   crumbs (about 10-11
   chocolate wafers)
8 large marshmallows,
   cut up

½ cup coarsely-chopped
   nuts
2 pints vanilla ice cream
   Chocolate syrup

In a small bowl, combine crumbs, marshmallows and nuts;
set aside. Place ice cream on aluminum foil; press ends
together. Return to freezer to harden. Press crumb mixture
over ice cream to completely coat. Wrap log in foil and freeze
until hard. To serve, slice the log and spoon 1 to 1½ tablespoons chocolate syrup over each serving. Yields 8 servings.

# CANNING AND FREEZING

## FREEZING VEGETABLES

*Select vegetables* that are at peak flavor and texture, the kind you would choose for immediate table use. When possible, harvest in cool part of the morning. Process as quickly as possible to retain top quality. If processing is delayed, cool vegetable in ice water or crushed ice and store in refrigerator to preserve flavor and quality and to prevent vitamin loss.

*Blanch* all vegetables before freezing to inactivate enzymes, otherwise flavor and vitamins will be lost during storage. Blanching will brighten the color and help retain texture. Blanch by scalding in boiling water.

*Assemble* the following equipment: large kettle (enamelware, aluminum, or stainless steel) with 2 or more gallon capacity; fine wire mesh basket or large, loose cheesecloth bag; pans for cooling; timer or clock with second hand.

*To blanch in boiling water,* allow 1 gallon water for each pound of vegetable except for leafy greens, which need 2 gallons per pound.

Bring water to rolling boil. Immerse wire basket or loose cheesecloth bag containing vegetable. Cover kettle and boil at top heat the required length of time (see table). Begin counting time as soon as you place the vegetable in water.

Cool immediately in cold running water or ice water for same time used for blanching. Drain and pack in containers. If vegetables are to be taken to a locker plant, store in refrigerator. *Not more than 2 hours should elapse between preparation, packaging and freezing.*

*To steam blanch,* put 1 inch of water in kettle, bring to a rolling boil. Suspend a thin layer of vegetable in a wire basket or loose cheesecloth over rapidly boiling water. Cover and process vegetable required amount of time (see table).

## WHEN YOU COOK FROZEN VEGETABLES

All vegetables may be cooked from the frozen state except corn-on-the-cob, which should be partially defrosted. Cook frozen vegetables in a small amount of salted water (about ½ cup or less). Cook only until tender — about half as long as if the same vegetable were fresh. You can use a pressure saucepan for cooking frozen vegetables. Follow manufacturer's directions for cooking time. A pack should be thawed enough to break it up before pressure cooking.

## HOW TO PREPARE VEGETABLES
### FOR FREEZING

| Vegetables | Varieties | Preparation |
|---|---|---|
| Asparagus | Martha Washington, Mary Washington, F1 Hybrid. | Wash and sort medium and large stalks. Leave whole or cut in 1- to 2-inch lengths. Blanch medium stalks 3 minutes, large stalks (½- to ¾-inch diameter) 4 minutes. Cool. |
| Beans (Green Podded) | Use strains of Blue Lake Bush and Tendercrop varieties. | Wash, snip off tips, and sort for size. Cut or break into suitable pieces or freeze small beans whole. Blanch 3½ minutes. Cool. |
| Beans (Yellow Podded) | Cherokee, Kinghorn Wax. | Process same as green podded beans. |
| Beans, Lima | Fordhook No. 242, Triumph, Burpee Improved Bush. | Wash, shell, and sort. Blanch small and medium beans, 3 minutes; large beans, 4 minutes. Cool. |
| Beans, Snap (Italian) | Any good garden variety. | Wash, snap off ends, and cut or break into 1- or 1½-inch lengths. Blanch 3½ minutes. Cool. |
| Beets | Use Ruby Queen and other garden varieties of good quality and color. | Select small- or medium-sized beets. Remove tops and wash. Cook until tender. Chill. Remove skins. Slice or dice large beets. |
| Broccoli | Waltham 29 and Spartan Early. | Discard off-color heads or any that have begun to blossom. Remove tough leaves and woody butt ends. Cut stalks to fit container. Cut through stalks lengthwise, leaving heads 1 inch in diameter. Soak ½ hour in salt brine (½ cup salt to 1 quart water) to drive out small insects. Rinse and drain. Blanch 4 minutes in water. Steam-blanch 5 minutes. Cool. Pack heads and stalk ends alternately in container. |

## FREEZING VEGETABLES, CONTINUED

| Vegetables | Varieties | Preparation |
|---|---|---|
| Brussels Sprouts | Catskill, Jade Cross. | Wash and trim. Soak ½ hour in salt brine (see broccoli). Rinse and drain. Blanch medium heads, 4 minutes; large heads, 5 minutes. Cool. |
| Carrots | Nantes, Chantenay. | Use tender carrots harvested in cool weather. Top, wash, and scrape. Dice or slice ¼-inch thick. Blanch 3½ minutes. Cool. |
| Cauliflower | Use Snowball strains. | Trim and wash. Split heads into individual pieces 1 inch in diameter. Soak ½ hour in salt brine (see broccoli). Rinse and drain. Blanch 4 minutes. Cool. |
| Sweet Corn | Sugar and Gold, Golden Beauty, Golden Cross Bantam, and Sugar King preferred for corn-on-the-cob. For cut corn, any good table corn, especially hybrid corn. | Husk, remove silks, and trim ends. Use a large kettle (12- to 15-quart capacity). Blanch whole grain corn to be cut from the cob 4½ minutes. Use schedule on page 333 for corn-on-the-cob. |
| Eggplant | Any variety with good color and quality. | Precooked eggplant is usually more satisfactory for freezing than blanched eggplant. Peel, cut into ¼- to ⅓-inch slices, or dice. To retain light color, drop pieces immediately into cold water containing 4 tablespoons salt per gallon. Blanch 4½ minutes in the same proportion salted water. Cool and package in layers separated by sheets of locker paper. |
| Garden Herbs | Any common varieties. | Wrap sprigs or leaves in foil or seal in film bags and store in a carton or glass jar. Wash, but do not scald leaves. |

| | | |
|---|---|---|
| Mushrooms | | Wash and remove stem base. Freeze small mushrooms whole; cut large ones into four or more pieces. When blanching mushrooms, add 1 teaspoon citric acid (or 3 teaspoons lemon juice or ½ teaspoon ascorbic acid) per quart of water to prevent darkening. Blanch medium or small whole mushrooms 4 minutes; cut pieces, 3 minutes. Cool. *OR:* Slice mushrooms ¼-inch thick. Saute in butter, 2 minutes. Cool. |
| Onions | Sweet Spanish types preferred. Can use good garden varieties. | Peel onions, wash, and cut into quarter sections. Chop. Blanch 1½ minutes. Cool. (They will keep 3-6 months.) |
| Peas | Little Marvel, Frosty, Laxton's Progress, and Dark Seeded Perfection. | Shell small amount at a time. Blanch 1½ to 2 minutes. Blanch black-eyed peas 2 minutes. Cool. |
| Peas (Edible-Podded, Sugar, or Chinese) | Any variety. | Wash. Remove stems, blossom ends, and any string. Leave whole. Blanch 2½ to 3 minutes. Cool. |
| Peppers, Green | Any variety. | Wash, cut out stem, and remove seeds. Halve, slice, or dice. Blanch halved peppers, 3 minutes; sliced or diced ones, 2 minutes. Cool. You can freeze chopped peppers without blanching them. |
| Peppers, Pimiento | | Oven roast at 400° F. for 3 to 4 minutes. Cool, skin, and pack dry without additional heating. |
| Pumpkin | Any good pie pumpkin. | Cut or break into fairly uniform pieces. Remove seeds. Bake at 350° F., or steam until tender. Cool, scoop pulp from rind, and mash or put through ricer. You can prepare pie mix for freezing, but omit cloves. |

FREEZING VEGETABLES, CONTINUED

| Vegetables | Varieties | Preparation |
|---|---|---|
| Potatoes | Any good quality potato. | Wash, peel, remove deep eyes, bruises, and green surface coloring. Cut in ¼- to ½-inch cubes. Blanch 5 minutes. Cool. For hash browns: Cook in jackets until almost done. Peel and grate. Form in desirable shapes. Freeze. For French fries, peel and cut in thin strips. Fry in deep fat until very light golden brown. Drain and cool. |
| Spinach and other Greens | Spinach, Bloomsdale Long Standing, New Zealand, America; Swiss Chard, Fordhook, Lucullus, Burgundy. | Sort and remove tough stems. Wash. Blanch most leafy greens 2 minutes. Blanch collards and stem portions of Swiss chard 3 to 4 minutes. Blanch very tender spinach 1½ minutes. Cool. |
| Summer Squash | Summer Crookneck, Zucchini, Summer Straightneck. | Wash, peel, and cut in pieces. Blanch ¼-inch slices, 3 minutes; 1½-inch slices, 6 minutes. Cool. |
| Winter Squash | For pies, Banana, Golden Delicious, Greengold, Hybrid R. For table use, Buttercup, Greengold, Rainbow, Hybrid R. | Prepare same as pumpkin. You can blend two or more varieties or blend squash with pumpkin. |

## PREPARATION FOR CORN-ON-THE-COB

| Size of ears | Number ears blanched with 12 quarts water | Diameter (inches) | Blanch (minutes) |
|---|---|---|---|
| Midget | 24 | 1¼ or less | 8 |
| Small | 14 | Between 1¼ and 1½ | 8 |
| Medium to large | 10 | Over 1½ | 11 |

## CONTAINERS

Use containers designed for freezing or use wide-mouthed glass canning jars. Some common types are: *Film bags,* with twist and tie tops. *Rigid cartons,* waxed or plastic-lined. *Glass jars,* wide-mouthed types are convenient. *Metal cans,* use enamel-lined types. *Polyester film boil-in-the-bag containers,* they have good protective qualities in the freezer.

## FREEZING FRUITS

*Select fruits that are* fully ripe, but not soft or mushy. Tree or vine-ripened fruits have the best flavor, color and food value.

*Sort* fruits carefully, discarding parts that are green or poor quality.

*Prepare* fruits as you use them — stem, pit and so forth.

*To make sugar syrup,* dissolve needed sugar in cold water. Stir and let stand until solution is clear. (You may substitute light corn syrup cup for cup for ⅓ of the sugar without noticeably affecting the flavor.)

*For sugar pack,* sprinkle required amount of sugar over fruit. Gently stir fruit until pieces are coated with sugar and juice.

*Use of ascorbic acid:* In freezing peaches, apricots, nectarines, or sweet cherries, add ½ teaspoon ascorbic acid for each 4 cups of water used in making the syrup. Do not beat. If you use commercial ascorbic acid preparations, follow manufacturer's directions.

*Fill containers* with syrup-packed fruit to within ½ inch of the top. Keep fruits that tend to darken, such as peaches, under the syrup by placing crumpled wax paper between lid and fruit.

*To freeze fruits without sweetening:* Freeze apricots and peaches in liquid containing 1 teaspoon ascorbic acid to 1 quart of water. Crush and freeze most berries in their own juice.

*Label containers* with name of fruit, type of pack and date.

## WHEN YOU USE FROZEN FRUIT

Thaw fruit at room temperature in its original package to preserve quality and nutritive value. If faster defrosting is required, place package in front of an electric fan or submerge (if watertight) in cool or lukewarm water. Serve as soon as defrosted, preferably while a few ice crystals remain.

## HOW TO PREPARE FRUITS FOR FREEZING

| *Fruits* | *Varieties* | *Preparation* |
|---|---|---|
| Apples | Most firm-fleshed cooking varieties, especially apples suitable for pies or sauces. | Peel and cut into pie slices. To prevent darkening, submerge slices in sodium bisulfite (USP grade) solution (1 teaspoon in 1 gallon water) for 5 minutes. Mix solution in glass, earthenware, stainless steel, or enamel container. Drain. Pack in sugar using 10-12 cups apples to 1 cup sugar. *OR:* Soak apple slices in brine solution (½ cup salt to 1 gallon water) for 15 minutes. Drain. Pack in sugar syrup using 2 cups sugar and ½ teaspoon ascorbic acid to 1 quart water. *OR:* Wash whole apple, drain, and dry. Place in polyethylene or similar plastic bags. Freeze. To use for pie, sauce, or other cooked desserts, run cold water over each frozen apple just before peeling. Peel, slice, and use immediately. |
| Apricots | Moorpark, or other well-ripened fruits of uniform golden-yellow color. | Dip six fully-ripened apricots into boiling water until skins loosen, about 15 to 20 seconds. Chill, peel, halve, and remove pits. Fill containers one-third full of syrup — 3 cups sugar to 1 quart water with ½ teaspoon ascorbic acid. Pack apricots in sirup. *OR:* Halve soft ripe fruit, steam 4 minutes, crush, and pack with 1 cup sugar to 8-9 cups fruit. Apricots are better canned than frozen. |
| Blackberries, Boysenberries, Dewberries, Loganberries, Youngberries, and Nectarberries | Any available varieties. | Pack in sugar syrup using 3 cups sugar to 1 quart water. *OR:* Crush and pack in sugar using 1 cup sugar to 7-8 cups fruit. For pies, pack berries dry without sugar. |

## FREEZING FRUITS, CONTINUED

| Fruits | Varieties | Preparation |
|---|---|---|
| Blueberries | Any available variety, cultivated or wild. | For desserts, pack in sugar syrup using 3 cups sugar to 1 quart water. *OR:* Pack in sugar using 1 cups sugar to 8-9 cups fruit. For pies, pack dry without sugar or sugar syrup. |
| Pie cherries | Any good quality cherry. | For pies, use 1½ to 2 cups sugar to 4 cups cherries for 9-inch pie. To improve color, add ¼ teaspoon ascorbic acid. |
| Sweet cherries | Bing, choose bright, fully ripe cherries. | Pack in syrup using 2 cups sugar to 1 quart water, ¼ teaspoon ascorbic acid, and either 1 teaspoon citric acid or 4 teaspoons lemon juice. |
| Citrus Fruit Mixes | Available citrus fruits. | Sprinkle sugar over each layer of citrus fruit, sweetening to taste. Let stand in refrigerator until fruit forms its own juice. If you wish to keep the mix 3-4 months, add ¼ teaspoon ascorbic acid to the sugar used for each 2 pints fruit. |
| Cranberries | Any available variety. | Wash and pack without sugar. |
| Currants | Red Lake and similar large fruit varieties. | Pack in sugar using 1 cup sugar to 8-9 cups fruit. For cooking, pack dry without sugar. |
| Gooseberries | Any good cooking variety | Pack without sugar or syrup or mix berries and sugar called for in pie recipe. |
| Ground Cherries | Any available varieties. | Husk, then scald cherries for 2 minutes. Pack in sugar syrup, 3 cups sugar to 1 quart water. |
| Muskmelons | Burpee Hybrid, Hybrid 16, Honey Dew, and other firm-fleshed varieties. | Cut flesh into ½- to ¾-inch cubes or balls. Cover with sugar syrup, using 2 cups sugar to 1 quart water. You can add whole seedless grapes. Serve partially frozen. |

| | | |
|---|---|---|
| Nectarines | Any available variety. | Same as apricots for preparation and packing. |
| Peaches | Elberta, July Elberta, J. H. Hale, Fireglow, Halehaven. There are some non-browning varieties that do not need ascorbic acid. | Dip 3 or 4 peaches into boiling water until skins loosen. Chill and follow instructions given for apricots. *OR:* Freeze non-browning varieties with dry sugar using ½ teaspoon ascorbic acid and 4 cups sugar with 8 pounds fruit (about 4 quarts). |
| Pineapple | Any fruit of bright appearance, dark orange-yellow color. | Peel and core. Dice, slice or cut into wedges. Cover with syrup, 3 cups sugar to 1 quart water. *OR:* Pack in dry sugar, 1 cup sugar to 8-9 cups fruit. Do not use uncooked pineapple in gelatin molds. |
| Raspberries | Red—Latham, Taylor, Chief, September, Newburgh; Purple—Sodus, Black Bristol. | Pack raspberries in syrup, 3 cups sugar to 1 quart water. *or:* Pack in dry sugar, 1 cup sugar to 7-8 cups fruit. Pack purple raspberries for jam without sweetening. |
| Rhubarb | Valentine, Chipman's Canada Red, McDonald Crimson. | Remove leaves and woody ends, wash, and cut in 1-inch lengths. Do not blanch. For sauce, pack in sugar syrup using 3½ cups sugar to 1 quart water. For pies, pack in dry sugar using 1 cup sugar to 4 cups rhubarb, or pack without sugar for a few months' storage. |
| Strawberries | Earlimore, Trumpeter, Red Rich, Sparkle are preferred; Dunlap, Gem, and Superfection. Beaver and Premier are acceptable. | Pack whole, sliced (preferred), or crushed berries in 1 cup sugar to 7-8 cups fruit. *OR:* Pack whole berries in syrup, 3-4 cups sugar to 1 quart water. |

## PRESSURE CANNER CANNING
*Recommended for processing vegetables, meats*
*and low-acid foods as it gives*
*a greater degree of safety.*

*Wash jars,* which are free of nicks and cracks, in hot soapy water. Scald and invert on clean cloth. Scald lids and keep in water until used.

*Select* firm, fresh, not overripe, foods and prepare according to recipe.

*Fill jars,* packing corn, peas, lima beans, meats and fish loosely, to 1 inch of top of jars — other food to ½ inch of top.

*Add liquid:* Raw pack fruits — fill jar 1½ inches from top with syrup, fruit juice or water. Hot pack fruit — fill jar ½ inch from top with syrup, fruit juice or water. Raw pack meat — pack loosely 1 inch from top of jar. Add no liquid. Natural meat juices will form. Hot pack meat — pack loosely 1 inch from top of jar. Add 3 to 4 tablespoons liquid (grease, broth or water).

*Wipe top* of jars clean and place scalded lid on jar with sealing composition next to glass. Screw bands firmly tight. Do not use rusty or bent screw bands or jars will not seal.

*Place rack* in bottom of pressure canner, add 1 to 2 inches of boiling water.

*Set capped jars* on rack in canner. Pack only enough jars at one time to fill cooker. Set jars apart so steam can circulate freely.

*Adjust canner cover* and fasten securely. Leave petcock open until steam has been flowing steadily 10 minutes. Close petcock. Start counting processing time when required pressure is reached on pressure gauge. Keep pressure uniform throughout processing time. See charts.

*When processing time is up,* remove canner from heat. Let canner set until gauge returns to zero. Then slowly open petcock and remove cover. If canner has weight control gauge, nudge it; if no steam escapes, open canner.

*Food in jars* may be boiling vigorously; if so, allow jars to remain in canner for a few minutes, then remove. Set jars on folded cloth, out of draft, to cool. Do not uncover. Do not tighten screw bands after processing.

*Test for seal* when jars are cold: Tap lid with a spoon; a clear ringing sound means a seal. See if lid is curved down; if so, jar is sealed. Press center of lid; if it is down and will not move, jar is sealed.

*Remove screw bands* from sealed jars, wash and store.

*Boil all home-canned* vegetables, meats, poultry and fish in an open vessel for 10 to 15 minutes before tasting or using.

## APPROXIMATE YIELDS

Legal weight of a bushel of fruits or vegetables varies in different states. These are average weights.

| FOOD | FRESH | CANNED |
|---|---|---|
| Apples | 1 bu. (48 lbs.) | 16 to 20 qts. |
| Berries, except strawberries | 24 qt. crate | 12 to 18 qts. |
| Peaches | 1 bu. (48 lbs.) | 18 to 24 qts. |
| Pears | 1 bu. (50 lbs.) | 20 to 26 qts. |
| Tomatoes | 1 bu. (53 lbs.) | 15 to 20 qts. |
| Beans, lima, in pods | 1 bu. (32 lbs.) | 6 to 8 qts. |
| Beans, snap | 1 bu. (30 lbs.) | 15 to 20 qts. |
| Beets, without tops | 1 bu. (52 lbs.) | 17 to 20 qts. |
| Corn, sweet, in husks | 1 bu. (36 lbs.) | 8 to 9 qts. |
| Peas, green, in pods | 1 bu. (30 lbs.) | 12 to 15 qts. |

## CANNING SOUPS

| | Boiling Water Bath | Pressure Canner | |
|---|---|---|---|
| | Minutes | Minutes | Pounds |
| Asparagus<br>Use tough part, boil. Press through sieve, Pour into jars. | | 40 | 10 |
| Chowder, Fish, Clam<br>Mix ingredients. Boil ten minutes. Pack into jars. | | 90 | 10 |
| Pea Soup<br>Boil peas until soft, press thru sieve. Pour into jars. | | 60 | 10 |
| Soup Stock Chicken<br>Cover bones and trimmings with water. Season. Cook 2 hours. Remove bones. Pour into jars. | | 45 | 10 |
| Tomato Soup<br>Mix vegetables. Cook tender; sieve. Add flour and butter; bring to boil; pour into jars. | 30 | | |
| Tomato Puree<br>Cook all ingredients until soft. Press thru sieve, pack. Use pint jars. | 35 | 10 | 5 |
| Vegetable Soup Mixtures<br>Use any vegetable combinations. Boil 5 minutes or pack raw. Pack into jars. Process time necessary for vegetable requiring longest processing. | | 85 | 10 |

# CANNING MEATS

| | Description | Pressure Canner Minutes | | |
|---|---|---|---|---|
| | | Pts. | Qts. | Lbs. |
| Lamb, Veal, Beef, Steak | Bleed well. Cool thoroughly. Pack raw without liquid or precook and add 3 to 4 tablespoons liquid. | 75 | 90 | 10 |
| Pork, Pork Chop | Bleed well. Cool thoroughly. Pack raw without liquid or precook, pack, add salt 1 teaspoon to quart, add 3 or 4 tablespoons liquid. | 75 | 90 | 10 |
| Tenderloin, Ham | Sear until lightly browned. Pack. Add 3 to 4 tablespoons water or broth. Or pack raw without liquid. | 75 | 90 | 10 |
| Sausage | Fry or bake cakes until brown. Pack. Add 3 to 4 tablespoons liquid. | 75 | 90 | 10 |
| Chicken, Rabbit, Duck, Turkey | Bleed well. Cool thoroughly. Pack raw without liquid or precook and add 3 to 4 tablespoons liquid. | 75 | 90 | 10 |
| Venison, Wild Birds, Geese | Bleed well, cool thoroughly, soak in brine 30 minutes or parboil. Precook, pack, add salt 1 teaspoon to quart, add 3 or 4 tablespoons liquid. Or pack raw without liquid. | 75 | 90 | 10 |
| Fish, All Kinds | Use only firm, fresh fish. Bleed well. Wash. Pack raw without liquid. Use pint jars. | 90 | | 10 |

# CANNING VEGETABLES

| | Preparation | Pressure Canner Minutes | | |
| --- | --- | --- | --- | --- |
| | | Pts. | Qts. | Lbs. |
| Asparagus | Wash, pack raw or boil 3 minutes and pack. | 25 | 30 | 10 |
| Beans (Green-Wax) | Wash, string, cut, pack raw or boil 5 minutes and pack. | 20 | 25 | 10 |
| Beans, Lima | Shell, wash, pack raw or bring to boil. Pack loosely, 1 inch from top. | 40 | 50 | 10 |
| Beets | Wash, leave roots and tops long, boil 15 minutes. Skin. Pack. | 30 | 35 | 10 |
| Brussels Sprouts or Cabbage | Remove outer leaves, wash, cut, boil 5 minutes, pack. | 45 | 55 | 10 |
| Carrots | Wash, peel, slice or leave whole. Pack raw or boil 3 minutes. | 25 | 30 | 10 |
| Cauliflower or Broccoli | Remove outside leaves, wash, cut. Pack raw or boil 3 minutes. | 25 | 40 | 10 |
| Corn (Whole Grain) | Remove shucks. Cut from cob. Pack raw or bring to boil. Pack loosely to within 1 inch of top of jar. Use pint jars. | 55 | | 10 |
| Greens (All Kinds) | Wash thoroughly. Steam or boil to wilt. Pack loosely. | 70 | 90 | 10 |
| Hominy | Boil 3 minutes. Pack loosely. | 60 | 70 | 10 |
| Mushrooms | Clean, wash, cut large ones, boil 3 minutes. Pack loosely. | 30 | 35 | 10 |
| Okra | Wash, boil 1 minute. Pack. | 25 | 40 | 10 |

| Vegetable | Instructions | | | |
|---|---|---|---|---|
| Onions | Peel, wash, boil 5 minutes. Pack. | 40 | 40 | 10 |
| Peas | Shell, wash and grade tender peas. Pack raw or bring to boil. Pack loosely to within 1 inch of top of jar. | 40 | 40 | 10 |
| Peppers, Bell | Wash, remove seed pod, boil 3 minutes. Pack. | 35 | 35 | 10 |
| Peppers, Pimiento | Place in moderate oven 6 to 8 minutes or 12 to 15 minutes in boiling water. Peel, stem, cut out seeds, flatten. Pack. | 10 | 10 | 5 |
| Potatoes Irish | Wash, and scrape small, new potatoes. Pack raw or boil 3 minutes. Add boiling water. | 40 | 40 | 10 |
| Pumpkin | Cut in pieces. Peel. Steam, boil or bake tender. Pack. | 65 | 80 | 10 |
| Rutabagas | Wash, peel, slice or cube, boil 5 minutes. Pack. | 35 | 35 | 10 |
| Spinach | Wash, steam or boil to wilt. Pack loosely, to 1 inch of top of jar. | 70 | 90 | 10 |
| Squash (Summer) | Cut in uniform pieces. Pack raw or bring to boil and pack. | 25 | 30 | 10 |
| Squash (Winter) | Cut in pieces. Peel. Steam, boil or bake tender. Pack. | 65 | 80 | 10 |
| Sweet Potatoes | Dry Pack. Wash, boil or steam 20 minutes, remove skins. Pack. | 65 | 95 | 10 |
| Sweet Potatoes | Wet. Wash, boil or steam 20 minutes, remove skins. Pack. Add liquid. | 55 | 90 | 10 |
| Turnips-Parsnips | Wash, peel, slice or cube. Pack raw or boil 3 minutes. | 20 | 25 | 10 |

## BOILING WATER BATH CANNING
*Recommended for processing fruits,*
*including tomatoes. These are acid foods and can be*
*canned safely at boiling temperature.*

*A boiling water bath canner* or any kettle with cover may be used. It must be deep enough for water to cover jars 1 to 2 inches over top and must be fitted with a rack. The rack may be wooden strips, wire or other perforated material. The rack must hold jars at least ½ inch off bottom of canner.

*Place canner on heat* with correct amount of boiling water needed to cover jars. Water should be boiling when jars of food are placed in it.

*Prepare jars and food* as directed for Pressure Canner Canning — paragraphs 1 through 5.

*Place filled jars* in canner of boiling water, far enough apart to allow free circulation of water. Start counting processing time as soon as water comes back to a rolling boil. Keep water boiling during entire processing time. If water boils down, add enough boiling water to keep jars covered by 1 inch.

*Process* food required length of time. See chart. Remove jars from canner and set on folded cloth, out of draft, to cool. Do not cover jars. Do not tighten screw bands after processing.

*When jars are cold,* test for seal as described under Pressure Canner Canning; remove screw bands.

*Remember* food will spoil if not processed for the correct length of time at the correct temperature. *And* home-canned vegetables, meat, poultry and fish should not be processed using this method.


## CANNING TIME TABLES

*Time for different size jars* — The time in these tables for water bath canning applies to half-pint, pint and quart jars. If canning fruit in water bath with half-gallon jars add 10 minutes to process time; for pressure canner add 5 minutes to processing time.


*Altitudes above sea level* — The time given in the time tables is for the half-pint, one-pint or one-quart pack. For all jars the time must be increased when boiling water bath is used at an altitude of 1,000 feet or more. For each 1,000 feet above sea level, add 1 minute to processing time if the time called for is 20 minutes or less. If the processing time called for is more than 20 minutes, add 2 minutes for each 1,000 feet.

When the pressure canner is used at an altitude of 2,000 feet or more, the pressure must be increased by 1 pound for each 2,000 feet altitude.

*Make Applesauce Special:* Add lemon juice or grated lemon peel for tang. *Or* when canning, try a few jars of minted sauce by adding a drop (be light-fingered) or two of mint extract and just a tint of green food coloring. *Or* add a little cinnamon to taste and some red food coloring. *Or* note that nutmeg tastes wonderful in fresh applesauce, though when sauce is canned it sometimes leaves a bitter taste.

## CANNING FRUITS

| | | Boiling Water Bath Minutes | | Pressure Canner Pts. & Qts. | |
|---|---|---|---|---|---|
| | | Pints | Quarts | Minutes | Lbs. |
| Apples | Wash, pare, core, cut in pieces. Drop in slightly salted water. Drain. Boil 3 to 5 minutes in syrup. Pack. Add syrup or water. | 15 | 20 | 10 | 5 |
| Apricots | Wash, halve and pit. Pack. Add syrup, fruit juice or water. | 25 | 30 | 10 | 5 |
| Berries (except Strawberries and Cranberries) | Wash, stem, pack. Add syrup or water. | 10 | 15 | 8 | 5 |
| Cherries | Wash, stem, pit. Pack. Add syrup or water. | 20 | 25 | 10 | 5 |
| Cranberries | Wash, remove stems. Boil 3 minutes in heavy syrup. Pack. | 10 | 10 | | |
| Currants | Wash, stem, pack. Add syrup or water. | 20 | 20 | 10 | 5 |
| Dried Fruits | Soak in cold water overnight. Boil 10 minutes in same water. Pack. | 15 | 15 | | |
| Fruit Juices | Crush fruit, heat slowly, strain. Heat juice according to recipe. Pour into jars. | 10 | 10 | | |
| Grapes | Wash, stem, pack. Add syrup or water. | 20 | 20 | 8 | 5 |

| | Preparation | | | | |
|---|---|---|---|---|---|
| Peaches | Peel, pack, add syrup, or boil 3 minutes in syrup, pack, add syrup. | 20 | 25 | 10 | 5 |
| Pears | Select not overripe pears, pare, halve, boil 3 to 5 minutes in syrup. Pack. Add syrup. | 20 | 25 | 10 | 5 |
| Pineapple | Slice, peel, remove eyes and core. Boil in syrup 5 to 10 minutes. Pack. Add syrup. | 30 | 30 | 15 | 5 |
| Plums | Wash, prick skins. Pack. Add syrup. | 20 | 25 | 10 | 5 |
| Preserves | Prepare as per recipe. Cook until thick. Pack. Process in water bath. (180° — simmering) | 20 | 20 | | |
| Rhubarb | Wash, cut into pieces. Pack. Add syrup. Or bake until tender. Pack. Add syrup. | 10 | 10 | 5 | 5 |
| Strawberries | Wash, stem, boil gently for 3 minutes in syrup. Cover the kettle and let stand for several hours. Pack. | 15 | 15 | 5 | |
| Tomatoes | Scald ½ minute, cold dip, peel, core, quarter. Pack. | 40 | 50 | 15 | 5 |
| Tomato Juice | Wash, peel, cut in pieces. Simmer until soft, press thru fine sieve. Bring to boil. Pour to within ¼ inch of top of jar. | 35 | 35 | | |

## HOW TO EXTRACT FRUIT JUICES FOR JELLY

Put prepared fruit in a damp, cheesecloth jelly bag and allow juice to drip through it into an enamel or glass bowl. *Clearest* jelly comes from juice which has dripped through a jelly bag *without pressing*. For a greater yield of juice, twist the bag of fruit tightly and squeeze or press. Pressed juice should be re-strained through a double thickness of damp cheesecloth . . . this time, the bag should not be squeezed.

*Use embroidery hoops* for holding the ends of a jelly bag open. The bag can be hung from a clean wire coat hanger, bent to hook under the hoops from the outside.

### FRUIT SYRUPS
*Try Thimbleberry, Dewberry, Raspberry —*
*plus the fruits listed in recipes below.*
*Serve on pancakes, custards, waffles and ice cream.*

*Basic Fruit Syrup:* Use this recipe with many flavorful fruits. First extract juice from fruit or berries as for jelly. Add 2 cups sugar and 1 cup light corn syrup to 4 cups juice. Bring to boil; boil hard 3 minutes. Pour into scalded, hot jars and seal. Yields 4 pints of syrup which can be diluted.

*Rose Hip Syrup:* Wash rose hips; remove stems and flower remnants; measure out 4 cups. Boil hips and 2 cups water for 20 minutes in a covered pan. Strain through jelly bag; add 2 cups sugar to juice and boil mixture 5 minutes. Remove from heat and pour into scalded, hot jars. Refrigerate. Yields about 1½ pints syrup.

*Blackberry Syrup:* Crush berries and strain through jelly bag as for jelly. Mix 4 cups juice with 4 cups sugar and ¼ cup lemon juice. Simmer mixture until sugar dissolves. Pour syrup into scalded jars; tighten lids and process for 10 minutes in boiling water bath. Yields about 6 pints syrup.

*Chokecherry Syrup:* Prepare chokecherry juice as for jelly page 351. Mix 4 cups juice, 4 cups sugar, ½ cup lemon juice and ½ package powdered pectin. Boil hard 2 minutes. Pour into scalded jars; tighten lids. Process for 10 minutes in boiling water bath. Yields about 6 pints syrup.

*Wild Pincherry Syrup:* Prepare pincherry juice as chokecherries are prepared for jelly, page 351. Bring 2 cups juice, ½ cup white corn syrup and 3 cups sugar to a boil in large saucepan. Turn down heat and simmer about 15 minutes. Skim off scum. Cool. Bottle in hot, scalded jars and refrigerate. Yields about 2 pints syrup.

*Blueberry Syrup:* Mash 2 quarts blueberries, sprinkle with 4 cups sugar. Cover and let stand overnight. Add ¾ cup cold water and bring mixture to a boil. Cook 20 minutes. Strain through cheesecloth jelly bag. Heat to boiling point and pour into scalded, hot jars and seal. Yields about 6 pints syrup.


## LAYERED JELLIES AND JAMS

Prepare a quick-setting jelly or jam for the bottom layer (tart apple, blackberry, crabapple, cranberry, currant, gooseberry, grape, quince or sour plum).

Place jelly glasses on a slant, using a V-shaped roasting rack or other suitable prop. Ladle jelly or jam into glasses, filling each glass about half full. When jelly or jam in glasses begins to set and will remain in place when glass is set upright, prepare second jelly or jam recipe. Recipes made of apricots, cherries, strawberries or peaches have a longer setting time and are more suitable on top.

Set glasses upright, ladle jelly or jam into them quickly. Cover at once with ⅛-inch hot paraffin.

You may wish to layer only part of a recipe. If so, ladle remainder into other glasses, filling to within ½-inch of top.


## BLACKBERRY JELLY
*Deep flavor!*

| | |
|---|---|
| 3½ cups juice (about 2 quarts ripe blackberries, not black caps) | 5 cups sugar 1 box powdered fruit pectin |

Prepare juice by crushing fully ripe berries thoroughly. Strain juice through cheesecloth bag. Measure 3½ cups into a large pan. Juice may be brought to a boil then canned or frozen in jars for future use.

*To make jelly:* Measure sugar, set aside. Add pectin to juice, mix well. Place over high heat, stir until mixture comes to a boil. At once stir in sugar, bring to full rolling boil, boil hard 1 minute, stirring constantly. Remove from heat, skim off foam, pour quickly into sterilized glasses. Cover jelly at once with ⅛-inch paraffin. Yields about 8 glasses, 6 ounces each.

## GRAPE JELLY
*Without added pectin.*

4 cups grape juice (takes
about 3½ pounds
Concord grapes and
½ cup water)

3 cups sugar

Select about ¼ under-ripe and ¾ fully-ripe grapes. Sort, wash, and remove grapes from stems. Crush grapes, add water, cover, and bring to boil on high heat. Reduce heat and simmer for 10 minutes. Strain juice through a cheesecloth bag. To prevent formation of tartrate crystals in the jelly, let juice stand in a cool place overnight, then strain through two thicknesses of damp cheesecloth to remove crystals.

*To make jelly:* Measure juice into a kettle. Add sugar and stir well. Boil over high heat to 8° F. above the boiling point of water, or until jelly mixture sheets from a spoon.

Remove from heat; skim off foam quickly. Pour jelly immediately into hot containers and seal with ⅛ -inch paraffin. Yields about 5 glasses, 6 ounces each.

## RED CURRANT JELLY
*Use only ripe currants or the jelly will be cloudy —
no pectin added.*

2 quarts ripe currants
½ cup water

1½ cups sugar for each cup
currant juice

Remove leaves, but not the stems, from the fruit. Wash and drain well. Combine currants and water; mash. Cook 10 minutes, stirring frequently. Strain through cheesecloth jelly bag. Juice may be returned to a boil then canned or frozen for future use.

*To make jelly:* Measure juice, pour into large pan. Bring to full rolling boil, boil 10 minutes. Remove from heat, stir in sugar — 1½ cups per 1 cup juice — until sugar is completely dissolved. Skim, pour at once into hot, sterile jars. Seal or cover with ⅛- inch paraffin. Yields 8 half-pint glasses.

## CHOKECHERRY JELLY
*Do not crush cherry pits during simmering.*

3 cups chokecherry juice
6½ cups sugar
½ teaspoon cinnamon
¼ teaspoon cloves

6½ cups sugar
1 bottle liquid fruit
pectin

Stem about 3½ pounds fully ripe, wild chokecherries or other wild cherries. Add 3 cups water; bring to boil and simmer, covered, 15 minutes. Crush fruit during cooking with a potato masher. Place fruit in jelly bag to strain off juice. Juice may be brought to a boil again then canned for future use. Sediment forms as juice stands. Pour juice carefully off this sediment — clearer jelly, with less "choke," results.

*To make jelly:* Measure juice into a large saucepan, add spices and sugar; mix well. Place over high heat and bring to boil, stirring constantly. Stir in liquid pectin. Bring to full, rolling boil and boil hard 1 minute, stirring constantly. Remove from heat, skim off foam with metal spoon and pour into glasses. Seal at once with ⅛-inch paraffin. Yields about 9 glasses 6 ounces each.

## PLUM JELLY
*Use some wild fruit, too.*

4 cups plum juice (takes
about 4½ pounds plums
and ½ cup water)

7½ cups sugar
½ bottle liquid pectin

Sort and wash fully ripe plums and cut them in pieces; do not peel or pit. Crush the fruit, add water, cover, and bring to boil over high heat. Reduce heat and simmer for 10 minutes. Extract juice by straining through a jelly bag. Juice may be brought to a boil then canned or frozen for future use.

*To make jelly.* Measure juice into a kettle. Stir in the sugar. Place on high heat and, stirring constantly, bring quickly to a full rolling boil that cannot be stirred down.

Add pectin; bring again to full rolling boil. Boil hard 1 minute. Remove from heat; skim off foam quickly. Pour jelly immediately into hot containers and seal with ⅛ - inch paraffin. Yields about 11 glasses, 6 ounces each.

## APPLE JELLY
*Without added pectin.*

| | |
|---|---|
| 4 cups apple juice (takes about 3 pounds apples and 3 cups water) | 2 tablespoons strained lemon juice, if desired |
| | 3 cups sugar |

Select about ¼ under-ripe and ¾ fully-ripe tart apples (Dolgo Crab apples are excellent). Sort, wash, and remove stem and blossom ends; do not pare or core. Cut apples into small pieces. Add water, cover, and bring to boil on high heat. Reduce heat and simmer for 20 to 25 minutes, or until apples are soft. Extract juice by straining through a jelly bag. Juice may be brought to a boil, then canned or frozen for future use.

*To make jelly.* Measure apple juice into a kettle. Add lemon juice and sugar and stir well. Boil over high heat to 8° F. above the boiling point of water, or until jelly mixture sheets from a spoon.

Remove from heat; skim off foam quickly. Pour jelly immediately into hot containers and seal with ⅛ -inch paraffin. Yields 4 or 5 glasses, 6 ounces each.

## TOMATO JELLY
*Rather unusual . . . and just a bit tart.*

| | |
|---|---|
| 18-20 large tomatoes | ½ lemon |
| 1 box powdered fruit pectin | 4½ cups sugar |

Cut ripe, but not over-ripe, tomatoes in quarters or thick slices. Cook over low heat in saucepan until soft; drain in jelly bag without pressure. Boil juice 20 minutes in uncovered kettle.

Measure out 3 cups of the boiled juice; add lemon which has been very thinly sliced (each slice then cut in quarters). Stir in pectin. Stir over high heat until mixture boils hard. At once stir in sugar. Bring to a full rolling boil which steams, tumbles and cannot be stirred down; boil hard one minute, stirring constantly.

Remove jelly from heat; skim off foam with metal spoon. Pour at once into sterilized jelly glasses and seal with ⅛ -inch paraffin. Cool a few inches apart. Yields 6 glasses, 6 ounces each.

## BLACKBERRY-RASPBERRY-RHUBARB JAM
*Spread on thick, warm slices of fresh bread.*

5 cups prepared fruit
  (about 1 quart each ripe
  blackberries and red
  raspberries plus 1 pound
  rhubarb)

7 cups sugar
1 box powdered fruit pectin

Crush berries. Slice or chop (do not peel) rhubarb. Mix fruits.

Measure 5 cups into a very large saucepan. Measure the sugar; set aside. Stir pectin into fruit. Place over high heat; stir until mixture comes to a hard boil. At once, stir in sugar. Bring to a full, rolling boil and boil hard 1 minute, stirring constantly. Remove from heat; skim off foam with metal spoon. Stir and skim for 5 minutes to cool slightly and prevent floating fruit. Ladle quickly into hot jars and seal. Yields about 8 half-pint jars of jam.

## ROSY MELBA PEACH JAM
*So pretty.*

1½ pounds ripe peaches
¼ cup lemon juice
2 cups red raspberries
7 cups sugar

1 bottle liquid fruit pectin
Few drops almond
  extract

Peel, pit and crush peaches. Measure 2 cups. Add 2 tablespoons of lemon juice, stir gently and let stand while preparing raspberries. Crush berries and add remaining 2 tablespoons lemon juice.

Combine peaches and raspberries with sugar in heavy kettle. Mix well and bring to a full, rolling boil, stirring constantly. Boil 1 minute. Remove from heat and add pectin. Stir and skim for several minutes to prevent fruit floating. Add extract. Pour into hot, sterilized jars. Seal. Yields 8 half-pint jars of jam.

## RHUBARB AND STRAWBERRY JAM
*Enjoy a summer garden taste all winter.*

4 cups prepared fruit
  (about 1 pound rhubarb
  and 1 quart fully ripe
  strawberries)

5½ cups sugar
1 box powdered fruit
  pectin

Slice thin or chop (do not peel) about 1 pound rhubarb. Thoroughly crush, one layer at a time, about 1 quart of strawberries. Combine fruits and measure 4 cups into a large saucepan.

Measure sugar and set aside. Mix fruit pectin into fruit in saucepan. Place over high heat and stir until mixture comes to a hard boil. Immediately add all sugar. Bring to a full rolling boil and boil hard 1 minute, stirring constantly. Remove from heat and skim off foam with metal spoon. Then stir and skim for 5 minutes to cool slightly and prevent floating fruit. Ladle quickly into hot jars and seal. Yields about 5 half-pint jars of jam.

## GRAPE AND PLUM JAM
*Try your own grapes and plums.*

5½ cups prepared fruit
  (about 2 pounds each
  fully ripe Concord
  grapes and Italian
  plums, and ½ cup
  water)

8 cups (3½-pounds) sugar
½ bottle liquid fruit pectin

Slip skins from about 2 pounds Concord or other loose-skinned grapes. Bring pulp to a boil and simmer, covered, 5 minutes. Sieve. Chop or grind skins and add to pulp. Pit (do not peel) about 2 pounds plums. Cut in small pieces and chop. Add ½ cup water; bring to a boil and simmer, covered, 5 minutes. Combine fruits and measure 5½ cups into a *very large* saucepan.

Thoroughly mix sugar into fruit in saucepan. Place over high heat, bring to a full rolling boil and boil hard 1 minute, stirring constantly. Remove from heat and at once stir in fruit pectin. Skim off foam with metal spoon. Then stir and skim for 5 minutes to cool slightly and prevent floating fruit. Ladle quickly into hot jars. Seal. Yields about 8 half-pint jars of jam.

## TUTTI-FRUTTI JAM
*A winter treat.*

3 cups chopped *or* ground pears
1 large orange
¾ cup drained crushed pineapple
¼ cup lemon juice

¼ cup chopped maraschino cherries (3-ounce bottle)
1 package powdered fruit pectin
5 cups sugar

Sort and wash ripe pears; pare and core. Chop or grind the pears. Peel the orange, remove seeds, and chop or grind the pulp.

Measure chopped pears into a kettle. Add orange, pineapple, lemon juice and cherries. Stir in the pectin. Place on high heat and, stirring constantly, bring quickly to a full boil. Add the sugar, continue stirring, and heat again to a full bubbling boil that cannot be stirred down. Boil hard for 1 minute, stirring constantly. Remove from heat; skim and seal. Yields about 7 half-pint jars of jam.

## SPICY GRAPE JAM
*New taste treat.*

3 pounds Concord grapes
1 cup water
¼-1 teaspoon each cinnamon, ginger and allspice

1 box powdered fruit pectin
7 cups sugar

Wash grapes and separate skins from pulp. Add water and spices to pulp; heat to boil; cover and simmer 5 minutes. Sieve to remove seeds.

Chop skins and add to pulp. Measure 5½ cups of grape mixture into a large saucepan and place over high heat. Mix in pectin and stir until mixture comes to hard boil. Stir in sugar at once. Heat to a rolling boil that cannot be stirred down; boil hard for 1 minute, stirring constantly.

Remove from heat, skim and seal in jars. Yields 9 half-pint jars of jam.

## BLUEBERRY JAM
*Wild blueberries are best.*

4½ cups prepared fruit
   (about 1½ quarts fully
   ripe blueberries)
 2 tablespoons lemon juice
   (1 lemon)

7 cups (3-pounds) sugar
1 bottle liquid fruit
   pectin

Thoroughly crush, one layer at a time, about 1½ quarts blueberries. Measure 4½ cups into a *very large* saucepan. Squeeze the juice from 1 lemon; add 2 tablespoons to fruit.

Thoroughly mix sugar into fruit in saucepan. Place over high heat, bring to a full rolling boil and boil hard 1 minute, stirring constantly. Remove from heat and immediately stir in fruit pectin. Skim off foam with metal spoon. Then stir and skim for 5 minutes to cool slightly and prevent floating fruit. Ladle quickly into jars and seal. Yields about 7 half-pint jars of jam.

*Spiced Blueberry Jam.* Prepare Blueberry Jam as directed, adding ¼ to ½ teaspoon of cloves, cinnamon and allspice, or any desired combination of these spices to berries before cooking.

*Bright jams and jellies.* Cut fruit patterns from different-colored felt or other fabric. Glue to jar and lid. Decorate for gifts or a bazaar.

## RASPBERRY-BLUEBERRY JAM
*Northern Minnesota wild fruits create a gourmet treat.*

1 quart red raspberries
1 quart blueberries

7 cups sugar
1 box powdered fruit pectin

Wash and crush fruit; combine. Measure 4 cups. If necessary, fill last cup with water.

Add pectin; mix well; heat to full, rolling boil. Stir in sugar at once. Bring to a rolling boil that cannot be stirred down and boil hard 1 minute, stirring constantly.

Remove from heat, skim, seal. Yields about 8 half-pint jars of jam.

## NO-COOK STRAWBERRY-RHUBARB JAM
*The kitchen doesn't even get warm.*

2 cups prepared fruit (about
 1½ pints ripe straw-
 berries and ½ pound
 rhubarb)

4 cups (1¾-pounds) sugar
¾ cup water
1 box powdered
 fruit pectin

Thoroughly crush about 1½ pints strawberries. Measure
1½ cups into a large bowl or pan. Grind (do not peel) about
½ pound rhubarb. Measure ½ cup. Add to the strawberries.
Thoroughly mix sugar into fruit; set aside. Mix water and
fruit pectin in a small saucepan. Bring to a boil and boil 1
minute, stirring constantly. Stir into fruit. Continue stirring
about 3 minutes. (A few sugar crystals will remain.) Ladle
quickly into jars. Cover at once with tight lids. Let stand at
room temperature until set (may take up to 24 hours); then
store in freezer. If jam will be used within 2 or 3 weeks, it
may be stored in the refrigerator. Yields 5 half-pint jars of
jam.

## NO-COOK PEACH-RASPBERRY JAM
*Enjoy fresh fruit taste all winter.*

1¼ cups prepared peaches
 (about 1¼ pounds
 ripe fruit)
2 tablespoons lemon juice
1 cup prepared red rasp-
 berries (about 1 pint
 ripe fruit)

5 cups sugar
¾ cup water
1 box powdered
 fruit pectin

Peel, pit and finely chop peaches. Measure 1¼ cups into
large bowl. Add lemon juice. Thoroughly crush raspberries, a
layer at a time; measure 1 cup into bowl.
Add sugar to fruits; mix well. Mix water and pectin in
small pan, bring to a boil and boil 1 minute, stirring
constantly. Stir in fruits. Continue stirring about 2 minutes. A
few sugar crystals will remain. Quickly ladle into glasses;
cover with tight lids. Let stand until set — about 24 hours.
Store in freezer. For use within 2 to 3 weeks, store in
refrigerator. Yields 4 half-pint jars of jam.

## UNCOOKED BERRY JAM
*Fruit tastes fresh.*

3 cups crushed berries
 (about 1½ quarts black-
 berries, raspberries *or*
 strawberries)

5 cups sugar
1 package powdered fruit
 pectin
1 cup cold water

Sort, wash, drain and hull fully ripe fruit; then crush berries.

Measure 3 cups prepared fruit into large mixing bowl. Add sugar, mix well; let stand 20 minutes, stirring occasionally.

Dissolve pectin in the cold water, bring to a boil and boil for 1 minute. Add pectin solution to fruit-sugar mixture and stir for 2 minutes. Pour jam into freezer containers or canning jars, leaving ½ inch space at the top. Quickly cover containers and let stand for 24 hours or until jam is set. Jam may be stored in refrigerator for a few weeks or frozen up to 1 year. Do not store at room temperature or jam will ferment. Yields about 7 half-pint jars of jam.

*Note:* If the jam is too firm, it can be softened by stirring. If it tends to separate, stirring will blend it again.

## GREAT GRANDMA'S STRAWBERRY JAM
*A soft spread that's good on ice cream.*

4 cups crushed strawberries
2 cups sugar
 Butter, size of walnut

2 cups sugar
2 tablespoons lemon juice

Combine first 3 ingredients and boil 3 to 5 minutes. Add remaining ingredients and boil 3 to 5 minutes more. Cover loosely with cheesecloth and let stand overnight. Then let stand in sun 1 whole day. Pour into hot, scalded bottles and cover with ⅛ inch hot paraffin, or screw on jar lids. Store. Jam keeps best in freezer or refrigerator. Yields about 4 glasses, 6 ounces each.

## GRAPE MARMALADE
*From the 1928 Country Kitchen Cook Book.*

Pick over grapes; wash; drain and remove stems. Separate pulp from skins. Cook pulp slowly until seeds separate. Rub through a fine strainer. Add skins, measure and add ¾ amount of sugar. Cook slowly 30 minutes. Seal in hot jars.

*Conserve:* Add grated rind and juice of orange to grape pulp and skin and sugar before cooking as in marmalade recipe. Five minutes before removing from fire, add nuts. Proportions: 4 pints grapes, 1 orange, 1 cup nuts.

## WINTER MARMALADE
*If your jam supply runs low, try this.*

1 can (Number 303) crushed pineapple, undrained

1 package (11-ounce) dried apricots
3 cups sugar

Put half pineapple, juice and apricots into blender; cover and process at high until apricots are chopped fine. Pour into 3-quart saucepan. Repeat with remaining pineapple, juice and apricots. Bring to boil and boil 5 minutes. Stir constantly, mixture is quite thick. Remove from heat, add sugar and continue to boil, stirring constantly until a small portion dropped from a spoon is thick when cool (about 5 to 7 minutes). Pour into sterilized jars and seal. Yields 2 pints.

## AMBER MARMALADE
*From the 1928 Country Kitchen Cook Book.*

1 grapefruit
1 orange
1 lemon

3½ quarts water
Sugar

Wash the fruit; cut in paper-thin slices, using a very sharp knife. Add the water and let stand overnight. Cook until the peel is tender and again let the mixture stand overnight. Measure and add an equal amount of sugar and cook until the syrup thickens when dropped on a cold dish.

It is best to use the finest quality of thick-skinned, juicy fruit for this recipe, as its thickening depends to a great extent upon the amount of thick, white skin which goes into it. To save all of the juice, cut on a narrow board placed over a wide-mouthed bowl. Seal in hot jars. Yields about 6 half-pint jars.

## APPLE MARMALADE
*New taste.*

| | |
|---|---|
| 8 cups thinly-sliced apples (about 3 pounds) | 1½ cups water |
| | 5 cups sugar |
| 1 orange | 2 tablespoons lemon juice |

Select tart apples. Wash, pare, quarter and core apples. Slice thinly. Quarter the orange, remove any seeds and slice very thin.

Then, heat water and sugar until sugar is dissolved. Add lemon juice and fruit. Boil rapidly, stirring constantly to 223° F. or until mixture thickens. This may take as long as 20 minutes after mixture comes to full boil. Remove from heat; skim, ladle into hot jars and seal. Yields about 4 half-pint jars.

## TOMATO MARMALADE
*A soft, delicious marmalade like Grandma's.*

| | |
|---|---|
| 4 quarts tomatoes | 6 medium cinnamon sticks |
| 3 oranges | 1 tablespoon whole cloves |
| 2 lemons | |

Blanch the tomatoes with boiling water and pare them. Slice them into a large shallow pan. Slice the oranges and lemons very thin and quarter the slices. Pour off half the juice from the tomatoes. Weigh the sliced tomatoes and add an equal weight of granulated sugar. Stir until the sugar is dissolved. Add the oranges, lemons, cinnamon sticks and cloves.

In order to preserve the beautiful color, a large shallow kettle should be used over a high flame so that the marmalade will rapidly reach the boiling point. Stir often and reduce the heat somewhat after the marmalade has begun to boil. Test by cooling a teaspoonful in a saucer. When the mixture shows signs of jelling, (about 1 hour) it is ready to be sealed in jars. Yields about 6 pints.

## WILD PLUM BUTTER
### *Zingy!*

Wash plums and cook until soft. If necessary, add a little water to prevent sticking. Press through a sieve or food mill to remove seeds and skins. Measure pulp, add ⅔ as much sugar as pulp, mix and cook until thick, stirring frequently. Allow 1 to 2 teaspoons of mixed spices, such as ground cinnamon, allspice and cloves, to 1 gallon of fruit butter. Seal in hot jars.

## CAUSES OF PICKLE TROUBLES

*Soft or slippery pickles: Cause* — Action of bacteria due to too weak brine or pickles exposed above brine. *Remedy* — Follow directions for brine, adding more salt if long process is used. Keep pickles weighted. Seal or cover with paraffin when fermentation is over. *Cause* — Fermentation sets in because of a weak vinegar solution. *Remedy* — Use good quality vinegar with 5% to 6% acidity. Do not heat more than 2 or 3 times. *Cause* — Bacteria in scum cause spoilage. *Remedy* — Remove frequently. *Cause* — jars not sealed by processing. *Remedy* — Process quarts of fermented whole pickles 15 minutes in boiling water bath (method on page 344); unfermented pickles, 20 minutes. Process quarts of most sliced pickles and relishes for 10 minutes; bread and butter pickles, 10 minutes; corn relishes, 30 minutes.

*Poor color: Cause* — Over-dark pickles may be caused by hard water. *Remedy* — Use soft water, or with hard water use more vinegar. *Cause* — Dark because of free spice. *Remedy* — Tie spices in bag and remove when flavored. *Cause* — Light or dull in color pickles may be due to scalded or poor-colored cucumbers. *Remedy* — Use good-colored cucumbers. Add a few grape leaves to each jar to brighten color. *Cause* — Using iodized table salt. *Remedy* — Use pure, granulated salt. Un-iodized table salt may be used, but the materials added to prevent caking may make pickle brine cloudy.

*Hollow pickles: Cause* — Poor development of cucumber or keeping cukes too long between gathering and pickling. *Remedy* — Use only firm, well-developed cucumbers and brine within 24 hours after gathering.

*Shriveled pickles: Cause* — Too strong salt or vinegar solution. *Remedy* — Increase strength of brine or vinegar gradually. Use 10% salt brine; 1 measure of plain salt to 9 measures of water. *Cause* — Allowing too much time between gathering and pickling. *Remedy* — Place cucumbers in brine within 24 hours of gathering. *Cause* — Too-sweet pickling syrup. *Remedy* — Let cured pickles first stand in plain vinegar, then add sugar to vinegar, reheat and pour over. Use no more than ¾ as much sugar, by measure, as vinegar.

## NINE-DAY SWEET PICKLES
*Worth the time!*

Use only 2-inch (or shorter) pickles. Use a 3-gallon crockery or enamel container. An enamel, water bath cooker works well.

*First day:* Fill container with whole pickles and cover with cold water. Container should be placed in a cool spot  such as the basement on the cool cement floor. Soak in cold water for 24 hours.

*Second, third and fourth days:* Drain. Cover again with a mixture made of 2 cups salt to 1 gallon of water. Soak pickles for 3 days. Stir each day so salt doesn't settle. Make certain it doesn't by pouring liquid off into another container. Stir up pickles and remix any salt in the bottom; then recover pickles with the same remixed liquid.

*Fifth day:* At the end of this 3-day soaking, pour off brine and cover pickles with boiling water. Soak 12 hours. Pour off this water and cover with mixture made of 1 tablespoon alum to 1 gallon boiling water. Let stand another 12 hours. Begin early in the morning so you don't find yourself on a schedule that will require getting up in the middle of the night.

*Sixth day:* Drain off alum water and split cukes vertically into halves or quarters to get small, slim pieces. Prepare mixture of 1 quart cider vinegar, 2 cups sugar, 1 tablespoon celery seed, 1 tablespoon cassia buds (a cinnamon), 1 tablespoon mustard seed (optional). Bring to a boil and pour over pickles, to cover. Make one batch at a time until pickles are covered. Let pickles soak in this mixture for 24 hours.

*Seventh day:* Drain off syrup and bring it to a boil. Then add 1 cup sugar for each quart of pickles. Stir syrup until sugar dissolves. Re-cover pickles with syrup and let them stand 24 hours.

*Eighth day:* Drain off syrup again, bring to boil, re-cover pickles and let stand 24 hours.

*Ninth day:* Drain off syrup and bring it to a boil. Pack pickles into jars (pints are nicest), fill jars with hot syrup and seal. Yields 16 pints of pickles. These pickles do not have to age, but may be used immediately. Process 10 minutes in boiling water bath to insure seal.


## HAMBURGER PICKLES
*Age a couple of weeks before using.*

| | |
|---|---|
| 1 cup cider vinegar | 1 slice, ⅛-inch-thick, onion |
| 1 cup sugar | for each jar (*or* 2 small |
| 1 teaspoon salt | garlic cloves for each jar) |
| ¼ teaspoon mustard seed | 1 sprig dill for each jar |
| ¼ teaspoon celery seed | Cucumbers |

Bring first 5 ingredients to a rolling boil. Place onion or garlic and a sprig of dill in each pint jar. Slice cucumbers into jars until almost full. Cover with boiling syrup and seal. Process in boiling water bath 15 minutes to insure seal. Recipe yields about 2 pints of juice — enough to cover about 3 pints of pickles, if pickles are sliced and packed down quite tightly.

## MA'S DILLS
*Flavor's great!*

12 cups water
1 cup canning *or*
   barrel salt
½ cup cider vinegar
   Whole cucumbers,
   3-4 inches long

2 large sprigs dill for
   each jar
3-4 small cloves of garlic
   for each jar when you
   want to make Kosher
   dills

Bring water, salt and vinegar to a boil and pour over whole cucumbers which have been packed in quart jars with the dill weed (and garlic if you are making Kosher pickles). Put one sprig of dill at the bottom of each jar, one at the top. Tighten lids and allow to age for several weeks. Process 15 minutes in boiling water bath to insure seal, avoid spoilage. Or store in refrigerator or other cool place after curing. Yields brine for 6 to 7 quarts of pickles.

## MUSTARD PICKLES
*Superb with cold roast beef.*

2 large heads cauliflower
1 quart small, white onions
2 quarts green tomatoes,
   quartered (include both
   large and small
   tomatoes)
10 green peppers, diced
½ pound dry mustard
1 quart large cucumbers,
   sliced

1 quart small-size
   cucumbers (gherkins)
1 gallon vinegar
½ cup salt
3 cups sugar
5 tablespoons turmeric
1½ cups flour

Separate cauliflower into flowerettes. Combine with other vegetables, except cucumbers, and place in a large kettle.

Heat vinegar to boiling point; pour over vegetables; bring to a boil. Mix salt, sugar, turmeric, flour and dry mustard to a thin paste with a little cold vinegar; add to hot mixture, stir to avoid lumping.

Add cucumbers, bring to a boil, stirring constantly. Pour into hot sterilized containers. Seal and process pints and quarts 10 minutes in boiling water bath to insure seal. Yields about 8 quarts pickles.

## BEET PICKLES
*Try Early Blood Turnip beets because*
*they are a really dark red and early.*
*Detroit Dark Red are a good, later beet.*
*Use beets about 2 inches in diameter.*

Pull beets and wash well by putting pressure nozzle on garden hose. Prepare for kettle. Leave 2-inch top intact and the root. If these are cut off, beets will bleed, get pale and aren't tasty looking.

Place beets in cooking kettle, cover with water and cook until tender. Beets are done when they can be pierced with a toothpick. Pour off hot water and cover beets with cold water. Slip off skins and cut into desired slices or chunks. About 8 beets fill a quart jar when quartered. More are needed if beets are cut in smaller, serving pieces.

*Syrup for about 4 quarts beets:* Bring mixture of 2 cups sugar, 2 cups water, 2 cups cider vinegar and egg-size bag of pickling spices to a rolling boil. Add beets to syrup and heat beets through. Do not boil beets. Pack into sterilized pint or quart jars and seal and process 30 minutes in boiling water bath for pints and quarts. No aging is needed.

## ONION PICKLES

| | |
|---|---|
| 1 gallon pickling onions | 2 tablespoons horseradish |
| 1 cup salt | 6 cups white vinegar |
| 1-2 cups sugar | Small red peppers |
| 3 tablespoons white mustard seed | Bay leaves |

Scald onions 2 minutes in boiling water. Dip in cold water. Drain and peel. Sprinkle with salt. Add cold water to cover. Let stand 12 to 18 hours.

Rinse onions; drain. Combine sugar, mustard seed, horseradish and vinegar. Simmer 15 minutes. Pack onions into hot sterile jars. (Add 1 bay leaf and 1 dry red pepper when each jar is half-filled).

Heat pickling liquid to boiling. Pour, boiling hot, over onions. Seal and process 10 minutes in boiling water bath to insure seal. Yields 8 pints of pickled onions.

## PICKLED DILL CARROTS

30 small carrots
2 cups water
1⅓ cups sugar
⅔ cup white vinegar

4 teaspoons pickling spices tied in bag
Dill

Wash and prepare carrots. Cook until tender. Drain. Combine remaining ingredients. Bring to boil and pour over carrots. Simmer 3 minutes. Pack into sterilized jars. Add a spray of dill and seal. Process 10 minutes in boiling water bath to insure seal. Yields about 4 pints carrots.

## WATERMELON PICKLES
*Delicate and delicious.*

Trim off all pink and green sections of watermelon rind and cut in squares. Soak overnight in salt water (1 quart cold water and ⅓ cup salt to 2 pounds prepared rind). Drain; cover with clear water and cook until tender. Drain; make a pickling syrup and add rind as soon as the syrup comes to a boil. Cook until clear and syrup is fairly thick. Pack in hot, scalded jars, add syrup; seal. Process 10 minutes in boiling water bath.

*Syrup for 3 quarts pickles:* Combine 1 quart sugar, 1 pint cider vinegar, 1 pint water, 2 to 3 sticks cinnamon, 1 teaspoon whole cloves. Bring first 5 ingredients to a boil, add rind.

## GREEN TOMATO RELISH
*"This superb, spicy-sweet relish is great with beef,"*
*says a Jackson County, Minnesota farm woman.*

1 peck (12½ pounds) green tomatoes, cored
12 large onions
2 tablespoons plain salt
2 quarts vinegar

4 pounds brown sugar
2 tablespoons celery seed
2 tablespoons mustard seed
2 tablespoons allspice

Grind green tomatoes and onions. Add salt. Let mixture stand overnight in a cloth bag to drain. Next day, mix remaining ingredients with tomatoes and onions. Bring mixture to a boil and boil gently for 30 minutes. Remove from heat and seal in sterile jars. Process 10 minutes in boiling water bath to insure seal. Yields 12 pints of relish.

## CORN RELISH
*Pretty in the jars, delicious to eat.*

16 ears sweet corn
 5 sweet red peppers, chopped fine, (*or* use canned pimiento)
 5 green peppers, chopped fine
2-3 medium-size onions
 2 medium-size stalks of celery, cut up

2 tablespoons plain salt
1 pint white vinegar
1 pint water
1 cup sugar
1 tablespoon mustard seed
1 tablespoon dry mustard

Cook corn, then scrape from the cobs. Mix remaining ingredients and simmer for 15 minutes. Add corn and simmer 10 minutes more. Pour into sterilized, pint jars and seal. Process 30 minutes in boiling water bath to insure seal. Yields 9 pints relish.

## APPLE CHUTNEY
*An old-y!*

12 large tart apples
 2 medium onions
 2 green peppers
 2 cups vinegar
 1 cup raisins
 ½ cup tart jelly

2 cups sugar
4 lemons, juice and grated rind
1 teaspoon ginger
1 teaspoon salt

Pare, core and slice apples. Mince onions and peppers; add to apples with vinegar. Boil until soft. Add remaining ingredients; mix well. Boil until thick (stirring constantly as it thickens). Pack boiling hot, into hot sterilized jars. Seal. Process 10 minutes in boiling water bath to insure seal. Yields about 10 pints chutney.

## CHILI SAUCE
*A Country Kitchen must.*

2 quarts peeled, sliced, ripe tomatoes
3-4 large onions, chopped
4 green peppers, chopped
1 red pepper, chopped

1¼ cups brown sugar
1 tablespoon salt
2 cups vinegar
½ teaspoon each allspice, cloves and cinnamon

Combine tomatoes, onions, green and red peppers, sugar and salt. Cook until it begins to thicken. Add the vinegar and spices. Cook slowly until thick. Seal in jars. Process 10 minutes in boiling water bath to insure seal. Yields about 8 pints chili sauce.

## SAUERKRAUT
*Only 32 calories per cup — and a good source of vitamin C.*

Kraut is fermented cabbage and must have air to allow for proper development of lactic acid bacteria. Best results are secured by first making kraut in an earthenware crock, keg or sturdy plastic waste basket. Do not use a metal container. After fermentation, kraut may be packed in jars if desired.

Use only fresh, firm cabbage. Do not wash leaves, because bacteria on inner leaves are needed for fermentation. Shred cabbage fine. Place in crock in layers — about 3½ pounds shredded cabbage sprinkled with 2½ tablespoons plain, non-iodized salt. Pack down each layer as tightly as possible with a wooden mallet or two-by-four. Pack crock to within 4 or 5 inches of top.

Cover crock with a clean cloth and plate, then weight down. Remove scum when necessary. Keep at about 85° F. for 10 days, or at room temperature for 6 to 8 weeks. Keep temperature above 60° F.

Then store kraut in a cooler place. It will keep indefinitely in the crock, as long as the top is not exposed to air. Kraut should not be too acid when ready to use. Too little salt results in soft kraut; too much salt makes kraut pink.

To can kraut, pack in jars, not too tightly. Fill jars with kraut brine or fresh brine (2 tablespoons salt to 1 quart water). Process 30 minutes in boiling water bath.

## TOMATO CATSUP
### *Old-fashioned flavor.*

1 gallon tomato pulp
(about 1 peck fruit)
2 sweet red peppers
2 tablespoons salt
2 tablespoons sugar
1 tablespoon paprika

1 teaspoon celery seed
(optional)
1 tablespoon dry
mustard
1 pint vinegar
1 ounce (⅓ cup) mixed
pickling spice

Use fully ripe tomatoes. Cut in pieces, removing discolored parts. Cut peppers; remove seeds, and add to tomatoes. Cook together until soft and strain through sieve. Measure, and to each gallon of pulp use given amounts of other ingredients. Boil pulp rapidly a little, add other ingredients, with whole spices tied in a bag. Cook until quite thick, stirring frequently; remove spice. Fill clean, hot jars; seal. Process 10 minutes in boiling water bath to insure seal. Yields about 8 pints catsup.

## GRAPE CATSUP
### *Excellent with meat.*

3 pounds ripe Concord
grapes
1 pound tart apples, cut
1½ pounds sugar

1 cup cider vinegar
¼ teaspoon salt
1 tablespoon cinnamon
1 tablespoon cloves

Wash grapes; simmer until soft. Cook apples until tender. Rub both through colander. Add sugar and boil until quite thick; add spices and vinegar; boil 5 minutes longer. Seal in jars. Process 10 minutes in boiling water bath to insure seal. Yields 5 to 6 pints catsup.

## SWEET PICKLED FRUIT
*So easy; so elegant!*

3 quarts peaches, pears *or*
  crab apples
1 pint white vinegar
4 cups granulated *or*
  light brown sugar

1 pint water
2-3 cinnamon sticks
1 teaspoon whole cloves

Prepare fruit. Combine sugar, vinegar, water and spices tied in a bag. Bring syrup to boil. Boil 10 minutes and drop in fruit. Cook until partly tender, but not soft or easily pierced through. Remove fruit from boiling syrup and pack in hot, scalded jars. Remove spices and pour syrup over fruit to fill jars within ½-inch of top. Tighten jar lids and process 10 minutes in boiling water bath. Yields 6 pints fruit.

## SPICED GOOSEBERRIES
*A pioneer recipe from Traill County, North Dakota*

Clean and wash 4 cups ripe gooseberries. For special occasions, select the largest and have them all the same size. Then put 3 tablespoons white vinegar and 2 tablespoons water in a pan; add berries; cover and steam until fruit looks white . . . just a few minutes. Next, add ½ teaspoon cinnamon, ½ teaspoon cloves and 1 package powdered fruit pectin. Stir carefully. Add 4 cups sugar, juice and slivered rind of ½ lemon and ½ orange. White membrane should be scraped from rind before slivering. Simmer fruit mixture, stirring gently until sugar is completely dissolved. Seal in sterile jars. Process 10 minutes in boiling water bath to insure seal. Yields 6 jars of relish, ½ pint each.

## RASPBERRY VINEGAR
*Printed in The Farmer, 1893.*

Fill a jar with berries; pour in as much white vinegar as jar will hold; let it stand for 10 days; then strain through a sieve. Do not press the berries while straining. To every pint add 1 pound sugar; boil 20 minutes; skim; bottle when cold.

# RECIPES FOR LARGE GROUPS

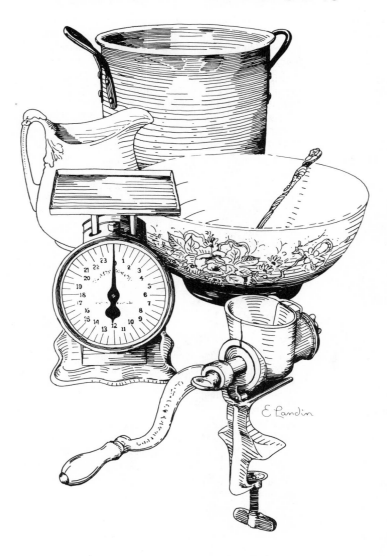

E. Landin

# HOW MUCH
## TO PREPARE FOR 50

| | *Ingredients* | *Amount* |
|---|---|---|
| **APPETIZERS** | Fruit juice (½ cup per serving) . . . . . . . . | 6 quarts |
| | Canned fruit cup (⅓ cup per serving) . . | 4½ quarts |
| | Soup (1 cup per serving) . . . . . . . . . . . . | 3 gallons |
| **VEGETABLES AS PURCHASED** | Potatoes to mash . . . . . . . . . . . . . . . . . . | 15 pounds |
| | Potatoes to bake, by count, about . . . . . . | 20 pounds |
| | Canned vegetables (½ cup per serving) . . | 13 cans, 1 pound each |
| | Carrots for dicing . . . . . . . . . . . . . . . . . . | 12 pounds |
| | Peas, frozen (½ cup per serving) . . . . . . . | 10 pounds |
| **SALADS** | Cabbage (for coleslaw) . . . . . . . . . . . . . . | 8 pounds |
| | Head lettuce (wedges or slices) . . . . . . . . | 10 heads |
| | Lettuce for garnish . . . . . . . . . . . . . . . | 3 to 5 heads |
| | French dressing . . . . . . . . . . . . . . . . . . . | 1 quart |
| | Salad dressing . . . . . . . . . . . . . . . . . . . . | 1⅓ quarts |
| **RELISHES** | Olives (3 per serving) . . . . . . . . . . . . . . . | 2 quarts |
| | Celery (curls 2½ inches) . . . . . . . . . . . . . | 2 stalks |
| | Carrots (strips, 3 inches) . . . . . . . . . . . . | 2½ pounds |
| | Pickles . . . . . . . . . . . . . . . . . . . . . . . . . | 1½ pounds |
| **CEREAL PRODUCTS** | Spaghetti or macaroni (generous 1 cup per serving) . . . . . . . . . . . . . . . . . . | 6 pounds |
| | Noodles (½ cup per serving) . . . . . . . . . . | 2 pounds, 4 ounces |
| | Rice (generous ½ cup per serving) . . . . . . | 4 pounds |
| **DESSERT** | Ice cream (No. 12 dipper, approximately ⅓ cup) . . . . . . . . . . . . . . . . . . . . . . . . | 2 gallons |
| | Whipping cream (2 tablespoons per serving) . . . . . . . . . . . . . . . . . . . . . . . . | 1 quart |
| **BEVERAGES** | Coffee (50 cups) . . . . . . . . . . . . . . . . . . . | 1 pound |
| | Tea (50 cups) . . . . . . . . . . . . . . . . . . . . . | 3 ounces |
| | Milk . . . . . . . . . . . . . . . . . . . . . . . . . . . | 3 gallons |
| | Coffee cream . . . . . . . . . . . . . . . . . . . . . | 1 quart |
| | Sugar, loaf . . . . . . . . . . . . . . . . . . . . . . | 2 pounds |
| **MISCEL- LANEOUS** | Butter, for table (1 to 1½ pats) . . . . . . . | 1½ pounds |
| | Butter for vegetables . . . . . . . . . . . . | ½ to ¾ pound |

## SPICED TOMATO JUICE
*A stand-up first course with cheese and crackers.*

6 quarts tomato juice
2 tablespoons Worcester-
   shire sauce

1 teaspoon salt
  Lemon wedges

Combine first three ingredients together, mix well. Chill. Serve with lemon wedge. Yields about 50 servings, ½ cup each.

## BESS ROWE'S PARTY PUNCH
*Favorite of an old-time Home Editor of The Farmer.*

1 dozen lemons
4 cups sugar
4 cups water

2 quarts tea, made using
  ⅓ cup black tea
2 cups pineapple juice
1 quart ginger ale

Grate yellow rind from lemons. Make syrup of sugar and water. When syrup has boiled, remove it from heat and add grated rind. Let mixture stand overnight. Make tea and after it has steeped, drain it off the leaves. Squeeze juice from lemons. Shortly before you are ready to use the punch, combine lemon juice, syrup, tea, pineapple juice and, last of all, add the ginger ale. Yields about 30 servings, 6 ounces each.

## GRAPE ORANGE PUNCH
*Teens like this.*

2 cans (6-ounce each)
  frozen, concentrated
  grape juice
3 cans (6-ounce each)
  frozen, concentrated
  orange juice

9 cups cold water
9 bottles (7-ounce each)
  cold lemon soda,
  about 7½ cups

Mix concentrated juices and cold water. Add cold soda and pour into punch bowl over block of ice; garnish with mint leaves and quartered orange slices. Yields 5 quarts or 40 servings, 4 ounces each.

## ICE RING FOR PUNCH
*Cools, but doesn't dilute, the punch.*

Dilute frozen orange and/or lemonade concentrate according to can directions. Make enough juice to fill a ring mold. Pour about 1 inch juice into bottom of mold. Arrange maraschino cherries and pineapple tidbits in juice. Carefully place on freezer shelf — rearrange fruit in juice if necessary. Freeze until solid. Pour rest of juice into mold, cover and freeze until needed for punch. Yields 1 ice ring.

## WASSAIL BOWL
*Serve with Christmas cookies and fruit cake.*

| | |
|---|---|
| 2 quarts apple cider | 6 cinnamon sticks |
| 2 cups sugar | 1 quart cranberry juice |
| 2 teaspoons whole allspice | 1 pint orange juice |
| 2 teaspoons whole cloves | 1½ cups lemon juice |

Combine cider and sugar in large pan. Tie spices in a cloth; add to cider. Cover; simmer 15 minutes. Remove spices; add remaining ingredients; simmer 10 minutes. Garnish with lemon and orange slices; serve hot. Makes about one gallon. Yields about 32 servings, 4 ounces each.

## OVERNIGHT BEAN SALAD
*Midwest favorite for outdoor barbecues —*
*or with cold meat and cheese buffet.*

| | |
|---|---|
| 4 cans (1-pound each) wax beans | 2 cups salad oil |
| 4 cans (1-pound each) cut green beans | 2 cups sugar |
| | 2 teaspoons salt |
| 4 cans (1-pound each) red kidney beans | 1 teaspoon pepper |
| | Garlic salt (optional) |
| 4 cups thinly-sliced onions | 2 cups cider vinegar |

Drain beans; place in large bowl with onions. Combine oil, sugar, salt, pepper, garlic salt and vinegar in a jar; shake until well blended. Pour over beans and onions. Yields about 40 servings.

## VEGETABLE SALAD
*Church dinner treat.*

6 large, solid heads of
  cabbage
3 stalks celery
24 medium carrots
9-10 tomatoes

3 medium onions
3 cucumbers, if desired
Salt, pepper to taste

Put cabbage and carrots through salad chopper. Finely dice other vegetables. Toss lightly with dressing made as follows: Thin 1½ quarts mayonnaise with cream and sweet pickle juice to desired consistency. Add vinegar if desired. Yields 150 servings.

## CRANBERRY-PINEAPPLE SALAD
*Serve with turkey, chicken or pork.*

2 cans (number 10) sliced
  pineapple
3 cans (1-pound each)
  cranberry sauce

6 heads lettuce
1 cup commercial
  fruit dressing

Arrange 50 lettuce cups on plates. Put pineapple slice in each. Slice cranberry sauce and cut in wedges. Arrange on pineapple slices. Top with dressing. Chill until ready to serve. Yields 50 salads.

## BESS ROWE'S CHICKEN SALAD
*The Farmer Home Editor used this recipe often;*
*made it in quantity for groups in the 1930's.*

3 cups cubed, cooked
  chicken
1½ cups diced celery
1 cup cooked peas,
  drained
3 teaspoons lemon juice
½ teaspoon salt

Mayonnaise
Lettuce
½ cup seedless green
  grapes
½ cup toasted, slivered
  almonds

Combine first 5 ingredients. Add enough mayonnaise to hold mixture together, but not enough to make it paste-y. Serve in a bowl lined with lettuce leaves; garnish with grapes and almonds. Yields 12 servings, ½ cup each.

## MOLDED CHICKEN OR TURKEY SALAD
*Garnish with olives, radish roses, carrot curls.*

4 cups chicken *or* turkey broth
2 tablespoons unflavored gelatin
½ cup cold water
10 cups diced, cooked chicken *or* turkey
2 cups diced, canned pineapple, drained
⅓ cup pineapple syrup
2 tablespoons lemon juice
1½ cups celery, finely chopped
7 hard-cooked eggs, sliced
½ pound process cheddar *or* Swiss cheese, finely cubed
Salt and pepper
½ teaspoon onion juice
1 cup mayonnaise
Lettuce *or* watercress

Heat chicken broth to boiling, season with pepper and salt. Soften gelatin in the cold water, dissolve in broth; pour over chilled chicken. Stir in pineapple and syrup, lemon juice, celery, eggs, cheese, salt, pepper (to taste) and onion juice. Chill until thick and syrupy; fold in mayonnaise. Pour into oblong pans, refrigerate overnight. To serve, cut in squares. Serve on a lettuce leaf and garnish; pass mayonnaise. Yields 18 to 20 servings.

## BAKED TUNA-CHEDDAR SALAD
*Serve with potato chips, fresh raw relishes, or sliced tomatoes, and warm rolls.*

8 pounds tuna, drained and flaked
16 cups finely-chopped celery
3 cups chopped onion
1⅓ cups chopped pimiento
4 tablespoons Worcestershire sauce
2 tablespoons salt
1 quart mayonnaise
1½ pounds sharp cheddar cheese, shredded
4 cups bread crumbs
1⅓ cups butter, melted

Combine tuna, celery, onions, pimiento, Worcestershire sauce, salt and mayonnaise; toss lightly. Place mixture in two 12x20x2-inch steam-table pans.

Combine cheese, bread crumbs and melted butter. Sprinkle evenly over 2 casseroles of the tuna mixture. Bake in preheated, 350° F. oven for 25 to 35 minutes. Yields 50 servings, 1 cup each.

## CHOW MEIN HOT DISH
*Serve with chow mein noodles and an*
*orange-grapefruit-apple salad.*

1 cup uncooked rice
1 pound ground beef
½ pound ground pork
1 large onion, chopped
2 cups coarsely-chopped
  celery

2 tablespoons brown sugar
1 can (10½-ounce) con-
  densed cream of mush-
  room soup
1 bottle (5-ounce)
  soy sauce

Pour 2½ cups of boiling water over rice and let stand while preparing other ingredients. Brown meat and onions together. Add celery and soy sauce. While browning add soup and brown sugar to rice mixture and stir together. Pour into casserole and cover. Bake in preheated, 350° F. oven for 1¼ hours. Double or triple recipe. Yields 10 to 12 servings.

## TURKEY-NOODLE CASSEROLE FOR A CROWD
*Double for a big group and garnish with*
*sliced tomatoes or jellied cranberry sauce.*

¾ pound medium noodles
8 cups cooked turkey
  meat, coarsely cubed
¼ cups turkey fat *or* butter
¾ cup chopped onion
¼ cup chopped green
  pepper
2 cups frozen peas

1¼ cups turkey fat *and/or*
  butter
1¼ cups flour
2½ quarts turkey stock *or*
  broth made with
  chicken boullion cubes
  Salt and pepper to taste
  Buttered crumbs
  (optional)

Cook noodles according to package directions; drain. Cook onions and green peppers in ¼ cup turkey fat. Cook peas until tender. Melt 1¼ cups turkey fat; blend in flour until smooth; add the turkey stock. Cook and stir until thick and smooth. Stir turkey, noodles, onion, green pepper and peas into sauce. Pour into 2 greased 9x13-inch baking pans and bake in preheated, 325° F. oven for 20 to 30 minutes. Buttered crumbs may be sprinkled over top of casserole, if desired, before baking. Yields 16 to 18 servings.

## GLORIFIED HAMBURGER
### *Double recipe if necessary.*

7½ pounds hamburger
¼ cup crumbled beef
   bouillon base
½ gallon chopped celery
½ gallon chopped onion
2½-3 gallons catsup

2 tablespoons prepared
   mustard
⅛ -¼ cup salt
Pepper to taste
Flour for thickening
100 hamburger buns,
   sliced

Brown the hamburger; add beef base, celery and onions. Simmer until soft. Add the rest of the ingredients; simmer about 20 to 30 minutes. Thicken with flour if necessary. Toast bun halves if desired and serve sauce over the buttered buns. Yields 100 servings.

## LASAGNE
### *Great square-dance supper.*

1 cup all-purpose flour
1 can (number 10) tomatoes
3 pounds ground beef
2 cloves garlic, minced
½ cup cooking oil *or* fat
1 cup chopped green
   pepper
1 cup chopped onion
1½ cups thinly-sliced celery
2 teaspoons oregano
1½ tablespoons salt

1 teaspoon pepper
4 cups (1-pound, 5-ounce)
   drained, pitted
   ripe olives, chopped
   very coarsely
¼ cup salt
2 gallons boiling water
4 pounds dry-curd
   cottage cheese
1 pound cheddar-type
   cheese, shredded

Make paste of flour and 3 cups juice from tomatoes. Bring remaining tomatoes to boil; add paste and boil 2 minutes longer, stirring constantly.

Lightly brown ground beef in oil; add garlic and onion and cook until clear, but not brown. Add to tomato mixture; also add green pepper, celery and seasonings; simmer 20 minutes, stirring occasionally. Add olives.

Add noodles to boiling, salted water. Cook 10 minutes or until tender. Rinse in cold water; drain.

Spread noodles equally over the bottom of two 12x20x2-

inch baking pans. Divide cottage cheese equally and spread over noodles in each pan.

Pour hot sauce over cottage cheese. Sprinkle half of shredded cheese over top of each pan. Bake, uncovered, in preheated, 350° F. oven for 20 to 30 minutes. If desired, let stand about 15 minutes for easier serving. Yields 50 servings, ¾ cup each.

## SWEDISH MEAT BALLS
### *Smorgasbord must!*

| | | | |
|---|---|---|---|
| 1 | pint shortening | 6 | tablespoons sugar |
| 1 | pint finely-chopped onions | 1½ | teaspoons pepper |
| ¾ | gallon ground beef, ground twice | 1½ | teaspoons nutmeg |
| | | 1½ | cups nonfat, dry milk |
| 1½ | quarts ground pork, ground twice | 1½ | gallons water |
| | | 2 | tablespoons beef concentrate |
| 2¼ | quarts dry bread crumbs | 1 | pint all-purpose flour |
| 1½ | cups whole eggs | ½ | cup lemon juice |
| 6 | tablespoons salt | 18 | bay leaves |

Melt ¼ cup shortening in each of two large skillets; add onion and saute until tender. Combine onions with beef, pork, bread crumbs, eggs, salt, sugar, pepper, nutmeg and milk. Mix thoroughly. Blend in 1½ quarts water. Shape meat mixture with #24 scoop into 144 balls, by pressing meat into scoop against rounded side of bowl. Add ¾ cup shortening to skillets. Place over medium heat until shortening melts; add meat balls and brown. Remove from skillet. Dissolve beef concentrate in remaining 4½ quarts water. Divide flour and blend into shortening in each skillet. Gradually add half of beef and water mixture, and half of lemon juice to flour and shortening in skillets. Heat slowly until mixture thickens, stirring constantly. Add bay leaves and browned meat balls to gravy. Cover and simmer 45 minutes to 1 hour. Remove bay leaves and serve over buttered egg noodles, rice or with mashed potatoes.

Meat and gravy may be put into steam-table pan and finished in a slow oven, instead of cooking on surface unit. Yields 48 servings, 3 meat balls each.

## ROAST BUFFALO MEAT (PIT METHOD)
*Meat prepared this way is worth all the effort —
the taste is out of this world,
according to Fort Totten, North Dakota trail riders.
Try beef roasts using this method, too.*

Dig a pit 5½ feet deep, 6 feet long and 3 feet wide. Place 3½ feet of coals in the bottom and cover with about 1 inch of dry sand. Cut meat into 10 to 15-pound roasts. Salt each roast and wrap with a bay leaf and 1 cup barbecue sauce (recipe below) in heavy aluminum foil. Place packets of meat in the pit. Cover pit with tin, then cover with 6 to 8 inches of dirt to seal in the heat. It takes 8 to 9 hours of burning to get the coals needed to line the bottom of the pit. Meat should be sealed in the pit at least 12 hours; a few more hours for larger roasts. Allow about ¼ pound meat per person.

*Barbecue Sauce:* Mix the following ingredients in a large kettle — 4 cups (2 pounds) brown sugar; 1 cup (8-ounce) paprika; 2 cups (1 pint) Worcestershire sauce; 4 cups (1 quart) vinegar; 4 cups (1 quart) catsup; 16 cups (1 gallon) tomato juice; ⅓ cup salt; ⅓ cup dry mustard; ⅓ cup ground cloves; 3 tablespoons garlic powder; 4 teaspoons chili powder; 2 teaspoons red pepper; 12 medium onions, grated. Bring mixture slowly to a boil and simmer 1 hour; stir often. Yields about 2 gallons sauce.

## TUNA TRIUMPH
*This elegant tuna dish goes together in minutes.
Serve with broccoli spears. Choose a lemony dessert.*

3 cans (10½-ounce each)
   condensed cream of
   mushroom soup
1 soup can milk
2 cans (9¾-ounce each)
   tuna
1 cup diced celery

¼ cup minced onion
1 package (8-10-ounce)
   chow mein noodles
2 cups cashew nuts
   Stuffed green olives
   (optional)

Add milk to soup gradually, stirring constantly until smooth. Add celery, tuna and onion; mix well. Add noodles and nuts; mix gently. Pour into 2 ungreased 2-quart casseroles and bake in preheated, 300° F. oven for 45 minutes or 1 hour. Slice stuffed olives. During last 15 minutes of baking add sliced olives to top of casserole. Double or triple recipe, as needed. Yields 12 to 14 servings.

## JUMBO PIZZA SANDWICH
*Couples Club favorite.*

1 loaf (1-pound) unsliced
French *or* Vienna bread
¼ cup sliced *or* chopped
ripe olives
⅛ teaspoon pepper
¼ teaspoon ground
oregano
¾ teaspoon salt
2 tablespoons finely-
chopped green onion
tops *or* chives

½ pound ground beef
¼ cup grated Parmesan
cheese
1 can (6-ounce) tomato
paste
14 thin slices tomato, *or*
2 cups drained, canned
tomatoes
1 package (9-ounce)
ready-sliced, processed
cheese

Cut bread in half, horizontally. Combine olives, pepper, oregano, salt, green onion, beef, Parmesan cheese and tomato paste. Divide mixture equally and spread over cut sides of bread. Arrange tomato slices over meat on each loaf. Place on cookie sheet, spread side up, and bake in preheated, 400° F. oven for 15 minutes. Remove from oven. Cut cheese slices in half, diagonally. Cover tomato slices with 8 overlapping triangular slices of cheese. Return to oven for 5 minutes. Slice each sandwich into 12 sections. Yields 24 pieces.

# APPLE CRISP
*A favorite for money-making meals.*

6 cups brown sugar
1 tablespoon cinnamon
2 teaspoons nutmeg
2 teaspoons salt
2 tablespoons lemon juice
2 cans (number 10) apples

4 cups brown sugar
6 cups all-purpose flour, sifted
2 teaspoons salt
1½ pounds butter

Mix first 4 ingredients together in large mixing bowl. Add lemon juice and apples; mix well. Put into baking pans. Mix together the remaining brown sugar, flour and salt. Cut in butter and mix until crumbly. Sprinkle over apples. Bake in preheated, 350° F. oven for about 45 minutes. Serve warm or cold with cream, lemon sauce or plain. Yields about 50 servings, ½ to ⅔ cup each.

# DARK, SPICY BRIDE'S CAKE
*Delicious, old-fashioned tradition.*
*A girl carefully saves and takes home a crumb of this cake;*
*sleeps on it — and believes she'll marry the man*
*she dreams of that night.*

2 cups butter
2½ cups sugar
8 eggs
4 cups all-purpose flour
4 teaspoons baking powder
4 teaspoons baking soda
1 teaspoon salt
4 cups graham cracker crumbs

2 cups chopped dates
2 cups broken walnuts *or* pecans
2 tablespoons grated lemon rind
2 teaspoons ground cinnamon
½ teaspoon ground cloves
1½ cups milk
2 cups apricot preserves

For middle and top layer, grease 12x8x2-inch and 10x6x2-inch baking dishes. In large bowl, with mixer at medium speed, beat 1 cup butter, 1¼ cups sugar until creamy. Add 4 eggs, one at a time, beating until light and fluffy. Sift together half of flour, baking powder, baking soda and salt. Combine half of next 6 ingredients with flour mixture, blending well. At low speed, alternately beat cracker crumb-

flour mixture and half of milk into butter mixture. Divide
into the 2 prepared baking dishes. Bake in a preheated, 350°
F. oven for 30 to 35 minutes, or until cake tests done. Remove
cake from oven and let stand 5 minutes; then loosen around
edges and turn out on rack to cool.

For bottom layer, mix remaining ingredients, except
preserves, according to above method and turn into a greased
13x8x2-inch baking dish. Bake 35 to 40 minutes, or until
cake tests done. Remove from oven and cool as above.

Cut each layer into two thin layers. Spread with apricot
preserves; reassemble. Frost with Rum Butter frosting, below.
This cake may be made several days ahead and refrigerated
until needed. Yields about 100 servings.

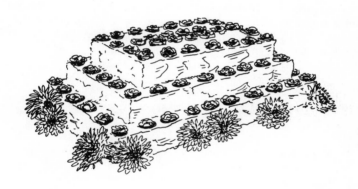

*Rum-Butter Frosting:* In large bowl, with mixer at medium
speed, beat 2 cups butter until creamy. Add 2 teaspoons
vanilla; then alternately add 8 cups sifted confectioners' sugar
and ½ cup milk. Mix in 1 teaspoon rum flavoring and beat
until smooth. Refrigerate 2¼ cups frosting.

Use remaining frosting to spread a thin layer over top and
sides of cakes; then stack one on top of the other on large
serving plate.

To 1¾ cups reserved frosting, add just enough food
coloring to tint it a pale color. Using pastry tube and #1 tip,
decorate top and sides of cake with swirls. Use remaining ½
cup white frosting to make rosettes, using same size pastry
tube. Top rosettes with gold or silver dragees.

In case frosting gets too soft while decorating, refrigerate to
make firm. Refrigerate cake when completed.

## MAKE-AHEAD BLUEBERRY DESSERT
*Ask several people to bring this for a big dinner.*

1 pound crushed graham
   crackers
½ cup sugar
⅔ cup butter, melted
72 large marshmallows
1½ cups milk

3 cups whipping cream
   whipped
1 package (10½-ounce)
   miniature marshmallows
2 cans (15½-ounce)
   blueberry pie filling

Mix crushed crackers, sugar and soft butter. Reserve ¼ cup crumb mixture. Press remaining crumb mixture into bottoms of two 9x13-inch pans. Melt large marshmallows in milk in top of double boiler placed over hot water. When melted remove from heat; cool mixture. Fold miniature marshmallows into whipped cream and blend into cooled milk mixture. Pour over two crusts; top with blueberry pie filling and sprinkle on reserved crumbs. Refrigerate overnight. Yields 20 pieces.

## MAKE-AHEAD LEMON DESSERT
*Easily doubled.*

1 pound graham crackers
½ cup butter, melted
2 cups sugar
14 eggs, separated
6 small lemons *or*
   2 lemons and ¾ cup
   bottled lemon juice

2 tablespoons unflavored
   gelatin
½ cup cold water
½ cup sugar

Roll graham crackers into fine crumbs; mix with melted butter. Reserve ½ cup crumb mixture and press remainder into bottom of two 9x13-inch pans.

Beat egg yolks, add 2 cups sugar, juice and grated rind of the lemons. Cook in double boiler over hot water until mixture thickens and coats a spoon.

Soften gelatin in cold water; add to hot lemon mixture. Cool.

Beat egg whites until stiff; beat in ½ cup sugar; fold into cooled lemon mixture. Pour over crumb crusts, dividing equally between two pans. Sprinkle reserved crumbs evenly over lemon mixture. Refrigerate overnight. Yields 20 servings.

# MEASURES AND SUBSTITUTIONS

## MEASURE THIS WAY

*Ingredient-amounts in this book have been determined using these standard measures:*

*Use graduated measuring spoons:* Pour in thin liquids until level-full. Spoon in solid or dry ingredients. Level by scraping across top with flat surface of a table knife or spatula.

*Measure liquids* in a liquid measuring cup. Read the measurement at eye-level.

*Use graduated, nested measuring cups* for measuring non-liquids because these cups can be easily leveled.

*Pour* cereals, confectioners' sugar or crumbs into cup; level.

*Dip* flour or sugar into cup and level.

*Spoon cake flour* and biscuit mixes lightly into cup; level.

*Spoon* shredded and chopped mixtures into cups and pack down lightly.

*Sift* confectioners' sugar and spoon gently into cup; level.

*Pack* brown sugar and shortenings firmly into cups; level.

## TABLE OF MEASURES

Dash=less than ⅛ teaspoon
Pinch (thumb plus 2 fingers)=¼ teaspoon
3 teaspoons=1 tablespoon
Lump the size of a walnut=1 tablespoon
4 tablespoons=¼ cup
Lump the size of a small egg=2 tablespoons
Lump the size of a large egg=¼ cup
5 tablespoons plus 1 teaspoon=⅓ cup
16 tablespoons=1 cup
2 cups=1 pint
4 cups=1 quart
4 quarts (liquid measure)=1 gallon
8 quarts (dry measure)=1 peck
⅓ cup bread crumbs, dry=1 slice bread
¾ cup bread crumbs, soft=1 slice dry bread
½ pound cheese, brick=2-plus cups grated
3 ounces cheese, cream=6 tablespoons
8 ounces cheese, cream=1 cup *or* 16 tablespoons
6 ounces chocolate chips=1 cup
4 ounces cocoanut, flake *or* shred=1½-1¾ cups
8 ounces cream, dairy sour=1 cup
½ pint cream, whipping=1 cup *or* 2 cups whipped
7-10 egg whites=1 cup
12-18 egg yolks=1 cup
Juice of 1 medium lemon=3-4 tablespoons
Grated rind of 1 medium lemon=about 3 teaspoons
1 large marshmallow=10 miniature marshmallows
25 large *or* 250 miniature marshmallows=1 cup
Juice of 1 medium orange=⅓-½ cup
1 cup precooked rice=1-2-plus cups cooked
1 cup regular rice=3-plus cups cooked

## WHAT 1 POUND YIELDS

*Apples,* 3 medium *or* 3 cups sliced
*Bananas,* 3 medium *or* 2½ cups sliced
*Beans,* dried, 2½ cups
*Butter,* lard or other fat, 2 cups
*Cheese,* cottage, 2 cups
*Cheese,* grated cheddar and other bricks, 4 cups
*Cocoa,* 4 cups
*Cocoanut,* shredded, 7 cups
*Coffee,* ground, 5 cups *or* 80 tablespoons
*Cornmeal,* 3 cups

*Eggs,* 8 large
*Flour,* sifted, all-purpose, 4 cups
*Flour,* sifted cake, 4¾ cups
*Flour,* graham *or* whole wheat, 3¾ cups
*Flour,* rye, 5 cups
*Macaroni,* 4½ cups
*Marshmallows,* 100 large
*Meat,* cooked, 3⅓ cups diced
*Milk,* 2 cups
*Oats,* rolled, 5½ cups
*Rice,* precooked, 4⅔ cups
*Rice,* regular, 2½ cups
*Salt,* table, 1½ cups
*Sugar,* brown, 2¼ cups packed
*Sugar,* granulated, 2¼ cups
*Sugar,* sifted confectioners', 3-4 cups

## WHAT 1 POUND DRIED FRUIT OR NUTS YIELDS

*Almonds in the shell,* 1-1¼ cups meats
*Almond meats,* 3 cups whole
*Candied fruit and peel,* 2⅔ cups, cut up
*Dates,* 2½ cups, pitted
*Filbert nuts in the shell,* 1½ cups meats
*Filbert meats,* 3½ cups
*Pecans in the shell,* 2¼ cups meats
*Pecan meats,* 2½ cups halves, 4 cups chopped
*Peanuts in the shell,* 2⅓ cups meats
*Peanut meats,* 3 cups
*Prunes,* 2 cups whole, dried
*Raisins,* 2¾ cups seedless
*Walnuts in the shell,* 2 cups meats
*Walnut meats,* 2 cups halves, 4 cups chopped

## GUIDE TO COMMON CAN SIZES

| Can Size* (Weight or Fluid Content) | Approx. Cup Yield (undrained) | Approx. Servings | Principal Products Packed in this size |
|---|---|---|---|
| 5 to 7 oz. . . . . . . . . | ⅔ to 1 cup . | 4 . . . . . . | Mushrooms, pimientos, poultry, sea food, meat spreads and fruit juices. |
| 10½ or 10¾ oz. (9½ fluid oz.) . . . . . | 1¼ cups . . . | 3 . . . . . . | Condensed soups and some vegetables. |
| 12 oz. (12 fluid oz.) . . . . . | 1½ to 1¾ cups . . . | 3 or 4 . . | Some fruits, vegetables, meat, poultry and sea food. |
| 14 to 15½ oz. (13½ fluid oz.) . . . . | 1¾ cups . . . | 3 or 4 . . | Baked beans, pork and beans, meat products, nut breads, cranberry sauce and a few fruits, such as blueberries. |
| 1 lb. or 1 lb. 1 oz. (15 fluid oz.) . . . . . | 2 cups . . . . . | 4 . . . . . . | Principal size for fruits and vegetables, plus some meat products and specialties. |
| 1 lb. 4 oz. (1 pt. 2 fluid oz.) . . | 2½ cups . . . | 5 . . . . . . | Juice, some fruits, ready-to-serve soups and meat products. |
| 1 lb. 13 oz. (1 pt. 10 fluid oz.) . | 3½ cups . . . | 7 . . . . . . | Fruits and some vegetables, such as tomatoes, sauerkraut and pumpkin. |
| 3 lb. 2 or 3 oz. (1 qt. 14 fluid oz.) . | 5¾ cups . . . | 12 . . . . . | Juices and "institutional or restaurant" size condensed soups. |
| 6½ lb. to 7 lb. 5 oz. ("No. 10 can") . . . . | 12 cups (3 qt.) . . . . . | 25 . . . . . | "Institutional or restaurant" size fruits and vegetables. |

*Cans and jars of identical size may show a net weight for one product that differs slightly from that of another product — this is due to the difference in the density of food.

# SUBSTITUTIONS
*Do not substitute ingredients in recipes unless absolutely
necessary. However, if the occasion demands, these
substitutions may be used safely.*

*Baking powder*, 1 teaspoon=¼ teaspoon baking soda plus ½ teaspoon cream of tartar.

*Butter*, 1 cup=⅞-1 cup hydrogenated shortening plus ½ teaspoon salt *or* ⅞ cup oil plus ½ teaspoon salt *or* ⅞ cup lard plus ½ teaspoon salt. Do not make these substitutions in cookies and expect the same quality cookie.

*Chocolate*, 1⅔ ounces semisweet=1 ounce unsweetened chocolate plus 4 teaspoons sugar.

*Chocolate*, 1 square unsweetened=3 tablespoons cocoa plus 1 tablespoon shortening.

*Cracker crumbs*, ¾ cup=1 cup bread crumbs.

*Cream*, 1 cup half-and-half= ⅞ cup milk plus 3 tablespoons butter.

*Cream*, 1 cup whipping=¾ cup milk plus ⅓ cup butter.

*Eggs*, 1 whole=2 yolks plus 1 tablespoon water in cookies. No water is added to custards and like mixtures.

*Flour*, 1 cup sifted, all-purpose=1 cup plus 2 tablespoons cake flour *or* ⅞ cup cornmeal *or* 1 cup rolled oats.

*Flour*, 1 tablespoon for thickening=½-¾ tablespoons cornstarch or arrowroot *or* 1 tablespoon granular tapioca *or* 2 teaspoons quick-cooking tapioca.

*Garlic*, 1 small clove= ⅛ teaspoon garlic powder.

*Herbs*, 1 tablespoon finely-cut, fresh=1 teaspoon dried herbs.

*Macaroni*, 2 cups uncooked (4 cups cooked)=4 cups uncooked noodles.

*Milk*, 1 cup sweet=½ cup evaporated milk plus ½ cup water *or* ⅓ cup non-fat dry milk plus 1 cup water.

*Milk*, 1 cup sour or buttermilk=1 tablespoon lemon juice *or* vinegar, plus sweet milk to make 1 cup. Let stand 5-10 minutes.

*Mustard*, 1 teaspoon dry=1 tablespoon prepared.

*Onion*, 1 small=1 tablespoon instant, minced onion, rehydrated.

*Rice*, 1 cup regular (3-4 cups cooked)=2 cups precooked.

*Shrimp*, 1 cup cooked, cleaned=¾ pound raw shrimp in shell *or* 1 can (4½-5 ounce) *or* 1 package (7-ounce) frozen, peeled shrimp.

*Sugar*, 1 cup granulated=1 cup firmly-packed brown sugar. Add about ⅛ teaspoon soda to cakes, if it isn't called for. *Or* 1 cup honey or syrup. Reduce liquid in recipe by ¼ cup. Do not substitute honey for more than ½ sugar called for in cakes.

*Tomatoes*, 1 cup canned=about 1⅓ cups cut up, fresh tomatoes, simmered 10 minutes.

*Tomato catsup* or chili sauce, 1 cup=1 cup tomato sauce plus ¼ cup sugar and 2 tablespoons vinegar — use in cooking only.

*Tomato juice*, 1 cup =½ cup tomato sauce plus ½ cup water — use in cooking only.

## LIST OF ILLUSTRATIONS

Many of the older items illustrated in this book came with the pioneers who settled Minnesota, Nebraska, North Dakota and Wisconsin . . . others were purchased or made at home during the years that followed. Items from across Minnesota were made available through the cooperation of Lolly Lundquist, registrar, and John Yust, curator, Minnesota Historical Society Museum. Matilda Rupp, wife of The Farmer editor, loaned things from North Dakota and Nebraska. Ethel Lilly offered items she has collected since her grandparents came to Minnesota in the late 1860's. Other old china, silver, glass and kitchen utensils illustrated are from the Gow-Berg and Landin-Larson households . . . and came to the Midwest in the 1860's or 1870's with settlers from England, Sweden, Germany, Norway and the state of Maryland.

*Page number*

i......Illustration from the Vegetable chapter in the 1917 Country Kitchen Cook Book.

ii......Coverplate from the first edition of Country Kitchen Cook Book, published in 1894.

vii.:...Illustration from a chapter on Frozen Dishes in the 1917 Country Kitchen Cook Book.

viii......Illustration from a chapter on Pastry in the 1917 Country Kitchen Cook Book.

1......Clockwise: sterling silver tea ball, 1919; Gorham sterling silver sugar tongs, 1930; Haviland demitasse cup and saucer, c. 1910; handpainted chocolate pot, c. 1900; yellow enamel 12-cup coffee boiler, c. 1920; large white coffee cup, c. 1910; etched-crystal lemonade glass, 1919; 2-piece china lemon squeezer, c. 1920.

2......Wood and cast metal coffee grinder, c. 1900.

7......Wood lemon squeezer, c. 1900.

9......Clockwise: cut glass celery dish, c. 1920; sterling cocktail fork, c. 1870; pierced sterling silver nut spoon, c. 1960; miniature aspic cutters, c. 1960; footed cut glass compote, c. 1880; Haviland gold-band chop plate, c. 1920; Dresden handpainted china plate, c. 1910; metal-wood whisk, c. 1920; Brown-tan Dunlap crockery bowl with blue markings, c. 1910.

13.....Gray granite-ware pan, c. 1920.

15.....Can opener, c. 1950.

17.....Clockwise: steel chopping knife, c. 1910; apple corer-wedger, c. 1960; cut glass cruet, c. 1910; anodized aluminum mold, c. 1960; collapsible vegetable-washing basket, c. 1950; large wood chopping bowl, c. 1920; handpainted pottery salad bowl, c. 1930; white ceramic pestle and mortar, c. 1960.

21.....Wood and steel 2-blade chopper, c. 1920.

25.....Tin-plated apple corer-wedger, c. 1920.

33.....Clockwise: slotted enamel spoon, c. 1960; steel slicing knife, c. 1920; wood-handle peeler, c. 1930; tin-lined copper pan, c. 1890; vegetable grater, c. 1930; wood cabbage slicer, c. 1910; aluminum colander, c. 1930.

35.....Glazed 2-pound butter crock, c. 1910.

36.....Silver-plated cake basket, c. 1860.

39.....Pressed glass footed fruit compote, c. 1890.

41.....Handwoven wicker basket, c. 1900.

42.....Gray granite-ware colander, c. 1920.

45.....Pierced wood dipper or ladle, c. 1900.
47.....Wood potato masher, c. 1900.
53.....Woven basket, c. 1950.
55.....White Haviland soup tureen, c. 1870.
61.....Square-bottom wooden spoon, c. 1920.

62.....Clockwise: steel and wood table fork, now called "granny fork," c. 1890; steel boning knife, c. 1910; steel cleaver, c. 1910; wood meat mallet, c. 1920; cast iron skillet, c. 1930; footed cast iron soup kettle with round bottom, c. 1880; Blue Willow platter, a coffee premium, c. 1890; tin-plated fish steamer, c. 1960.
64.....Basting brush, c. 1950.
66.....Lemon garnishes.
70.....Bone-handled steak carving set, 1930.
75.....Round covered aluminum roasting pan, c. 1910.
83.....Fondue fork, c. 1970.
84.....Hammered copper meat fondue pot, c. 1970.
87.....Silver-plated Swedish soup ladle, c. 1950.
91.....Pressed glass double salt basket, c. 1900, and silver-plated salt spoon, c. 1930.
95.....Ridged-bottom cream-colored crockery Dutch oven with glazed inside. Made in Red Wing, Minnesota, c. 1900.
97.....Sterling silver serving spoon, c. 1880.
101....Crown roast of pork.
103....Silver-plated meat serving fork, c. 1885.
107....Steel and wood 3-tine table fork, c. 1890.
111....Cast iron sausage stuffer, c. 1890.
120....Silver-plated gravy ladle, c. 1880.
123....Silver-plate and glass condiment set, c. 1917.
127....Baster, c. 1960.
131....Frills for meat.
132....Handpainted china salt dish, 1895; English silver salt spoon, c. 1850.
142....Wood and steel potato peeler, c. 1940.
145....Cast iron tea kettle, c. 1900.
155....Cut glass knife rest, c. 1915.
156....Handmade birch bark wild ricing basket, c. 1960.
159....Haviland meat platter, c. 1910.
161....Quart-size crockery vinegar jug, c. 1900.

163....Clockwise: small wood cutting board, c. 1960; cheese slicer, c. 1970; handpainted blue egg cup, c. 1920; glazed brown pottery souffle dish, c. 1960; nickel-plated chafing dish, c. 1900; cast iron omelet pan with orange baked-enamel surface, c. 1960.
169....Wood egg crate with cardboard liners, c. 1910.
170....Tin-plated egg cooker, c. 1910.

173....Norwegian handcarved wood-pegged whisk, c. 1890.
174....Wood cheese mold, c. 1890.


177....Clockwise: tin-plated picnic cup, c. 1935; steel camp fork, c. 1935; gallon-size metal beverage jug with glazed crockery liner, c. 1915; woven split birch picnic basket, c. 1935; woven fringed picnic cloth, c. 1910.
184....Tin-plated pop corn popper, c. 1900.
191....Blue enamel gallon-size coffee boiler, c. 1910.


193....Clockwise: wood pig cutting board, c. 1910; chrome-plated spreader, c. 1950; stainless steel table knife and spoon, c. 1970; blue glass 1-pint canning jar, c. 1910; 2-pound butter crock, c. 1920; pound-size wood butter mold, c. 1890; wood butter spoon, c. 1890; glass butter churn, c. 1920; blue-brown spatter crockery bowl, c. 1920.
195....Etched-crystal cheese dish, c. 1900.
197....Hotpoint electric flip toaster, c. 1920.
198....Loaf of Sandwiches.
200....Base for Party Sandwich Loaf from bread slices.
203....Silver-plated butter knife with twisted handle to fit pronged butter dish, c. 1890.


205....Clockwise: cast iron griddle, c. 1910; short 1-piece rolling pin, c. 1910; crockery bread bowl, c. 1940; wooden mixing spoon, c. 1910; wood-handled doughnut cutter, c. 1920
207....Ridged butter paddle, c. 1910.
213....Fan-tan rolls; crescent rolls.
214....Cloverleaf rolls; parker house rolls.
215....Kolacky.
219....Coffee bread braid.
221....Glazed Pineapple Almond Ring.
222....Woven coffee bread.
224....Knockebröd rolling pin, c. 1890.
231....Range-top cast iron waffle baker, c. 1910.
232....Lefse rolling pin, c. 1890.
237....Metal cake tester, c. 1950; corn broom straw cake tester, 1973.
239....Tin-plated flour sifter, c. 1920.
240....Cast iron muffin pans, c. 1880.


243....Clockwise: aluminum gingerbread man cookie cutter, c. 1940; aluminum measuring spoon, c. 1940; sandbakkel tin, c. 1920; cast rosette iron, c. 1915; footed glass candy dish, c. 1950; crockery cookie jar, c. 1910; tin-plated candy and bar-cookie pans, c. 1920; pink etched-crystal candy jar, c. 1920; tin-plated cookie press, c. 1915.

247.... Tin-plated sugar scoop, c. 1910.
248.... Round tin-plated lemon grater, c. 1920.
255.... Wood rolling pin, c. 1850.
258.... Springerle cookie rolling pin, c. 1940.
262.... Tin-plated nut chopper, c. 1930.
265.... Plastic gingerbread man cookie cutter, c. 1970.

273.... Clockwise: tin-plated pudding mold, c. 1900; cast metal cutter and pastry fluter, c. 1920; tin lard pail, c. 1910; footed pressed glass cake plate, c. 1895; galvanized steel 1-quart ice cream freezer, 1914; tin-plated angel food cake pan, c. 1930; cast metal ice cream mold, c. 1920.

283.... Steel egg beater, c. 1900.
284.... Hollow blown-glass pastry rolling pin to be filled with ice water, c. 1880.
290.... Wood pie peel used to lift pies from oven which has stationary racks, c. 1880.
295.... Aluminum double boiler, c. 1930.
297.... Japanese tin-ware cake storage box, c. 1890.
301.... Drum Cake.
302.... Clown Cup Cakes.
313.... Blue-banded glazed crockery cream pitcher, c. 1910.
314.... Set of wooden spice boxes, patented 1858.
317.... English tin-plated pudding mold, c. 1970.
320.... Pierced steel cream skimmer, 1900.
323.... Nickel-plated wood-handled ice cream scoop, c. 1915.
325.... Wood sugar pail with wood pegs, c. 1860.

327.... Clockwise: steel jar tongs, c. 1920; jelly glass, c. 1930; gallon-size glazed crockery vinegar jug, c. 1915; fruit basket, c. 1930; 2-quart clear glass canning jar, c. 1920; tin-plated quart measure, c. 1910.

334.... Wood berry-picking box, c. 1930.
339.... Aluminum food sieve and kettle, c. 1930.
345.... Blue enamel boiling water bath canner, a premium from The Farmer, c. 1935.
350.... Wood berry press, c. 1900.
352.... Wood-handled, plated steel can opener, c. 1930.
360.... Wooden masher for potatoes, fruit, c. 1920.
362.... Glazed 2-gallon pickle crock with blue marking, c. 1900.
368.... Wood sauerkraut stomper, c. 1900.

371.... Clockwise: food grinder, c. 1940; blue kitchen scale, c. 1930; white English Ironstone pitcher, c. 1890; handmade 2-gallon tin-lined copper kitchen kettle, c. 1870; handpainted, heavy Swedish china punch bowl, c. 1870; silver plated Swedish ladle, c. 1960.

381.... Tin-lined copper kettle, c. 1850.

383.... Dark Spicy Bride's Cake.

385.... Gallon-size gray granite-ware cream pail, c. 1910.

387.... Dishwasherproof plastic liquid measure, marked in U.S. cups and ounces, plus Metric milliliters, 1973.

390.... Small steel skillet, c. 1920.

395.... Handcarved wood scoop with hanging handle, c. 1860.

# INDEX OF RECIPES

## A

Antelope, barbecued ribs, 162

## B

Baked beans
  Boston, 58
  Boston sandwich, 194
  "doctored," 59
  fruited, 58
  skillet, 58

Bars

  apricot shortbread, 244
  brownies
    double take, 249
    mincemeat, 248
  cherry
    cocoanut, 245
    delights, 247
  date, 245
  French, 246
  honey-fruit, 249
  lemon, 248
  peanut butter, unbaked, 250

pecan surprise, 246
toffee
  plain, 247
  English squares, 244

Beef
  braising chart, 67
  broiling chart, 80
  corned jumbo jigg sandwich, 202
  dried
    burning bush canape, 10
    creamed with peas, 90
  fondue
    chunks, 82
    how to serve, 81-82
    meatball, 83
    mixed, 83
    sauces, 84-85
  ground
    cabbage rolls, 76
    chili con carne, 73, 78
    chow mein hot dish, quantity, 377
    corn chip-stuffed tomatoes, 76
    5-layer field dinner, 192
    glorified, quantity, 378
    grilled dinner in package, 181

meat balls, 12, 74, 379
meat loaf, 74
multi-purpose mix, 72
noodle skillet, 73
old fashioned hot dish, 77
onion-stuffed tomatoes, 76
pastie, 75
pie, 77
pizza
burgers, 196
sandwich, quantity, 381
rice skillet, 73
sandwiches
crumble, 196
filled buns, 73
taverns, chiliburgers, 196
spaghetti sauce, 73, 78
stuffed green peppers, 73
stuffed rolls, 73
stroganoff, 73
thermos hot dish, 190
hash, baked, 91
heart, 94
jerky, 186
kabobs, 179
how to cook in liquid, 85
liver
casserole, 97
turkey in casserole, 97
dumplings, 96
with sour cream gravy, 98
meat roll, 90
meat-potato sandwich, 197
pressed loaf, 89
quickie creamed, 90
roasts
everyday pot, 68
glazed, rolled, 64
pit-cooked, quantity, 380
roasting chart, 65

spicy pot, 69
Sunday best pot, 68
salad with greens, 31
shepherd's pie, 89
short ribs, barbecued, 70
soup
boiled beef, 88
croutons, 88
goulash, 91
stock, 87
winter, 88
steak
cowboy's, 81
farmer's, 69
flank, 70
toppings, 79-80
stew
canned, plus, 92
kidney, 96
let 'em be late, 86
oxtail, 99
party, 71
rutabaga, 87
savory, 71
sweetbread-Canadian bacon grill, 99
tongue, 98


Beverages
citrus-peach julep, 7
coffee
boiled, 2
cappuccino, 3
drip or filter, 3
perked, 3
spiced dessert, 3
steeped, 2
grape juice, spiced, 8
lemonade syrup, 6
milk
brown cow, 6
eggnog, 5
maple shakes, 6
sleigh ride chocolate, 5
punch
Bess Rowe's party, quantity, 373

grape-orange, quantity, 373
golden glow, 7
ice ring, 374
mulled cider, 8
orange, 6
rhubarb, 8
wassail bowl, quantity, 374

tea
hot, 4
iced, 4
minted, 4
spiced mix, 4
tomato juice, spiced, quantity, 373

Boiling water bath canning, 344-347

Breads, yeast
flat, 224
instant blend yeast, how to use, 206
oatmeal, 210
pumpernickel, 211
·raisin-orange, 210
tips, 206
white
with nuts or dry fruit, 208
plain, 208
plain, from starter sponge, 209
basic roll dough, 214
biscuit starter, 212
double buns, 212
shaping rolls, 213-214
whole wheat
biscuits from starter, 212
with nuts or dry fruit, 208
plain, 208

Breads, yeast, sweet
apple cake from starter, 209
basic sweet dough, 217
caramel rolls, 218
cardamom coffee braid, 219
Danish coffee twist, 218
doughnuts, raised, 223
Easter egg buns, 218
German, Christmas coffee cake, 220
glazed pineapple almond ring, 220
hot cross buns, 216
kolacky, 215
kolacky fillings, 216
orange rolls, 218
pocket books, from starter, 209
poppy seed coffee cake, 222
rosebuds, 217

Breads, quick
banana, 238
baking powder biscuits
cut, 233, 235
drop, 233
bacon, 234
make-at-home mix, 234
Boston brown bread, 230
bread-on-a-stick, 184
cinnamon rolls, 233
corn bread
bacon, 233
camp fire, 186
plain, 233
cranberry-honey, 237
deep fat frying chart, 231
dumplings
cheese, 92, 173
plain, 139
hasty coffee cakes
biscuit bubble ring, 240
caramel cherry coffee cake, 241
pineapple bubble ring, 240
hasty hot rolls

apricot, quick, 242
caraway, 241
celery, 241
cranberry-mincemeat,
  242
parmesan, 241
pineapple sticky buns,
  241
griddle cakes, rice, 227
Indian fried
  biscuits, 230
  plain, 230
  raisin, 230
Irish batter, 232
lefse, 232
maple bran, 240
milk toast, 227
mincemeat-topped coffee
  cake, 236
muffins
  apple, 229
  biscuit mix, 235
  blueberry, 229
  cooked cereal, 229
  corn meal, bran, 229
  cranberry, 229
  date or nuts, 229
  graham, 229
  Lizzie's cream, 229
  maple syrup, 229
  sour cream, 229
  sour milk, 229
  sweet milk, 228
  whole wheat, 229
nut
  cherry, 239
  date or raisin, 239
  orange-sunflower, 239
  prune, 239
  quick, 238
onion, from mix, 236
orange biscuits, 233
pancakes
  apple, 226
  blueberry, 226
  buttermilk, 225
  gingerbread, 226
  ham, 225
  from mix, 235

onion, 226
pan-sans, 226
peach, 226
sausage, 226
from starter, 212
sweet milk, 225
popovers, 228
pumpkin, 238
Scotch scones, from mix,
  234
short cake from mix
  cardamom, 234
  golden, 234
  plain, 234
streusel coffee cake
  blueberry, 237
  plain, 237
Sunday bread, 236
waffles, 227
Yorkshire pudding, 228

Buffalo roast, pit method,
  quantity, 380

Bulgar
  boiled, 59
  oven-cooked, 59

Building a cooking fire, 178

Butter
  flavored for breads, 207
  flavored for pancakes, 224
  flavored for vegetables, 56
  how to make, 204

## C

Cake
  angel food, 296
  apple sauce, 293
  black walnut, 297
  bride's dark spice, quantity,
    382
  burnt sugar, 292
  chocolate
    Dutch family, 293
    old-fashioned, 291
    plain, 292
    pound, 294
  clown cupcakes, 302
  cocoanut, 292
  corn starch, 295
  cranberry-orange, 299
  drum, 301
  foundation yellow, 291
  fruit cake
    dark, 298
    white, 298
  gold or Lord Baltimore, 292
  hazel nut, 292
  honey-almond cupcakes,
    294
  Lady Baltimore, 291
  lingonberry cream, 300
  orange
    cake mix, 301
    layer, 292
  pound
    chocolate, 294
    plain, 294
    pyramid, 295
  spice
    fluffy, 292
    Spanish, 291
  tunnel-of-love, 300
  yolk sponge, 296
  white, 291

Canapes (also look under chief
  ingredient)
  hor d'oeuvre dates, 11

nuts and bolts, 13

Candy
  burnt sugar, 270
  candy apples, 271
  caramels, rich, 270
  chocolate nut crunch, 269
  divinity, maple, 271
  fudge
    light, beef, 268
    dark, super, 269
  honey-spiced walnuts, 267
  peanut brittle, 268
  pinoche, 270
  pop corn balls, 272
  stuffed dates, prunes, figs,
    272
  taffy, pull, 272

Caramelizing sugar, 281

Catsup
  grape, 369
  tomato, 369

Cheese
  burning bush canape, 10
  cheddar-tuna salad, baked,
    quantity, 376
  Christmas ball, 15
  cottage cheese, how to
    make, 176
  dips
    deviled, 15
    party, for apples, 16
    pumpkin hollow, 14
    zesty, for vegetables, 14
  dumplings, 92, 173

fondue, 172
golden crown casserole, 174
Hungarian noodle hot dish,
175
lasagne
    with pork sauce, 106
    quantity, 378
macaroni and
    celery, 171
    plain, 171
pizza
    burgers, 196
    jumbo sandwich, quan-
    tity, 381
quiche lorraine, 173
rice, baked
    peanut, 171
    plain, 171
sandwiches
    Bavarian, 204
    broiled, 194
tacos, baked sour cream,
174
welsh rarebit, 172


Chicken
baked
    caraway, 137
    cinchy, 137
    hens in the oven, 137
    orange, 136
    roast, stuffed, 136
    spit-roasted, 136
barbecued, 182
barbecue sauces, 182
boiled, with dumplings, 139
casserole of fowl and vege-
    tables, 138
Clara's poultry seasoning,
138
gravy, creamy, 137
ham supper dish, 141
pie, 140
pressed, 139
salad
    Bess Rowe's, 375

chef's, with ham, 31
cherry, 30
ham canapes, 11
molded, quantity, 376
sandwich, gourmet, 203
sauced squares, 141
soup
    classic, 139
    canned, dressed-up, 142
stew, creamy, 140
sunflower, 138


Condiments, meat, 64


Cookies
almond bubbles, 256
anise sticks, pallilos, 261
bateau bonbons, 263
cherry cocoanut macaroons,
258
chocolate chip, 251
Christmas tree, 262
cinnamon angels, 259
date pinwheels, 264
double decker, 257
fattigman, 264
filled, 252
florentines, 260
French lace, 260
ginger, 255
hermits, 253
lemon
    bonbons, 259
    pudding, 250
mincemeat marvel, 260
molasses
    cut-outs, 265
    peanut butter, 255
noels, 261
nut balls, 257
oatmeal
    bran, 253
    nuts, 253

spiced, 253
sweet milk, 253
orange
    cranberry, 258
    drop, 254
peanut blossoms, 256
raisin jumbo, 254
rosettes, 266
sandbakkelse, 266
Shrewbury cakes, 250
sour cream drop, 251
spritz, 267
sugar, 252
sunflower, champion, 252
Swedish cream wafers, 263
tart, 267
Vienna crescents
    brazil nut, 261
    plain, 260

Croutons, for soup
    buttered, 88
    cheese, 88
    garlic, 88
    lemon-buttered, 88
    herb, 89

D

Desserts (also see cake, ice
cream, pie, pudding, sherbet)
apple
    baked with dates, 311
    baked, glazed, 311
    cobbler, 312
    crisp, quantity, 382
    dumplings, 311
    speedy sauce dessert,
        321
    snaps pudding, 312

banana yum-yums, camp,
    188
berry swirl, 320
blueberry
    angel, 320
    make-ahead, quantity,
        384
    quickie dumplings, 187
cherry
    angel, 320
    melange, 321
    spiced, 314
cheese cake, elegant, 306
chocolate dream, 310
cream puffs
    blueberry, 307
    cherry, 307
    chocolate-orange, 307
    whipped cream, 307
Danish puff, 306
fruit rolls, 313
fruit soup, 308
upside-down cake, ginger-
    bread, 309
ice cream log, 326
jelly roll, 309
lemon, make-ahead, quan-
    tity, 384
meringue shells, 308
peach cobbler, quickie, 312
pecan bombe, 326
pineapple almond torte, 310
purple plum cobbler, 312
rhubarb
    casserole, 313
    pie plant pan-dowdy,
        311
short cake
    banana-strawberry, 308
    berry, 308
    mixed fruit, 308
    peach, 308

Dips (also look under chief
ingredient)
    brunch fruit sauce, 16

Duck
  baked wild and rice, 154
  duckling and vegetable cas-
    serole, 143
  roast wild, 154-155
  stuffed duckling, 142

souffle
  day-off tuna, 168
  plain, 168
  stuffed eggs
    chicken, 170
    crabmeat, 170
    deviled, 171
    ham, 170
    surprise sausage, 166

E

Eggs
  baked
    crisp-coated, 166
    crisp-coated with bacon,
      166
    tomato, 167
  creamed, 167
  eggnog
    chocolate, 5
    plain, 5
  French toast
    scrambled, 165
    scrambled molasses, 165
  hard-cooked, 164
  omelet
    cheese-vegetable, 169
    puffy, 168
    sauces, 169
  picnic, 170
  in potato soup, 49
  salad
    ham, 32
    oven-toasted  sandwich,
      194
    plain, 32
  scrambled
    cheese, 165
    egg buns, 164
    herbed, 165
    homestead skillet, 165
    olive, 165
    plain, 164
  shrimp foo yung, 166
  soft-cooked, 164

F

Fillings
  chocolate, cookie, 257
  cream cheese, cake, 304
  lemon, cake, 305
  orange, cake, 305
  party sandwich loaf, 200
  prune, cake, 305
  whipped cream, cake
    chocolate, 303
    fruit, 300
    orange, 303
    pineapple, 304
    sherry, 303

Fish
  chowder, 150
  how to cook, 146
  crab, cream salad filling, 11
  fresh baked
    fillets and vegetables,
      147
    fillets in sour cream, 148
    fish bake, 148
    stuffed bass, 147
  how to freeze, 145
  lutefisk
    baked, 150
    boiled, 150

marinated fillets, 183
salmon casserole, 152
oysters, scalloped, 153
poached pike, 149
sauces, 149
shrimp
  fondue, 151
  almond hot dish, 151
sticks
  cheese, 151
  deviled, 151
  herbed-baked, 151
  savory, 151
  spicy, 151
trout sauteed with bacon,
  148
tuna
  cinchy rice, 152
  pate, 14
  salad, 31
  salad, baked cheddar,
    376
  sandwich spread, 202
  stuffed baked potato,
    153
  sunflower, 152
  triumph, 380
  wrap-ups, 199

Flaming foods, 101

Freezing
  fruits, 333-337
  vegetables, 328-333

Frills for turkey, lamb, crown
  roast, 131

Frosted grape clusters, 310

Frostings and icings
  bonbon, 259
  chocolate
    cookie dip, 266
    cream, 300
    easy, 302
  cocoanut, 307
  coffee creamy, 302
  confectioners' sugar, 250,
    256, 261, 263
  creamy, 263, 301
  decorative cookie, 265
  lemon, 287, 293
  orange creamy, 246, 302
  party sandwich loaf, 201
  rum butter, 383
  seven-minute
    chocolate, 303
    marshmallow, 303
    white, 303
  strawberry creamy, 302
  uncooked honey, 303
  whipped cream
    chocolate, 303
    orange, 303
    sherry, 303

Fruit, canning
  boiling water bath, 344-347
  extracting juices, 348
  freezing, 333-337
  pressure canner, 338-339
  syrups, 348

**G**

Goose
  braised, 143
  roast
    domestic, 144
    wild, 155

Granola, 59

Gravy
    brown sauce base, 72
    creamy chicken, 137
    meat ball, 75
    turkey with bacon, 128

Grouse
    in cream, 157
    roast with almonds, 156
    smothered, 156


I

Ice Cream
    caramel, 323
    chocolate, 323
    French vanilla, 322
    fresh fruit, 324
    peanut brittle, 323
    peppermint, 323


J

Jam
    berry, uncooked, 358
    blackberry-raspberry-
        rhubarb, 353
    blueberry, 356
    grape
        plum, 354

    spicy, 355
layered, 349
peach
    raspberry, uncooked,
        357
    rosy melba, 353
raspberry-blueberry, 356
strawberry
    great grandma's, 358
    rhubarb, 354
    rhubarb, uncooked, 357
tutti-frutti, 355


Jelly
    apple, 352
    blackberry, 349
    chokecherry, 351
    currant, red, 350
    grape, 350
    juice for, 348
    layered, 349
    plum, 351
    tomato, 352


L

Lamb
    braising chart, 67
    broiling chart, 122
    Italian chops, 123
    kalypso kabobs, 180
    roast
        breast with sausage, 119
        stuffed shoulder, 118
        leg with cucumber-dill
            sauce, 119
        roasting chart, 118
    soup, hot pot with barley,
        121

Swedish shanks, 120
stew
let 'em be late, 87
sour cream, 121
surprise, 122
zucchini casserole, 120

rump roast, 161
steak tarragon, 160

P

Pastas
caraway noodles, 60
how to cook, 60
homemade noodles, 61
parmesan, 60

M

Marmalade (conserves, butters)
amber, 359
apple, 360
grape, 358
grape conserve, 359
tomato, 360
wild plum butter, 361
winter, 359

Peanut butter
cookies, 256
bars, 250
sandwiches
honey-sweet, 202
grilled with bacon, 194

Measuring
guide to can sizes, 388
how to, 385
table, 386
what 1 pound yields, 386-387

Meat (see specific kinds)
canning chart, 341

Pickles
beet, 365
carrot, 366
causes of trouble, 361
dills, Ma's, 364
fruit, sweet, 370
gooseberries, spiced, 370
hamburger, 363
mustard, 364
nine-day sweet, 362
onion, 365
sauerkraut, how to make, 368
watermelon, 366

Meringue, 276

Moose
meat loaf, 160

Pie, crust
chocolate crumb, 275

corn flake, 275
graham cracker, 276
mix-and-press, 274-275
supreme, 274

Pie, custard
  banana cream, 278
  butterscotch, 281
  orange-carrot, 281
  plain carrot, 280
  cherry cream, Washington,
    282
  chocolate, 279, 289
  cocoanut cream, 278
  cottage cheese, 281
  baked custard
    cocoanut, 279
    plain, 278
  date
    cream, 290
    nut, 282
  lemon meringue, 276
  fudge-nut, 282
  pecan, 282
  pumpkin, 280
  rhubarb meringue, 279

Pies, fruit
  apple
    German, 284
    praline, 284
  apricot, mile-high, 289
  banana cream, 278
  blackberry, 285
  blueberry
    blue cheese, 285
    graham cracker, 290
    wild, 285
  cherry
    almond, 288
    cream, 282
  cranberry, 287
  currant, 285
  gooseberry, 285

lemon meringue, 277
mincemeat
  brandied, 287
  cheese, 287
  how to make, 286
  pastry squares, 286
  squash, 286
pineapple upside-down, 288
raspberry, 285
rhubarb meringue, 279
strawberry
  plain, 285
  glace, 283
  pink moon rhubarb, 283

Pheasant
  with almonds, 156
  in cream, 157
  smothered, 156

Pork, cured
  bacon
    baked, crisp, 117
    Canadian with sweet
      breads, 99
    Spanish rice, 117
    sandwiches
      breakfast-lunch-
        supper, 194
      grilled with pea-
        nut better, 194
    wrap-ups, canapes, 12
  bratwurst sandwich, grilled,
    184
  broiling chart, 117
  ham
    cheese pie, 115
    chicken supper dish, 141
    glazes, 112
    honey loaf, 113
    'n rice deluxe, 116
    salad
      chef's with chicken,
        31
      chicken, canape, 11
      egg, 32

ground spread, 203
sandwiches
asparagus deluxe, 197
Bavarian, 204
sauces, 112
savory slice, 113
scalloped potatoes, 115
soup with cabbage, 116
Swedish balls, 114
turnovers, 114
with vegetables on toast, 116
wieners
with beans, 189
franks in a blanket, 183
special hot dogs, 198

Pork, fresh
braising chart, 67
broiling, how to, 107
casserole with biscuit topping, 107
chops
barbecued, 181
with beans, 189
escalloped, 104
oinky hot slaw, 192
stuffed, 104
hocks
kraut 'n caraway, 109
vegetable dinner, 109
lasagne, 106
lunchmeat sandwiches
ground, grilled, 183
liver sausage, hot, 197
loaf of, hot, 198
saucy burgers, 199
roast
crown, 101
chart, 100
sauces, 102
sausage
apples, stuffed, 111
cabbage casserole, 108
cabbage-caraway casserole, 108

with creamy gravy on biscuits, 110
fruit kabobs, 185
how to make, 110
pizza, 110
with squash, 111
soup, chodder, 108
souse, jellied pork, 108
spareribs
barbecued, 181
crispy baked, 102
on lentils, 103
stuffed, 103
stew
make-ahead savory, 105
sweet-sour, 106
sesame spread
canapes, 10
sandwiches, 203
steaks, barbecued, 181
tenderloin, stuffed, 102

Pudding
blueberry, in-a-bowl, 315
custard
Danish, 314
grandma's, 316
steamed
cranberry, 316
English plum, 317
holiday, 318
rice, Swedish, 315
tutti-frutti, 316

# Q

Quantity (see chief ingredient for recipes)
preparation chart, 372

## R

Rabbit
    fried, 158
    pie, 157

Relishes
    apple chutney, 367
    beet, 68
    chili sauce, 368
    corn, 367
    orange-cranberry, 128
    tomato, green, 366

Rice
    boiled, 61
    fried, 62
    oven-baked, 61
    oven-baked with celery, 62
    wild, fried, 62

## S

Salad dressings
    boiled, 20
    cheese, 20
    cole slaw
        honey, 22
        sour cream, 22
        syrup, 22
    creamy
        maple, 29
        patio, 27
        plain, 28
    French, 24
    fruit, 29
    Italian, 20
    mayonnaise, blender, 26
    oil-vinegar, 21
    piquant, 30
    sour cream, 23
    thousand island, 19
    zippy, 19

Salads, fruit
    apple-orange, whipped, 25
    banana, 28
    canned fruit, 29
    cranberry-pineapple,
        quantity, 375
    frozen, 27
    grapefruit-avocado, 27
    broiled grapefruit, 29
    mandarin orange, 27
    melon rings, 28
    orange-endive, 21
    pineapple-cucumber mold,
        26
    raspberry gelatin mold, 26
    spur of the moment, 18
    waldorf, 28

Salads, vegetable
    bean
        mixed, 20
        overnight, quantity, 374
    cabbage or carrot, shred-
        ded, 22
    cauliflower-beet, 20
    lettuce, bacon-wilted, 19
    olives, oregano-garlic, 21
    potato
        cold, 24-25
        hot, with cheese, 24
    spinach
        bacon-wilted, 19
        crisp, 18
    spur of the moment, 18
    tomato aspic, 23
    tomato shells
        and flowers, 23
        fillings, 23

vegetable, quantity, 375

Sandwiches (also look under chief ingredient)
orange-cocoanut toasties, 194
party loaf, 199-201
super variety, 188-189
tea fillings, 10

Sauces
beef
brown, 72
horseradish, 64
mushroom, 72
piquant, 72
beef steak
sunflower, 79
Roquefort, 80
mustard-butter, 80
sesame seed-butter, 80
cake
blueberry, 304
orange cream, 304
spicy, 304
chicken, barbecue
lemon, 182
mustard-molasses, 182
parmesan, 182
rosemary butter, 182
tomato, 182
fish
herbed mayonnaise, 149
lemon-garlic butter, 149
maitre d'hotel, 149
tartar, 149
fondue, 84-85, 134, 151, 172
game, 72
gravy
creamy chicken, 137
turkey with bacon, 128
ham glazes
apple sauce, 112
brown sugar, 112
currant jelly, 112
orange-honey, 112
ham sauces
cherry, 112
cherry, spiced, 113
honey, 112
jewelled, 112
plum 'n spice, 112
ice cream
chocolate, 319
fruit, 319
strawberry cooler, 322
strawberry-rhubarb, 322
lamb
cucumber dill, 119
mint, 118
omelet, 169
pancake
blueberry, 304
brown sugar spread, 224
caramel syrup, 225
maple apple slices, 225
orange, 304
peach, 225
spicy, 304
pork, fresh
apricot glaze, 102
rosy peach, 102
spicy barbecue, 102
pudding
brandy, 318, 319
brown sugar, 318
cocoa, 319
chocolate, 319
foamy, 318
fruit, 319
hard, 318-319
lemon, 319
orange, 318
vanilla, 319
wine, 319
vegetable
carrot golden, 57
cheese, 57
cream, 57
East Indian, 57
egg, 57
hollandaise, 56
lobster, 57

oyster, 57
paprika, 57
parsley, 57
pimento, 57
shrimp, 57
tomato, 57
white, 57

Sherbet
banana cream, 325
lemon cream, 325
orange cream, 325
pineapple cream, 324
snow cream, 325
strawberry, 325

Squirrel
fried, 158
pie, 157

Soup (also see chief ingredient)
canning chart, 340
clarifying stock, 87·
croutons, 88-89

Stuffing
apple-prune, turkey, 129
apple-raisin, wild duck, 155
caraway, chicken, 136
corn bread, turkey, 129
cranberry, turkey, 130
double dress the turkey, 128
favorite bread, turkey, 129
giblet
chicken, 136
turkey, 130

mashed potato, goose, 145
fruit, duckling, 142
rice
duckling, 142
heart, 95
turkey, 130, 131
sauerkraut, goose, 145
sausage
goose, 144
turkey, 130
tips, 129

Substitutions, 389

Sunflowers
roasting meats, 12
roasting in shell, 13

Syrups, fruit, how to make, 348-349

T

Toast cups, 91

Turkey
barbecue on a spit, 178-179
cooked meat
green bean bake, 132

make-ahead supper, 133
skillet and stuffing, 132
wild rice casserole, 133
crispy, 135
fondue, 134
liver in casserole, 97
noodle casserole, quantity,
377
roast
charts, 125-127
boneless, 126
lemon-roasted, whole,
126
rotisseried, whole, 127
savory hot dish, 190
salad
cole slaw, 32
molded, quantity, 376
plain, 30
sandwiches
red devil, hot, 195
savarin club, 195
soup
corn chowder, 134
cream, 134
steak, 135
teriyaki kabobs, 180
how to thaw, 124

**V**

Veal
brain and egg saute, 94
braising chart, 67
with cashews, 92
city chicken, 93
heart, 94
kalvsylta, jellied veal, 93
loaf, 94
roasting chart, 92

Vegetables
asparagus and eggs, 34

beets, boiled, 51
broccoli-cheese casserole, 34
cabbage
boiled, 51
glorified, 35
tomato casserole, 36
carrots
baked, 37
boiled, 51
glazed with onions, 37
green beans au gratin,
37
mashed with potatoes,
38
O'Brien, 55
special occasion ring, 38
crown cauliflower with peas,
38
celery and carrots, baked, 39
corn
baked, 39
escalloped, 40
grilled, 184
stewed with tomatoes, 40
cucumber a la dill, 40
dippable garden vegetables,
13
eggplant, fried, 40
freezing, 328-333
green beans
herbed, 42
supreme, 41
greens, 42
mixed vegetables, grilled,
185
mushrooms, baked, 43
onions
au gratin, 44
batter-fried, 43
parsnips and carrots, scalloped, 44
peas
Dutch, 45
gourmet touch, 44
peppered, 45
shelling, 44
potatoes, sweet
baked, stuffed, 50
cranberry glazed, 49

grilled packs, 185
potatoes, white
  baked, frozen, 48
  creamed with peas, 46
  fried, sweet-sour, 46
  grilled, 185
  with herbs, 47
  mashed casserole top-
    ping, 75
  pancakes, 46
  parmesan, 186
  poppy seed, 186
  puff, 49
  strips with cheese, 47
  stuffed, 48
  tuna-stuffed, 153
pressure canner canning,
  338-343
pumpkin
  baked, 50
  creamed with almonds,
    50
rutabagas, boiled, 51
salsify
  escalloped, 52
  fritters, 52
soups
  cheese-corn chowder,
    175
  early garden, 55
  French onion, camp, 187
  potato, 48
  quickie green velvet, 34
  tomato supper, 55
special butters, 56
spinach loaf, 53
squash
  apple-baked, 51
  baked, 50
  creamed with almonds,
    50
  fried, summer, 52
  summer, with bacon, 52
  treat, 51
Swiss chard, 54
tomatoes
  broiled, 54
  casserole dinner, 172
  scalloped, 54

turnips O'Brien, 55


Venison
  barbecued burgers, 158
  casserole, 160
  hunter style, 159
  meat loaf, 160
  roast, 158


Vinegar, raspberry, 370


**W**

Wild game (see specific meat)